Building Your Next Big Thing with Google Cloud Platform

A Guide for Developers and Enterprise Architects

S. P. T. Krishnan

Jose L. Ugia Gonzalez

Apress®

Building Your Next Big Thing with Google Cloud Platform: A Guide for Developers and Enterprise Architects

ISBN-13 (pbk): 978-1-4842-1005-5

ISBN-13 (electronic): 978-1-4842-1004-8

Distributed to the book trade worrldwide by Springer Science+Business Media New York, 233 Spring Street, 6th Floor, New York, NY 10013. Phone 1-800-SPRINGER, fax (201) 348-4505, e-mail orders-ny@springer-sbm.com, or visit www.springeronline.com. Apress Media, LLC is a California LLC and the sole member (owner) is Springer Science + Business Media Finance Inc (SSBM Finance Inc). SSBM Finance Inc is a Delaware corporation.

For information on translations, please e-mail rights@apress.com, or visit www.apress.com.

Apress and friends of ED books may be purchased in bulk for academic, corporate, or promotional use. eBook versions and licenses are also available for most titles. For more information, reference our Special Bulk Sales–eBook Licensing web page at www.apress.com/bulk-sales.

Any source code or other supplementary materials referenced by the author in this text is available to readers at www.apress.com. For detailed information about how to locate your book's source code, go to www.apress.com/source-code/.

Krishnan: I would like to dedicate this book to my parents, wife, and children. I would like to specifically thank my wife Kavitha, who is a key motivating factor in everything I do and who strongly believes I am capable and destined for even greater things in life. I am not sure I would have reached where I am today without you, and I can't imagine a life without you now.

Jose: To Alejandro.

Contents at a Glance

About the Authors.......xvii

Acknowledgments.......xix

Introduction.......xxi

■Part I: Introducing Cloud Computing and Google Cloud Platform....... 1

■Chapter 1: The Google Cloud Platform Difference....... 3

■Chapter 2: Getting Started with Google Cloud Platform....... 13

■Chapter 3: Using Google APIs....... 27

■Part II: Google Cloud Platform - Compute Products....... 51

■Chapter 4: Google Compute Engine....... 53

■Chapter 5: Google App Engine....... 83

■Chapter 6: Next Generation DevOps Initiatives....... 123

■Part III: Google Cloud Platform - Storage Products....... 157

■Chapter 7: Google Cloud SQL....... 159

■Chapter 8: Cloud Storage....... 185

■Chapter 9: Google Cloud Datastore....... 211

■Part IV: Google Cloud Platform - Big Data Products....... 233

■Chapter 10: Google BigQuery....... 235

■Chapter 11: Google Cloud Dataflow....... 255

■Chapter 12: Google Cloud Pub/Sub....... 277

■Part V: Google Cloud Platform - Networking and Services 293

■Chapter 13: Google Cloud DNS.. 295

■Chapter 14: Google Cloud Endpoints 309

■Part VI: Google Cloud Platform - Management and Recipes 331

■Chapter 15: Cloud Platform DevOps Toolbox... 333

■Chapter 16: Architecture Recipes for Google Cloud Platform 349

Index.. 365

Contents

About the Authors xvii

Acknowledgments xix

Introduction xxi

■Part I: Introducing Cloud Computing and Google Cloud Platform 1

■Chapter 1: The Google Cloud Platform Difference 3

What Is Cloud Computing? 3

Technical Benefits of Using a Public Cloud 4

- Uptime 4
- Resource Utilization 5
- Expertise 5

Economic Benefits of Using a Public Cloud 5

- TCO 5
- Economies of Scale 5
- CapEx and OpEx 6
- ROI and Profit Margins 6

Business Benefits of Using a Public Cloud 6

- Time to Market 6
- Self-Service 7
- Pay per Use 7
- Uncertain Growth Patterns 7

Why Google Cloud Platform? 7

- Hardware Innovations 8
- Software Innovations 8
- Economic Innovations 10

A Quick Comparison to AWS 11
Summary 12
■ **Chapter 2: Getting Started with Google Cloud Platform 13**
Cloud Platform Building Blocks 13
Projects 13
Regions, Zones, Resources, and Quotas 14
The Developers Console 16
Permissions and Auth 17
The Cloud SDK and the gcloud Tool 20
APIs and Cloud Client Libraries 21
Cloud Platform Products 24
Summary 25
■ **Chapter 3: Using Google APIs 27**
Auth Essentials 27
API Keys 28
OAuth 2.0 30
Translate API 41
Accessing Translate REST API 41
Discovering Languages Supported by Translate API 43
Accessing Translate API using Client Programs 47
Summary 49
■ **Part II: Google Cloud Platform - Compute Products 51**
■ **Chapter 4: Google Compute Engine 53**
Virtual Machines 53
Persistent Disks 55
Networks and Firewalls 55
Deploying High-Performance Virtual Machines Using Compute Engine 56
Associating the gcloud Command-Line Tool with a Google Account 56
Selecting a Google Cloud Platform Project 59

Creating and Starting an Instance 59
Allowing Ingress Network Access 60
Creating a Web Presence with Compute Engine in 8 Minutes Flat 60
Handling Unpredictable Traffic with the Compute Engine Load Balancer 65
Forwarding Rules 65
Target Pool 66
Load-Distribution Algorithm 66
Health Checks 66
Going Live 66
Building a Global Multi-Datacenter Web Tier in an Hour 69
Global Forwarding Rules 70
Target HTTP Proxy 70
URL Maps 70
Backend Services 70
Instance Groups 71
Load-Distribution Algorithm 71
Going Live 71
Automatically Resizing a Web Tier with the Compute Engine Autoscaler 76
Managed Instance Group 76
Utilization Metric 76
Target Utilization Level 77
Autoscaling Integrations 77
Going Live 78
Summary 81
■Chapter 5: Google App Engine 83
The SDK 83
About Web Applications 84
Time for the Much-Beloved "Hello World" 84
Pretty "Hello World" 86
Storing Information 89

Key Properties and Ancestor Paths 95
Batching and Asynchronous Operations 96
Request Routing 98
Queries 99
Transactions 102
User Management 103
Memcache 105
E-mail 107
Task Queues 109
Push Queues 110
Pull Queues 112
Handling Tasks 113
Task Queues in the Administration Console 115
Deleting Tasks 116
Deferred Tasks 116
Scheduled Tasks 118
Schedule Format 118
Updating Cron Information 119
Logs 120
Deploying 120
Summary 121
■ Chapter 6: Next Generation DevOps Initiatives 123
Containers 124
Operating System–Level Virtualization 126
LXC and Control Groups 126
Namespaces 126
Docker 127
Docker Images 127
Docker Containers 128

Kubernetes 129
Pods 129
Replication Controllers 130
Volumes 130
Labels and Annotations 131
Networking 132
Services 133
Namespace 133
DNS 134
Google Container Engine 134
App Engine Managed Virtual Machines 139
Getting Started 140
Deploying Docker Containers 143
Live Debugging 149
Configuring a Managed VM 152
Summary 155
■ Part III: Google Cloud Platform - Storage Products 157
■ Chapter 7: Google Cloud SQL 159
Building a Reliable MySQL Back End with Cloud SQL 160
Creating a Cloud SQL Instance 160
Setting Up Access to Cloud SQL Instance 162
Connecting to your Cloud SQL Instance 164
Securing Access to your Cloud SQL Instance 165
Building a Scalable MySQL Cluster with Cloud SQL 168
Step 1: Checking and Enabling (If Required) Database Backups 169
Step 2: Checking and Enabling (If Required) Binary Logs in the Master Instance 170
Step 3: Waiting for a Database Backup to Be Available 170
Step 4: Creating a Cloud SQL Read Replica 171
Setting Up WordPress CMS with Cloud SQL as Backend 172

Expanding the Cloud SQL MySQL Cluster with External Nodes 174
Setting Up a MySQL Server External to Cloud Platform 175
Measuring the Performance of Cloud SQL 180
Summary 183
Chapter 8: Cloud Storage 185
Your First File Upload 185
Installing gsutil 185
Enabling Cloud Storage 186
Enabling Billing 186
Authorizing Your Google Account at the Command Line 186
Running Commands with gsutil 187
Creating a New Bucket 187
Uploading Your First File 187
Cleaning Up 188
Why Use Cloud Storage? 188
Strong Consistency in Cloud Storage 189
Applications of Cloud Storage 189
Access Control 190
Resumable Uploads 192
Signed URLs 196
URL Structure 197
Signature 198
Handling Errors 200
ACLs (Access Control Lists) 201
Permissions and Scopes 202
Default and Predefined ACLs 204
Lifecycle Management 208
Automation 209
Summary 210

■Chapter 9: Google Cloud Datastore.......... 211
Why Is Cloud Datastore Scalable?.......... 211
Why Is Cloud Datastore Highly Available?.......... 212
Why Is Cloud Datastore Fast?.......... 212
The Building Blocks of Cloud Datastore.......... 212
Properties.......... 213
Identifiers, Keys, and Ancestor Paths.......... 214
Cross-Group Transactions.......... 219
Cloud Datastore Indexes.......... 220
Exploding Indexes.......... 222
Queries.......... 224
Operating with Large datasets: OFFSET, LIMIT, and Cursors.......... 227
Filtering.......... 229
Optimizing for Costs: Keys-Only and Projection Queries.......... 229
Sorting.......... 230
Pricing.......... 231
Summary.......... 231
■Part IV: Google Cloud Platform - Big Data Products.......... 233
■Chapter 10: Google BigQuery.......... 235
Building Blocks and Fundamentals.......... 236
Importing Data.......... 238
Transform Apache Access Log Files.......... 239
Loading Transformed Data to BigQuery via Cloud Storage.......... 243
Querying Data.......... 245
Exporting Data and Creating Views.......... 250
Summary.......... 253

■ **Chapter 11: Google Cloud Dataflow 255**

Setup 256

The Building Blocks of Cloud Dataflow 258

Pipelines 258

PCollection 259

Transforms 260

Data Sources and Sinks 264

Constructing and Executing Jobs in Cloud Dataflow 266

1. Filter Log to Extract Response Code 269

2. Count Occurrences for Each Response Code Found 270

3. Get the Top Five Response Codes 271

4. Format Response Codes and Counts into a Printable String 271

Executing your pipeline 273

Showing Results 275

Summary 275

■ **Chapter 12: Google Cloud Pub/Sub 277**

Setting Up Your System 278

Topics 279

Subscriptions 282

Push Subscriptions 283

Pull Subscriptions 284

Acknowledgement Deadline 285

Messages 286

Processing Messages 288

Pull Subscriptions 288

Push Subscriptions 290

Summary 292

■ **Part V: Google Cloud Platform - Networking and Services 293**

■ **Chapter 13: Google Cloud DNS 295**

Publishing Your Internet Identity 296

Summary 307

■ **Chapter 14: Google Cloud Endpoints 309**

Cloud Endpoints and ProtoRPC 309

Setting Up Your Environment: The SDK 310

The Foundations of Your Application: app.yaml 310

Your API and api_server 311

The model: A Bridge between NDB Datastore and Cloud Endpoints 314

Services and Request Handlers 318

EndpointsModel.method 320

EndpointsModel.query_method 321

The APIs Explorer 324

Generating Client Libraries for Your Application 325

Accessing Your API from Your Android client 326

Summary 330

■ **Part VI: Google Cloud Platform - Management and Recipes 331**

■ **Chapter 15: Cloud Platform DevOps Toolbox 333**

Google Cloud Deployment Manager 333

Building Blocks 333

Launching the Compute Engine VM using Deployment Manager 334

Developing Configuration and Template Files 337

Managing Deployments 343

Source and Binary Code Management 345
Cloud Repositories 345
Push-to-Deploy 346
Source Code Tools 346
Google Container Registry 347
Hosted Security Services 347
Cloud Debugger 347
Cloud Security Scanner 347
Cloud Trace 347
Summary 348
■ **Chapter 16: Architecture Recipes for Google Cloud Platform 349**
Use Case 1: Using an Unmanaged Infrastructure to Host Internet-Scale Web Apps 349
Think Big, Start Small, Scale Fast 350
Use Case 2: Using Managed Infrastructure to Host Internet-Scale Web Apps 353
Use Case 3: Doing Big Data Analytics, Google Style 355
Use Case 4: The MVP Approach 355
Use Case 5: LunchMates—Getting the World to Learn During Lunch 358
What's Next in Google Cloud Platform 360
Google Compute Engine 361
Google App Engine 361
Google Container Engine 362
Google Cloud SQL 362
Google Cloud Storage 362
Google Cloud DNS 362
Summary 363
Index 365

About the Authors

S.P.T. Krishnan has more than 15 years of professional software development experience. He has expertise and experience in multiple computing domains: information systems security, cloud computing, high-performance computing, data analytics, and embedded systems. Krishnan is a Google Developer Expert in Google Cloud Platform and is currently working as a research scientist with the Institute for Infocomm Research, Singapore. Learn more about Krishnan at `https://developers.google.com/experts/people/krishnan-s-p-t` and `http://bit.ly/sptkrishnan`.

Krishnan graduated with a doctorate degree in computer engineering and a master's degree by research in computer science from National University of Singapore. He graduated with a bachelors of engineering degree in electronics and communication engineering from University of Madras, India. Krishnan currently lives in Singapore with his wife, Kavitha, and daughters, Balini, Bhadra, and DhanyaDeveshi.

Jose L. Ugia Gonzalez is a tech engineer and an entrepreneur. His main activities are generally related to software and product development in tech startups, with a greater focus on mobile and cloud computing technologies. Jose is currently working as a consultant for technological companies, as well as on own initiatives. Learn more at `https://linkedin.com/in/joseluisugia` and `ugia.io`.

Acknowledgments

The authors would like to thank the following 30 Googlers who reviewed the technical content in this book, provided guidance and feedback, and offered advice on best practices.

Adam Lydick
Amy Unruh
Anthony Moore
Brad Adams
Brian Dorsey
Chris Crall
Chris Sells
Craig Mcluckie
Dan Ciruli
Daniel Tang
Danielle Aronstam
Dominic Preuss
Ed Davisson
Frances Perry
Francesc Compoy Flores
Jason Allor
Jeremy Condit
Joerg Heilig
John Cormie
Jordan Tigani
Katie McCormick
Kim Cameron
Mandy Waite
Paul Newson
Rae Wang
Rafael Fernandez
Rohit Khare
Takashi Matsuo
Vilas Jagannath
Weston Hutchins

And the authors would like to thank the following Googlers who played key roles in making this book a reality:

Amit Chopra
Alex Maier
Kathy Kam
Laurence Moroney

The authors would also like to thank the three amazing women at Apress who made sure the book was released on time for Google IO 2015.

Rita A. Fernando
Susan McDermott
Tiffany Taylor

Finally, we would like to apologize to the people we may have missed in these lists. Please know that we will always be grateful for the catalytic role you played.

Introduction

Cloud computing, specifically the public cloud, is revolutionizing the way application developers design, build, deploy, maintain, and retire their software. Just a decade ago, it took several weeks to make a website public. Today, thanks to public cloud platforms like Amazon Web Services, Google Cloud Platform, and Microsoft Azure, the same task can be done in a hour, if not in a couple of minutes.

When we became Google Developer Experts in Google Cloud Platform, we interacted with the developer communities in several countries and asked them what they needed to in order to start using Cloud Platform. The unanimous responses were the need for books. We scoured the market, and although a few books talked about specific Cloud Platform technologies, we couldn't find a single book that introduced application developers to the entire Cloud Platform. So, we decided to fill the gap—and the result is this book.

We started writing with one clear objective: to help you benefit from the power of Cloud Platform to make an impact onyour present and future projects at work, on the side, in your hobbies, or in any other area where taking advantage of the experience acquired by Google in recent years can get you further and faster than before.

Let's step back for a second and see how technological progress has affected the way you work. Think about a day of work in your life, starting with small things like commuting, organizing meetings, managing productive time, and so on. The important point is not how much these have changed but the fact that a few years ago we never would have expected to be working with the Internet or reading an ebook on our way to work; meeting with colleagues in different parts of the world in a productive way; or controlling our work habits, focus times, and breaks with tools that you can install on your computer. We did not see many of these things coming; and even when we did, we tended not to accept them until they penetrated our culture sufficiently that not adopting them would have left us behind.

Because of the pace at which technology progresses, this process repeats itself every few years. So regardless of how new you are to technology, it is likely that you have seen this cycle a couple of times already. It does not matter how many times this happens—most of us arestatic and defensive in the face of change, because it is easier to think in retrospective than to apply broad new knowledgeto our daily lives. If we did, it would be clear to us that in the near future, information will surround us in less invasive ways than it does today when we use computers or mobile devices. We would also know that artificial intelligence and machine learning will likely keep handling moreduties for humans; and that our lives will be connected not only to other lives, but also to the objects that surround us—houses, cars, streets, buildings—and so on. Likewise, and most important, we know that developing server applications, in most cases, will not require usto set up machines, databases, and load balancers—at least, not by ourselves. If we need to analyze and process big chunks of information, we will not need to set up the entire infrastructure; or if we need massive amounts of computing power to make calculations that are still out of reach today, we will be ready to run the logic in a matter of seconds.

This book is intended to help you make that transition inCloud Platform and build a foundation that will make you comfortable in such a flexible and changing environment. You can consume this book in two different ways. You can read it the way you read most books, starting with chapter one and reading all the way to the end. If you do, you will get a broad and experimental understanding of the entire stack of services that Cloud Platform offers. This will give you the assets you need to design and tackle today's challenges when it comes to cloud computing.

Conversely, you can use this book as a travel companion through your ideas, projects, or work, jumping between chapters based on your needs at specific points in time. For example, suppose you decide to start gathering and processing analytics in your company. You can open Chapter 10 of this book, learn about Google BigQuery, and get your system set up and ready in a few pages. Or consider a different project: you want to build something very fast in order to get your product or service out as soon as possible. In that case, you can jump directly to Chapter 5, where we cover Google App Engine, or Chapter 14, about Google Cloud Endpoints, and get your backend set up in a matter of hours. Don't worry; when we think it is relevant for you to read about other technologies, we point you to the right resources inside and outside of this book.

Who This Book Is For

This book is targeted at two classes of developers: those new to cloud computing and those new to Cloud Platform. We take an on-ramp approach and gradually introduce you first to cloud computing and the public cloud and then to Cloud Platform. We adopt a "getting things done" approach (versus a "tell-all" approach) and share only essential knowledge that is required for you to get going with Cloud Platform.

Downloading the Code

The source code forthe examples in this book can be downloaded from `github.com/googlecloudplatformbook`, and the errata will be posted at `www.cloudplatformbook.com`. The source code for this book is available in zip file format at `www.apress.com/9781484210055`.

Contacting the Authors

The authors can be reached at `cloudplatformbook@gmail.com`.

PART I

Introducing Cloud Computing and Google Cloud Platform

CHAPTER 1

The Google Cloud Platform Difference

Cloud computing as a vision is just 54 years young in 2015 (much older than either of this book's authors!). In 1961, John McCarthy introduced the idea of "computation being delivered as a public utility." Over the next five decades, various technological innovations enabled today's cloud computing, including the following:

- In 1960s, J. C. R. Licklider developed ARPANET—the forerunner to the Internet and what is considered to be the biggest contributor to the history of cloud computing in this era.
- In 1971, Intel engineer Ray Tomlinson developed software that allowed users to send messages from one computer to another. This subsequently was recognized as the first e-mail.
- In 1976, Xerox's Robert Metcalfe introduced Ethernet, essentially standardizing the wired network interface in computers.
- In 1991, CERN released the World Wide Web for general (that is, noncommercial) use.
- In 1993, the Mosaic web browser allowed graphics to be shown on the Internet. In the same year, private companies were allowed to use the Internet for the first time.
- During the late 1990s and early 2000s (famously known as the dot-com era), the availability of multitenant architectures, widespread high-speed bandwidth, and global software interoperability standards created the right environment for cloud computing to finally take off.

The realization of a global high-speed network and a utilities-based business model are the two major driving principles behind cloud computing.

What Is Cloud Computing?

Cloud computing is about abstracting the computing infrastructure and other associated resources and offering them as service, usually on a pay-per-use basis, over the Internet. The service can be targeted for human consumption or consumption by other software systems. Users just need a web browser to access services; software systems can consume services using a web application programming interface (API). This abstraction is often realized through a technical process called *virtualization*.

WHAT IS VIRTUALIZATION?

Virtualization is a process through which a hardware resource (such as a server or network) is cloned as an in-memory resource and is used as the (virtual) foundation to support a software stack. Virtualization is not an entirely new concept; virtual memory, for example, is used extensively in modern operating system(s) for security, for process isolation, and to create an impression that more memory is available than is actually present. Virtualization also makes it easy to transfer a virtual resource to another system when the underlying hardware fails.

A good analogy to cloud computing is the electric grid that centralized the production, transmission, and distribution of electricity to consumers. Consumers simply plug in to the grid, consume power, and pay for what they use without worrying about the nitty-gritty details of how electricity is produced, transmitted, and distributed. (You may be interested to know that, before the electric grid was invented, each organization produced its own electricity. Obviously, this required a large capital expense and was affordable only for the elite and rich.)

Cloud technology standardizes and pools IT resources and automates many of the maintenance tasks done manually today. Cloud architectures facilitate elastic consumption, self-service, and pay-as-you-go pricing. *Cloud* in this context refers to cloud computing architecture, encompassing both public and private clouds. But the public cloud has its own distinct set of advantages, which are hard to replicate in a private setting. This chapter focuses on these from both technical and nontechnical perspectives.

Technical Benefits of Using a Public Cloud

Several key performance benefits may motivate you to migrate to the public cloud. This section covers a few of these benefits.

Uptime

Most public cloud providers have redundancy built in as part of their system design. This extends from foundational utilities like electricity, Internet, and air conditioning to hardware, software, and networking. As a result, providers typically can offer uptime of 99.9% or more. This translates to expected downtime of just 8.76 hours per year (~1/3 day). All businesses can benefit from such high uptime for their IT infrastructure.

As independent businesses, public cloud service providers are able to provide legally binding service-level agreements (SLAs) that state the guaranteed uptime for their infrastructure and the penalties when those guarantees are not met. Such SLAs are not typically available from internal IT departments. The following URLs are for the SLAs of some of the popular cloud platform products covered in this book. In general, once a product is out of beta and into general availability (GA), the corresponding SLA should be available at `https://cloud.google.com/<product>/sla`:

- `https://cloud.google.com/compute/sla`
- `https://cloud.google.com/appengine/sla`
- `https://cloud.google.com/sql/sla`
- `https://cloud.google.com/storage/sla`
- `https://cloud.google.com/datastore/sla`
- `https://cloud.google.com/bigquery/sla`

Resource Utilization

Many organizational applications' resource needs vary by time. (Here, *resource* is a generic term and may refer to CPU, RAM, disk traffic, or network traffic.) As an example, an employee-facing app may be used more during the day and require more resources; it uses fewer resources at night due to reduced demand. This time-of-day variability leads to low overall resource usage in a traditional data-center setup. When you use a public cloud infrastructure, more resources can be (instantly) deployed when required and released when not needed, leading to cost savings.

Public cloud service providers have wide visibility on resource usage patterns across their customers and typically cluster them based on industry. Any application's resource usage may vary across individual system components; this is known as *multi-resource variability*. Resource usage patterns across industries are known as *industry-specific variability*.

Due to resource usage visibility, a public cloud service provider can reassign resources released by one customer to another customer, thereby keeping resource utilization high. If there is no demand for a particular resource, the provider may shut down the corresponding infrastructure to save operational costs. This way, the provider is able to handle applications whose resource needs are spiky in nature.

Expertise

Pubic cloud service providers have experienced system and network administrators along with 24×7 hardware maintenance personnel on site, owing to the tight SLAs they provide. By using a public cloud, companies can indirectly tap on this expert pool.

It would be challenging for a small or medium-size business to recruit, train, and maintain a top-notch team of domain experts, especially when deployment size is limited. Even larger companies are sometimes unable to match the deep expertise available at a public cloud service provider. For example, the well-known file-sharing company DropBox, which has millions of users, runs entirely on a public cloud.

Economic Benefits of Using a Public Cloud

In addition to the technical benefits of using a public cloud, there are several economic advantages to doing so. This section discusses the economic benefits of deploying on a public cloud, based on typical business yardsticks.

TCO

Total cost of ownership (TCO) refers to the total cost of acquiring, using, maintaining, and retiring a product. When you understand TCO, you will realize that many hidden costs usually are not accounted for. Specifically, TCO should include core costs such as the actual price of hardware/software and non-core costs such as time spent on pre-purchase research, operating costs including utilities, manpower, maintenance, and so on. Non-core costs typically are not included with traditional purchases and are bundled into administrative costs.

In the context of public cloud computing, TCO usually refers to software and/or hardware made available via lease. Interestingly, it avoids many non-core costs such as purchase-order processing, shipping, installation and so on.

Economies of Scale

Businesses (or customers) save more when they make a bulk purchase—the seller is willing to reduce its profit margin per unit for large sales. This is how big buyers, such as large companies, are able to get better deals compared to smaller companies in traditional transactions.

In the case of a public cloud, the buyer is the public cloud service provider such a Google Cloud Platform or Amazon Web Services. The larger the public cloud service provider, the more hardware it is likely to purchase from OEMs and the lower the price per unit. Public cloud service providers typically pass some of these savings to their customers (similar to a cooperative society model). This practice puts individual developers and companies of all sizes on the same level playing field, because they get the same low pricing for hardware/software.

CapEx and OpEx

Capital expenditures (CapEx) and *operational expenditures (OpEx)* are linked and refer to expenses incurred at different points in a product's consumption lifecycle. CapEx usually refers to large upfront expenses incurred before commencing use of a product, such as building a data center or acquiring hardware such as servers and racks and procuring Internet connectivity. OpEx refers to the associated operational expenses after a product is purchased and during its lifetime, such as manpower, utilities, and maintenance. The traditional wisdom is that high CapEx leads to low OpEx, whereas low CapEx leads to higher OpEx. Largely due to economies of scale, a public cloud service consumer enjoys low CapEx and low OpEx while transferring the large CapEx to the public cloud service provider, essentially creating a new economic model.

ROI and Profit Margins

Return on investment (ROI) and *profit margins* are strongly linked to one another and are key selling points for adopting a public cloud. ROI refers to the financial gain (or return) on an investment, and the profit margin is the ratio of income to revenue. By using a public cloud, an organization reduces its expenditures, and thus its ROI and profit margins are higher. Such higher returns are more visible in small and medium-sized businesses that have relatively high CapEx (because of low purchase quantities) when starting up.

Business Benefits of Using a Public Cloud

In addition to the technical and economic benefits, there are several business-process advantages to using a public cloud. This section describes a few of them.

Time to Market

Responsiveness is crucial in today's business environment. Business opportunities often arrive unannounced and are short-lived. Winners and losers are often determined by who is able to move faster and grab opportunities. Such opportunities typically require new/additional IT resources, such as computational power or bandwidth. A cloud service provider can provide these almost instantaneously. Hence, by using a public cloud, any business can reduce the time it takes to bring a product to market. In comparison, using the traditional route of building/acquiring infrastructure first, introducing a new product would require days if not weeks of onsite deployment.

Using a public cloud leads to reduced opportunity costs, increases agility, and makes it easy to respond to new opportunities and threats. The same quick response times also apply to shedding unneeded capacity. In summary, public cloud computing enables just-in-time procurement and usage for just as long as needed.

Self-Service

One of the hallmarks of the public cloud is the easy-to-use, remotely accessible interface based on modern web standards. All large public cloud service providers offer at least three interfaces: a web-based, graphical, point-and-click dashboard; a console-based command-line tool; and APIs. These enable customers to deploy and terminate IT resources anytime. These facilities make it easy for customers to perform self-service and further reduce time to market. In a traditional setting, even if IT deployment is outsourced to a third party, there is usually a lot of paperwork to be done, such as a request for quotes, purchase orders, and invoice processing.

Pay per Use

One of the promises of a public cloud is no lock-in through contracts. *No lock-in* means no upfront fees, no contractual time period, no early termination penalty, and no disconnection fees. Customers can move to another public cloud provider or simply take things onsite.

Google Cloud Platform adopts this definition and charges no upfront fees, has no contractual time period, and certainly charges no termination/disconnection fees. But Amazon Web Services offers a contract-like reservation plan that requires an initial payment to reserve resources and have lower usage costs during the reservation period. The downside of this reservation plan is that the promised savings are realized only if the same resource type is used nonstop the entire time.

The pay-per-use business model of a public cloud allows a user to pay the same for 1 machine running for 1,000 hours as they would for 1,000 machines running for 1 hour. Today, a user would likely wait 1,000 hours or abandon the project. In a public cloud, there is virtually no additional cost to choosing 1,000 machines and accelerating the user's processes.

WHAT IS SCALABILITY?

Scalability is a process through which an existing resource can be expanded on an on-demand basis either vertically or horizontally. An example of vertical scalability would be to upgrade a server's RAM from 2GB to 4GB, whereas horizontal scalability would add a second server with 2GB RAM. Scalability can be automatic or manual, but the end user should be able to update resources on an on-demand basis using either a web-based dashboard or an API.

Uncertain Growth Patterns

All organizations wish for exponential growth, but they can't commit sufficient IT infrastructure because they are not certain about the future. In a traditional setup, such scenarios result in unused capacity when growth is less than predicted or result in unhappy customers when the installed capacity is not able to handle additional load. Arbitrary loads are best handled by using public cloud deployments.

Why Google Cloud Platform?

Google Cloud Platform is built on the same world-class infrastructure that Google designed, assembled, and uses for corporate products like Google search, which delivers billions of search results in milliseconds. Google has also one of the largest, most geographically widespread, most advanced computer networks in the world. Google's backbone network comprises thousands of miles of fiber-optic cable, uses advanced software-defined networking, and is coupled with edge-caching services to deliver fast, consistent, scalable performance. Google is also one of the few companies to own a private fiber-optic cable under the Pacific Ocean.

Google Cloud Platform empowers software application developers to build, test, deploy, and monitor applications using Google's highly scalable and reliable infrastructure. In addition, it enables system administrators to focus on the software stack while allowing them to outsource the challenging work of hardware assembly, maintenance, and technology refreshes to experts at Google.

Hardware Innovations

Whereas a typical cloud service provider's strategy is wholesale-to-retail using standard hardware and software components, Google's approach has been to innovate at every level: hardware, networking, utilities, and software. This is evident from the multitude and variety of innovations that Google has introduced over the years. Needless to say, Google Cloud Platform benefits from all these innovations and thus differentiates itself from the competition:

- *Highly efficient servers:* In 2001, Google designed energy-efficient servers using two broad approaches: it removed unnecessary components like video cards, peripheral connections, and casing; and it used energy-efficient power supplies (that do AC-to-DC conversion) and power regulators (DC-to-DC conversion) and backup batteries on server racks.
- *Energy-efficient data centers:* In 2003, Google designed portable data centers using shipping containers that held both servers and cooling equipment. This modular approach produced better energy efficiency compared to traditional data centers at the time. Since 2006, Google has achieved the same efficiency using alternate construction methods.
- *Carbon neutrality:* In 2007, Google became a carbon-neutral Internet company, and it remains so today. Its data centers typically use 50% less energy compared to traditional data centers.
- *Industry-leading efficiency:* The cost of electricity is rapidly increasing and has become the largest element of TCO (currently 15%–20%). Power usage effectiveness (PUE) tends to be significantly lower in large facilities than in smaller ones. Google's data centers have very low PUE: it was 1.23 (23% overhead) in Q3 2008 and came down to 1.12 (12% overhead) in Q4 2014. This is significantly lower than the industry average of 1.7 (70% overhead).

All of these hardware innovations result in lower operational costs for Google, and the difference is passed to Google Cloud Platform users. This means customers save on costs.

Software Innovations

Infrastructure innovation is not just about hardware. Google has also led the industry with innovations in software infrastructure:

- *Google File System:* In 2002, Google created the Google File System (GFS), a proprietary distributed file system designed to provide efficient, reliable access to data using a large cluster of commodity hardware.
- *MapReduce:* In 2004, Google shared the MapReduce programming model that simplifies data processing on large clusters. The Apache Hadoop project is an open source implementation of the MapReduce algorithm that was subsequently created by the community.

- *BigTable:* In 2006, Google introduced the BigTable distributed storage system for structured data. BigTable scales across thousands of commodity servers and is used by several Google applications.
- *Dremel:* In 2008, Google shared the details of a system called Dremel that has been in production since 2006. Dremel is a scalable, interactive, ad hoc query system for analyzing read-only nested data that is petabytes in size. Dremel combines multilevel execution trees, uses a columnar data layout, and is capable of running aggregation queries over trillion-row tables in seconds. Dremel is the backend of Google BigQuery.
- *Pregel:* In 2009, Google created a system for large-scale graph processing. The principles of the system are useful for processing large-scale graphs on a cluster of commodity hardware. Examples include web graphs, among other things.
- *FlumeJava:* In 2010, Google introduced FlumeJava. FlumeJava is a pure Java library that provides a few simple abstractions for programming data-parallel computations. These abstractions are higher-level than those provided by MapReduce and provide better support for pipelines. FlumeJava makes it easy to develop, test, and run efficient data-parallel pipelines of MapReduce computations.
- *Colossus:* In 2010, Google created the successor to GFS. Details about Colossus are slim, except that it provides a significant performance improvement over GFS. New products like Spanner use Colossus.
- *Megastore:* In 2011, Google shared the details of Megastore, a storage system developed to meet the requirements of today's interactive online services. Megastore blends the scalability of a NoSQL datastore with the convenience of a traditional RDBMS in a novel way, and provides both strong consistency guarantees and high availability. Megastore provides fully serializable ACID semantics within fine-grained data partitions. This partitioning allows Megastore to synchronously replicate each write across a wide area network with reasonable latency and support seamless failover between datacenters.
- *Spanner:* In 2012, Google announced this distributed database technology. Spanner is designed to seamlessly operate across hundreds of datacenters, millions of machines, and trillions of rows of information.
- *Omega:* In 2013, Google introduced Omega—a flexible, scalable scheduler for large-scale compute clusters. Google wanted to move away from current schedulers, which are monolithic by design and limit new features. Omega increases efficiency and utilization of Google's compute clusters.
- *Millwheel:* In 2014, Google introduced Millwheel, a framework for fault-tolerant stream processing at Internet scale. Millwheel is used as a platform to build low-latency data-processing applications within Google.

All of these innovations are used to make Google Cloud Platform products, just as they are used to build Google's internal products. By using Google Cloud Platform, customers get faster access to Google innovations, thereby distinguishing the effectiveness of applications hosted on Google Cloud Platform.

Figure 1-1 shows a few important innovations from the above list to help visualize the continuous innovations by Google.

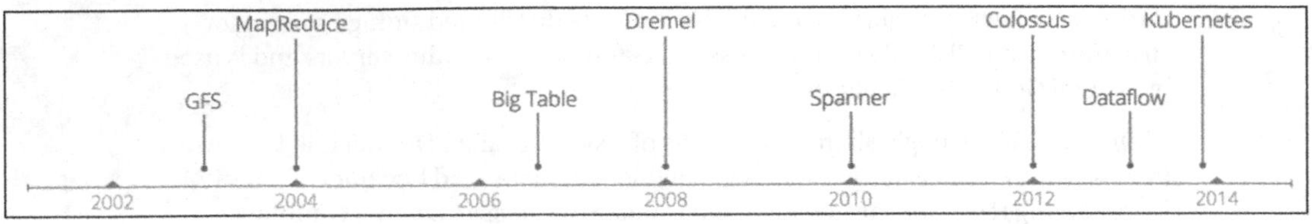

Figure 1-1. *Google's software innovations that are actively used in Google Cloud Platform*

Economic Innovations

In addition to making technical and infrastructure innovations, Google has also taken a fresh look at how to charge for cloud computing resources. Let's consider the economic innovations that Google has introduced in Google Cloud Platform, many of which benefit cloud platform users.

Typical public cloud providers, in particular Amazon Web Services, provide two types of pricing options for products: *on-demand* and *reserved* pricing. The guiding principle behind these two types of pricing options is to secure longer-term commitments from users. In the on-demand pricing model, the customer is free to use the resource for as long as needed and is free to leave anytime. There is no time contract or penalty for termination; this is typical of cloud hosting. In the reserved price model, the customer is required to pay a nonrefundable upfront fee and select the type of resource. As a result, the customer enjoys lower hosting charges for the specified time period.

There are several shortcomings in the reserved pricing model. First, because lower pricing is tied to the resource type, if the customer decides to switch resource types (say, due to different traffic patterns than expected), they are thrown back to the higher pricing model. Second, the upfront fees are time bound and not based on the number of hours of usage. Third, the upfront fees are not refundable if the customer decides to terminate early. In essence, the onus of choosing the right resource type and time duration is with the customer; there is no reconciliation if the actual workload is different from the expected workload.

Google's approach is that customers should be want to host on Google Cloud Platform due to its meritocracy and technical superiority. They should be able to leave anytime and not be tied through contract-like approaches. They should also be able to switch resource types anytime, as their needs change. Finally, while customers are hosting on Google Cloud Platform, they should enjoy the best pricing, on par with the industry.

To realize these objectives, Google has created a new type of pricing model called a *sustained-use discount*. Under this model, Google Cloud Platform automatically applies discounts to resources that run for a significant time. The discount is based on the cumulative amount of time a resource of a particular type is up rather than being tied to a single instance. This means two instances of equivalent specs running simultaneously or concurrently are given the same discount as long as the cumulative hosting period is above a threshold. Sustained-use discounts combined with per-minute billing ensure that customers get the best deal. The following list shows the sustained-use discounts as of this writing (March 2015):

- *0%-25%:* 100% of base rate
- *25%-50%:* 80% of base rate
- *50%-75%:* 60% of base rate
- *75%-100%:* 40% of base rate

Google has ventured to decipher the sometimes-complex world of cloud pricing by explaining how to calculate the cost of a cloud deployment. See the following post in the official Google cloud platform blog for details: `http://googlecloudplatform.blogspot.sg/2015/01/understanding-cloud-pricing.html`.

A Quick Comparison to AWS

This section highlights a few select features of Google Cloud Platform and how they compare with the incumbent public cloud provider, Amazon Web Services:

- Google Compute Engine, the Internet-as-a-service (IaaS) product from Google Cloud Platform, adopts a per-minute charging model except for the initial minimum 10-minute tier. On the other hand, AWS charges on an hourly-basis.

  Let's consider two example use cases. First, if you use an instance for 11 minutes, you pay for 11 minutes in Google Cloud Platform, but you pay for 60 minutes with Amazon Web Services. Second, if you use an instance for 1 minute, you pay for 10 minutes in Google Cloud Platform or 60 minutes in Amazon Web Services. In either case, you can see that Google Cloud Platform is cheaper than Amazon Web Services.

- Google Compute Engine is better suited to handle traffic spikes. This is because the Compute Engine load balancers don't require pre-warming, unlike AWS load balancers. In addition, pre-warming AWS load balancer requires customers to subscribe to AWS support. Compute Engine load balancers are able to scale instantly when they notice a sudden traffic spike.

  In 2013, Google demonstrated that its load balancers could serve 1 million requests per second on a sustained basis and within 5 seconds after setup. You are advised to read the full article at `http://googlecloudplatform.blogspot.in/2013/11/compute-engine-load-balancing-hits-1-million-requests-per-second.html`.

- Compute Engine's persistent disks (PDs) support a larger disk size (currently 10TB) compared with AWS. In addition, Google includes the I/O costs in the cost of the PD, thereby giving customers predictable costing. In the case of AWS, the cost of I/O is separate from the cost of the raw disk space. Moreover, other nice features include the ability to mount a PD to multiple VMs as read-only or a single VM in read-write mode.

- Compute instances are hosted as virtual machines in IaaS. Periodically, the IaaS service provider needs to do maintenance (host OS or hardware) on the platform. The hardware may also fail occasionally. In such cases, it is desirable to have the VM automatically migrate to another physical host. Compute Engine can do live migration.

- Google App Engine, the platform-as-a-service (PaaS) product from Google Cloud Platform, is in our view a pure PaaS product when compared with Beanstalk from Amazon Web Services. This is because Beanstalk is a management layer built on top of AWS EC2. The implication of this design choice is that Beanstalk needs to have at least one EC2 instance up all the time, which adds to hosting costs. App Engine, on the other hand, charges only when there is traffic and includes a monthly free tier.

- BigQuery, the big-data analytics product from Google Cloud Platform, is an integrated and fully hosted platform that scales to thousands of nodes and charges only for space and computation time. In comparison, the AWS equivalent (Red Shift) requires users to configure the system and also charges by the hour rather than based on usage.

- Google data centers (that host Google Cloud Platform's regions and zones) are spread globally and interconnected by Google's private fiber network. This means network traffic between two cloud platform zones passes through a private network and not over the public Internet. As of today, AWS does not have such a private network.

Overall, Google's approach with Google Cloud Platform is not to achieve feature parity with Amazon Web Services but to build products that are by far the best in the industry and in the process fill in the gaps in the AWS portfolio. Hence, the question to ask is whether your needs are being met by what Google Cloud Platform has today, rather than talking about what Google Cloud Platform doesn't have.

When talking about the strengths of Google Cloud Platform, it is important to acknowledge that Amazon Web Services currently has a broader portfolio of products and services than Google Cloud Platform. This is primarily due to the fact that AWS started much earlier, while Google was busy building the fundamentals right, as shown in the list of major software innovations earlier in this chapter.

Summary

We started this chapter by defining the concept of cloud computing. Following this, we leaped into public clouds, which we cover in this book. We shared with you the advantages of a public cloud from several perspectives: technical, economic, and business. Following this, we highlighted several Google research publications that are used to build the strong foundation of Google Cloud Platform. We concluded this chapter by listing the strengths of Google Cloud Platform when compared with Amazon Web Services.

The promise of the public cloud is not just cheaper computing infrastructure, but also faster, easier, more flexible, and ultimately more effective IT.

CHAPTER 2

Getting Started with Google Cloud Platform

Welcome to Google Cloud Platform!

Cloud Platform is a set of modular cloud-based services that provide building blocks you can use to develop everything from simple web sites to sophisticated multitier web-based applications. This chapter introduces the core components of Cloud Platform and guides you through the process of getting started with it.

Cloud Platform Building Blocks

This section gives you an overview of the products in Cloud Platform and explains the technology clusters they belong to. This approach will help you select which chapters of this book you need to read to quickly get started with Cloud Platform. We do, however, encourage you to read the book cover to cover!

Projects

Projects are top-level containers in Cloud Platform. Using projects, you can consolidate all related resources, IT and non-IT, on a project-by-project basis. This enables you to work on several projects at the same time while ensuring that the resources are in separate control domains. Each project is identified by a tuple consisting of the following three items:

- *Project name*: This is a text field that lets you store a friendly, descriptive string about the project's purpose. This is only for your reference and can be changed any number of times during the project's lifetime.
- *Project ID*: The Project ID is a globally unique string across all Cloud Platform products. A random project ID, made of three words delimited by hyphens between them, will be automatically generated during project creation. You can change the suggested ID as long as it's unique across all Cloud Platform projects from all Cloud Platform users. Project ID can include lowercase letters, digits, or hyphens, and it must start with a lowercase letter. Once the choice is made, the ID cannot be changed during the project's lifetime.
- *Project number*: Cloud Platform automatically assigns a project number at creation time for the project's lifetime. You have no control over this number.

The command-line developer tool called gcloud (described later) requires a project ID for identifying and accessing various IT resources. Public-facing Cloud Platform APIs may require either the project ID or the project number for resource-identification purposes. Cloud Platform uses project numbers almost exclusively to identify projects.

In addition to IT resources, a Cloud Platform project also stores information about billing and authorized users. In Cloud Platform, a billing account is considered separate from a project account. One billing can be linked to more than one project account. A billing account is identified by a set of the following four items:

- *Billing account ID*: This is automatically generated by Google billing. You don't have any control over it and don't need to worry about it.
- *Billing account name*: Tis a friendlier description of the billing account. You can set it during account creation and change it any time during the account's lifetime.
- *Status*: The status of a billing account is either active or closed.
- *# Of projects*: Each billing account, after being created, is attached to projects. One billing account can be attached to one or more projects, whereas one project can be attached to only one billing account.

By using projects, you can provide services to different customers and separate the associated costs. Cloud Platform generates a separate bill for each project. At the same time, you can pay for all your projects using the same billing account.

As of this writing, a project can only be created using the web-based Developers Console, not with the gcloud command-line tool or the Cloud Platform API. You also can't list all the projects associated with a Google account using gcloud or an API. This restriction is in place because the project-creation feature is not part of the public-facing APIs, which are also used by gcloud. However, you can store project information using gcloud and use it automatically for subsequent requests. You can create a project by visiting http://console.developers.google.com and filling in the required details.

Regions, Zones, Resources, and Quotas

Cloud Platform resources are hosted in multiple locations worldwide. These locations are composed of *regions*, and each region is further broken into *zones*. A zone is an isolated location within a region. Zones have high-bandwidth, low-latency network connections to other zones in the same region.

Cloud Platform resources can be classified as *global*, *regional*, or *zonal*. IT resources in the same region or zone can only use resources that are specific to the region or zone. For example, Compute Engine, the Infrastructure-as-a-Service product from Cloud Platform, instances and persistent disks are both zonal resources. If you want to attach a persistent disk to an instance, both resources must reside in the same zone. Similarly, if you want to assign a static IP address to a Compute Engine instance, the instance must reside in the same region as the static IP. Not all resources are region or zone specific; some, such as disk images, are global resources that can be used by any other resources at any location.

During the resource-creation stage, depending on the scope of the resource, Cloud Platform prompts you to choose either a region or a zone. For example, when you create an instance or disk, you are prompted to select a zone where that resource should serve traffic. Other resources, such as static IPs, live in regions; when you select a region, the system chooses an appropriate regional IP address.

Cloud Platform makes it easy to programmatically query for current regions and zones and to list all of a region's or zone's public details. Although regions and zones do not change frequently, Google wants to make it easy for you to retrieve this information without having to browse through a web site or documentation. Let's look at how to use the gcloud command-line tool to query information about regions and zones. For now, focus on the results; you learn about gcloud later.

All generally available Cloud Platform resources that have regional scope, such as Compute Engine, are available in all regions/zones. For products that have global scope, such as App Engine and BigQuery, you do not need to select a region or zone. Let's list the regions where Compute Engine (and, by extension, persistent disks, load balancers, autoscalers, Cloud Storage, Cloud Datastore, and Cloud SQL) is available, using gcloud:

```
$ gcloud compute regions list
NAME           CPUS          DISKS_GB      ADDRESSES RESERVED_ADDRESSES STATUS TURNDOWN_DATE
asia-east1     2.00/24.00    10/10240      1/23      1/7                UP
europe-west1   0.00/24.00     0/10240      0/23      0/7                UP
us-central1    0.00/24.00     0/10240      0/23      0/7                UP
```

This output shows that there are currently three regions in Cloud Platform, one on each major continent. This choice was made strategically to accommodate applications and data that need to reside on the respective continent.

In addition to the regions, the previous output shows quota information. A *quota* in Cloud Platform is defined as a soft limit for a given type of resource. If you need more than the stated limit, you can request additional resources by filling out an online Google form. The previous output shows that this particular Google account has instantiated two CPUs, has a 10BG persistent disk, and is using two public IPs, one of which is a reserved IP address. All regions are operating normally, and there is no announced teardown date for any of them.

Let's examine one of the regions in detail:

```
$ gcloud compute regions describe asia-east1
creationTimestamp: '2014-11-18T14:51:15.377-08:00'
description: asia-east1
id: '1220'
kind: compute#region
name: asia-east1
quotas:
- limit: 24.0
  metric: CPUS
  usage: 2.0
- limit: 10240.0
  metric: DISKS_TOTAL_GB
  usage: 10.0
- limit: 7.0
  metric: STATIC_ADDRESSES
  usage: 1.0
- limit: 23.0
  metric: IN_USE_ADDRESSES
  usage: 1.0
- limit: 1024.0
  metric: SSD_TOTAL_GB
  usage: 0.0
- limit: 1500.0
  metric: LOCAL_SSD_TOTAL_GB
  usage: 0.0
- limit: 240.0
  metric: INSTANCES
  usage: 0.0
```

```
selfLink: https://www.googleapis.com/compute/v1/projects/www-redcross-sg/regions/asia-east1
status: UP
zones:
- https://www.googleapis.com/compute/v1/projects/www-redcross-sg/zones/asia-east1-a
- https://www.googleapis.com/compute/v1/projects/www-redcross-sg/zones/asia-east1-b
- https://www.googleapis.com/compute/v1/projects/www-redcross-sg/zones/asia-east1-c
```

This output shows more interesting and useful information about the region. First, you can see that Google publicly discloses when this zone went live (or was upgraded). Second, just like any other entity in Cloud Platform, the region has an ID, a name, and a description. Finally, the output states that the region contains three zones.

Let's now list all the zones in all the regions in Cloud Platform:

```
$ gcloud compute zones list
NAME           REGION         STATUS NEXT_MAINTENANCE TURNDOWN_DATE
asia-east1-a   asia-east1     UP
asia-east1-c   asia-east1     UP
asia-east1-b   asia-east1     UP
europe-west1-b europe-west1 UP
europe-west1-c europe-west1 UP
europe-west1-d europe-west1 UP
us-central1-f  us-central1    UP
us-central1-a  us-central1    UP
us-central1-c  us-central1    UP
us-central1-b  us-central1    UP
```

This output shows that there are a total of 10 zones across 3 regions. Of course, this is as of this writing; Google is expected to add new regions and zones regularly.

From the region and zone names, you can decipher that the fully qualified name for a zone is made up of `<region>-<zone>`. For example, the fully qualified name for zone a in region `us-central1` is `us-central1-a`.

Let's look at the details for one particular zone:

```
$ gcloud compute zones describe asia-east1-a
creationTimestamp: '2014-05-30T18:35:16.575-07:00'
description: asia-east1-a
id: '2220'
kind: compute#zone
name: asia-east1-a
region: https://www.googleapis.com/compute/v1/projects/www-redcross-sg/regions/asia-east1
selfLink: https://www.googleapis.com/compute/v1/projects/www-redcross-sg/zones/asia-east1-a
status: UP
```

Just like a region, a zone has a creation date, an ID, a kind, and a name.

The Developers Console

The Developers Console is a web-based interface that you can use to create and manage your Cloud Platform resources. You can also view and manage projects, team members, traffic data, authentication, and billing through the Developers Console; see `https://developers.google.com/console/help/new` to learn about its capabilities. Figure 2-1 shows the Google Developers Console overview screen.

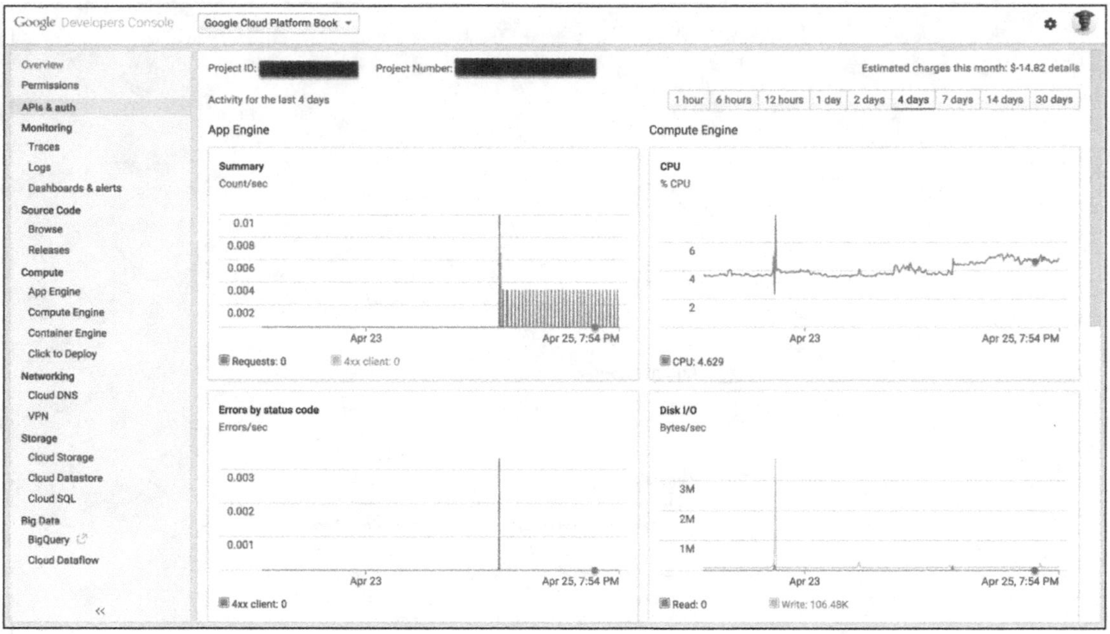

Figure 2-1. *Google Developers Console*

This section looks at some of the Developers Console functionality that is generally applicable for deploying Cloud Platform products.

Permissions and Auth

Each Cloud Platform project can be accessed by one or more Google accounts. The Google account that creates a project is automatically designated as its owner. In addition to an owner, two other roles are allowed that have different levels of access to a project:

- *Owner*: An owner can change project settings and manage team members.
- *Editor*: An editor can change project settings.
- *Viewer*: A viewer can read all project settings and information.

The owner, using the web-based Developers Console, can add additional owners, editors, and viewers. To do so, choose Developers Console ➤ Permissions ➤ Add Member, as shown in Figure 2-2. In addition to regular Google accounts (which are accessed by humans), Cloud Platform also supports a category called Service Accounts. These are automatically added by Cloud Platform and are used to authenticate the project to other Google services and APIs.

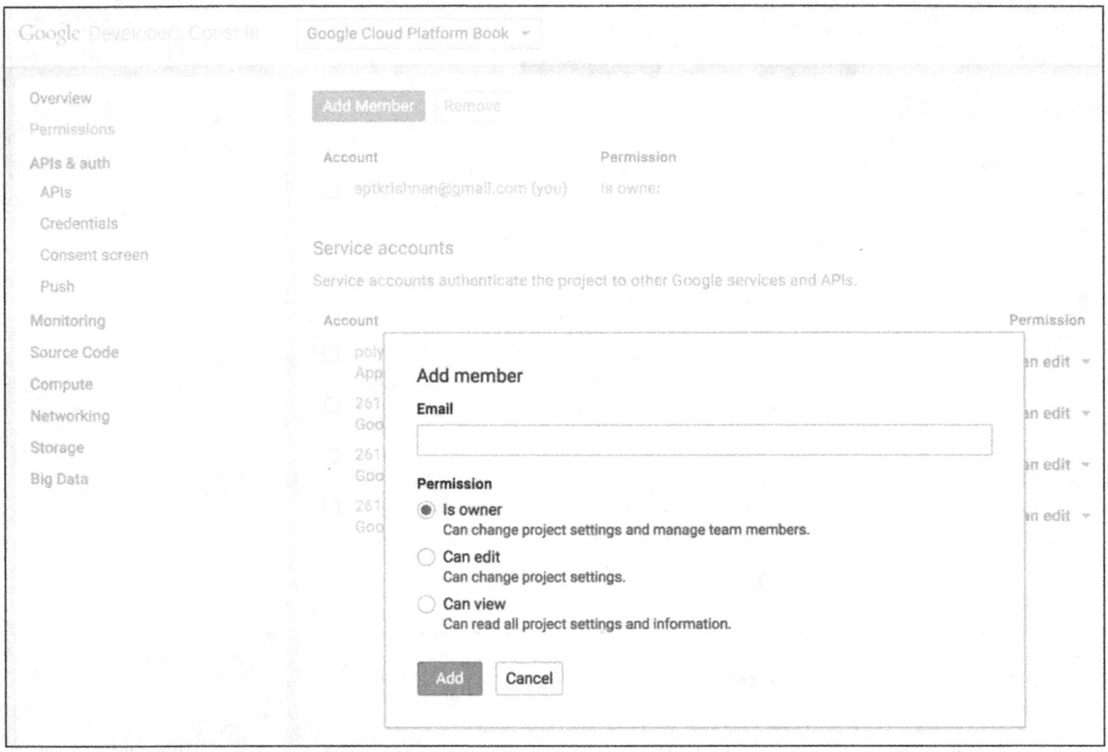

Figure 2-2. *Adding team members to a project*

Permissions allow a project's resources to access various Cloud Platform APIs. Some APIs allow unlimited and unmetered access, such as the Compute Engine API. Other APIs impose daily quotas and access-rate limits. Auth (short for authentication) allows one or more client applications to access APIs that have been enabled in a particular project. In addition, it lets applications access your private data (for example, contact lists). We examine the OAUTH technology in Chapter 3. For now, you just need to know how to create new client ID or key using the Developers Console. Go to Developers Console ➤ APIs & Auth ➤ Credentials to create an OATH2 client ID or a public API access key, as shown in Figure 2-3.

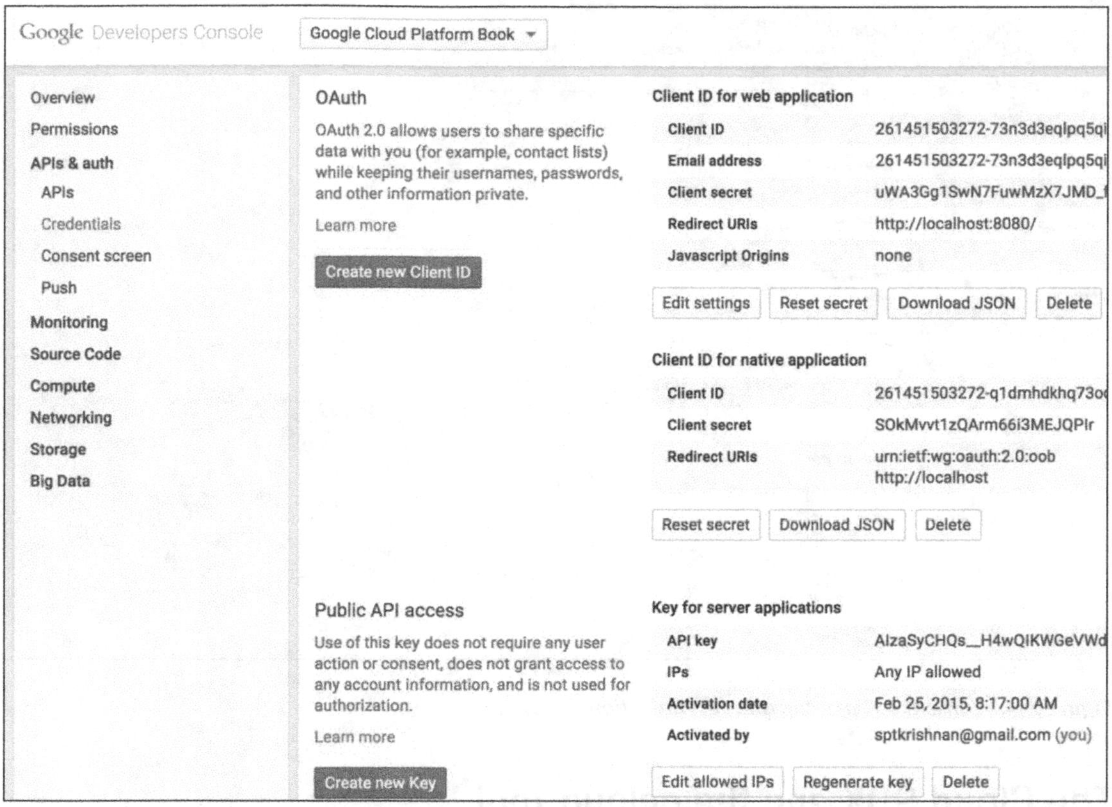

***Figure 2-3.** Creating new credentials*

When you use the version of OAUTH called *three-legged authentication (3LO)*, your users are shown a consent screen that they need to accept before Google will authorize your application to access their private data. This is explained in the OAUTH section in Chapter 3. For now, to customize the consent screen in the Developers Console, choose Developers Console ➤ APIs & Auth ➤ Consent Screen as shown Figure 2-4.

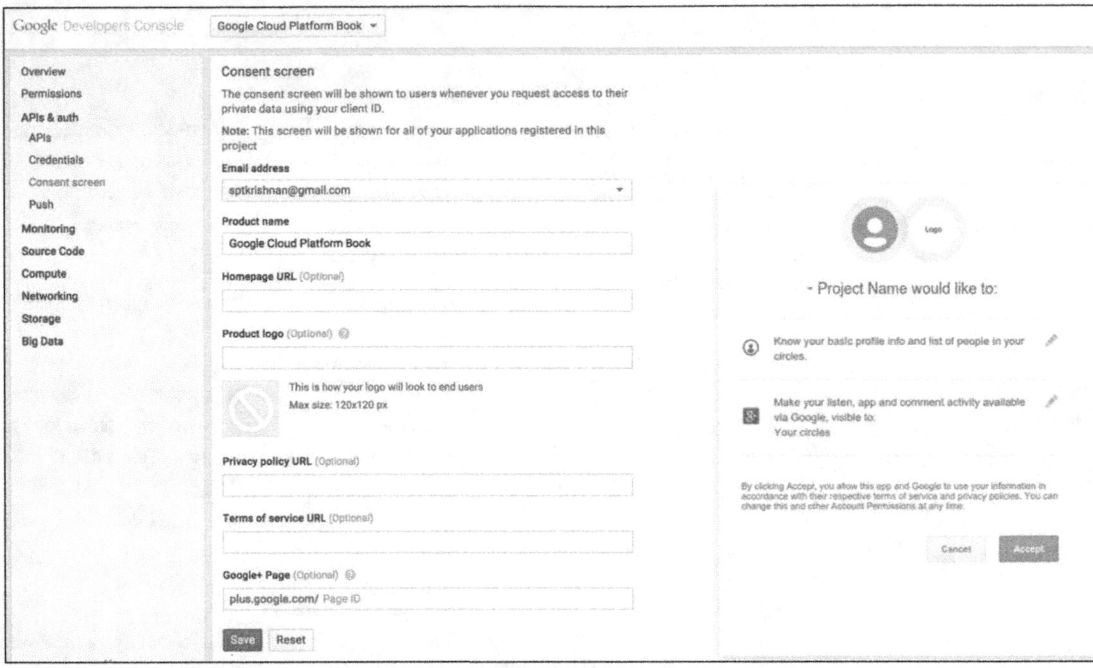

Figure 2-4. *Consent screen setup and customization*

The Cloud SDK and the gcloud Tool

The Google Cloud SDK contains tools and libraries that enable you to easily create and manage resources on Cloud Platform. It runs on Windows, Mac OS X, and Linux, and it requires Python 2.7.x or greater or another language runtime for language-specific support in the SDK. Installing the Cloud SDK is operating system dependent and is well documented at `https://cloud.google.com/sdk`. Follow the instructions there to install the Cloud SDK.

The most common way to manage Cloud Platform resources is to use the `gcloud` command-line tool. `gcloud` is included as part of the Cloud SDK. After you have installed the Cloud SDK, you need to authenticate the `gcloud` tool to access your account. Run the command `gcloud auth login` to do this, as follows:

```
$ gcloud auth login
Your browser has been opened to visit:
https://accounts.google.com/o/oauth2/auth?redirect_uri=http%3A%2F%2Flocalhost%3A8085%2F&
prompt=select_account&response_type=code&client_id=32555940559.apps.googleusercontent.com&
scope=https%3A%2F%2Fwww.googleapis.com%2Fauth%2Fuserinfo.email+https%3A%2F%2F
www.googleapis.com%2Fauth%2Fcloud-platform+https%3A%2F%2Fwww.googleapis.com%2Fauth%2F
appengine.admin+https%3A%2F%2Fwww.googleapis.com%2Fauth%2Fcompute&access_type=offline

Saved Application Default Credentials.

You are now logged in as [cloudplatformbook@gmail.com].
Your current project is [cloud-platform-book].  You can change this setting by running:
  $ gcloud config set project PROJECT
```

gcloud opens a new browser window when you execute this command. After you click Accept, control returns to the gcloud tool, and your gcloud instance is configured to access your Google account and project. If you would like to switch to another account or project, you can use the following commands (replacing the account and project values):

```
$ gcloud config set account cloudplatformbook@gmail.com
$ gcloud config set project cloud-platform-book
```

gcloud has a comprehensive built-in help system. You can request help at multiple levels. Here are a few examples:

- `gcloud -h`: Produces help at the outermost level. The tool lists various command groups, commands, and optional flags that are permissible.
- `gcloud compute -h`: Lists the command groups, commands, and optional flags that apply to Google Compute Engine.
- `gcloud compute instances -h`: Lists the commands and optional flags that apply to the `instances` command group in Google Compute Engine.

This way, you can request help at multiple levels. To learn about all of gcloud's features, visit `https://cloud.google.com/sdk/gcloud`. You can list the various components supported in gcloud by using the command `gcloud components list`.

APIs and Cloud Client Libraries

Google follows an API-first development philosophy, and APIs are the primary developer interface for Google's products, including Cloud Platform. Hence, before you can use a product—say, Compute Engine—you need to enable that particular API in your project. API enablement is on a project-by-project basis. Google makes it easy for you to enable a particular API using the Developers Console. You can access the APIs section by choosing Developers Console ➤ APIs & Auth ➤ APIs. The tabbed screen shows the list of all available APIs and the APIs that have been enabled in a project. Figure 2-5 shows a subset of the APIs available, and Figure 2-6 shows the APIs that have been enabled for this project.

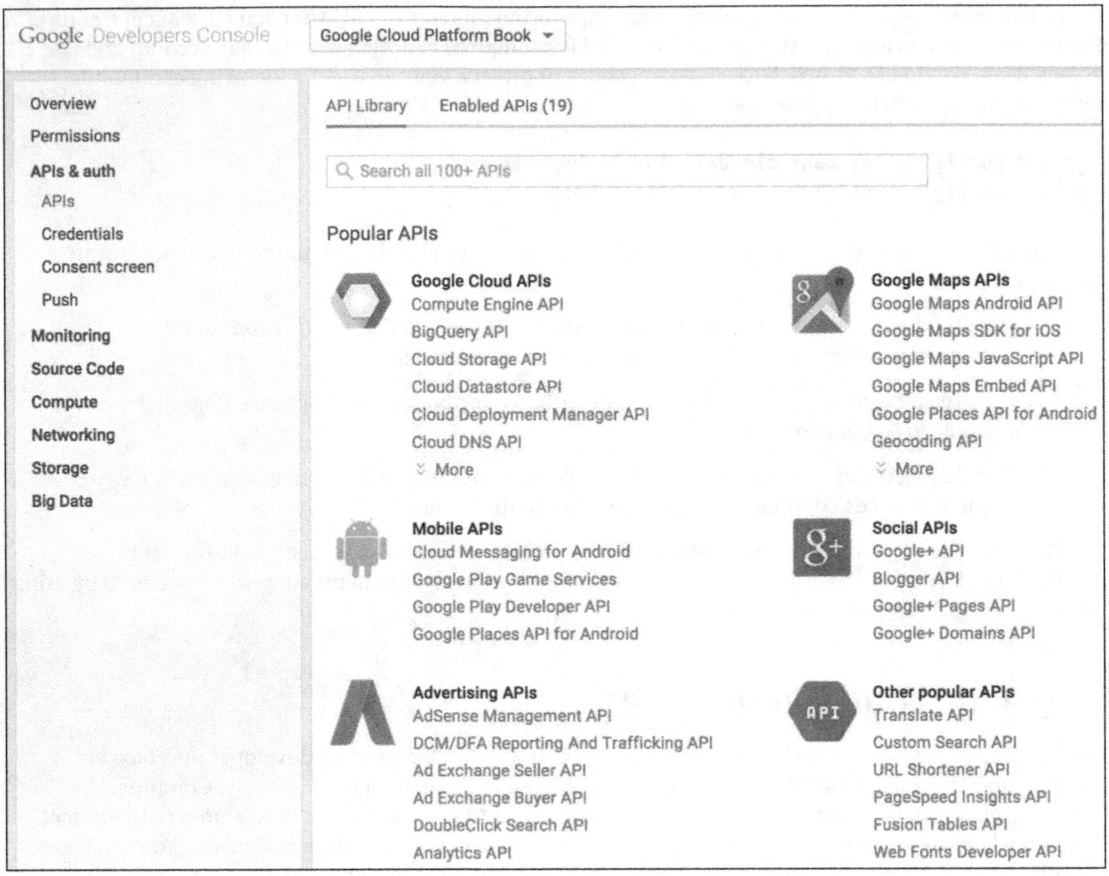

Figure 2-5. *Subset of APIs available to Google developers*

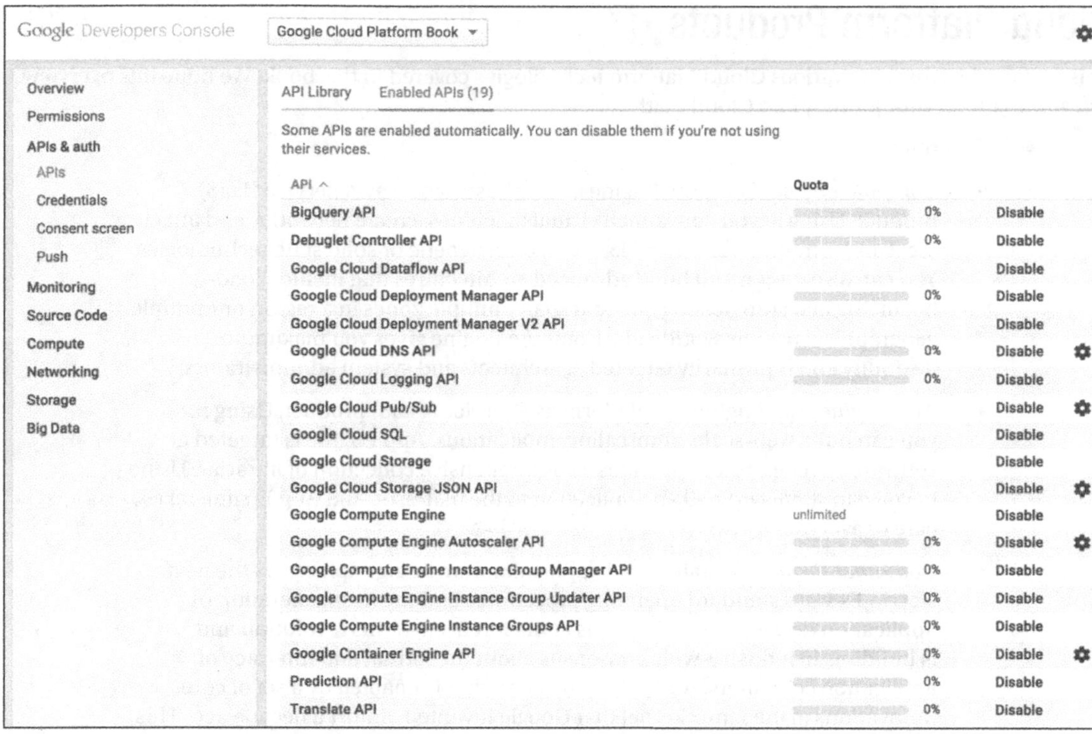

Figure 2-6. *List of APIs enabled in one project*

Deploying resources on demand and releasing them when they aren't needed realizes the power of the Cloud Platform. This workflow can be achieved using several methods. When you use the Developers Console, the response time is slow and the process is manual. When you use the `gcloud` tool, the response time is faster, and you can automate the process by using a script. However, Google designed `gcloud` to be used by developers and not programs, so you have to write code to parse the command output. You can use the Cloud Platform APIs to allocate and release resources as needed, but because the APIs are RESTful and stateless, you need to maintain state between API calls.

Cloud Client libraries fill the gap of programmatically accessing the Cloud Platform while integrating into the respective programming language so that the client can use other language features. The Cloud Platform APIs have been implemented as library functions in several programming languages. As of this writing, Google officially supports the Python, Node.js, and Go languages.

Cloud Platform Products

This section describes the various Cloud Platform technologies covered in this book. We hope this overview will guide you on your journey into Cloud Platform:

- Compute
    - *Compute Engine*: Compute Engine is an infrastructure as-a-service (IaaS) product. Using it, you can launch virtual machines, create networks, and attach local and remote persistent disks based on magnetic or solid state technologies. You can also design and build advanced architectures that include load-balancing and auto-scaling and that span multiple zones in a region or multiple geographical regions worldwide. Compute Engine gives you maximum flexibility and is primarily targeted at architects and system administrators.
    - *App Engine*: App Engine is a platform as a service (PaaS) product. Using it, you can build web-scale, autoscaling applications. App Engine is targeted at software developers and provides a comprehensive collection of libraries. Using it, you can simply upload an application to the platform, and App Engine takes care of everything else.
    - *Container Engine*: Containerized applications are being explored as the next step in DevOps standard operating procedures and the next generation of application development. Docker is at the forefront of this revolution and is building an industry-wide consensus about the format and interface of application containers. An application container is enabled by a set of core innovations in the Linux kernel that Google invented almost a decade ago. This places Google at the forefront of driving container adoption among developers. Container Engine is covered in Chapter 6; it is still in an early stage of evolution.
    - *Managed VMs*: Managed virtual machines are the next generation of App Engine and feature many new capabilities such as Docker-formatted application containers, writable local disks, and live debugging of applications over SSH. Whereas Container Engine enables you to build sophisticated multi-tier applications where each node is a Docker container, managed VMs take care of all of them. In essence, Container Engine is an unmanaged platform for Docker-based applications, and a managed VM is a managed platform for Docker-based applications. Managed VMs are also covered in Chapter 6.
- Storage
    - *Cloud SQL*: Cloud SQL is a managed RDBMS product and is 100% binary compatible with open source MySQL server software. Google manages all the database-management tasks, and you can focus on building an app that needs a SQL back end. Cloud SQL supports advanced configurations such as read replicas (internal and external) and SSL connections.
    - *Cloud storage*: Cloud storage is object-based file storage that you can use to store data files without worrying about file system setup and maintenance. Cloud storage also includes automatic transparent global edge caching so that you don't have to set up another entity manually. Cloud storage offers different product flavors based on durability characteristics.
    - *Cloud Datastore*: Cloud Datastore is a managed, NoSQL, schemaless database for storing non-relational data. You can use this service to store key:value-based data. Cloud Datastore scales as your data needs increase, and you pay only for space that you consume.

- Big Data
    - *BigQuery*: BigQuery is a hosted Big Data analytics platform. BigQuery lets you query datasets that are multiple terabytes in size and features data ingestion at the rate of 100,000 rows per second per table.
    - *Cloud Pub/Sub*: Cloud Pub/Sub is a hosted messaging and queuing product that lets you connect multiple producers and consumers and enable low-latency, high-frequency data transfer between them.
    - *Cloud Dataflow*: Cloud Dataflow is a simple, flexible, powerful system you can use to perform data-processing tasks of any size. It lets you build, deploy, and run complex data-processing pipelines.
- Services
    - *Cloud Endpoints*: Cloud Endpoints enables you to create RESTful services and make them accessible to iOS, Android, and JavaScript clients. It also automatically generates client libraries to make wiring up the front end easy. With built-in features include denial-of-service protection, OAuth 2.0 support, and client key management, Cloud Endpoints lets you host API endpoints in Cloud Platform.
    - *Google APIs*: Applications can consume both Cloud Platform product APIs (for example Google Storage) and Google products APIs (for example Google Maps). This book includes an example of using the *Translate API* to translate content among 90 pairs of human languages.
- Networking
    - *Cloud DNS*: Cloud DNS is a reliable, resilient, low-latency DNS service from Google's worldwide network of Anycast DNS servers. You can manage your DNS records using the Developers Console UI, the `gcloud` command-line tool, or a full-featured RESTful API.
    - *Authentication*: Authentication is an essential step for governing access to your Cloud Platform resources or Google user data. Google uses the OAUTH 2.0 protocol exclusively for both authentication and authorization. We cover OAuth 2.0 and the various operational models in this book.
    - *Developer Toolbox*: Cloud Platform provides several tools to assist you in building, deploying, and maintaining awesome applications. We cover a few of them in this book, such as cloud repositories, container registries, click-to-deploy, and so on.

Summary

This chapter introduced you to the Cloud Platform's intricacies. We started by explaining the core building blocks of Cloud Platform, the various components of a project, and the steps you need to follow to get started.

We also explained the developer tools and gave a brief overview of the Cloud Platform products discussed in this book. Welcome aboard—let's get going!

CHAPTER 3

Using Google APIs

Virtually all of Google's products are built according to an API-first philosophy. This approach encompasses both Cloud Platform products like Google Compute Engine and consumer-facing products like Google Maps. On Google Cloud Platform, although Google makes it easy to consume products using either the web-based Developers Console or the console-based `gcloud` tool, the real power of the platform is best appreciated by using the core building blocks: the product APIs. In addition, certain developer-targeted products are made available solely through APIs.

API access is subject to access control. Access control comprises authentication and authorization and is collectively referred to as *Auth*. In order to consume an API, an application should be properly authenticated and authorized. The level of access control depends on whether the application is requesting access just to a public API (for example Translate API) or to an API that has access to protected information (for example Cloud Storage). In the first case, the application needs to be authenticated; in the second case, the application needs to be both authenticated and authorized to access the user's data.

Google supports OpenID Connect for authentication and OAuth 2.0 for authorization. OpenID Connect is also known as OAuth for authentication. Google uses the OAuth 2.0 open-standard protocol with Bearer tokens[1] for both web and installed applications. This chapter first covers the essentials of OAuth 2.0 required to access Google APIs. All Google APIs are available as REST APIs, so it is easy to consume them through HTTP(S) requests.

In addition, Google provides application support libraries for many of its APIs in several programming languages. This makes it easier to develop client applications that consume Google APIs and simpler for Google APIs to be deeply integrated with the respective programming language's features and capabilities. For information about the availability of client libraries in your programming language of interest, see `https://developers.google.com/accounts/docs/OAuth2#libraries`. To aid your understanding of both Auth and API access, in this chapter's example you use a relatively simple API from Cloud Platform—the Google Translate API—and access it using both REST APIs and client libraries.

Auth Essentials

Every application that attempts to access Google APIs needs to prove its identity. The level of identification depends on the access scope requested by the application. For example, for APIs like Google Translate that do not access application or users' private data, the level of identification is a simple API key. An application that needs access to protected information must use an OAuth 2.0–based identification process. In addition to that, there are different types of authorization in OAuth 2.0. 3-legged flows are common when requests

[1]Bearer tokens are a type of access tokens. Access tokens represent credentials that provide third-party clients with the necessary rights to access protected information. These tokens are issued by an authorization server that has the approval of the resource owner.

need to be done on behalf of a concrete user. This type of flow normally requires user interaction to obtain access. Because of that, this flow is suitable for applications that have a user interface, like web server or mobile applications. On the other hand, 2-legged flows are used by clients with limited capabilities -e.g.: clients that are not able to store secret keys privately like JavaScript client side applications- or in situations where requests are sent on behalf of applications, hence there is no need for user consent -e.g.: server to server communication. For example, the Prediction API reads data from files stored in Google Cloud Storage and so uses OAuth 2.0 to request access to the API. Conversely, the Translate API does not need to access private data from users or the application itself, so the only authentication mechanism needed is an API key. This is used by Google to measure usage of the API. Let's examine the difference between using an API key and user/application specific OAuth 2.0.

■ **Note** In order to keep tokens, secrets, and keys safe, it is strongly encouraged that you operate over secure connections using SSL. Some endpoints will reject requests if they are run over HTTP.

API Keys

An API key has the following form:

```
AIzaSyCySn7SBWYPCMEM_2CBJgyDGO5qNkiHtTA
```

This key is all you need to authenticate requests against services that do not access users' private data or specific permissions like Directions API, such as the Directions API. Here is an example of how to request directions for the Via Regia—from Moscow to Berlin—using the Directions API[2]:

```
GET https://maps.googleapis.com/maps/api/directions/json?
origin=Moscow&
destination=Santiago%20de%20Compostela&
key=AIzaSyCySn7SBWYPCMEM_2CBJgyDGO5qNkiHtTA
```

The key used in the previous example is not valid. Because of that, if you try to run a request using the previous URL, it fails stating that access is denied for the key provided. To obtain a new API key, do the following:

1. Go to the Developers Console in Google: `https://console.developers.google.com`.
2. Select a project, or create a new one.
3. Go to Credentials, and create a new API key under Public API access.

---

[2]Via Regia is a historic road dating back to the Middle Ages that travels from Moscow to Santiago de Compostela (`http://en.wikipedia.org/wiki/Via_Regia`).

When you do that, you are offered four different options or types of keys to create. Choose the type that fits your needs, depending on the platform or system you are using to access an API:

- Choose a *server key* if your application runs on a server. Keep this private in order to avoid quota theft.

  When you select this method, you can specify the IP addresses of the allowed clients that you expect to connect to this server. You do that by adding a query parameter with the IP address: userIp=<user-ip-address>. If access is started by your server—for example, when running a cron job—you can provide a quotaUser parameter with a value limited to 40 characters. For example: quotaUser=myemail@gmail.com. These two parameters are also used to associate usage of an API with the quota of a specific user.

- Use a *browser key* if your application runs on a web client. When you select this type of key, you must specify a list of allowed Referers. Requests coming from URLs that do not match are rejected. You can use wildcards at the beginning or end of each pattern. For example: www.domain.com, *.domain.com, *.domain.com/public/*.

- If you plan to access a Google API from an Android client, use an *Android key*. For this key, you need to specify the list of SHA1 fingerprints and package names corresponding to your application(s). To generate the SHA1 fingerprint of the signature used to create your APK file, use the keytool command from the terminal:

  ```
  keytool -exportcert -alias androiddebugkey -keystore <path-to-keystore-file> -list -v
  ```

  When you run your app from your development environment, the key in ~/.android/debug.keystore is used to sign your APK. The password for this signature is normally "android" or an empty string: "".

  Here is an example of the requested string to identify your application.

  ```
  B6:BB:99:41:97:F1:1F:CF:84:2A:6E:0B:FE:75:78:BE:7E:6C:C5:BB;com.lunchmates
  ```

- Use an iOS key if your application runs on an iOS device. When using this key, you need to add the bundle identifier(s) of the whitelisted app(s) to the dedicated field in the API key creation process. For example: com.gcpbook.

■ **Note** In Windows machines, keytool.exe is usually located under C:\Program Files\Java\<jdk-version>\bin\

Remember that prior to accessing a Google API, you must enable access to it and billing where it applies.

You do that as follows:

1. Go to the Developers Console in Google: https://console.developers.google.com.
2. Select a project, or create a new one.
3. In the left sidebar, Expand APIs and Auth and navigate to APIs.
4. Look for the API you are interested in, and change its status to On.

To enable billing, click on the preferences icon next to your profile in the top right side of the screen. If a project is selected, you see an option to access "project billing settings". From there, you can see the details of the billing account associated with that project. To see all the billing accounts that you registered click on "Billing accounts" from the same preferences menu.

OAuth 2.0

This protocol was created with the intention of providing a way to grant limited access to protected content hosted by third-party services in a standardized and open manner. This protected content can be requested on behalf of either a resource owner or an external application or service. This protocol has been adopted by Google to enable access to its APIs, by providing a way to authenticate and authorize external agents interested in exchanging information with Google APIs.

The following steps describe the complete process of requesting access to specific content:

1. The client requests authorization from the resource owner.
2. The resource owner sends back an authorization grant.
3. The client uses this authorization grant to request an access token to the authorization server.
4. If the process is successful, the authorization server provides the client with an access token.
5. The client accesses protected content, authorizing requests with the access token just acquired.
6. If the token is valid, the client receives the requested information.

This process is very similar to how you obtain access to APIs in Google, although that varies depending on the type of application or system you are building. We cover each of these cases in the following paragraphs.

■ **Note** Given the many steps involved in this process, the chances of making a mistake are high, which has security implications. It is highly recommended that you use one of the available libraries that enable and simplify the fulfillment of this protocol. Google provides a variety of client libraries that work with OAuth 2.0[3] in programming languages like Java, Python, .NET, Ruby, PHP, and JavaScript. The Internet also offers valuable resources related to this topic.

In this chapter, you use `oauth2client`. You can find this library in the Google APIs Client Libraries for Python or through the link to the code repository in GitHub: `https://github.com/google/oauth2client`.

Each of the application types follow different OAuth 2.0 flows (2-legged, 3-legged) and thus require different associated information. In the following sections you see how to operate with each of them.

[3]Google OAuth 2.0 client libraries: `https://developers.google.com/accounts/docs/OAuth2#libraries`.

OAuth 2.0 Application Authentication

You use this kind of authentication when you need to access content on behalf of your application, typically in server-to-server communications: for example, managing internal files stored in Cloud Storage. Because of this, the authorization process does not require the authentication of any specific user in order to obtain an access token. Instead, you use the identity of your application.

Some services in Cloud Platform - like App Engine or Compute Engine - already have associated default credentials that are used to perform requests to the different APIs through the client libraries. If you are calling a Google API from somewhere else, you can still use this functionality by creating a new client ID for your service in Developers Console:

1. Go to the Developers Console in Google: `https://console.developers.google.com`.
2. Select a project, or create a new one.
3. In the left sidebar, Expand APIs and Auth, and navigate to Credentials.
4. Create a new client ID by clicking the button for that purpose.
5. Select the application type based on needs and click on Create.

Now you can generate and download the JSON key associated to this client ID. Place it somewhere private within your system. The client libraries attempt to use this key by looking under the path set in the environmental variable `GOOGLE_APPLICATION_CREDENTIALS`. Set this variable to the path where you stored your key.

Figure 3-1 shows the application authorization process.

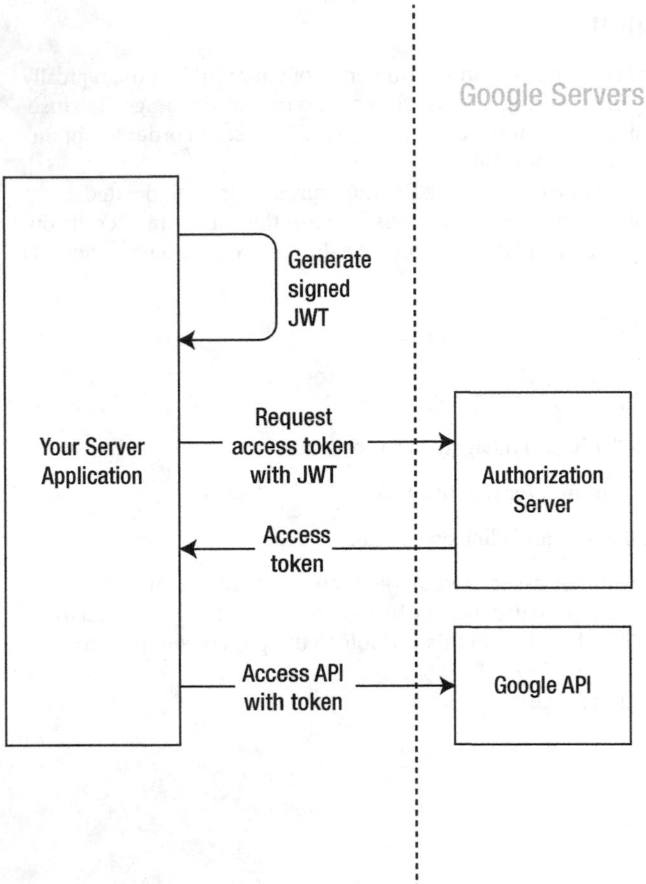

***Figure 3-1.** Oauth 2.0 authorization flow for service accounts*

To create the credentials based on the key associated to your account you do the following:

```
from oauth2client.client import GoogleCredentials

credentials = GoogleCredentials.get_application_default()
```

Before making requests to the API, you need make sure that the credentials have the right scope to access the information you are interested in. In this case, you need read permissions:

```
CLOUD_STORAGE_SCOPE = 'https://www.googleapis.com/auth/devstorage.read_only'

if credentials.create_scoped_required():
    credentials = credentials.create_scoped(CLOUD_STORAGE_SCOPE)
```

Now, these credentials have all the necessary information to obtain an access token. The API client does that internally by wrapping the creation of every new request and adding a pre-execution trigger that checks for the existence of an access token. If the access token is invalid or inexistent, the method obtains a new access token; otherwise, it adds the access token to the request as a means of authorization before it is executed. You can create a client representing a concrete Google API that you can use to make requests against it. In this case, we are using the Python client library. For example, if you are interested in listing the files stored on a bucket in Cloud Storage, you do the following:

```
from apiclient.discovery import build

# ...previous code generating credentials

gcs_service = build('storage', 'v1', credentials=credentials)
content = gcs_service.objects().list(bucket='lunchmates_document_dropbox').execute()
print json.dumps(content)
```

■ **Note** You can learn more about the `discovery` and `build` directives at `https://cloud.google.com/appengine/articles/efficient_use_of_discovery_based_apis`.

If you want to see the full implementation, check the script `api_access_application_authentication.py` under `oauth2` in the `code_snippets` repo. `https://github.com/GoogleCloudPlatformBook/code-snippets/tree/master/oauth2`.

If you are interested in obtaining an access token manually for testing or other purposes, you can do so by executing the `_refresh()` method from the class `OAuth2Credentials` directly, passing a dummy request: `Http().request`. This internal method is called each time you execute a request—after you authorize your credentials with an instance of `httplib2.Http()`—if there is no access token yet or the access token is invalid. The following snippet generates and prints the obtained access token:

```
credentials._refresh(Http().request)
print credentials.access_token
```

Note that once you have an access token, you can, for instance, perform requests from any system that operates with the HTTP standard. For example, you can execute the previous request using only HTTP:

```
GET https://www.googleapis.com/drive/v2/files?alt=json
Authorization: Bearer <access_token>
```

OAuth 2.0 User Authentication

This type of authentication is used when there is the need to access protected information on behalf of a concrete user. This is common in user facing applications so that users can grant access to the required scopes.

The most common version is the 3-legged OAuth 2.0 user authentication flow, shown in Figure 3-2.

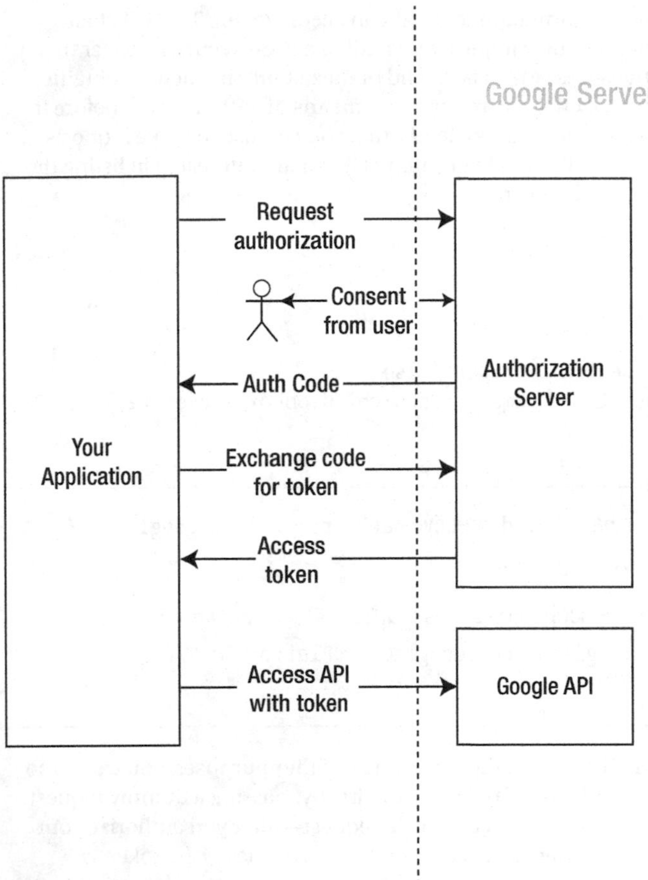

Figure 3-2. *Oauth 2.0 user authentication flow*

As you can see in the figure, this flow asks for user consent. This is because the content is accessed on behalf of that user. The first thing you need to do is obtain the authorization URI to redirect the user, in order for the user to authenticate with their Google credentials and authorize the specified scope:

```
from oauth2client import client

client_secrets_json_path = <path_to_your_client_secrets_file.json>
api_scope = <api_scope_url>
redirect_uri = <redirect_uri_in_client_id>

flow = client.flow_from_clientsecrets(
     client_secrets_json_path,
     scope=api_scope,
     redirect_uri=redirect_uri,
     include_granted_scopes=True)

auth_uri = flow.step1_get_authorize_url()
```

client_secrets_json_path is the path to the file containing the secrets and other relevant information related to your client ID. Remember that you can download this JSON file at any point from the Developers Console, under APIs & Auth ➤ Credentials.

You can also execute this first step through HTTP:

```
POST https://accounts.google.com/o/oauth2/auth?
access_type=offline&
response_type=code&
client_id=<client_id>&
redirect_uri=<redirect_uri>&
scope=<api_scope>&
included_granted_scopes=true
```

This request accepts the parameters listed in Table 3-1.

Table 3-1. *List of accepted parameters for the authorization endpoint in Google APIs* *https://accounts.google.com/o/oauth2/auth*

Parameter	Description
response_type	Determines the expected response. Options are code for web server and installed applications or access_token for JavaScript client-side applications.
client_id	Identifies the client ID used for this request. You can get this value from the client ID used to perform this request in the Developers Console.
redirect_uri	Defines the mechanism used to deliver the response. This value must match one of the values listed under Redirect URIs in the client ID in use. In web applications, this URI is called to deliver a response after the authentication phase. It must also contain the scheme and trailing /.
scope	Determines the API and level of access requested. It also defines the consent screen shown to the user after authorization succeeds.
state	Allows any type of string. The value provided is returned on response; its purpose is to provide the caller with a state that can be used to determine the next steps to take.
access_type	Determines whether the application needs to access a Google API when the user in question is not present at the time of request. Accepted values are online (the default) and offline. When using the latter, a refresh token is added to the response in the next step of the process, the result of exchanging the authorization code for an access token.
approval_prompt	Accepts force or auto. If force is chosen, the user is presented with all the scopes requested, even if they have been accepted in previous requests.
login_hint	Provides the authorization server with extra information that allows it to simplify the authentication process for the user. It accepts an e-mail or a sub-identifier of the user who is being asked for access.
include_granted_scopes	If the authorization process is successful and this parameter is set to true, it includes any previous authorizations granted by this user for this application.

■ **Note** In scenarios where applications cannot catch redirects to URLs—for example on mobile devices other than Android or iOS—`redirect_uri` can take the following values:

urn:ietf:wg:oauth:2.0:oob: The authorization code is placed in the title tag of the HTML file. The same code is also exposed in a text field where it can be seen and from which it can be copied manually. This approach is useful when the application can load and parse a web page. Note that if you do not want users to see this code, you must close the browser window as soon as the operation has completed. Conversely, if the system you are developing for has limited capabilities, you can instruct the user to manually copy the code and paste it into your application.

urn:ietf:wg:oauth:2.0:oob:auto: This value behaves almost identically to the previous value. This procedure also places the authorization code in the title tag of the HTML page, but instead of showing the code in the body of the HTML, it asks the user to close the window.

This request responds with a redirect to the URI specified under `redirect_uri`, including an `error` or `code` parameters in the query string, depending on whether the authorization process succeeded or failed, respectively. If the authorization succeeds, the redirect is as follows:

```
<redirect_uri>?code=<authorization_code>
```

And this is the redirect if the authorization fails:

```
<redirect_uri>?error=access_denied
```

Now you can use the code to obtain an access token with it:

```
from oauth2client import client

code = <auth_code_from_previous_step>
credentials = flow.step2_exchange(code)
...
```

Just as before, you can use the `discovery` classes and `build` directive to instantiate a service representing the API to interact with:

```
from apiclient.discovery import build

gcs_service = build('storage', 'v1', credentials=credentials)
content = gcs_service.objects().list(bucket='lunchmates_document_dropbox').execute()
```

If you prefer to obtain the access token manually through HTTP, you can do so by using the following endpoint:

```
POST https://www.googleapis.com/oauth2/v3/token

Content-Type: application/x-www-form-urlencoded
```

```
client_id=<client_id>&
client_secret=<client_secret>&
code=<code_from_previous_request>&
grant_type=authorization_code&
redirect_uri=<redirect_uri>
```

This includes the following:

- `client_id` is the identifier for the client ID used throughout the process.
- `client_secret` is the secret corresponding to that client ID.
- code is the resulting authorization code extracted from the previous request.
- `grant_type` determines the type of authorization.
- `redirect_uri` has to match the specified value during the previous step.

If the request is successful, you should see something like this:

```
{
  "access_token": <access_token>,
  "token_type": "Bearer",
  "expires_in": 3600,
  "refresh_token": <refresh_token>
}
```

Note that you get a property called `refresh_token`. This is because in the first step, when obtaining the authorization code, you set `access_type` to `offline`. This refresh token allows you to obtain renewed access tokens until the user deliberately revokes access to your application.

To obtain a new access token from a refresh token, perform the following request:

■ **Note** This step also applies to other scenarios and account types.

```
POST https://www.googleapis.com/oauth2/v3/token

Content-Type: application/x-www-form-urlencoded

client_id=<client_id>&
client_secret=<client_secret>&
refresh_token=<refresh_token>&
grant_type=refresh_token
```

In this case, `grant_type` is set to `refresh_token`, and you need to add the refresh token under the parameter `refresh_token`. As before, the expected response is

```
{
  "access_token": <access_token>,
  "token_type": "Bearer",
  "expires_in": 3600
}
```

■ **Pro Tip** In order to obtain new tokens from a refresh token, you must store the latter in your application for as long as you want to have this ability.

■ **Note** As you may have noted, there is no Python implementation for the generation of new tokens from a refresh token. This process is encapsulated and automated in the client libraries. As mentioned previously, you can trigger this process manually in the Python library by calling `credentials._refresh(Http().request)`.

Some applications may need to revoke access to authorized scopes and invalidate tokens when users unsubscribe or delete their account from your system. You can do that by requesting the following:

```
GET https://accounts.google.com/o/oauth2/revoke?token=<access_or_refresh_token>
```

The value for the query parameter can be either an access token or a refresh token. If the revoked access token has an associated `refresh_token`, both are revoked. This request responds with `200 OK` if executed successfully or `400` in case of error.

2-Legged OAuth 2.0 User Authentication

This scenario is aimed to support OAuth 2.0 on applications running on the side of the client. Because of that they are not assumed to have the ability to keep a secret. For example, JavaScript client side applications do not have a way to store a private key, used in the 3-legged user authentication flow.

The flow for this scenario is slightly different from those seen so far. However, the requests that need to be performed to obtain access are consistent with what you used in earlier examples. You begin as in other scenarios by calling to `the /o/oauth2/auth` endpoint. The difference this time is that instead of asking for a code, you directly request an access token. Figure 3-3 shows the process.

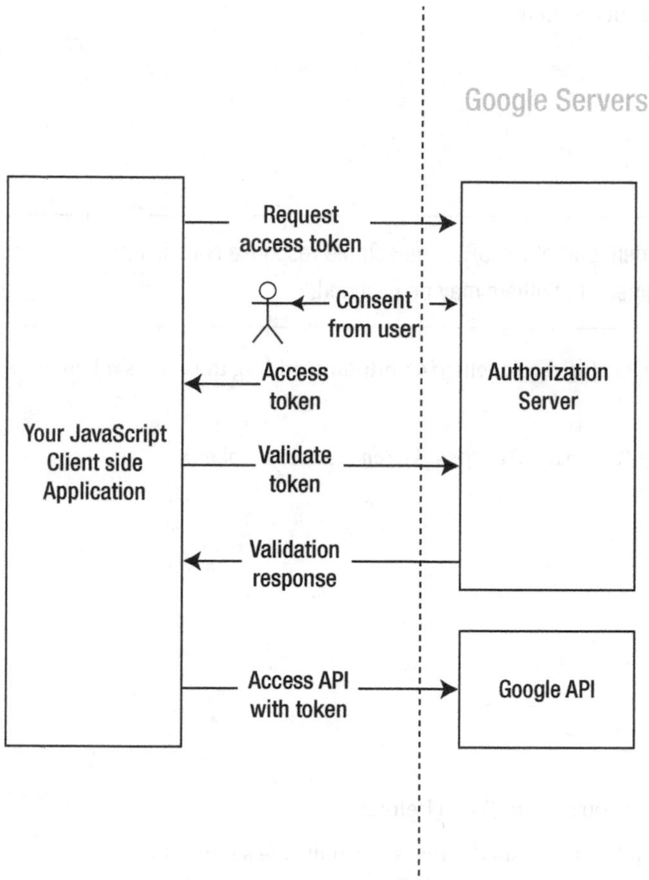

Figure 3-3. *Oauth 2.0 authorization flow for JavaScript client-side applications*

To request the access token, start by calling the authorization server:

```
POST https://accounts.google.com/o/oauth2/auth?
response_type=token&
client_id=<client_id>&
redirect_uri=<redirect_uri>&
scope=<api_scope>&
included_granted_scopes=true
```

The expected response for this request is as follows if the request failed to authorize a combination of user and scope:

```
<redirect_uri>#error=access_denied
```

Or as follows if the process was completed successfully:

```
<redirect_uri>#
access_token=<access_token>&
token_type=Bearer&
expires_in=3600
```

■ **Pro Tip** Your client needs to parse the fragment part of the URL. The sample response contains the minimum set of parameters returned in the fragment, but others may be included.

Before using this token, you must validate it using the `TokenInfo` endpoint, adding the access token in the query string:

```
GET https://www.googleapis.com/oauth2/v1/tokeninfo?access_token=<access_token>
```

A successful response looks like this:

```
{
   "issued_to": <issuer_of_the_token>,
   "audience": <audience>,
   "scope": <requested_scope>,
   "expires_in": 3578,
   "access_type": "online"
}
```

This response includes two parameters that you have not seen before:

- `issued_to`: Specifies to whom the token was issued. This is normally the same as `audience`.
- `audience`: The identifier of the application that is intended to use the token to query Google APIs.

There is one last critical step before using the recently obtained access token: you need to confirm that the value returned under `audience` exactly matches the client ID of your application. As you know very well at this point, you can find this value in the Developers Console.

You can now use the access token to access the Google API you are targeting through one of the client libraries offered for this purpose or simple HTTP. For example, you can use the `curl` command:

```
curl -H "Authorization: Bearer <access_token>" https://www.googleapis.com/drive/v2/
files?alt=json
```

If the token has expired or was revoked, the request to `TokenInfo` will respond with an error `400` and a body similar to the following:

```
{
   "error": "invalid_token",
   "error_description": "Invalid Value"
}
```

Translate API

Google Translate (`https://translate.google.com`) is an online service that automatically translates text from one language to another (for example, English to Italian). Google Translate supports dozens of languages and hundreds of language pairs for translations. The Google Translate API is a RESTful API that lets developers programmatically translate text using either server-side or client-side applications. This API can also detect the language of input text.

The first step in using any Google API, including the Translate API, is to enable it for a project. The Translate API is a paid service and hence needs the API key for a successful transaction. You perform these steps using the web-based Developers Console at `https://console.developers.google.com`.

Following are the high-level steps required to use the Translate API:

1. Open a browser window to URL `https://console.developers.google.com`.
2. Select a project, or create a new one.
3. Switch on the Translate API using the following steps:
    a. In the left sidebar, Expand APIs and Auth.
    b. Select APIs.
    c. Change the status of the Google Translate API to On.
4. Click Credentials, and create a new API key under Public API Access. The OAuth client ID is required for APIs that need access to user's data.
5. Enable Billing, if required, as follows.
    a. In the left sidebar, select Billing and Settings.
    b. In the Billing section, click Enable Billing.
    c. Fill in the required details, and click Submit and Enable Billing.

Accessing Translate REST API

The following key phrases are relevant to the Translate API:

- *Source text*: The input text provided to the Translate API for translation
- *Source language*: The language of the input text, as declared by the application developer
- *Target language*: The language into which the source text needs to be translated

The following three methods make up the Translate API:

- `Translate`: Translates source text (from source language) into target language
- `Languages`: Lists the source and target languages supported by the translate methods
- `Detect`: Detects the source language of the input text

All of these methods are available as REST APIs. Translate REST APIs are different from cloud platform REST APIs in the way they provide access to a service, whereas cloud platform REST APIs provide access to a resource. As a result, the API provides a single URI that acts as a service endpoint, is accessible using the HTTP GET method, and accepts service requests as query parameters.

The base URL for requesting service from the Translate API is `https://www.googleapis.com/language/translate/v2?PARAMETERS`, where `PARAMETERS` is the list of keywords and values that applies to the query. `v2` in the URL refers to version 2 and is the current version of the Translate API. Listing 3-1 constructs a translation query using this base URL template and replacing `PARAMETERS` with actual query names and values.

Listing 3-1. HTTP Query for a Translation Request

```
https://www.googleapis.com/language/translate/v2?
key=INSERT-YOUR-KEY&q=good%20morning&source=en&target=it
```

This example includes four query words:

- `key`: Translate API is a paid service, and in order to use it, you need to activate billing and obtain an API access key. The key is also a means to identify your application.
- `q`: Identifies the source text that needs to be translated into the target language. The text is URL encoded to represent special characters like spaces.
- `source`: A language code that identifies the source language of the input text as declared by the application developer.
- `target`: A language code that identifies the target language of the translation request.

Suppose the query in Listing 3-1 succeeds. The Translate API returns a `200 OK` HTTP status code along with a simple JSON object-based reply, as shown in Listing 3-2.

Listing 3-2. HTTP Response for the Translation Query in Listing 3-1

```
200 OK

{
    "data": {
        "translations": [
            {
                "translatedText": "buongiorno"
            }
        ]
    }
}
```

In this query invocation, the API is called by specifying the source language. However, the source language specification is optional; when the query does not specify a source language, the API figures it out and does the translation. The Translate API charges an additional (nominal) fee for source-language detection in addition to the translation fee.

The example in Listing 3-3 and Listing 3-4 shows the query syntax without a specified source language, along with the corresponding JSON response. Note that the response object highlights that the source language is not specified by stating the detected input language.

Listing 3-3. HTTP Query for a Translation Request without the Source Language

```
GET https://www.googleapis.com/language/translate/v2?
key=INSERT-YOUR-KEY&target=it&q=Hello%20universe
```

Listing 3-4. HTTP Response for the Translation Request in Listing 3-3

```
200 OK

{
   "data": {
      "translations": [
         {
            "translatedText": "ciao universo",
            "detectedSourceLanguage": "en"
         }
      ]
   }
}
```

The Translate API also supports batch mode, with which the client can make translation requests consisting of a list of input text. The size of the HTTP request data is limited, due to the use of the `GET` or `POST` HTTP method. The request when using `GET` should be fewer than 2,000 characters including the input text. The request size when using `POST` should be fewer than 5,000 characters including the input text. To use the HTTP `POST` method, the client needs to set an HTTP method override as part of the `POST` request to be accepted by the Translate API, called `X-HTTP-Method-Override: GET`. The example in Listing 3-5 and Listing 3-6 shows a sample batch query using the HTTP `GET` method and the JSON response returned by the Translate API.

Listing 3-5. Batch Query Request

```
GET https://www.googleapis.com/language/translate/v2?
key=INSERT-YOUR-KEY&source=en&target=it&q=Good%20Afternoon&q=Good%20Evening
```

Listing 3-6. Batch Query Response

```
200 OK

{
   "data": {
      "translations": [
         {
            "translatedText": "buon pomeriggio"
         },
         {
            "translatedText": "buonasera"
         }
      ]
   }
}
```

Discovering Languages Supported by Translate API

The Translate API adds support for new languages and translations between new language pairs on a regular basis. Hence it is useful to know the list of languages supported by the API at any point in time. You can find this by using the API's `languages` subcommand. The language query can be invoked in two forms: with and without the target language specified. Listing 3-7 shows the URI template for making this request.

Listing 3-7. URI Template for Retrieving Language Codes Supported by the Translate API

```
https://www.googleapis.com/language/translate/v2/languages?PARAMETERS
```

You can use this URI template to retrieve the language codes supported by the Translate API; see Listing 3-8. The only required parameter for this API invocation is the key and corresponding value pair.

Listing 3-8. Retrieving the Language Codes Supported by the Translate API

```
https://www.googleapis.com/language/translate/v2/languages?key=INSERT-YOUR-KEY
```

If this succeeds, the server responds with a HTTP `200 OK` message along with a JSON object that lists all the languages supported by the Translate API, as shown in Listing 3-9.

Listing 3-9. Language Query Response

```
200 OK

{
    "data": {
        "languages": [
            {
                "language": "en"
            },
            {
                "language": "it"
            },
            ...
            {
                "language": "zh-TW"
            }
        ]
    }
}
```

This example assumes that you want the results returned in English—that is, the language codes are listed in English. Perhaps you want the list of languages to be returned in another language, such as traditional Chinese. Listing 3-10 shows the example URI to achieve this.

Listing 3-10. Retrieving the Translate API Supported Language Codes in Italian

```
https://www.googleapis.com/language/translate/v2/languages?key=INSERT-YOUR-KEY&target=it
```

If this API succeeds, the server responds with a HTTP `200 OK` message along with a JSON object that list the supported languages codes and their translation in the requested target language. Listing 3-11 shows the result.

Listing 3-11. Language Query Response in a Specified Target Language

```
200 OK

{
  "data": {
      "languages": [
          {
              "language": "af",
              "name": "Afrikaans"
           },
           {
               "language": "sq",
               "name": "Albanese"
           },
           . . .
           {
               "language": "zu",
               "name": "Zulu"
           }
      ]
   }
}
```

In some situations, it may not be possible to determine the source language of the input text, or the source language specified may not be correct or reliable. To handle these situations, the Translate API provides a method to predict the source language of the input text. You request this service by using the API's `detect` subcommand. Listing 3-12 shows the URI query template.

Listing 3-12. URI Query Template to Detect the Source Language

```
https://www.googleapis.com/language/translate/v2/detect?PARAMETERS
```

Listing 3-13 uses this URI template to detect the source language of an input string. The only required parameters for this API invocation are the key and corresponding value pair along with the query string.

Listing 3-13. Using the Detect Feature of the Translate API

```
https://www.googleapis.com/language/translate/v2/detect?
key=INSERT-YOUR-KEY&q=Este+mes+es+marzo
```

If the request succeeds, the server responds with a `200 OK` HTTP status code along with a set of values in a JSON object, as shown in Listing 3-14.

Listing 3-14. Language-Detection Query Response for Spanish Input

```
200 OK

{
   "data": {
        "detections": [
            [
                {
                    "language": "es",
                    "isReliable": false,
                    "confidence": 0.015852576
                }
            ]
        ]
   }
}
```

`confidence` is an optional parameter with a floating-point value between 0 and 1; *optional* means this parameter is not always returned. The closer the value is to 1, the higher the confidence in the language detection. `isReliable` has been deprecated, and Google plans to remove it in the near future. Hence you should not use this value to make decisions.

You may wonder why the confidence score is so low and whether it is reliable enough to be used in your applications. We wondered about that, too, and did another test using a simple English sentence; see Listing 3-15 and Listing 3-16.

Listing 3-15. Language-Detection Query Using an English Sentence

```
https://www.googleapis.com/language/translate/v2/detect?
key=YOUR_API_KEY&q=this+is+a+simple+english+sentence
```

Listing 3-16. Language-Detection Query Response for English Input

```
200 OK

{
   "data": {
        "detections": [
            [
                {
                    "language": "en",
                    "isReliable": false,
                    "confidence": 0.025648016
                }
            ]
        ]
   }
}
```

From this result, you can see that the English language-detection confidence score is low as well. This may indicate that the Translate API is strict about confidence scores, and hence even a low score provides usable results.

Just as in the `translate` command, you can pass in several query text inputs. The Translate API returns a list of detected languages.

Accessing Translate API using Client Programs

Although the HTTP-based Translate API is easy to use, Google also makes it simple to consume the Translate API from client applications. This is facilitated by the Google APIs client library (`https://cloud.google.com/translate/v2/libraries`). The Translate API is part of the Google APIs client library, and as of this writing the client library is available for six programming languages and is being developed for three more.

Let's take a brief look at the Python example provided as part of the Google APIs client library (`https://code.google.com/p/google-api-python-client/source/browse/samples/translate`). We only examine the relevant lines from the program—Listing 3-17 is a code snippet, not a complete program. To use this snippet, you need to install the Google API client library for Python.

Listing 3-17. Translate API Python Example Provided as Part of the Google APIs' Client Library

```
from apiclient.discovery import build
def main():
    service = build('translate', 'v2', developerKey='INSERT_YOUR_KEY')
    print service.translations().list(
        source='en',
        target='fr',
        q=['flower', 'car']
    ).execute()

if __name__ == '__main__':
    main()
```

Any Python programmer should be able to easily understand the standard Python parts in this code snippet. Hence we discuss only the distinctive parts. At the base level, the Google API client library builds a `service` object. This is facilitated by using the `discovery` class from the module `apiclient`. Specifically, you need the `build` method. The `build` method requires three parameters: the API name, API version, and API key. Once the `service` object is built, you can use the methods inside it. Again, depending on the API name provided to build, the methods available are different.

This example uses the `translations()` method to translate from English to French. The query text is provided as a standard Python list containing two items. When the `execute` method is called, the client library constructs the equivalent REST API using these values, makes the HTTP `GET` request, and returns either the result or an error from this API invocation.

More methods are available in this class. They detect the source language and get the list of languages supported by the Translate API. Listing 3-18 shows a more detailed example that uses most of the Translate API capabilities. This example reads the Unix English dictionary and translates it into all possible languages supported by the Translate API. We have added line numbers for easy reference.

Listing 3-18. Python Program to Translate the Unix English Dictionary into Multiple Languages

```
#!/usr/bin/env python

__author__ = 'sptkrishnan@gmail.com (S. P. T. Krishnan)'

from apiclient.discovery import build
import json


```

```
def main():
    # create a build object
    service = build('translate', 'v2', developerKey='INSERT_YOUR_KEY')

    # STEP 1 - Get the list of languages supported by Translate API
    languages = service.languages().list(target='en').execute()

    # [debug] print the JSON dump of HTTP response
    # print json.dumps(languages, sort_keys=True, indent=4, separators=(',', ': '))

    # Unpack the JSON object from HTTPResponse, extracts the language name,
    # code and creates a dictionary object from it.
    langdict = {}
    for key, value in languages.iteritems():
        for x in value:
            for y, z in x.iteritems():
                if y == 'name':
                    name = z
                elif y == 'language':
                    language = z
                    langdict[name] = language

    # [debug] print the language name and code langdict object
    # for name, code in sorted(langdict.iteritems()):
        # print name, code

    unidict = {}
    filename = '/usr/share/dict/words'
    filehandle = open(filename, 'r')
    for line in filehandle:
        line = line.rstrip('\n')
        for name in langdict.keys():
            if langdict[name] == 'en':
                continue
            else:
                translation = service.translations().list(source='en',
                target=langdict[name], q=line).execute()
            for key, value in translation.iteritems():
                for x in value:
                    for y, z in x.iteritems():
                        if line == z:
                            pass
                            # print line, '(' + name + ')', 'x'
                        else:
                            print line, '(' + name + ')', z


if __name__ == '__main__':
    main()
```

In this example, lines 1-8 and 55-56 are standard Python. They use the `json` module to programmatically process the Translate API return values. Lines 10-11 construct the `service` object, and lines 13-14 get the list of languages supported by the Translate API. By explicitly specifying the target language to be English, you get the language codes and also the language names. Lines 16-17 are a debug `print` statement to print the JSON response from the Translate API.

You parse the HTTP response and create a Linux data structure in lines 19-19. Once this code block completes execution, you have a Python dictionary data structure that maps the language code to its name in English. Lines 31-33 are a debug `print` statement that prints the contents of this dictionary data structure.

The primary purpose of this program is to read the English dictionary (assuming the default language is English) from a Unix system and translate each word into all the languages supported by the Translate API. This is achieved in lines 36-44. The dictionary file is opened, and words are read from each line. (Note that each line contains a single word.) Next the supported language dictionary is iterated over, and each word is passed to the `translations` method along with a single target language. It doesn't make sense to translate from English to English, so you skip that combination.

There are 235,886 words in the English dictionary on our Mac system running Yosemite. Note that the Translate API has daily API limits; see `https://cloud.google.com/translate/v2/pricing`. If you intend to run this program, you are advised to have a delay between invocations or to use a subset of the word list per day. Listing 3-19 shows the program output for a few words.

Listing 3-19. Partial Output from the English Dictionary Translation Example

```
abaca (Maltese) manilla
abaca (Portuguese) abacá
abaca (Japanese) アバカ
abaca (Spanish) abacá
abaca (Chinese (Simplified)) 蕉
abacate (Tamil) அபகடே என்றும்
abacate (Finnish) Abacate
abacate (Serbian) абацате
abacate (Galician) aguacate
abacate (Yiddish) אַבאַקאַטע
```

As you can see, the Translate API is able to translate between many language pairs. We leave it as an exercise for you to extend this program to save the output into a file, such as a CSV. You can offset the cost of using the Translate API by applying the $300 credit available from `https://cloud.google.com`.

Summary

In this chapter, you have learned about a fundamental concept that is applicable to all Cloud Platform products: Auth. Auth, which stands for authentication and authorization, is the gatekeeper of Cloud Platform. It is also responsible for safeguarding users' data and allowing access only from approved third-party applications. Cloud Platform Auth implements the authentication, authorization, and accounting (AAA) protocol.

You also learned about the Translate API, which can translate between 90 pairs of languages. We selected this API because it is relatively simple and showcases how to use a standalone API in Google Cloud Platform. You saw how to use this API both via HTTP and using a client library. This chapter has given you a good introduction to Auth and how to use it to access a Google API.

PART II

Google Cloud Platform - Compute Products

CHAPTER 4

Google Compute Engine

Google Compute Engine is an infrastructure service provided as part of the Google Cloud Platform. Compute Engine is made up of three major components: virtual machines, persistent disks, and networks. It is available at several Google datacenters worldwide and is provided exclusively on an on-demand basis. This means Compute Engine neither charges any upfront fees for deployment nor locks down the customer. At the same time, Compute Engine provides steep discounts for sustained use. These sustained-use discounts, without any upfront subscription fees, are an industry first; this pricing innovation shows that Google innovates outside of technology as well.

In this chapter, you continue to use the Cloud Platform project that you created earlier using the web-based Google Developers Console. Most of the examples in this chapter use the `gcloud` command-line interface tool.

The objective of this chapter is to introduce you to all the major components of Compute Engine. The chapter includes examples of the various components to make it easier for you to understand them. This chapter is written in a prescriptive manner, meaning it provides step-by-step instructions for how to create most common deployment architectures and solutions using Compute Engine components. Let us begin with an overview.

Virtual Machines

The core component of Compute Engine is the virtual machine (VM). Compute Engine allows you to create clusters of high-performance VMs comprising of thousands of virtual CPU cores. The VMs are available in multiple hardware configurations, making them suitable for different computational workloads. Changing the ratio of CPU cores and main memory per VM creates the hardware variations. This results in three types of VM instances:

- *Standard instances* have 3.75GB of RAM per CPU core.
- *High-memory instances* have 6.5GB of RAM per CPU core.
- *High-CPU instances* have 0.9GB of RAM per CPU core.

The graph in Figure 4-1 shows the difference between these instance types and lists all the types of VMs that can be created as of this writing. The specific instance types may change over time; see `https://cloud.google.com/compute/pricing` for current instance types and prices.

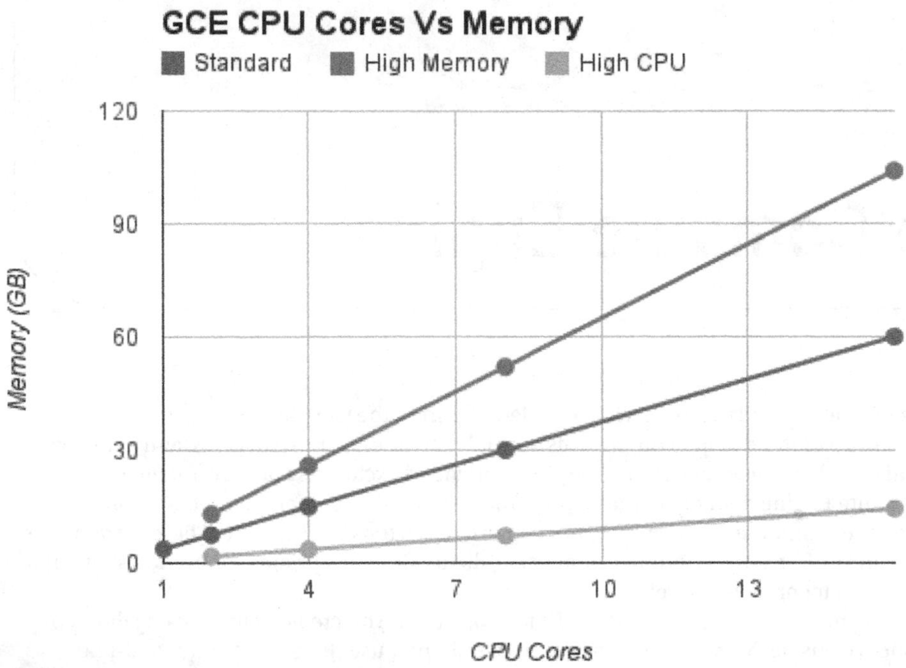

Figure 4-1. *VM classes and instance types*

WHAT IS A VIRTUAL MACHINE?

In computing, a *virtual machine* is a representation of hardware. The representation can be either emulation or simulation based. Emulation is the default method and is more efficient, whereas simulation is typically used for smaller targets. The hardware that is being represented can be either real or hypothetical. For example, semiconductor companies typically emulate hypothetical hardware to test its performance for common workloads before making a physical prototype. The emulation target can be either the local machine (that is, the underlying host hardware) or a remote target. Some enterprises are consolidating servers as VMs, and these VMs run on emulated hardware. Virtualization is one of the core technologies in cloud computing, as well.

Compute Engine, while offering consistent performance, supports several standard and customized operating systems. These include several distributions of Linux, UNIX and Windows. On the hardware front, Compute Engine supports 64-bit versions of x86-based processors only. An *instance* is a per-zone resource, meaning you have to specifically state the Cloud Platform zone in which you want to start the instance.

The action of adding an instance to a project also automatically starts the instance. Although it is not possible to add an instance without starting it, you can shut down an instance without terminating it and removing it from the project.

Persistent Disks

A persistent disk (PD) is network-based block storage that is attached to one or more VMs and used as a storage device. Hosting a PD external to an instance is critical because it helps to retain data in case of hardware failures in the physical host. Google Cloud Platform offers both magnetic and solid-state disk-based PDs. Magnetic disk-based persistent storage is the default, and its performance is sufficient for most applications. You can format the device using any file system you choose. Compute Engine also offers solid-state disks; you can use these for applications that require performance beyond what a magnetic medium can provide.

Each PD can be attached to a single VM instance in read-write mode or can be attached to multiple VM instances in read-only mode. When multiple disks are attached to a single VM instance, some of them can be in read-only mode while others are in read-write modes. A total of 16 persistent disks can be added to a VM, with cumulative storage space of 10TB.

From a system design perspective, persistent disks are hosted in multiple vantage points in a data center. This arrangement eliminates bottlenecks that would be present if the storage was hosted in single network location. Persistent disk data is also replicated for additional redundancy.

In addition to network-hosted persistent block storage, Compute Engine also offers local SSD-based storage for extreme low latency, high IOPS, and high throughput requirements. Local SSD is optimal for temporary data or for hosting high-performance databases. However, because the data is local to the instance, there is no redundancy in case of failure. For database systems, you should configure replication or regular backups. As with PDs, the contents are encrypted-at-rest. If a VM is migrated between physical hosts, the local SSD-based data is automatically migrated as well.

Networks and Firewalls

Networks are the means through which a VM communicates with the external world. This includes communicating with its PD as well, because the PDs are hosted external to the VM instance. The Cloud Platform's philosophy of network bandwidth is to provide dedicated bandwidth on a per-CPU-core basis. This means a VM that has more CPU cores has more network bandwidth compared to another VM with fewer CPU cores. The current bandwidth/core is set at 2 Gbits/sec.

There can be multiple networks in a Cloud Platform project. Each network can host several VM instances, but one VM instance can be attached to only one network. This means the Cloud Platform does not support multi-homed instance configurations. However, it is possible to achieve the same result by using a combination of IP forwarding and Compute Engine network components.

An associated feature of a Compute Engine network is its integrated firewall capability. By default, Compute Engine allows only a small set of ingress (incoming) traffic to reach an instance. The following standard firewalls are attached to Compute Engine's default network (this is the list at the time of this writing; see `https://cloud.google.com/compute/docs/networking#firewalls_1` for an updated list):

- `default-allow-internal`: Allows network connections of any protocol and port between any two instances
- `default-allow-ssh`: Allows TCP connections from any source to any instance on the network, over port 22
- `default-allow-icmp`: Allows ICMP traffic from any source to any instance on the network
- `default-allow-rdp`: Allows remote desktop protocol traffic to port 3389

All other ingress traffic must be explicitly allowed through firewall rules. Specifically, no ingress HTTP traffic is allowed to reach an instance. This "deny all by default" approach is very important from a security perspective.

You can customize the scope of Compute Engine network firewall rules. For example, a firewall rule can be applied to all VM instances in a network or to a single VM instance in a network. An example would be to allow incoming SSH from source IP 1.2.3.4 to access an instance called `vm1-nextbigthing-com`. All communication between instances, even if they are within the same network, needs to be explicitly allowed by corresponding firewall rules, whether user-defined or predefined by default.

The Compute Engine network firewall is capable of filtering ingress traffic only. The recommended way to filter egress (outgoing) traffic is to use routes (`https://cloud.google.com/compute/docs/networking#routing`) to force all outbound traffic to a specific instance or load balancer, and do the filtering there. This lets you configure software VPN connections to other sites. It is also possible to filter egress traffic using other methods in two special cases. First, when the destination is another VM in Compute Engine, the ingress rules at the target can be used to filter ingress traffic. When the OS platform in the source VM is a Linux distribution, you can use host-based firewall filters like `iptables to filter egress traffic`.

Deploying High-Performance Virtual Machines Using Compute Engine

This section describes the steps required to deploy VM instances in Compute Engine. Along the way, you learn about associated Compute Engine components. You use the `gcloud` command-line tool exclusively on this journey.

The following steps are required to realize this goal:

1. Associate the `gcloud` command-line tool with a Google account.
2. Select a Google Cloud Platform project.
3. Create and start your instance.
4. Allow ingress network access.

Let us delve into the technicalities involved in these steps.

Associating the gcloud Command-Line Tool with a Google Account

Before you can use the `gcloud` command-line tool to manage a Google cloud project, you need to associate the `gcloud` tool with a Google account. The following command makes this association:

```
$ gcloud auth login [--no-launch-browser]
```

When you type this command in a terminal window and press the Enter key, your default web browser launches. Depending on whether you have already logged in to a Google account, such as Gmail, you may encounter either one or both of the windows shown in Figure 4-2 and Figure 4-3.

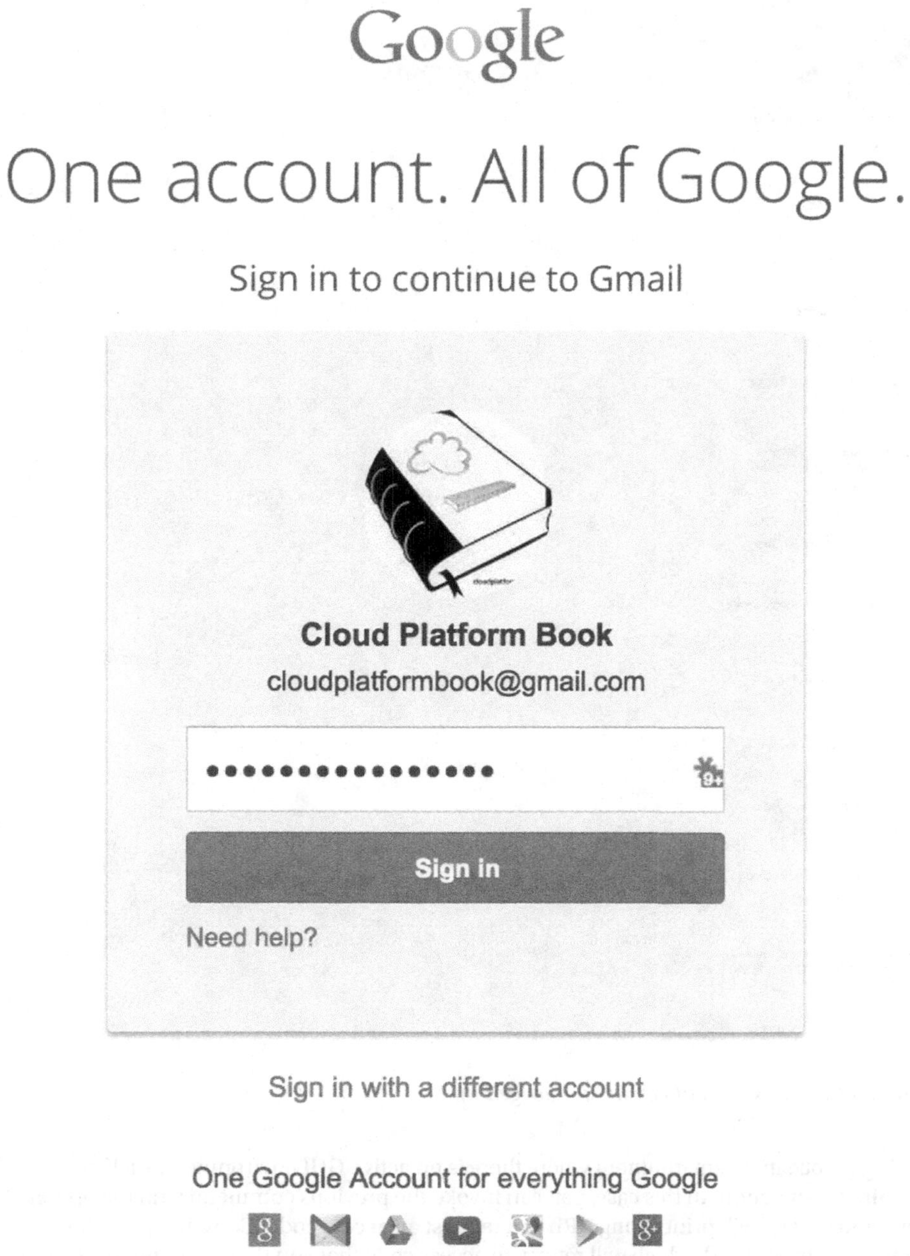

Figure 4-2. Google login screen if you are not currently logged in

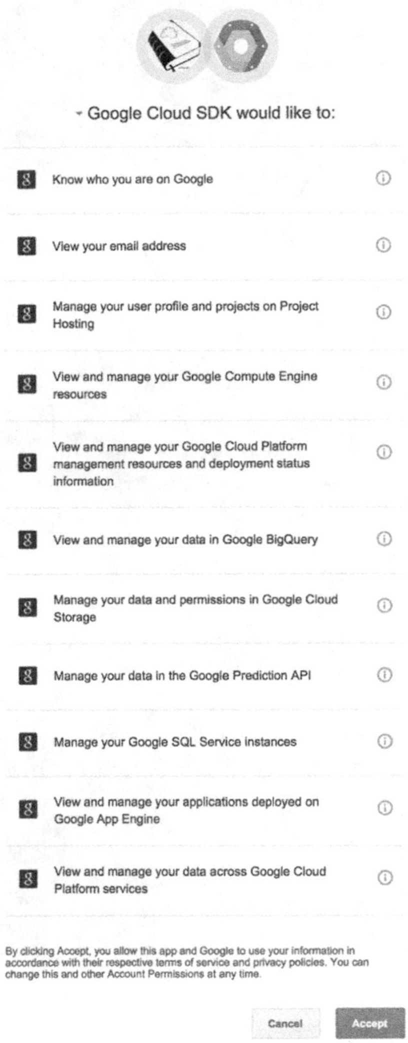

Figure 4-3. *Google authentication screen after you have logged in*

You may be running `gcloud` in an environment where there is no active GUI environment, such as a server or a remote terminal connection. In this case, you can invoke the previous command with the option `--no-launch-browser`, and `gcloud` will print a long URL and request an access code. Copy and paste the code into a web browser (on any system), which will return an access code that you then copy and paste into the command-line prompt. Figure 4-4 illustrates this workflow.

sptkrishnan — bash — 112×32
Last login: Sat Mar 14 15:23:33 on ttys000
Ss-MacBook-Pro:~ sptkrishnan$ gcloud auth login
Your browser has been opened to visit:
https://accounts.google.com/o/oauth2/auth?redirect_uri=http%3A%2F%2Flocalhost%3A8085%2F&prompt=select_account&response_type=code&client_id=32555940559.apps.googleusercontent.com&scope=https%3A%2F%2Fwww.googleapis.com%2Fauth%2Fappengine.admin+https%3A%2F%2Fwww.googleapis.com%2Fauth%2Fbigquery+https%3A%2F%2Fwww.googleapis.com%2Fauth%2Fcompute+https%3A%2F%2Fwww.googleapis.com%2Fauth%2Fdevstorage.full_control+https%3A%2F%2Fwww.googleapis.com%2Fauth%2Fuserinfo.email+https%3A%2F%2Fwww.googleapis.com%2Fauth%2Fndev.cloudman+https%3A%2F%2Fwww.googleapis.com%2Fauth%2Fcloud-platform+https%3A%2F%2Fwww.googleapis.com%2Fauth%2Fsqlservice.admin+https%3A%2F%2Fwww.googleapis.com%2Fauth%2Fprediction+https%3A%2F%2Fwww.googleapis.com%2Fauth%2Fprojecthosting&access_type=offline
Saved Application Default Credentials.
You are now logged in as [cloudplatformbook@gmail.com].

Figure 4-4. *Screenshot showing the long URL and code*

You may use different Google identities for different roles in your life—work, personal, and community project. If so, you have to repeat this process for each account the first time. After you have done this once, you can easily switch between accounts anytime. The following command sequence lists all linked account and lets you choose one of them:

```
$ gcloud auth list
$ gcloud config set account <email>
```

Selecting a Google Cloud Platform Project

You need to declare a `project-id` for use by the `gcloud` tool. You can get the `project-id` from the Developers Console at `https://console.developers.google.com`. Once you have the `project-id`, issue the following command from a terminal window to set the project:

```
$ gcloud config set project <project-id>
```

At this stage, it is important to know about the following limitations when selecting a project using `gcloud`:

- It is currently not possible to create a new project.
- It is currently not possible to list existing projects.
- The declared `project-id` is not validated on entry.
- Access rights to a project are not checked on entry.

Creating and Starting an Instance

Now it is time to create your first VM instance in the Compute Engine platform. You need to do decide which geographical region and zone you want to host your VM and the operating system to use. A geographical region may contain one or more zones. Compute Engine has packaged several widely used OSs as disk images. *Disk images*, or simply *images*, are templates for creating new disks. Root disks usually have an operating system installed, but an image may just be a data disk.

The following command lists all Google Cloud Platform regions and the count of certain resources you have created in each of them:

```
$ gcloud compute regions list
```

Google has multiple zones in each of these regions. You can use the following command to list the zones in each region:

```
$ gcloud compute zones list
```

For this first instance, you use a standard operating system. To determine which operating system images are currently supported in Compute Engine, use this command:

```
$ gcloud compute images list
```

With this information, using the defaults for the rest of the options, you can now create a VM instance using the following command:

```
$ gcloud compute instances create <instance-name> --image <image-name> --zone <zone>
```

This command lists all running instances in the Compute Engine platform:

```
$ gcloud compute instances describe <instance-name>
```

Allowing Ingress Network Access

With the instance up and running, all that remains is to allow access to it from the Internet. You do so by creating firewall rules. The Compute Engine network firewall processes all inbound traffic; hence the source addresses are always external, whereas the target addresses are hosted on the Compute Engine platform. The following command shows how to add a new firewall rule to allow ingress network traffic to access an instance:

```
$ gcloud compute firewall-rules create <name> --description <description> --allow
<protocol:port(s)>
```

With the completion of these commands, you have a VM instance that is accessible from the Internet. In the next section, using these command templates, you launch a new VM instance to host a web-based blog.

Creating a Web Presence with Compute Engine in 8 Minutes Flat

In this section, you use the `gcloud` commands you learned in the previous section to launch a VM instance with a web application that is accessible from anywhere on the Internet. The following instructions create a VM with default specifications running the Linux Debian 7 operating system. The instructions are in **bold** font, and the output is shown:

```
$ gcloud config set account cloudplatformbook@gmail.com

$ gcloud config set project cloud-platform-book
```

```
$ gcloud config list
[core]
account = cloudplatformbook@gmail.com
disable_usage_reporting = False
project = cloud-platform-book
user_output_enabled = True

$ gcloud compute instances list
NAME ZONE MACHINE_TYPE INTERNAL_IP EXTERNAL_IP STATUS
```

■ **Note** Some of "gcloud" command-line tool argument list and output string is longer than single line. We have manually split such long lines into two lines for ease of reading throughout this chapter. For input argument list we have added a " \" at the end of list just like with traditional bash shell inputs. You can ignore these two characters and input the two lines as a single continuous line in your console. For return values we have split them at ".../cloud-platform-book/" part of the output.

```
$ gcloud compute instances create frontend-master --image debian-7 --zone asia-east1-a
Created [https://www.googleapis.com/compute/v1/projects/cloud-platform-book/
zones/asia-east1-a/instances/frontend-master].
NAME            ZONE         MACHINE_TYPE  INTERNAL_IP    EXTERNAL_IP    STATUS
frontend-master asia-east1-a n1-standard-1 10.240.135.214 104.155.206.70 RUNNING
```

This command explicitly states the Compute Engine zone using the --zone flag. If you are going to work with instances that are in a single zone most of the time, you are advised to set that zone as the default in the project configuration for Compute Engine. This saves you the hassle of specifying the zone in all the commands. When you need to work with instances that are in other zones, you can explicitly use the --zone flag to override the default temporarily.

The following gcloud command sets the default zone for Compute Engine. Consequently, you can drop the --zone flag from subsequent commands:

```
$ gcloud config set compute/zone asia-east1-a

$ gcloud compute instances describe frontend-master
canIpForward: false
creationTimestamp: '2015-01-10T22:21:33.244-08:00'
disks:
- autoDelete: true
  boot: true
  deviceName: persistent-disk-0
  index: 0
  interface: SCSI
  kind: compute#attachedDisk
  mode: READ_WRITE
  source: https://www.googleapis.com/compute/v1/projects/cloud-platform-book/
zones/asia-east1-a/disks/frontend-master
  type: PERSISTENT
id: '13106361493425027 62'
kind: compute#instance
```

```
machineType: https://www.googleapis.com/compute/v1/projects/cloud-platform-book/
zones/asia-east1-a/machineTypes/n1-standard-1
metadata:
  fingerprint: P8RS5MYe1aA=
  kind: compute#metadata
name: frontend-master
networkInterfaces:
- accessConfigs:
  - kind: compute#accessConfig
    name: external-nat
    natIP: 104.155.206.70
    type: ONE_TO_ONE_NAT
  name: nic0
  network: https://www.googleapis.com/compute/v1/projects/cloud-platform-book/global/
networks/default
  networkIP: 10.240.135.214
scheduling:
  automaticRestart: true
  onHostMaintenance: MIGRATE
selfLink: https://www.googleapis.com/compute/v1/projects/cloud-platform-book/
zones/asia-east1-a/instances/frontend-master
serviceAccounts:
- email: 261451503272-compute@developer.gserviceaccount.com
  scopes:
  - https://www.googleapis.com/auth/devstorage.read_only
status: RUNNING
tags:
  fingerprint: 42WmSpB8rSM=
zone: https://www.googleapis.com/compute/v1/projects/cloud-platform-book/zones/asia-east1-a
```


By default, Compute Engine configures the network firewall to allow only a few default ports (SSH, ICMP, and RDP) from any source IP address to the VM instances. You need to add firewall rules to allow inbound connections to other software network ports. The most common such rule allows HTTP and HTTPS traffic to ports 80 and 443. You are setting a web server in the newly created instance, so you can now configure the network firewall to allow incoming HTTP and HTTPS traffic to this instance:

```
$ gcloud compute firewall-rules create allow-http --description "Incoming http allowed."
--allow tcp:80
Created [https://www.googleapis.com/compute/v1/projects/cloud-platform-book/
global/firewalls/allow-http].
NAME       NETWORK SRC_RANGES RULES  SRC_TAGS TARGET_TAGS
allow-http default 0.0.0.0/0  tcp:80
```

You can tweak the command to allow HTTPS connections as well:

```
$ gcloud compute firewall-rules create allow-https --description "Incoming https allowed."
--allow tcp:443
Created [https://www.googleapis.com/compute/v1/projects/cloud-platform-book/
global/firewalls/allow-https].
NAME        NETWORK SRC_RANGES RULES   SRC_TAGS TARGET_TAGS
allow-https default 0.0.0.0/0  tcp:443
```

Let us dissect one of these commands in detail, to understand some of the implicit assumptions made by Compute Engine when no explicit options are provided. Compute Engine uses these default options:

- When a firewall rule does not specify an instance, the firewall rule is applied to all live instances.
- When a firewall rule does not specify a network, the firewall rule is applied to the default network.
- When a firewall rule does not specify a source, the firewall rule allows *all* source IPs (both internal and external) to make requests to the target. In this case, all instances are added to the default network.

Now that you have added your own custom firewall rules, you may want to list all the active firewall rules. This can be accomplished using the following command:

```
$ gcloud compute firewall-rules list
This NAME                 NETWORK SRC_RANGES    RULES               SRC_TAGS TARGET_TAGS
allow-http                default 0.0.0.0/0     tcp:80
allow-https               default 0.0.0.0/0     tcp:443
default-allow-icmp        default 0.0.0.0/0     icmp
default-allow-internal default 10.240.0.0/16 tcp:1-65535,udp:1-65535,icmp
default-allow-rdp         default 0.0.0.0/0     tcp:3389
default-allow-ssh         default 0.0.0.0/0     tcp:22
```

If you want to describe any one rule in more detail, you can do so using the following command:

```
$ gcloud compute firewall-rules describe allow-http
allowed:
- IPProtocol: tcp
  ports:
  - '80'
creationTimestamp: '2015-01-18T21:35:09.045-08:00'
description: Incoming http allowed.
id: '15660039426868416436'
kind: compute#firewall
name: allow-http
network: https://www.googleapis.com/compute/v1/projects/cloud-platform-book/
global/networks/default
selfLink: https://www.googleapis.com/compute/v1/projects/cloud-platform-book/
global/firewalls/allow-http
sourceRanges:
- 0.0.0.0/0
```

The default options may not be suitable for every VM instance. For example, you may want to restrict SSH access from certain IP addresses, such as a bastion host, or allow HTTP from internal IP addresses only. In such cases, you can use the applicable options to these commands. To list the available options for any command, add the suffix --help to it. As an example, the following command shows the help page for firewall rule creation:

```
$ gcloud compute firewall-rules create -help
```

You have set up your instance and allowed both inbound HTTP(S) and SSH connections. Let us log in to the system and set up the required software to serve incoming requests. You use the following command to log in to the system:

```
$ gcloud compute ssh frontend-master
Warning: Permanently added '104.155.206.70' (RSA) to the list of known hosts.
Linux frontend-master 3.2.0-4-amd64 #1 SMP Debian 3.2.65-1 x86_64

The programs included with the Debian GNU/Linux system are free software;
the exact distribution terms for each program are described in the
individual files in /usr/share/doc/*/copyright.

Debian GNU/Linux comes with ABSOLUTELY NO WARRANTY, to the extent
permitted by applicable law.
Last login: Sun Jan 11 07:17:48 2015 from 103.224.116.114
user@frontend-master:~$
```

Let us examine some of this command's features. First, the `gcloud` command-line tool has the built-in ability to SSH into the remote system. Second, the default authentication method is to use public keys instead of passwords. This is safer and easier to use, as well. At the same time, you can use any other SSH tool to access VM instances. See the online documentation at `https://cloud.google.com/compute/docs/console` for more information. You can also log in over SSH using your browser from the web-based Developers Console; look for the SSH button when viewing information about a VM.

Once you are logged in, you can do anything on this Compute Engine VM instance that you can do on a standard Linux system. You have full root access in the VM. Next, you need to run the following three commands to update the Linux VM with any critical updates that may have been issued by the distribution owner since the image was created. Remote Compute Engine VM commands have the prefix `VM` before the $ symbol:

```
VM$ sudo apt-get update
<Snip>

VM$ sudo apt-get dist-upgrade
<Snip>

VM$ sudo reboot
<Snip>
```

After the VM has rebooted, you need to log in again via SSH. Let us set up a web server to serve the default web site from your instance. This example uses the most popular web server software: the Apache web server. Use the following command to set up the Apache web server software:

```
VM$ sudo apt-get install apache2
<Snip>
```

You should now be able to access the instance over HTTP using the URL `http://EXTERNAL_IP`. You can obtain the external IP address using the following command:

```
$ gcloud compute instances list
NAME            ZONE          MACHINE_TYPE  INTERNAL_IP    EXTERNAL_IP    STATUS
frontend-master asia-east1-a n1-standard-1 10.240.135.214 104.155.206.70 RUNNING
```

It is important to know that billing begins on VM deployment, and you are charged every month for the resources consumed: compute, storage, or network bandwidth. Hence, you should delete deployed resources when you do not need them anymore. The following command stops and deletes the VM instance and, depending on the setting, the associated PD as well. The default setting is to delete PDs on VM instance deletion:

```
$ gcloud compute instances delete frontend-master
```

Handling Unpredictable Traffic with the Compute Engine Load Balancer

Compute Engine offers VM instances of varying sizes. But each of these instances has a maximum computing capacity, as measured by CPU processing and/or network throughput. Hence, it is important for system architects to know how to design Internet-facing systems that can scale up as the incoming requests increase and scale down to shed extra capacity when not required, thereby leading to cost savings. You can achieve this automatic reconfiguration of systems using two entities called the *load balancer* and the *autoscaler*.

This section discusses the Compute Engine load balancer and shows an example of setting up a frontend web tier comprising a load balancer and two web servers in a single geographic region. The following section expands this architecture to build a truly global infrastructure consisting of nodes in multiple geographic regions. Let us start by defining a load balancer.

A *load balancer* is a device that acts as a proxy; it can be considered the first network hop for incoming network or application traffic. In a traditional three-tier architecture, consisting of web, application, and database tiers, the load balancer is in front of the web tier and distributes incoming traffic to healthy web server nodes. A load balancer can be either physical or virtual.

The Google Cloud Platform currently offers two types of load balancing: network and HTTP. *Network load balancing* is a regional capability that can load-balance incoming network traffic to a set of healthy compute nodes in a single region. Network load balancing operates on a low-level network protocol, such as TCP, and software ports on a VM instance, such as port 80. On the other hand, *HTTP load balancing* is a global capability; it can distribute incoming application-level traffic, such as web traffic, and distribute that traffic to VM instances in different Google Cloud Platform regions and zones. Let us look in detail at network load balancing in the following paragraphs; the following section covers HTTP load balancing.

The Compute Engine load balancer has two main building blocks—forwarding rules and target pools—and a supporting service called the health checker. Let us examine these along with the load-distribution algorithm.

■ **Note** Some components of the Google Cloud Platform are in beta as of this writing. This includes HTTP load balancing. To access these components, you need to install the `gcloud` preview component, using the following command: `gcloud` **`components update preview`**.

Forwarding Rules

A *forwarding rule* is like a filter that extracts selected traffic, which is interesting to you, from the total traffic entering a Cloud Platform zone. Technically, it can be seen as a regular expression that matches a subset of network traffic from the overall traffic. Forwarding rules reside in a forwarding rule collection managed by Compute Engine. A forwarding rule matches an external IP address and a protocol (TCP/UDP). Optionally, the forwarding rule can be restricted to a certain range of ports. The filtered traffic matching a forwarding rule is forwarded to a target pool.

Target Pool

A *target pool* is a resource that consists of one or more VM instances. Incoming network traffic is automatically assigned to a healthy VM instance based on a load-distribution algorithm (explained in the next section). The advantage of using network load balancing is that the endpoint VM receives the actual network traffic as if it was the instance exposed to the Internet in the first place.

Load-Distribution Algorithm

It is common for a load balancer to use a round-robin method to assign new incoming connections to healthy VM instances. Compute Engine uses a different and unique method: a hash of incoming IP and port, and target IP and port, to decide the target instance to which to deliver the connection. All subsequent connections that match the same hash will be delivered to the same VM instance. This characteristic ensures that a session is handled by the same VM instance. You can change this default behavior using a different hashing algorithm if better session affinity is required.

Health Checks

Compute Engine has a built-in ability to detect whether a VM instance is healthy. It determines this by sending an HTTP request to a preset URL hosted in each of the VM instances; it expects a valid response with HTTP code 200 OK, and it expected the HTTP to be closed normally within the timeout duration. If an instance does not respond within the timeout duration or does not return the expected response for a configurable X number of times, then it is marked as unhealthy and removed from the target pool. The target pool does not send any new requests to this VM instance; however, existing connections in the session are served by the same instance to allow for graceful shutdown. The Compute Engine health checker keeps pinging the unhealthy VM instance, and once it receives a configurable Y number of good responses, it marks the VM instance as healthy and returns the instance to the target pool.

It is important to note that the VM instance should be running a web server in order to respond to the health checker, even if the expected network traffic to the VM instance is not HTTP traffic. This usually is not a major issue, because you can limit incoming network traffic to the IP range of the health checker, thereby not exposing the web server to the Internet. Further, you can use a lightweight web server if the system resources are not sufficient to run a full-fledged web server like Apache. For HTTP load balancing, the health check requests come from addresses in the range 130.211.0.0/22. For network load balancing, the health check requests come from 169.254.169.254. See `https://cloud.google.com/compute/docs/load-balancing/health-checks#listing_health_checks` for the current health-checker IP range. This is useful if you configure firewall rules with narrower scopes.

Going Live

This section explores the details of setting up a network load balancer with two VM instances. Begin by following the instructions from the previous section and setting up a second VM instance. Then, log in to each of these instances and create different default `index.html` files to uniquely identify them over the Web. The following instructions achieve this (the commands are documented individually):

```
# Create a new instance in the same region but in a different zone
$ gcloud compute instances create frontend-slave --image debian-7 --zone asia-east1-b

# Login to the new instance
$ gcloud compute ssh frontend-slave --zone asia-east1-b
```

```
# Update the installed packages and install apache web server
VM$ sudo apt-get update
<Snip>

VM$ sudo apt-get dist-upgrade
<Snip>

VM$ sudo reboot
<Snip>

VM$ sudo apt-get install apache2
<Snip>
```

Now SSH into both VM instances and update the default `index.html` file to show different messages. You will use this for a future test case where you load-test the load balancer; by having different default pages, you can see which instance is responding to incoming queries. The following code shows the modified `index.html` files for the two instances:

```
user@frontend-master:/var/www$ pwd
/var/www

user@frontend-master:/var/www$ ls -l
total 4
-rw-r--r-- 1 root root 193 Jan 24 01:09 index.html

user@frontend-master:/var/www$ cat index.html
<html><body><h1>Frontend Master</h1>
<p>Welcome to FRONTEND MASTER server.</p>
</body></html>

user@frontend-slave:/var/www$ pwd
/var/www

user@frontend-slave:/var/www$ ls -l
total 4
-rw-r--r-- 1 root root 192 Jan 24 01:10 index.html

user@frontend-slave:/var/www$ cat index.html
<html><body><h1>Frontend Slave</h1>
<p>Welcome to FRONTEND SLAVE server.</p>
</body></html>
```

At this stage, you should have two Linux-powered VM instances that have Apache web server software installed and are accessible from the Internet. Verify that you can access them using a web browser:

```
# Verify the VM instances are accessible from a web browser
http://130.211.244.80/
http://104.155.206.70/
```

Note that this code uses the IP addresses of my instances. Your IP addresses will be different. You can find the external IP addresses by running `gcloud compute instances list`.

Next, you need to set up a health check, create a target pool, and associate the health check with the target pool. After this, you add these two instances to the target pool and create the required forwarding rules to direct traffic to the target pool. The following are the commands to run on your workstation, with explanations in the comments:

```
# Create an http health check using default settings
$ gcloud compute http-health-checks create http-check
Created
[https://www.googleapis.com/compute/v1/projects/cloud-platform-book/
global/httpHealthChecks/http-check].
NAME       HOST PORT REQUEST_PATH
http-check      80   /
```

Now let us add a target pool in the same region where you have created the instances. The instances can be in different zones in the same region, as is the case with the two example instances. The following commands list the regions, set an environment variable to remember the region, and then create the target pool linked with the HTTP check in the same region:

```
$ gcloud compute regions list
NAME          CPUS         DISKS_GB     ADDRESSES RESERVED_ADDRESSES STATUS TURNDOWN_DATE
asia-east1    2.00/24.00   20/10240     2/23      0/7                UP
europe-west1  0.00/24.00    0/10240     0/23      0/7                UP
us-central1   0.00/24.00    0/10240     0/23      0/7                UP

$ REGION="asia-east1"

$ gcloud compute target-pools create www-pool --region $REGION --health-check http-check
Created
[https://www.googleapis.com/compute/v1/projects/cloud-platform-book/
regions/asia-east1/targetPools/www-pool].
NAME     REGION     SESSION_AFFINITY BACKUP HEALTH_CHECKS
www-pool asia-east1 NONE                    http-check

$ gcloud compute target-pools add-instances www-pool --instances frontend-master --zone
asia-east1-a
Updated [https://www.googleapis.com/compute/v1/projects/cloud-platform-book/
regions/asia-east1/targetPools/www-pool].

$ gcloud compute target-pools add-instances www-pool --instances frontend-slave --zone
asia-east1-b
Updated [https://www.googleapis.com/compute/v1/projects/cloud-platform-book/
regions/asia-east1/targetPools/www-pool].
```

In this example, if the instances are in same zone, you can combine the two statements and list the instances. Also, it is possible to add a health check to an existing target pool. This is useful when new type of health checks are added to Compute Engine.

As a final step, let us add a forwarding rule to send traffic to the target pool. The forwarding rule needs a public IP address; you can use either static IP or an ephemeral IP address. In this case, use the default option (an ephemeral IP address):

```
$ gcloud compute forwarding-rules create www-rule --region $REGION --port-range 80 --target-pool www-pool
Created [https://www.googleapis.com/compute/v1/projects/cloud-platform-book/regions/asia-east1/forwardingRules/www-rule].
NAME     REGION     IP_ADDRESS             IP_PROTOCOL TARGET
www-rule asia-east1 104.155.234.199 TCP    asia-east1/targetPools/www-pool
```

Let us add the ephemeral IP address assigned to the forwarding rule and load-test the setup you have built to see if the target pool is working as expected:

```
$ IP="104.155.234.199"

$ while true; do curl -m1 $IP; done
<html><body><h1>Frontend Master</h1>
<p>Welcome to FRONTEND MASTER server.</p>
</body></html>
<html><body><h1>Frontend Slave</h1>
<p>Welcome to FRONTEND SLAVE server.</p>
</body></html>
<html><body><h1>Frontend Master</h1>
<p>Welcome to FRONTEND MASTER server.</p>
</body></html>
<html><body><h1>Frontend Slave</h1>
<p>Welcome to FRONTEND SLAVE server.</p>
</body></html>
<html><body><h1>Frontend Master</h1>
<p>Welcome to FRONTEND MASTER server.</p>
</body></html>
<html><body><h1>Frontend Slave</h1>
<p>Welcome to FRONTEND SLAVE server.</p>
</body></html>
```

As you can see, incoming queries to the forwarding-rule IP address are distributed to the VM instances behind the target pool. This completes the setup for the network load balancer.

Before you move on, a final note. It is my observation and experience that users usually set up one VM to begin with; once the software stack is set up and tuned properly, they scale out. You can do so by creating an image of your existing VM, using it as a mold to create a second VM, and attaching both of them to the same target pool. See https://cloud.google.com/compute/docs/images for extensive documentation of Compute Engine images.

Building a Global Multi-Datacenter Web Tier in an Hour

In the previous section, you created a network load balancer that is restricted to one region in the Google Cloud Platform. This type of setup works well for companies whose customers are in one geographical region. For global enterprises that have customers around the globe, having a setup in one geographical region means low-latency network access to customers in one region but medium- to high-latency network access to other groups of users. Hence, many organizations with customers spread globally need multiple points of presence for their IT footprint. This requirement is well served by the HTTP load balancer and is covered in this section.

The key components of the HTTP load balancer are as follows:

- Global forwarding rule
- Target proxy
- URL map
- Backend services
- Instance groups

Global Forwarding Rules

Global forwarding rules route incoming network traffic by IP address, port, and protocol to a load-balancing configuration, which consists of a target proxy, a URL map, and one or more backend services. Similar to the forwarding rules in network loading balancing, global forwarding rules assign a single global IP address, which can be either static or an ephemeral IP address. This single global IP address can be used in a DNS record, negating the need for traditional DNS-based round-robin load balancing.

Target HTTP Proxy

The *target HTTP proxy*, as the name suggests, is the endpoint on the Compute Engine side that terminates the incoming HTTP/TCP connection from the user. A new connection is then made by the proxy to the next internal network hop, known as the *URL map*. The proxy also adds additional request/response HTTP headers to the HTTP connection, as follows:

```
Via: 1.1 Google (requests and responses)
X-Forwarded-For: <client IP>, <global forwarding rule external IP> (requests only)
```

By inspecting the HTTP headers, the clients and the server can extract key information. For example, an analytics module on the server side should use the `<client IP>` in the `X-Forwarded-For` header instead of the `source-ip` of the TCP connection, because the latter is always the proxy IP. The clients can also parse the HTTP connection and know that a Google proxy is serving them, and not the actual server, although the DNS resolution of the domain provides the server's IP address.

URL Maps

URL maps define regular-expression matching patterns to filter the incoming requests and forward them to different sets of backend services. They are typically used in content-based routing architectures where different backend services serve different type of content, such as images, videos, and text. A default service is defined to handle any requests that are not matched by any other rule. This is sufficient for a multi-region load-balancing setup.

Backend Services

Backend services define groups of backend instances and their serving capacity. The serving capacity is defined either as CPU usage or requests per second (RPS). The backend service also specifies the health checks that will be performed against the available instances. The health checks are the same as described earlier for network load balancing.

Instance Groups

Instance groups are a grouping mechanism that defines VM instances that are available as a backend-services group. A backend service may list a set of instance groups instead of individual instances. You can add instances to and remove them from an instance group, and the instance group can be used for other cloud services in addition to load balancing.

Load-Distribution Algorithm

HTTP load balancing provides two methods of determining an instance load: RPS and CPU utilization modes. Both modes let you specify a maximum value. Incoming requests are sent to the region that is closest to the user and that has remaining capacity.

Going Live

This example uses the two instances you created in the previous two sections. In addition to these two instances in the Asia region, you add four more instances: two in Europe and two in the United States. All the instances are in different zones. In addition, you automate the installation of a web server using a startup script. Compute Engine executes the startup script as part of VM startup. Following are the required Linux commands and the output of these steps:

```
$ echo "apt-get update && apt-get install -y apache2 && hostname > /var/www/index.html" > \
$HOME/gce:startup.sh

$ gcloud compute instances create frontend-us1 --image debian-7 \
--zone us-central1-a --metadata-from-file startup-script=$HOME/gce:startup.sh
Created [https://www.googleapis.com/compute/v1/projects/cloud-platform-book/
zones/us-central1-a/instances/frontend-us1].
NAME         ZONE          MACHINE_TYPE  INTERNAL_IP    EXTERNAL_IP     STATUS
frontend-us1 us-central1-a n1-standard-1 10.240.154.170 130.211.186.207 RUNNING

$ gcloud compute instances create frontend-us2 --image debian-7 \
--zone us-central1-b --metadata-from-file startup-script=$HOME/gce:startup.sh
Created [https://www.googleapis.com/compute/v1/projects/cloud-platform-book/
zones/us-central1-b/instances/frontend-us2].
NAME         ZONE          MACHINE_TYPE  INTERNAL_IP   EXTERNAL_IP    STATUS
frontend-us2 us-central1-b n1-standard-1 10.240.124.81 104.154.39.159 RUNNING

$ gcloud compute instances create frontend-eu1 --image debian-7 --zone europe-west1-b
--metadata-from-file startup-script=$HOME/gce:startup.sh
Created [https://www.googleapis.com/compute/v1/projects/cloud-platform-book/
zones/europe-west1-b/instances/frontend-eu1].
NAME         ZONE           MACHINE_TYPE  INTERNAL_IP   EXTERNAL_IP     STATUS
frontend-eu1 europe-west1-b n1-standard-1 10.240.232.37 146.148.126.134 RUNNING

$ gcloud compute instances create frontend-eu2 --image debian-7 \
--zone europe-west1-c --metadata-from-file startup-script=$HOME/gce:startup.sh
Created [https://www.googleapis.com/compute/v1/projects/cloud-platform-book/
zones/europe-west1-c/instances/frontend-eu2].
NAME         ZONE           MACHINE_TYPE  INTERNAL_IP   EXTERNAL_IP   STATUS
frontend-eu2 europe-west1-c n1-standard-1 10.240.95.225 104.155.11.26 RUNNING
```

Using a web browser, verify that you can access each instance through its public IP address. If they are not accessible, check whether the firewall rules have been added to enable access at port 80.

The following are the logical steps to set up the HTTP load-balancing service:

1. Create instance groups, one per zone.
2. In these zones, add instances to the instance groups.
3. Add the required HTTP service to each instance group.
4. Create or reuse an HTTP health-check object.
5. Create a backend service linking the health check.
6. Add instance groups as backends to the backend service.
7. Create a URL map to direct ingress traffic to the backend service.
8. Create a target HTTP proxy to route requests to the URL map.
9. Create a global forwarding rule to send traffic to the HTTP proxy.

Here are the gcloud commands to carry out these steps:

■ **Note** Some gcloud commands use preview instead of the compute option. This is because they are in a beta state, and it is possible the API and gcloud options may change as the product goes into GA release. If the following commands do not work, check the current versions at http://cloud.google.com/compute/docs.

```
# Step 1 - gcloud commands to create instances groups

$ gcloud preview instance-groups --zone us-central1-a create ig-usc1a
Instance group ig-usc1a created.
$ gcloud preview instance-groups --zone us-central1-b create ig-usc1b
Instance group ig-usc1b created.
$ gcloud preview instance-groups --zone europe-west1-b create ig-euw1b
Instance group ig-euw1b created.
$ gcloud preview instance-groups --zone europe-west1-c create ig-euw1c
Instance group ig-euw1c created.
$ gcloud preview instance-groups --zone asia-east1-a create ig-ape1a
Instance group ig-ape1a created.
$ gcloud preview instance-groups --zone asia-east1-b create ig-ape1b
Instance group ig-ape1b created.

# Step 2 - gcloud commands to add instances to instance groups

$ gcloud preview instance-groups --zone us-central1-a instances \
--group ig-usc1a add frontend-us1
Instances added to instance group ig-usc1a.
$ gcloud preview instance-groups --zone us-central1-b instances \
--group ig-usc1b add frontend-us2
Instances added to instance group ig-usc1b.
$ gcloud preview instance-groups --zone europe-west1-b instances \
--group ig-euw1b add frontend-eu1
Instances added to instance group ig-euw1b.
```

```
$ gcloud preview instance-groups --zone europe-west1-c instances \
--group ig-euw1c add frontend-eu2
Instances added to instance group ig-euw1c.
$ gcloud preview instance-groups --zone asia-east1-a instances \
--group ig-ape1a add frontend-master
Instances added to instance group ig-ape1a.
$ gcloud preview instance-groups --zone asia-east1-b instances \
--group ig-ape1b add frontend-slave
Instances added to instance group ig-ape1b.

# Step 3 - gcloud commands to add required http service to each instance group

$ gcloud preview instance-groups --zone us-central1-a add-service ig-usc1a \
--port 80 --service http
Service http:80 added.
$ gcloud preview instance-groups --zone us-central1-b add-service ig-usc1b \
--port 80 --service http
Service http:80 added.
$ gcloud preview instance-groups --zone europe-west1-b add-service ig-euw1b \
--port 80 --service http
Service http:80 added.
$ gcloud preview instance-groups --zone europe-west1-c add-service ig-euw1c \
--port 80 --service http
Service http:80 added.
$ gcloud preview instance-groups --zone asia-east1-a add-service ig-ape1a \
--port 80 --service http
Service http:80 added.
$ gcloud preview instance-groups --zone asia-east1-b add-service ig-ape1b \
--port 80 --service http
Service http:80 added.
```

You created an HTTP health check earlier, in the network load-balancing section, and you reuse it here. If you have deleted it, you can create a new one using the following command:

```
# Step 4a - List any existing http health check objects
$ gcloud compute http-health-checks list
NAME        HOST PORT REQUEST_PATH
http-check       80   /

# Step 4b - Create a new http health check object (if required)
$ gcloud compute http-health-checks create http-check

# Step 5 - Create a backend service

$ gcloud compute backend-services create web-service --http-health-check http-check
Created [https://www.googleapis.com/compute/v1/projects/cloud-platform-book/
global/backendServices/web-service].
NAME         BACKENDS PROTOCOL
web-service           HTTP
```

```
# Step 6 - Add instance groups as backends to backend service

$ gcloud compute backend-services add-backend web-service \
--group ig-usc1a --zone us-central1-a
Updated [https://www.googleapis.com/compute/v1/projects/cloud-platform-book/global/
backendServices/web-service].
$ gcloud compute backend-services add-backend web-service \
--group ig-usc1b --zone us-central1-b
Updated [https://www.googleapis.com/compute/v1/projects/cloud-platform-book/global/
backendServices/web-service].
$ gcloud compute backend-services add-backend web-service \
--group ig-euw1b --zone europe-west1-b
Updated [https://www.googleapis.com/compute/v1/projects/cloud-platform-book/global/
backendServices/web-service].
$ gcloud compute backend-services add-backend web-service \
--group ig-euw1c --zone europe-west1-c
Updated [https://www.googleapis.com/compute/v1/projects/cloud-platform-book/global/
backendServices/web-service].
$ gcloud compute backend-services add-backend web-service \
--group ig-ape1a --zone asia-east1-a
Updated [https://www.googleapis.com/compute/v1/projects/cloud-platform-book/global/
backendServices/web-service].
$ gcloud compute backend-services add-backend web-service \
--group ig-ape1b --zone asia-east1-b
Updated [https://www.googleapis.com/compute/v1/projects/cloud-platform-book/global/
backendServices/web-service].

# Step 7 - Create URL Map to direct ingress traffic to backend service

$ gcloud compute url-maps create web-map --default-service web-service
Created [https://www.googleapis.com/compute/v1/projects/cloud-platform-book/
global/urlMaps/web-map].
NAME    DEFAULT_SERVICE
web-map web-service

# Step 8 - Create target HTTP proxy to route requests to URL map

$ gcloud compute target-http-proxies create web-proxy --url-map web-map
Created [https://www.googleapis.com/compute/v1/projects/cloud-platform-book/global/
targetHttpProxies/web-proxy].
NAME      URL_MAP
web-proxy web-map

# Step 9 - Create Global forwarding rule to send traffic to HTTP proxy

$ gcloud compute forwarding-rules create http-rule --global \
--target-http-proxy web-proxy --port-range 80
Created [https://www.googleapis.com/compute/v1/projects/cloud-platform-book/
global/forwardingRules/http-rule].
NAME      REGION IP_ADDRESS     IP_PROTOCOL TARGET
http-rule        107.178.245.89 TCP         web-proxy
```

At this stage, if you open a web browser with `http://<global-forwarding-rule-ip>`, your request is routed to the instance that is nearest to you. Let us send some traffic to the HTTP load balancer you have set up, and see its responses. Note that my workstation was in Singapore for this test:

```
$ while true; do curl -m1 107.178.245.89; done
frontend-master
frontend-master
frontend-master
```

Let us simulate system maintenance in the setup by shutting down the Apache web servers in both of Asian nodes and see if the traffic is automatically routed to the next-best location:

```
$ gcloud compute ssh frontend-master --zone asia-east1-a
...
Last login: Sun Jan 25 04:06:14 2015 from 1.2.1.1
VM$ sudo service apache2 stop
[ ok ] Stopping web server: apache2 ... waiting .
VM$ exit
logout
Connection to 104.155.206.70 closed.

$ gcloud compute ssh frontend-slave --zone asia-east1-b
...
Last login: Sat Jan 24 14:31:53 2015 from 1.2.1.1
VM$ sudo service apache2 stop
[ ok ] Stopping web server: apache2 ... waiting .
VM$ exit
logout
Connection to 130.211.244.80 closed.

$ while true; do curl -m1 107.178.245.89; done
frontend-us2
frontend-us2
frontend-us1
```

This experiment shows that the HTTP load balancer is transparently detecting backend failure and automatically routing traffic to the next-nearest node. When the nodes return to service, the routing will automatically reset. Using the HTTP load balancer, IT operations can be assured that customers always reach a good node.

A variation of the HTTP load-balancing setup is *content-based load balancing*. In this architecture, incoming traffic is distributed to various backend services based on predefined patterns in the request URLs. This is a very useful feature that can be used to select appropriate backend services to serve different type of data such as images, video, and text.

You can obtain this desirable behavior by making a minor modification to the HTTP load-balancing setup discussed in this section. You make the change in the step where you define a URL map. In addition to defining the default map, you also need to define more specific maps that route traffic to those URLs to a different backend. Let us look at an example:

```
# Example URL map
hostRules:
- hosts: ["*"]
  pathMatcher: pathmap
pathMatchers:
- name: pathmap
  defaultService: https://www.googleapis.com/compute/v1/projects/PROJECT_ID/
global/backendServices/www-service
  pathRules:
    - paths: ["/video", "/video/*"]
      service: https://www.googleapis.com/compute/v1/projects/PROJECT_ID/
global/backendServices/video-service
    - paths: ["/static", "/static/*"]
      service: https://www.googleapis.com/compute/v1/projects/PROJECT_ID/
global/backendServices/static-service
```

In this example, requests to URLs `/video/*` are sent to a backend service called `video-service`, and requests to `/static/*` are sent to a backend service called `static-service`. All other requests are sent to a backend service called `www-service`.

Automatically Resizing a Web Tier with the Compute Engine Autoscaler

The previous sections looked at the network load balancer and HTTP load balancer. A network load balancer has regional scale, whereas an HTTP load balancer has global scale, but neither load balancer scales automatically. You need to either scale them up manually (by adding more VM instances) to meet additional workloads or scale them down (by removing VM instances) to save costs.

This section looks at another technology called the *autoscaler* in the Compute Engine portfolio that automatically adds resources on demand and sheds overcapacity when not required, resulting in cost savings. The autoscaler can add resources based on several metrics: CPU utilization, serving metric, and other cloud-monitoring metrics. Let us first learn about the key building blocks and terminology of the Compute Engine autoscaler service.

Managed Instance Group

An *instance group* is a group of VM instances managed as a single entity. A *managed instance group* is a group of homogenous instances that is automatically managed by an instance group manager. The instance group manager can add homogenous instances (instances with the same specs) to the group or remove them.

Utilization Metric

The autoscaler requires a dynamic system metric that it can measure, in order to add and remove the VM resources that it is managing. This is known as the *utilization metric*; and depending on the type of computational resource, it is measured differently.

The following are some standard metrics:

- *CPU utilization metric*: Usage is measured as a percentage of total CPU capacity in the VM cluster.
- *Incoming requests*: Usage is counted as the number of new connections every second.

The utilization metrics are averaged over the total number of VM instances, and the average value is compared against the target utilization level. Selecting a good utilization metric is paramount to the proper functioning of the autoscaler. *Good* mean a metric that reflects the actual load the cluster is experiencing at that point in time. Examples of good metrics include CPU usage across the VMs and actual network ingress/egress traffic from the VMs. An example of an indirect metric is the amount of traffic to/from the persistent storage. Although this is a sign of how busy a VM/app is, it need not produce good results all the time, because apps may be CPU-bound instead of IO-bound. At the same time, choosing a bad metric negates the purpose of the autoscaler. An example of a bad metric is the number of cores in a VM. Because the number of cores is a static measure, the autoscaler is ineffective in this case.

Target Utilization Level

You can think of the *target utilization level* as a tipping point: when exceeded, it triggers the autoscaler to add more resources so the average utilization level is restored to being under this set level. By default, the autoscaler watches the resource every 5 seconds. When resource consumption exceeds this set level for two consecutive checks, additional VM resources are added. Similarly, when resource consumption falls below the set threshold level for two consecutive checks, VMs are discarded, resulting in cost savings.

The frequency of checks and the number of consecutive checks that trigger the autoscaler to either scale up or scale down VM resources are configurable. Also, the specification of the target utilization level is different for various resources. CPU utilization is defined as the average of CPU utilization across all VM instances, whereas RPS for ingress connections is defined per VM. Both the autoscaler and the managed VMs reside in the same zone.

Autoscaling Integrations

This section discusses how autoscaling can be integrated with the load-balancing configurations you saw in the previous sections. To recall, you learned about the regional-scale network load balancer and global-scale HTTP load balancer. In both cases, the number of instances is manually managed. Using an autoscaler, the number of instances can be auto-managed so the VM cluster size is optimal for the load factor.

In the case of a network load balancer, forwarding rule filters traffic based on network characteristics (IP, port, and protocol) and sends the traffic to a network pool, which is the entity that contains an instance group. In an earlier example, you used an unmanaged (static) instance group. When you are using the autoscaler, you can simply replace this unmanaged instance group with a managed (dynamic) instance group. The instance group manager of the managed instance group is passed to the autoscaler, which measures the load factor—say, CPU utilization—while the forwarding rules and network pool continue to deliver ingress traffic to the VM instances.

In the case of an HTTP load balancer, a global forwarding rule filters traffic to a target HTTP proxy that in turn consults an URL map and the source of the request and delivers that traffic to the corresponding backend services. The backend services form the unmanaged instance group in the classic configuration. With the autoscaler, you replace the unmanaged instance group with a managed instance group and pass the corresponding instance-group manager to the autoscaler. This way, each regional cluster autoscales regardless of the load factor at other regional clusters. This behavior is useful for content-based load balancing where certain parts of a web app, such as media (images and video), may require more backend resources compared to text-based resources like HTML, CSS, and JavaScript data. Let us look at the steps required to set up an autoscaler in the network load balancer.

Going Live

The following are the high-level steps to realize an autoscaling backend for a network load balancer:

1. Create an instance template.
2. Create a managed instance group.
3. Create an autoscaler.
4. Add autoscaled managed instance groups as endpoints.

Step 1: Create an Instance Template

Instance templates are deployment configurations for VMs that specify various system settings such as hardware configuration and operating system, among others. Creating an instance template does not automatically create an instance. An instance group manager creates instances in a managed instance group using the template. Let us use the gcloud cli tool to create an instance template using the default values:

```
$ gcloud compute instance-templates create debian-template
Created [https://www.googleapis.com/compute/v1/projects/cloud-platform-book/
global/instanceTemplates/debian-template].
NAME            MACHINE_TYPE  CREATION_TIMESTAMP
debian-template n1-standard-1 2015-01-26T21:38:14.412-08:00
```

The following are the default values for the various parameters. Using the default values has its pros and cons, as discussed in a moment:

- *Machine type*: n1-standard-1
- *Image*: The latest Debian backports image
- *Boot disk*: A new boot disk named after the VM
- *Network*: The default network
- *IP address*: An ephemeral external IP address

Recall that the purpose of creating instance templates is for the autoscaler to use them to create replica VMs in a managed VM. Suppose that a managed instance group contains only one VM under normal workloads. After a few weeks, the autoscaler detects an increased workload and creates a second VM based on the instance template. However, during the time between the creation of the first and second VMs, the Debian distribution is updated, and the "latest" refers to a newer software release version compared to the first VM. This creates variations between the VMs and may lead to unexpected and undesirable outcomes. Hence, it is recommended that you create a deterministic instance template using the custom instance template creation options. Here is an example command:

```
$ gcloud compute instance-templates create example-template-custom \
--machine-type n1-standard-4 --image debian-7 --boot-disk-size 250GB
```

You should be aware of two move caveats while using the instance template. These revolve around the usage of PDs and network IPs. In Compute Engine, a PD can be mounted in read-write mode in a single VM instance or read-only mode in more than one VM instance. Hence, if you specify a custom disk image by name, the VM template can be used to make only one VM instance—negating the purpose of the autoscaler. In order to use customized software in the new VMs, you can either use startup scripts that install required software or create snapshots from a master VM and use it to create new PDs. The same logic applies to IP address. In Compute Engine, a static IP address can be attached to only one VM. Hence, if you mention static IP addresses as part of the instance template, you cannot use it to create more than one instance. Therefore, it is best to use ephemeral addresses in the instance template specification.

You can list, describe, and delete instance templates using the following commands:

```
$ gcloud compute instance-templates describe debian-template
<snip>

$ gcloud compute instance-templates list
NAME            MACHINE_TYPE  CREATION_TIMESTAMP
debian-template n1-standard-1 2015-01-26T21:38:14.412-08:00

$ gcloud compute instance-templates delete example-template
<snip>
```

Step 2: Create a Managed Instance Group

After you have created an instance template, you can use it to create an instance group manager to manage the instance group. Here is an example command:

```
$ gcloud preview managed-instance-groups --zone ZONE create GROUP \
--base-instance-name BASE_INSTANCE_NAME --size SIZE \
--template TEMPLATE [--target-pool [TARGET_POOL ...]]
```

Let us dissect this example's various options:

- GROUP: The name of the managed instance group
- BASE_INSTANCE_NAME: The name prefix of all instances that are created in the managed instance group
- SIZE: The minimum number of instances in the managed instance group
- TEMPLATE: The instance template created in the previous step

You can use this example template to create a new managed instance group, as follows.

```
$ gcloud preview managed-instance-groups --zone asia-east1-a create debian-group \
--base-instance-name debian7c --size 1 --template debian-template
Managed instance group debian-group is being created. Operation: \operation-1422345108442-
8e29ad58-62a0-4a7e-b379-460d2af08e46
```

Let us list all the managed instance groups in this zone and describe the instance group debian-group:

```
$ gcloud preview managed-instance-groups --zone asia-east1-a list
https://www.googleapis.com/replicapool/v1beta2/projects/cloud-platform-book/
zones/asia-east1-a/instanceGroupManagers/debian-group

$ gcloud preview managed-instance-groups --zone asia-east1-a describe debian-group
---
baseInstanceName: debian7c
creationTimestamp: '2015-01-27T07:51:48.272Z'
```

```
currentSize: 1
description: ''
fingerprint: 5qidxR57jJo=
group: https://www.googleapis.com/resourceviews/v1beta2/projects/cloud-platform-book/
zones/asia-east1-a/resourceViews/debian-group
id: '3800371457892609647'
instanceTemplate: https://www.googleapis.com/compute/v1/projects/cloud-platform-book/
global/instanceTemplates/debian-template
kind: replicapool#instanceGroupManager
name: debian-group
selfLink: https://www.googleapis.com/replicapool/v1beta2/projects/cloud-platform-book/
zones/asia-east1-a/instanceGroupManagers/debian-group
targetSize: 1
```

To see the number and names of the instances in this instance group, you can use the get option of the instance-groups command to list the instances:

```
$ gcloud preview instance-groups --zone asia-east1-a get debian-group
---
creationTimestamp: '2015-01-27T07:51:48.272Z'
description: 'This instance group is controlled by Instance Group Manager ''debian-group''.
  To modify instances in this group, use the Instance Group Manager API: https://developers.
google.com/compute/docs/instance-groups/manager/'
fingerprint: dfaa54cf583111db
kind: resourceviews#resourceView
name: debian-group
network: https://www.googleapis.com/compute/v1/projects/cloud-platform-book/
global/networks/default
resources:
- https://www.googleapis.com/compute/v1/projects/cloud-platform-book/
zones/asia-east1-a/instances/debian7c-vpwn
selfLink: https://www.googleapis.com/resourceviews/v1beta2/projects/cloud-platform-book/
zones/asia-east1-a/resourceViews/debian-group
size: 1
```

Step 3: Create an Autoscaler

After you have created your managed instance group, you can create the autoscaler using the gcloud CLI tool. The following command template shows the important parts of the command:

```
$ gcloud preview autoscaler --zone ZONE create AUTOSCALER \
    --max-num-replicas MAX_NUM \
    --min-num-replicas MIN_NUM \
    --target INSTANCE_GROUP_MANAGER
```

Here are the details of each part of the command:

- ZONE: The same zone where the instance group manager was created.
- AUTOSCALER: The name of the autoscaler.

- `MAX_NUM`: The maximum number of VM replicas the autoscaler creates. This is a very important metric and has many indirect effects. You see an example scenario in a moment.
- `MIN_NUM`: The minimum number of VM replicas the autoscaler maintains. This is an optional argument, and the default value is 2. If your web app is not expected to receive a lot of traffic at normal times, you can set this to 1.
- `INSTANCE_GROUP_MANAGER`: The name of the instance group manager created in the previous step.

Suppose an autoscaled managed instance group is attached as an HTTP load balancer backend. Heavy network traffic has caused the load balancer to add new instance replicas, and `MAX_NUM` has been reached. Even if the load further increases, the load balancer won't add any new instance replicas. Let us say the utilization metric of the instance group has crossed the target utilization metric. At this stage, the load balancer shifts traffic away from this instance group to other instance groups. Depending on the setup, this may result in more network latency for customers based in some geographical regions, or in part of the web app experiencing more latency if content-based HTTP load balancing is used. Hence, it is important to understand the consequence of using a high value compared to a low value.

Step 4: Add Autoscaled Managed Instance Groups as Endpoints

This step is similar to what you did for both the classic network load balancer and the HTTP load balancer. Instead of using fixed-size instance groups, you use a managed instance group as the endpoint. In the case of a network load balancer, you add this managed instance group to the target pool; in the case of an HTTP load balancer, you attach the managed instance group as a backend.

Using the combination of the autoscaler and an HTTP load balancer, it is easy to create a scalable architecture for a web site that uses the HTTP protocol only. However, if you need to support HTTPS and other TCP protocols, you can use the combination of the autoscaler and the network load balancer. The latter has regional scale, and the former is global-scale architecture. This way, depending on the needs of your web application, your organization, and the geographical distribution of your customers, it is easy to architect a web site to handle large and spiky traffic automatically using Compute Engine on the Google Cloud Platform.

Summary

In this chapter, you learned about Compute Engine, Google Cloud Platform's Infrastructure-as-a-Service product,. The Compute Engine platform consists primarily of high-performance VMs, PDs, and networks. You learned about each of these components in detail and how they are interdependent with one another.

Following this, you looked at several practical examples of deploying high-performance VMs on Compute Engine. You started small, by deploying a single VM; and then you gradually upgraded the deployment by introducing the regional-scale network load balancer and the global-scale HTTP load balancer, which can load-balance a fixed backend of VMs. Next, you learned about making the backend dynamic; it autoscales, depending on the transient load factor, by adding resources when needed and shedding excess to achieve cost savings. This chapter has given you a foundation in Compute Engine and will enable you to build more sophisticated and customized native cloud architectures by using Compute Engine, integrating with other Cloud Platform products, and consuming public Google services.

CHAPTER 5

Google App Engine

Google App Engine (GAE) is commonly defined as a platform as a service (PaaS) part of Google Cloud Platform. The definition of such a service is based on the level of resources managed by the platform. Unlike infrastructure as a service (IaaS) or back end as a service (BaaS)—which primarily manage maintenance tasks such as hardware replacement—with a service like App Engine you do not need to care of things like load balancing, instance management or scaling, and so on. Think of it from a duty standpoint. When using IaaS, your responsibility begins with the operating system, whereas in PaaS, your responsibility starts with the code for your application.

App Engine is appropriate when your infrastructure needs are not particularly cumbersome, when you need to develop and iterate fast, or in any other scenario where avoiding handling the extra complexity of setting up a complete backend infrastructure by yourself adds any value towards your objectives. Since you can write your code just right away, App Engine is a great fit for fast development. It is also important to remember that App Engine has already demonstrated proficiency in ambitious projects such as Snapchat and Khan Academy, where scaling and concurrent access were important challenges. In this chapter, you get to know the power of App Engine from a practical standpoint as you learn about its APIs and services.

You can choose Python, Java, Go, or PHP to write your code. Objectively speaking, we would believe Python to be the most ideal option to take. At the time of this writing, Python and Java have the most advanced APIs and libraries for App Engine, because these were the first languages available to build apps. Also note the important contributions made by the core team at Google—including Guido van Rossum—when crucial parts of App Engine like the NDB Datastore were being brought into life. Finally, the nature of Python as a programming language—its flexibility and variety of frameworks—makes it a valid option. In this book, you work with Python. You can also find online documentation and printed material that provide great coverage for Java, PHP, and Go.

The SDK

The Python SDK includes all the tools you need to build, test, and manage your application code, data, and indexes. You do that locally first, by using the development server included in the SDK. You operate the local server from the Google App Engine Launcher, a small UI-based application that helps you organize your App Engine projects, run them locally, access logs, explore their status through a browser-based console that resembles a small part of what you can expect from the online dashboard, and finally deploy them to the world. Alternatively, you can use the `dev_appserver.py` and `appcfg.py` commands to perform these and other tasks; we mention them when you need specific functionality. Also note that you can use the two commands mentioned previously to integrate and automate specific operations in your development/deployment process.

You can find the SDK at `https://cloud.google.com/appengine/downloads`. It comes in the form of an installer file for Mac and Windows or a zip file for Linux. Installing the SDK on Mac and Windows also gives you access to the Google App Engine Launcher UI.

As of this writing, App Engine only supports Python 2.7. If your code is written in Python 2.5 (now deprecated), consider migrating to 2.7. You can find a complete guide on how to do that at `http://cloud.google.com/appengine/docs/python/python25/migrate27`.

To make sure Python is installed on your computer, simply run the following command on your console or terminal:

```
python -V
```

If the output looks something like `Python 2.7.x`, then you are good to go. Otherwise, go to the Python web site (`www.python.org/downloads/release/python-279/`) and download and install Python 2.7 on your machine.

About Web Applications

Let's take a short step back and consider the different types of applications you can build with App Engine. When you develop an application on the server side, its appearance can vary while its insides remain the same. For example, your application can render the same content both into a HTML template with CSS styles or simply responding with serialized content in formats like JSON, XML or plain text.

In contrast, we are now seeing the rise of client-centric web development, driven by the need to deliver a richer experience to the user and the variety of devices that can open a web. This type of application runs on the client, from where the user operates; hence it needs a mechanism to retrieve information from the Internet. This is generally referred to as a *web service*.

Note that the most relevant difference between the two scenarios, from a server standpoint, is how the information is serialized and sent through the channel. Once the data is fetched and processed, a web server application generates the code that the browser uses to draw the results, whereas a RESTful web service or API simply serializes the content and exposes it as a text-based response that clients—such as JavaScript client-centric applications—can then consume.

One size almost never fits all. This is why it is common nowadays to see hybrid approaches, combining development of web services with web server applications in the same project. On one hand, there is increasing awareness of making information more centralized and accessible, and conveniently designed and implemented APIs are key to achieving that. On the other hand, web server–generated sites have advantages over client-side applications in circumstances such as unified interpretation and content rendering, reducing client overhead on simple sites and minimizing latency among the agents involved. This hybrid approach applies to the example used in this chapter, where most of the data exchange is requested against a RESTful JSON API and other parts of the app are directly rendered into HTML.

Time for the Much-Beloved "Hello World"

All projects built on App Engine share a common denominator across runtime environments (Python, Go, Java, PHP). This is a group of YAML configuration files that make it simple to specify your app's building blocks. You see all of them over the course of this chapter. For now, let's focus on the main configuration file, `app.yaml`. This, as well as the other YAML files, lives in the root of your project and describes the basic aspects of your app. Here's an example:

```
version: 1
runtime: python27
api_version: 1
threadsafe: true
```

```
handlers:
- url: /.*
  script: helloworld.app
```

- The version number allows you to control versioning for your application. You can manage versions from the Google Developers Console, including doing things like rolling back to a previous version or splitting traffic among two different versions.
- Python 2.7, referred as python27, is currently the only actively supported runtime for Python. Other runtime environments or versions may be added in the future.
- api_version refers to the runtime environment in App Engine. As of this writing, only one version has been released. If the team at Google releases an iteration that is not compatible with the current runtime environment, they will do so under a different version name; thus your app will be unaffected until you actively migrate your code.
- Setting threadsafe to true allows App Engine to send concurrent requests to your handlers, or serially otherwise. Assuming that your code is thread-safe, you can default to allowing concurrency. This has an important effect on resource consumption because you are telling App Engine that there is no need to use a new instance to run other requests in parallel.
- Handlers host a list of URL patterns used to match incoming requests. There are two kinds of handlers: scripts, which run specific code you write to determine the response of an incoming request; and static, which serve the binary content of specific files. Handlers are matched from top to bottom, which means the first matched URL pattern in app.yaml will be chosen to handle the request.

Going back to the definition of app.yaml, in the handlers section you tell your app to take any incoming request to a Python script called helloworld.py. Let's create the file helloworld.py:

```
import webapp2

class MainController(webapp2.RequestHandler):
    def get(self):
        self.response.headers['Content-Type'] = 'text/plain'
        self.response.write('Hello World!')

app = webapp2.WSGIApplication([
    ('/', MainController),
], debug=True)
```

■ **Note** webapp2 is a WSGI framework included in App Engine's SDK. You can use any pure Python framework that speaks WSGI in App Engine, such as Django, Flask, or web2py. webapp2 is a simple and lightweight framework and a very convenient option to simplify your code by letting the framework take care things like URI routing, request method processing, and request and response preprocessing, and so on.

`webapp2.WSGIApplication` takes a list of routes represented by a path and the class to process the request. In this case, `MainController` is executed for incoming requests to the root URL (`/`). When the debug property is set to `True`, the application outputs errors or uncaught exceptions that happen during the execution of the request as HTTP responses. You may want to set this to `False` before deploying your application for production use.

To test your code locally, all you need to do is run the development server. As mentioned earlier, there are two ways you can do that with the Python runtime:

- If you prefer to work with applications with user interface instead of command line tools, launch Google App Engine Launcher, a simple UI that helps you manage, test, and deploy projects. Select the project you are working on, and click the play button that says Run. Remember that this app comes in the form of an installable package for Windows and Mac.
- You can also use the development server command-line tool directly. Start the server by pointing `dev_appserver.py` to the root folder of your App Engine application, which is where `app.yaml` is:

  ```
  dev_appserver.py <path_to_root_folder>
  ```

  To stop the server, stop the execution of the command: Ctrl+C on Unix machines or Ctrl+Break if you are running Windows.

WHAT HAPPENS WHEN YOU RUN THIS CODE?

Running the project and sending a `GET` request to the local root URL `http://localhost:8080` causes the following:

1. App Engine lands on your `app.yaml`, which passes the request to `helloworld.py`.
2. The application maps the root path to `MainController`.
3. `MainController` detects the HTTP request method and calls the corresponding method of the handler, which outputs the response content type and body.
4. The application sends the response to the browser or console.

Pretty "Hello World"

A "Hello World" example is always cool, but it gets boring very quickly. To get past that, we give you a taste of App Engine's front-end potential supported by integrated frameworks and libraries like Jinja and Django.

In this case, you will take “Hello World” a step further by rendering the response into HTML. For that, you use Jinja, a fast and powerful templating engine for Python included in App Engine’s Python runtime environment. This is what the template looks like:

```
<html>
    <body>
        <div style="background: #fefefe;">
            <p style="font-family: Helvetica Neue, Arial, sans-serif;
                   font-size: xx-large;
                   font-weight: 100;
                   position: absolute;
                   top: 50%;
                   left: 50%;
                   margin-right: -50%;
                   transform: translate(-50%, -100%);
                   -webkit-transform: translate(-50%, -100%);">Hello {{world_type}} World!
            </p>
        </div>
    </body>
</html>
```

Note that this is a very simple HTML structure with some embedded CSS code. Later you see how to access static files like images, JS and CSS files, and so on through an external link.

You can also include variables in your template, and this is just the beginning. Jinja2 offers other great features such as template inheritance, loops, conditionals, and more.

Enough talk. Let’s see how you need to modify the previous `app.yaml` and `helloworld.py` to bring Jinja into the game. You specify the libraries you need to use in `app.yaml`, under `libraries`. Note that this only applies to libraries that are already included in the SDK, such as Django, Jinja2, Google Cloud Endpoints, PyCrypto, and so on. The final result looks like this:

```
version: 1
runtime: python27
api_version: 1
threadsafe: true

handlers:
- url: /.*
  script: helloworld.app

libraries:
- name: jinja2
  version: latest
```

Note that you are telling your app to always use the latest version of Jinja2. This can lead to unexpected outcomes. Because of that, it is recommended that you use specific versions for the libraries as soon as your application goes into production:

```
libraries:
- name: jinja2
  version: "2.6"
```

■ **Pro Tip** If you want to include other Python libraries, you can do so by adding them in your app file tree and accessing them from your code by using package nomenclature. Remember that you can only add pure Python libraries to App Engine—libraries for which 100% of the code is written in Python. For example, if you placed the library `pybcrypt` in a `libs` folder that lives in the root of your application—`root/libs/pybcrypt`—and you wanted to load its `bcrypt.py` module, you would need to import it in the following way: `from libs.pybcrypt import bcrypt`.

The last and most relevant step to use Jinja is to define the parameters involved in the template before rendering it:

```
import webapp2
from jinja2 import Environment, FileSystemLoader

JINJA_ENV = Environment(loader=FileSystemLoader(''),
                        extensions=['jinja2.ext.autoescape'],
                        autoescape=True)

class MainController(webapp2.RequestHandler):
    def get(self):

        template_values = {
            'world_type': self.request.get('kind', default_value='Pretty')
        }

        template = JINJA_ENV.get_template('pretty_template.html')

        self.response.headers['Content-Type'] = 'text/html; charset=utf-8'
        self.response.write(template.render(template_values))

app = webapp2.WSGIApplication([
    ('/', MainController),
], debug=True)
```

After the imports, you need to set the environment to be used when loading templates. `FileSystemLoader` specifies the route to the templates in your app file tree. In this case, because the only template is in the root folder, this path is an empty string.

Next, you need to specify the key-value pairs to be used to populate the template. The render method you will use later accepts the same arguments as the `dict` constructor in Python, which can be a `dict`, a subclass of a `dict`, or keyword arguments:

```
template.render({'world_type': 'Beautiful'})
template.render(world_type='Beautiful')
```

For the sake of clean code, here you define a dictionary to hold these entries. On the next line, you read parameters from the request. Note how you set the value to `self.request.get('kind', default_value='Pretty')`. This looks for the parameter `kind` in the query string (GET request) or the body of the request (POST request), or it defaults to "Pretty" if the key is not found.

For example, if you request `http://localhost:<port>/`, the output will be "Hello Pretty World"; whereas if you specify the parameter `kind` and request `http://localhost:<port>/?kind=Lovely`, the output will be "Hello Lovely World".

After fetching the template, the last step is to set the `Content-Type` header to `text/html; charset=utf-8` and render the template into the response. If you now request the same URL from your browser, you will see something nicer than the previous example.

Storing Information

One of the most important parts of any application is information. Whether you are developing a web application or an API that acts as a bridge between different client applications, storing and being able to access information in a way that is quick, flexible, and scalable is key for good system operation.

App Engine offers multiple ways to store information, including the following three that are covered later in this book:

- *Google Cloud Datastore* is schema-less, fully-managed object storage with transactions and advanced querying that scales. See Chapter 9 for more information.
- *Google Cloud SQL* is a web service that allows you to operate a fully managed MySQL database that lives in Google's cloud. See Chapter 7 to learn more.
- *Google Cloud Storage* is Google's solution to store and serve larger files or other binaries such as media, compressed files, and so on. To read more about Cloud Storage, see Chapter 8.

The example used in this chapter—the LunchMates app—uses Cloud Datastore, mainly due to its ease of integration, its managed nature, and its ability to scale without extra effort. In addition, the Python library used to operate Cloud Datastore (NDB) includes many convenient features, such as automatic caching, more control on your transactions and more property classes to help you process your data.

LunchMates is intended to be a service that helps individuals who share a common passion about a given topic to get together to learn and enjoy discussing and sharing knowledge about that topic. Users can create any kind of informal meeting, such as lunch, a drink, brunch, and so on, and define the place and time for it so that potential lunch mates can check the map of their area and look for meetings. They should be able to send requests for meetings and be accepted or rejected as quickly as possible.

The file structure of the application is as follows:

```
model/
controllers/
util/
static/
app.yaml
index.yaml
main.py
```

Let's create the first part of the model. Here is the simplest version of `model.py`, stored in `model/`:

```
#!/usr/bin/env python

from google.appengine.ext import ndb

class Meeting(ndb.Model):
    created = ndb.DateTimeProperty(auto_now_add=True)
    venue_forsquare_id = ndb.StringProperty(required=True)
    location = ndb.GeoPtProperty()
    earliest_possible_start = ndb.DateTimeProperty(required=True)
```

```
    latest_possible_start = ndb.DateTimeProperty()
    topic = ndb.StringProperty(required=True)
    type = ndb.StringProperty(required=True, choices=['drink', 'lunch', 'brunch'])
    tags = ndb.StringProperty(repeated=True)
```

You can inherit from ndb.Model to define your own data models. This allows you to store information in Datastore in an object oriented way. If you are familiar with other relational database systems, you can think of kinds and entities as equivalent to tables and rows, respectively.

The `required` keyword makes it compulsory to specify a value at instantiation time for the ID of the venue where the meeting should take place and the starting date. Also note that the type property has `choices`, which constrain the possible values. Finally, the `repeated` keyword on tags allows this property to hold and store a list of values of the defined type (strings, in this case).

This is how you create and store an instance of a given meeting:

```
from datetime import datetime
from google.appengine.ext import ndb

dateformat_str = '%Y-%m-%dT%H:%M'

meeting = Meeting()
meeting.venue_forsquare_id = 'A9ABCD'
meeting.location = ndb.GeoPt('52.511165, 13.443115')
meeting.earliest_possible_start = datetime.strptime('2015-10-21T12:00', dateformat_str)
meeting.latest_possible_start = datetime.strptime('2015-10-21T13:00', dateformat_str)
meeting.topic = 'Polyglot backend systems'
meeting.type = 'drink'
meeting.tags = ['vegetarian', 'tech', 'programming', 'short']

meeting.put()
```

Given that the world cannot be built with only strings, dates, and lists; NDB provides a full set of property types:

- `IntegerProperty`: 64-bit signed integer
- `FloatProperty`: Double-precision floating-point number
- `BooleanProperty`: To be true or not to be true, that is the question.
- `StringProperty`: Unicode string, up to 500 characters. This property is always indexed.
- `TextProperty`: Unicode string with no length limit. This property cannot be indexed.
- `BlobProperty`: Uninterpreted byte string. If you set `indexed=True`, it can be up to 500 characters; if indexed is `False` (the default), it has unlimited length. The `indexed` keyword defines whether the property is included in indexes. You can read more about the implications of this in Chapter 9.

  BlobProperty, like some others, has an optional keyword argument: `compressed`. When this parameter is `True`, the content of the property is compressed on disk using gzip. That obviously requires less storage space but more time to process. Generally, there are no big wins from compressing properties unless the content is too big and sensitive to use gzip compression. Take PNG, JPEG, and MP3, for example: they are not affected much by gzip because they are built using a similar kind of compression. If the amount of data is large, it is sensible to consider other means of storage, such as Cloud Storage, explained in Chapter 8.

- `DateTimeProperty`: Date and time
- `DateProperty`: Date
- `TimeProperty`: Time

  Date and time properties describe certain points in time in UTC format; there is no associated time zone information. `DateTimeProperty`, the most commonly used of the three, is consistent across other APIs in Cloud DataStore. As the name indicates, it holds a value for a specific day in the year and a certain point in time with microsecond precision. The other two properties, as you have probably guessed, are useful in cases when you only need to hold a day of the year or time of day, respectively.

  These properties accept two keyword arguments that, when set to `True`, update the value of the property to the current date and/or time:

  - `auto_now_add`: The entity is created.
  - `auto_now`: The entity is created or updated.

  This is very handy when, for instance, you need to store a date with the creation of a specific entity, as you did in the previous example in the `Meeting` class.

- `GeoPtProperty`: A geographical location. This is an `ndb.GeoPt` object. The object has the attributes `lat` and `lon`, both floats. It can be constructed with two floats, as in `ndb.GeoPt(52.37, 4.88)`, or with a string, as in `ndb.GeoPt('52.37, 4.88')`.
- `KeyProperty`: Datastore key. This property accepts an optional keyword argument, `kind=kind`, which forces keys assigned to this property to always be of the indicated kind. The value specified may be a string or a `Model` subclass.
- `BlobKeyProperty`: Blobstore key.
- `StructuredProperty`: Includes one kind of model in another, by value.
- `LocalStructuredProperty`: Like `StructuredProperty`, but the on-disk representation is an opaque blob and is not indexed. Optional keyword argument: `compressed`.

  A structured property can be simply understood as a whole model object in the property. For example, given two models, `Dog` and `House`, each house can have a property storing its favorite dog, like so:

  ```
  favorite_dog = ndb.StructuredProperty(Dog)
  ```

  Structured properties are not a means to model relationships between entities in Cloud Datastore, because they are not referenced to any other part of the model: they do not have a key. Think of them as a bunch of content stored under a property that is unmarshalled into a class that you defined and know about, so you can operate with it. Use `StructuredProperty` if you need to filter on the internal properties of the structure. For example, consider you need to retrieve houses where the favorite dog is big. You can use the following query in Datastore:

  ```
  House.query(House.favorite_dog.size == 'big')
  ```

If you do not have such a need, you can use LocalStructuredProperty, which is treated as a not-indexed, compressible opaque blob on disk. Structured properties can use other arguments, except indexed.

- JsonProperty: Serialized using Python's JSON module.
- PickleProperty: Serialized using Python's pickle module.

  Pickle and JSON properties are simple inheritances of BlobProperty that use Python libraries to serialize and deserialize their content from blob into any given Python object. These properties are not indexed by default, but they are compressible using the optional argument compressed.

- ComputedProperty: Computed at runtime from other properties in the model by using a function you define. This is very handy when you need to store properties in different formats or combine other properties in order to query them later. Imagine, for example, that you need to implement Spartan search-by-username functionality in your app. It is convenient to store two versions of the property: one holding the standard value of the username (that is, the user's name exactly as typed—for example, "Marie") and a lowercase version of it ("marie"). That way, when another user searches for "MARIE", "MaRiE", or "MARie", you can normalize the search term to lowercase and use it to filter your query so that the same user is returned. Here is an example of how to use computed properties:

```
class User(ndb.Model):
  username = ndb.StringProperty(required=True)
  username_search = ndb.ComputedProperty(lambda self: self.username.
lower())
```

  Note that computed properties are read-only. Even though a property's value is persisted in Cloud Datastore so you can browse it internally, the final value of the property is always calculated when queried. An updated version is shown only if the properties it depends on change.

  Consider using computed properties only if you need to use the computed values in your queries. Otherwise, you can process them internally in your app code by using a regular function and optionally decorating it with @property to access the result of the function with dot notation, like so:

```
@property
def username_lower (self):
    return self.username.lower()
```

  print user.username_lower returns the user's name in a lowercase format.

- GenericProperty: As the name suggests, this property does not have a concrete type. Instead, it can hold any kind of value depending on the type assigned to it: int, long, float, bool, str, unicode, datetime, Key, BlobKey, GeoPt, or None.

  Generic properties are mostly used by the Expando class, which is a special kind that does not need a model expectation in order to store values and properties in Cloud Datastore. In other words, you can define a class that inherits from ndb.Expando without needing to define any of the model's properties:

```
class DynamicThing(ndb.Expando):
    pass
```

Then, after instantiation, you can dynamically add as many properties as you need, to persist like any other record in your Cloud Datastore. This is not applicable to most models, but it is useful in cases when you need to take a flexible approach. For example, if you have a table to track usage, metrics, or statistics, it is likely that new measurements, indicators, or variables are added to the model at some point in the future. By reusing the `DynamicThing` class, you can store one entity as follows:

```
thing = DynamicThing()
thing.material = 'cotton'
thing.count = 10
thing.put()
```

This code snippet stores your new record with the three newly defined properties.

Keep in mind that `Expando` models use generic properties under the hood, so when using filters in queries to `Expando` models, make sure you refer to them properly:

```
DynamicThing.query(ndb.GenericProperty('material') == 'cotton')
```

While looking at property types, you have seen keyword arguments like `repeated`, `choices`, `required`, and `indexed`. These keywords help make your model more specific and performant. There are three additional arguments you can use:

- `default` defines the value of a property if it is not given:

  ```
  coins = ndb.IntegerProperty(default=1)
  ```

- `verbose_name` represents a human-readable name for this property. This name can be used to bind your model with HTML forms, templates, marshalling, and so on.
- `validator` defines a function to acknowledge that a given value matches the conditions for it to be valid. The function takes the property and the proposed value as arguments. The returned result, which may be slightly modified in the validation function if necessary, is used and persisted. As a simple example, you can add validation to the property `earliest_possible_start` in the `Meeting` model to make sure you avoid creating meetings that are accidentally scheduled to start in the past:

  ```
  from datetime import datetime
  from google.appengine.ext import db

  def not_in_the_past(prop, value):

      if value < datetime.now()
          raise db.BadValueError

      return value

  ....
  ```

```
class Meeting(ndb.Model):
    ....
    earliest_possible_start = ndb.DateTimeProperty(required=True,
                                                    validator=not_in_the_past)
    ....
```

Now that you are familiar with how properties and kinds work in Cloud Datastore, you can define the entire model for the sample app:

```
#!/usr/bin/env python

import unicodedata

from google.appengine.ext import ndb
from google.appengine.api import users

DATE_FORMAT_STR = '%Y-%m-%dT%H: %M'

class BaseModel(ndb.Model):
    created = ndb.DateTimeProperty(auto_now_add=True)

class UserData(BaseModel):

    def normalize(self):
        return unicodedata.normalize('NFKD', unicode(self.name))
                        .encode('ascii','ignore')
                        .lower()

    auth_provider = ndb.StringProperty(choices=['google', 'facebook'], required=True)
    name = ndb.StringProperty(default='')
    search_name = ndb.ComputedProperty(normalize)
    email = ndb.StringProperty(required=True)

class Meeting(BaseModel):
    owner = ndb.KeyProperty(kind=UserData, required=True)
    venue_forsquare_id = ndb.StringProperty(required=True)
    location = ndb.GeoPtProperty()
    earliest_possible_start = ndb.DateTimeProperty(required=True)
    latest_possible_start = ndb.DateTimeProperty()
    topic = ndb.StringProperty(required=True)
    type = ndb.StringProperty(required=True, choices=['drink', 'lunch', 'brunch'])
    tags = ndb.StringProperty(repeated=True)

class MeetingRequest(BaseModel):
    meeting = ndb.KeyProperty(kind=Meeting, required=True)
    state = ndb.StringProperty(default='pending',
                          choices=['pending', 'accepted', 'rejected'])
```

You are creating a base model holding a property that you can use across the rest of your kinds. The final code in the book's repository (`https://github.com/GoogleCloudPlatformBook/lunchmates-api`) shows the other utilities you can add to this base class. The class `MeetingRequest` is in charge of storing requests from users who want to join a meeting. If you are familiar with other relational database systems, this structure may seem to resemble one-to-many relationships. But in Cloud Datastore, there are other mechanisms to create relationships among entities, and the kind `MeetingRequest` uses of two of them.

Key Properties and Ancestor Paths

As you saw in the previous example, the meeting for which a request is being created is referenced with a `KeyProperty`. Cloud Datastore uses a key to identify an object, consisting of at least the kind and identifier of the entity it belongs to. A key contains information about the entity itself and also about its ancestor path. This path defines how an entity is connected to other objects: In Cloud Datastore, objects can be connected to other entities using parent-child relationships, forming entity groups. Entity groups are a very important part of how Cloud Datastore works: special rules apply to objects in them, such as strong consistency, and the associated limitation of allowing only one write every second. You can read more about this in Chapter 9.

For now, to provide you with a clear picture of these concepts, let's use the example of `Meeting` and `MeetingRequest`. A meeting request needs to know about the user who is trying to join and the meeting to which the action applies. As mentioned previously, the meeting is referenced with a `KeyProperty` in the model, but what about the user? In the proposed design, users are part of the ancestor path of meeting requests. That is, the user who initiates the request to join a meeting is the parent of that request. That means querying meeting requests for a particular user is an ancestor query, thus it is strongly consistent: the user always sees up-to-date information about this entity. Additionally, the limit of creating one meeting request per second is acceptable in this instance, given that it is hard for a single user to try to join more than one meeting every second.

This is how you create a user request to join a meeting:

```
request = MeetingRequest(parent=self.user_key, meeting=ndb.Key(Meeting, meeting_id))
request.put()
```

In this example, the `parent` is specified using the entity key of the user that creates the request to join a meeting. Alternatively, you can use the entity itself. In contrast, the `meeting` is a key property referencing the meeting for which the request is being created. The value of this argument must be a `ndb.KeyProperty` as specified in the model definition.

A key can contain either a numeric ID or a string. If you do not specify the key for an object you are about to create, Cloud Datastore generates a numeric ID for you. If the operation of persisting a new object in Cloud Datastore is successful, it returns the key associated with this object:

```
request_key = request.put()
```

If you specify the identifier of the key yourself, it is your duty to make sure no other entity with that key is already stored. If that is the case, the existing content is replaced with the values provided in the last `put()`. This is how you specify a custom key identifier:

```
meeting_key = ndb.Key(MeetingRequest, 'custom-meeting-request-id')
meeting_request = MeetingRequest(key=meeting_key)
```

You can achieve the same goal by using the id keyword when instantiating a new entity:

```
meeting_request = MeetingRequest(id='custom-meeting-request-id')
```

Batching and Asynchronous Operations

When it comes to optimizing your dynamic handlers, you need to keep two strategies in mind; async and batch. Almost all operations in Cloud Datastore have batched and async counterparts. For example, the get() function has the alternatives get_async(), get_multi(), and get_multi_async().

Batching requests avoids the redundancy of executing each request separately by using a single batched RPC to handle all the operations at once. You do that by using the _multi versions of methods like get(), put(), and delete(). Here is an example:

```
# Deletes multiple objects at once
ndb.delete_multi(list_of_keys_to_delete)

# Retrieves multiple objects at once
entities = ndb.get_multi(list_of_keys_to_retrieve)

# Stores multiple entities at once
keys = ndb.put_multi(list_of_entities_to_store)
```

Each of the following _multi methods return a list of values depending on the results of the operations. You can use that list to determine if any of the operations did not complete successfully. ndb.delete_multi returns a list of None values, one for each deleted item. ndb.get_multi returns a list of Model instances or None objects if no object was found for a given key. Finally, ndb.put_multi returns a list of keys for each of the stored elements.

You may wonder though, how to leverage an asynchronous API call to reduce the latency, since most of the cases you may want to wait for the result of the asynchronous call before returning the results. It is true if you only call a single API call. However, in many practical applications, you may need to make multiple API calls to create a single HTTP response. In such cases, the asynchronous API calls will result in a significant improvement in terms of the overall latency of your application. Consider the following scenario.

TEST CASE: THE SOCIAL MERGER

Suppose you expose an endpoint in your API that merges information from a user in your data store with other details about them from third-party services—say, Google+ and Facebook. To do the merge, you first need to fetch the information from the three sources. For simplicity, assume that you already have valid tokens to access the two external services. The naive approach to perform this task would look something like this:

```
from google.appengine.api import urlfetch
from google.appengine.ext import ndb

user_info_google_url = 'http://...'
user_info_facebook_url = 'http://...'

user = ndb.Key(User, user_id).get()
user_info_google = urlfetch.fetch(user_info_google_url)
user_info_facebook = urlfetch.fetch(user_info_facebook_url)
```

```
merged_user = merge_user(user, user_info_google, user_info_facebook)
merged_user.put()
```

However, this code executes each operation sequentially—that is, the time the request takes to return is the total time needed to retrieve the user from the Cloud Datastore, fetch information from Google's API, fetch information from Facebook's API, and merge and persist the results:

```
total_time = t_user_datastore + t_user_google + t_user_facebook + t_merge +
t_persist_new_user
```

This is not a good idea, bearing in mind that some of the steps in this request may take a while to return. Instead, you should parallelize as many independent requests as you can until you need to use the results. In this case, you do not need the user information from the three sources until you merge the data. That is, the first three operations can be executed asynchronously:

```
...
user_future = ndb.Key(User, user_id).get_async()
user_google_rpc = urlfetch.make_fetch_call(urlfetch.create_rpc(), user_info_google_
url)
user_facebook_rpc = urlfetch.make_fetch_call(urlfetch.create_rpc(), user_info_
facebook_url)

merged_user = merge_user(user_future.get_result(), user_google_rpc.get_result(),
user_facebook_rpc.get_result())

merged_user.put()
```

Using this strategy, the total time for the request is reduced to the time of the asynchronous operation that takes longest to return:

```
total_time = max(t_user_datastore + t_user_google + t_user_facebook) + t_merge +
t_persist_new_user
```

When you use the `async` version of certain operations, they begin execution and return a promise immediately so the rest of your code can continue running. This promise holds a reference to the operation. When you need the result, you call `.get_result()`, which either returns immediately if the operation finished already or blocks execution until that happens. Note that you are not using the asynchronous version of the `put()` method when persisting the new user at the end of the request, since in this case there is no benefit on doing that. But suppose that many users are being updated at the same time, if `puts` happen synchronously you could experience greater contention. To avoid that you can perform this operation asynchronously. You can do that in various ways, for example using the asynchronous version of the `put` method: `put_async`.

By analyzing the needs of your application and the code involved, you can potentially identify areas where using asynchronous operations appropriately can lead to dramatic performance improvements. In App Engine, there is a complete set of asynchronous alternatives to commonly used operations, including NDB, queries and URL fetch operations.[1]

[1]The article "NDB Asynchronous Operation" explains how to take advantage of using asynchronous directives in your application: `https://cloud.google.com/appengine/docs/python/ndb/async`.

■ **Pro Tip** Avoid `DeadlineExceededErrors`. One of the biggest limitation of the App Engine runtime is `google.appengine.runtime.DeadlineExceededError`. This error is thrown when your handler takes too long handling a request. The current deadline is 60 seconds for frontend requests and 600 seconds for task queues and cron requests. Using asynchronous operations is a great way of avoiding this error especially if you are issuing multiple RPCs in a single request. There are also other strategies for avoiding this error like configuring properly your performance settings in App Engine –e.g.: number of maximum idle instances allowed–, handling external URL fetches properly or revising your data model to make sure there are no bottlenecks in the way it is structured – e.g.: using entity groups, and thus limiting throughput to a write per second, for entities with a very high update rate.

Request Routing

Now that the model for the application you are building is complete, it is time to interact with it. Just as before, you define the routes and paths in the application and point them to the appropriate handlers. Remember that it all starts in `app.yaml`:

```
version: 1
runtime: python27
api_version: 1
threadsafe: yes

handlers:
- url: /.*
  script: main.app

libraries:
- name: webapp2
  version: "2.5.1"
```

Your controller classes need to do more than print "Hello World", so you are going to place them in a folder called `controllers/`. The `main.py` application is now a means of routing. In the API of the LunchMates application, you need handlers for users, meetings, and requests to join those meetings. You expose these handlers through the paths `/api/users`, `/api/meetings`, and `/api/meetings/<meeting_id>/requests`, respectively. `webapp2.WSGIApplication` creates an application that accepts a list of routes. Consider something like the following:

```
(main.py)
#!/usr/bin/env python
# imports
...

# Requested URLs that are not listed here return with a 404

ROUTES = [

    routes.PathPrefixRoute(r'/api', [
```

```
        # Users
        Route(r'/users', handler=UserController),

        # Meetings
        Route(r'/meetings', handler=MeetingController),
        routes.PathPrefixRoute(r'/meetings/<meeting_id:\d+>', [
            Route(r'/requests', handler=MeetingRequestController, methods=['GET']),
            Route(r'/join', handler=MeetingRequestController, methods=['POST'])
        ])
    ])
]

app = webapp2.WSGIApplication(ROUTES, debug=True)
```

You use the method `PathPrefixRoute` to wrap all URIs under the same prepended path `/api`. You can use that as a means of separating different functionality in your API or the entire application. Each route needs to have at least a regex matching the requested URI path and a handler that is called to process the request. Other optional parameters are as follows:

- `name`: Builds a URI for the route with the method `webapp2.uri_for()`.
- `handler_method`: Specifies the method to execute in the handler. By default, the method in the handler is chosen based on the HTTP method of the request. For example, the `get()` method is called for an incoming `GET`.
- `methods`: Determines a list of HTTP methods accepted for that route.
- `schemes`: Specifies the allowed schemes used to request the route. For example, `'https'`.

Queries

Let's look at the meeting handler and see how to query Cloud Datastore for the list of meetings. Note that all handler classes must inherit from `webapp2.RequestHandler`:

```
(meetings.py)
import webapp2
import json

from model.model import Meeting
from util.json_serializer import JsonSerializer

class MeetingController(webapp2.RequestHandler):

    def get(self): # This method gets called for incoming GET requests to this endpoint.
        results = []
        query = Meeting.query().order(-Meeting.created)

        for meeting in query:
            results.append(meeting)

        self.response.status = 200
        self.response.write(json.dumps(results, cls = JsonSerializer))
```

All the method does is query for `Meeting` objects that match specific criteria, loop through the results, and write them to the response along with a response code.

■ **Note** `JsonSerializer` is a utility class that helps with serialization of complex objects. You can find it in the `util` folder in the `lunchmates-api` code repository[2]: `https://github.com/GoogleCloudPlatformBook/lunchmates-api`.

In the previous example, you can see how to query objects stored in Cloud Datastore. Simply call the `query` method and loop through the results. This is how you use other common functionalities in queries:

- To *limit the number of results* returned, append the `fetch(n)` method to the query, where `n` is the number of results to return:

  ```
  result = Meeting.query().fetch(20)
  ```

- If you want to *filter* using specific properties, you can add natural expressions for the respective properties in the `query` method:

  ```
  query = Meeting.query(Meeting.type == 'lunch',
  Meeting.earliest_possible_start >= given_date, ancestor=ndb.Key(AncestorKind,
  ancestor_id))
  ```

  As you can see, you can filter on properties of the queried kind by using equality or inequality filters. Similarly, you can query for entities with a concrete parent on their entity path (in other words, an ancestor).

- You can also specify one or multiple *sort orders* in which the query returns its results. The `order()` method accepts a list of arguments for the properties used in the sorting process. To specify descending order, prepend a minus sign to the property (`-`). This example sorts results by the date when a meeting takes place and the date of its creation, both descending:

  ```
  query = Meeting.query().order(Meeting.earliest_possible_start, -Meeting.
  created)
  ```

Coming back to the meeting handler, let's explore the logic that allows the creation of new entities through the `POST` method on the same endpoint:

```
...

def post(self):

    if self.request.body:

        body = json.loads(self.request.body)
```

[2]All the examples used in this book are publicly available in repositories for the user GoogleCloudPlatformBook in GitHub: `https://github.com/GoogleCloudPlatformBook`.

```
        # Pre-format
        date_format = '%Y-%m-%dT%H:%M'
        body['owner'] = self.user_key
        body['earliest_possible_start'] =
                datetime.strptime(body['earliest_possible_start'], format)
        body['latest_possible_start'] =
                datetime.strptime(body['latest_possible_start'], format)
        body['location'] = GeoPt(body['location'])

        # Put meeting
        meeting = Meeting(**body)
        meeting.put()

        self.response.status = 201
        response = meeting

    else:
        self.response.status = 422
        response = {base.ERRORS: 'Request must have a body'}

    self.response.write(json.dumps(response, cls = JsonSerializer))
```

First the code checks for the existence of a body in the request. This is the associated body you send with the HTTP requests. Before the entity is written to Cloud Datastore, dates and location objects are converted from the string values obtained from the body into their final types. This is a great time to do data validation, to avoid corrupting the stored information or having the system raising unexpected errors at write time. Once integrity is checked, you can create a new entity of the kind `Meeting`, unpacking the dictionary obtained in the body into keywords using the double star operator (**). Note in the example how the currently authenticated user is being added as the owner of the meeting—you see where this authenticated user comes from in the next section. After that, your code is ready to persist the new entity through the `put()` method. If the operation succeeds, this method returns the resulting Key for the newly created object.

This is an example HTTP request that triggers the method as just explained:

```
POST http://localhost:15080/api/meetings

Content-Type: application/json

{
    "venue_forsquare_id":"A9ABCD",
    "location":"52.511165, 13.443115",
    "earliest_possible_start":"2015-10-21T12:00",
    "latest_possible_start":"2015-10-21T12:30",
    "topic":"Polyglot backend systems",
    "type":"drink",
    "tags":["scaling","polyglot","beer"]
}
```

■ **Note** Similar to `request.body`, which returns the entire body of the request, `request.get (parameter_name)` retrieves a single value for the given argument name specified in either the query string of the URL or the body of the request.

To find out more about types of queries, features, and the nature of Cloud Datastore, see Chapter 9.

■ **Note** This application has other handlers, utilities, and convenience strategies. Most, but not all, of them are used in this book. Refer to the code repository hosted in GitHub to explore and test the entire application.

Transactions

In some situations you may want to have atomicity on two or more operations, that is, all operations are treated as an indivisible unit that either succeeds or fails as a whole. In the case of failure, the entire transaction is rolled back and the data's state remains unaffected. Consider the following scenario: To show some statistical data in your users' profiles, you decide to track the number of meetings each user creates and show it in their profile. It is generally not a good idea to count entities in very large datasets due to performance implications. In Cloud Datastore, because of the way it operates, queries could slow down for a user who creates a couple of meeting entities every day.

■ **Pro Tip** A common practice to circumvent this limitation, especially in scenarios with a need for higher throughput, is to use external sharded counters[3] holding the total number of entities of one specific kind.

This example is not demanding, in the sense that users cannot create meetings very quickly, so it uses a simple counter for each user. Every time a user creates a new meeting, the counter needs to be increased. These two operations need to happen as a unit. If the creation of the meeting fails but the counter is incremented, the information the user sees will be inconsistent:

```
class MeetingCounter(ndb.Model):
    count = ndb.IntegerProperty(default=0)

    @classmethod
    @ndb.transactional
    def increment(cls, user_key):
        counter = cls.get_by_id(user_key.id())
        if counter is None:
            counter = cls(id=user_key.id())

        counter.count += 1
        counter.put()
```

[3]Joe Gregorio, "Sharding Counters," Google Inc., 2008, `https://cloud.google.com/appengine/articles/sharding_counters`.

NDB exposes a simple decorator `@ndb.transactional` that wraps the entire method and executes it in the context of a transaction. In this method, you retrieve the counter for a specific user, or create it if it does not exist, and increment the counter by one before persisting it again.

If the transaction collides with another transaction, the operation fails. NDB automatically retries failed transactions a few times -3 times by default- before failing permanently and raising a `TransactionFailedError`. You can configure this by setting the keyword `retries` in the decorator:

```
ndb.transactional(retries=5)
```

Now you can modify the logic used to create a new meeting and increment the counter by one:

```
@ndb.transactional(xg=True)
def post(self):

    if self.request.body:

        body = json.loads(self.request.body)

        # Pre-format
        ....

        # Put meeting
        meeting = Meeting(**body)
        meeting.put()

        # Increment meeting counter for the user
        MeetingCounter.increment(self.user_key)
        ....
```

Notice how you also add the transactional decorator to this method. You do so because you need the meeting to be created and the counter to be incremented atomically and fail as a whole if either operation does not succeed. In this case, you also need to add the keyword `xg=True`. This allows for a maximum of 25 entity groups to operate in the same transaction. Note that `Meeting` and `MeetingCounter` do not share a common ancestor, so they belong to different entity groups.

■ **Note** In this specific case, creating entities of `MeetingCounter` and setting the `User` they belong to as their parent would have been an acceptable alternative because it is in practice almost impossible for users to create meetings more quickly than once a second.

User Management

Just when everything looked perfect, you decide to add user management and authentication logic to your app, and it suddenly starts to rain. User management is an important aspect of your application that requires care and dedication. This is why it is relevant to ask yourself, first, whether to include it in your application and at which level and, second, what strategy to use to tackle this requirement.

These days, implementing, testing, and securing your own authentication solution requires a decent amount of effort. You have to consider the most appropriate way to secure passwords, how to control user sessions, how to protect your system against external attacks, and so on. In addition, there is extra effort for users, who have to sign up and manage a collection of accounts and passwords for services they may not use more than once or twice. Altogether, this proposes a brief but deep exercise about which way to go. This book shows how to authenticate users in your App Engine project with Google accounts, using the libraries provided for this purpose.

■ **Pro Tip** If you are planning to integrate your application with other authentication services, you can follow the authorization flows in providers such as Google, Facebook, GitHub, and so on. There is increasing interest in using third-party authorities to authenticate users, which results in simpler integration and more support from providers. For the same reason, new open source libraries to help integrate many providers at once into your auth solution are increasingly appearing onto the scene.

App Engine comes with a module to handle user authentication with Google Accounts, Google Apps: `com.google.appengine.api.users`. To retrieve the user who is currently signed in, you simply call

```
users.get_current_user()
```

You can use this method to test whether a user is currently signed in and, if necessary, redirect them to a URL where they can log in and then return:

```
if not users.get_current_user():
    self.redirect(users.create_login_url(destination_url))
```

`destination_url` is the address to which you need users to return as soon as they sign in successfully. This is normally the same URL they were trying to access.

Similarly, you can obtain a logout URL using the `create_logout_url(destination_url)` method. And if you need to know whether the currently signed-in user is an administrator of the application, use `is_current_user_admin()`.

You do not want to fill your application logic with `if` clauses in every handler that needs to check for an authenticated user. In Python, there is a convenient pattern called a *decorator* to extend the functionality of methods and functions. Decorators wrap the code they enclose, giving you the ability to perform any logic prior to or after executing the code in question. Decorators can be specified above the definition of the method or function using the following syntax:

```
@decorator
def method():
    # Method logic
```

A common requirement for web server applications and APIs is to have protected and public areas. Using the decorator pattern and the libraries provided by App Engine to authenticate users gives you a simple way to control access to different parts of the API. Suppose you want to restrict the ability to create meetings in LunchMates to authenticated users. You can do the following:

```
def login_required(handler):
    """Wrapper to test for a signed in user"""
```

```
    def user_or_redirect(self, *args, **kwargs):
        if not users.get_current_user():
            self.redirect(users.create_login_url(self.request.path)) # Redirects to login
        else:
            return handler(self, *args, **kwargs) # User is signed in, execute the request

    return user_or_redirect

class MeetingController(webapp2.RequestHandler):

    @login_required
    def post(self):
        ....
```

Every time a user attempts to create a meeting by POSTing to the meeting endpoint, `login_required` will be called, executing the request on behalf of the user who is signed in or redirecting to a login URL to proceed with the authentication process prior to continuing with the request.

■ **Pro Tip** To generalize this behavior, you can create a base `RequestHandler` class from which all your handlers inherit. In this base class, you can define functions that you can use to decorate any method on any of the child classes. (for example, : `login_required`). To see an example of this and other strategies, check `base.py` under `controllers/` in the LunchMates API repository: `https://github.com/GoogleCloudPlatformBook/lunchmates-api`.

Instances of the `User` class expose the name, e-mail, and user ID of the user via `.nickname()`, `.email()`, and `.user_id()`, respectively. When you use third-party auth providers to authenticate users and you want to store additional user information, it is recommended that you not rely on the e-mail as a means of identification. Instead, use the auth ID of the provider, which is not meant to—or is less likely to—change: `.user_id()` in this case.

Memcache

Data storage systems persist data on disk drives. Thus these systems are not the fastest solution when it comes to writing and reading information. Even though these devices have gotten an important boost recently with the introduction of solid state drives (SSDs), memory access still operates on a different order of magnitude in terms of speed. For this reason it is useful to consider using memory caches to briefly hold commonly accessed information, to alleviate high load in your data-storage system caused by a demanding operation or set of users.

Memcache is a distributed, scalable, high-performance memory cache for objects that allows you to access certain information much more quickly than retrieving the same data from disk storage. Memcache is integrated into App Engine and comes with a simple set of APIs to use it in Python, Java, Go, and PHP.

Think of the data added to Memcache as transient information that is quickly available when you need it, but that can be out of sync with the data in your primary storage. This is why information that is not updated often but is commonly accessed, and for which seeing the latest snapshot is not crucial to your application, is a great candidate for memory caching. Examples are a list of headlines on the front page of your site, global configurations of your application, user preferences, user sessions, and so on.

However, Memcache operations are not transactional, which means that Memcache does not coordinate concurrent access. In other words, when two or more clients try to update the value of the same key at the same time, the final value stored may be incorrect or corrupted. To avoid that, you can use the `cas`[4] (compare and set) function in combination with the `gets` function. When using this strategy, you have to account for errors and retry handling.

Another aspect to consider is that information stored in Memcache can be evicted at any time under memory pressure or other reasons. This event can happen before the expiration time you specified when you write the data.

Let's apply Memcache to a tangible scenario. In the LunchMates application, one of the great candidates for memory cache is the query that retrieves the list of available meetings in a user's city or area. This information is the starting point for every user who is looking for a meeting and the first thing that the application shows when it is opened so that you want to make it as fast as possible. Also note that this information does not change drastically over short periods; and when it does, it does not affect the user experience so badly as long as the refresh time is adequate.

This is a fantastic candidate for Memcache. Let's see how this looks in code:

```
from google.appengine.api import memcache
....

TOP_MEETINGS_KEY = 'top_meetings'

class MeetingController(base.BaseHandler):

    def get(self):

        results = memcache.get(TOP_MEETINGS_KEY) # Attempt to fetch from memcache

        if results is None:

            results = []

            # Fetch from Datastore
            query = Meeting.query().order(-Meeting.created).fetch(30)

            for meeting in query:
                results.append(meeting)

            # Store in memcache - TTL: 30 s
            memcache.set(TOP_MEETINGS_KEY, results, 30)

        self.response.status = 200
        self.response.write(json.dumps(results, cls = JsonSerializer))
```

[4]"Using compare and set in Python," Google Inc., 2015, `https://cloud.google.com/appengine/docs/python/memcache/#Python_Using_compare_and_set_in_Python`.

You attempt to fetch results from Memcache using the specified key. If the value is None, you fetch, process, and add the list of items to your memory cache, so that when another user requests the same information, the result is returned directly from Memcache. Notice how you specify a time to live of 30 seconds for this key. You can also use an absolute Unix epoch time in the future—that is, a number of seconds since midnight January 1, 1970. This means the value in question is removed 30 seconds after it was added, so the next time after the key is evicted, the list is fetched from your data store and set to Memcache.

The time to live that you specify depends on the type of request, the expected load, how rapidly the data changes, and how much you and your users care about that. In this case, you make sure users never see information older than 30 seconds, but you also obtain significant improvements in terms of access and load. Suppose you receive traffic in an area and requests per second increases to 500. With a time to live of 30 seconds, you are saving your application from issuing (500 QPS × 30s) - 1 = 14,999 Datastore RPCs. This has a dramatic impact in performance at scale.

■ **Note** Sorting entities with geolocation information only by creation date is generally not what you want in an application with these characteristics. Instead, you want to be able to prompt users with meetings nearby. Cloud Datastore currently is not the best solution to perform geolocation-based fetches. But there are alternatives that operate on the data-processing side, such as geomodel[5]; search solutions in App Engine, like Search API[6]; and independent services like the widely known Elastic Search.[7]

E-mail

After exploring the list of currently available meetings nearby, Kris, who has a free spot for lunch today, finds one he would like to join, so he decides to create a meeting request that can later be accepted by the owner. To do that, the owner needs to be notified of the new meeting request. To fulfill this need, you decide to send an e-mail to the owner every time a new request to join a meeting is filed.

This is one scenario among many where you need the ability to send e-mails from your application. The sender can either be an application administrator or a user with a Google account. App Engine exposes this functionality through the Mail API. This API allows you to not only send e-mails but also lets you process incoming e-mails by transforming them into HTTP requests to your handler.

Going back to the handler that takes care of meeting requests, you now add the necessary logic to send an e-mail to the owner every time a new user asks to join the meeting:

```
....
def post(self, meeting_id): # Posts a request to join a meeting

    # Creation of the request to join a meeting
    meeting = Meeting.get_by_id(int(meeting_id))
    join_request = MeetingRequest(parent=self.user_key, meeting=meeting.key)
    join_request.put()
```

---

[5]"geomodel: Indexing and Querying Geospatial Data in App Engine," https://pypi.python.org/pypi/geomodel.
[6]Amy Unruh, "Getting Started with the Python Search API, Google Inc., 2015, https://cloud.google.com/appengine/training/fts_intro.
[7]elastic, https://www.elastic.co.

```
        # Notify meeting owner
        owner_email = meeting.owner.get().email
        if mail.is_email_valid(owner_email):
            self._send_join_request_notification(owner_email)

        self.response.status = 201
        self.response.write(json.dumps(join_request, cls = JsonSerializer))

    def _send_join_request_notification(self, email_address):

        sender_address = 'LunchMates <lunchmates@appid.appspotmail.com>'
        subject = 'Request to join your meeting'
        body = 'Somebody requested to join your meeting. Check it out!'

        mail.send_mail(sender_address, email_address, subject, body)
```

As you can see, the code is self-explanatory. When a new meeting request created, an e-mail with the specified subject and body is sent to the owner's e-mail address. This time, the administrator is an e-mail under the domain of your application. If you need a dedicated e-mail address for this purpose, you can create it and add it as an administrator in your application. Remember that you can do that from the Permissions section in your project in the Developers Console.

■ **Note** By default, the development server prints a log record with the information for the e-mail to be sent, without actually sending it.

As of this writing, an e-mail's size is limited to 10MB, including attachments. You can check the current limit using the following link: `https://cloud.google.com/appengine/docs/python/mail/#Python_Quotas_and_limits`

You can also configure your application to receive e-mails of the following form: `<value>@appid.appspotmail.com`. These e-mails are turned into HTTP requests that your application can handle just as you would for the rest of the handlers.

First you need to enable this service and specify the app that handles it in `app.yaml`:

```
....

inbound_services:
- mail

- url: /_ah/mail/.+
  script: mail_handler.app
  login: required

....
```

Now, in the mail_handler.py file, you create a handler to process the incoming e-mails and an application wrapping it. This handler inherits from InboundMailHandler, which is conveniently prepared for this purpose with methods like def receive(self, mail_message): that you can override to directly process the mail object:

```
import webapp2
from google.appengine.ext.webapp.mail_handlers import InboundMailHandler

class IncomingEmailHandler(InboundMailHandler):
    def receive(self, mail_message):
        # Process InboundEmailMessage

app = webapp2.WSGIApplication([IncomingEmailHandler.mapping()], debug=True)
```

The receive method gives you an instance of InboundEmailMessage. From this object, you can access the following details:

```
mail_message.subject
mail_message.sender # The address of the sender. e.g. 'Kris <kris@domain.com>'
mail_message.to  # 'To' recipients separated by comma
mail_message.cc # 'CC' recipients separated by comma
mail_message.date
mail_message.attachments # Contains a list of google.appengine.api.mail.Attachment
mail_message.original # Contains the original message in an instance of
email.message.Message
```

You can use this information to perform associated tasks in your application. For example, suppose you have an application that allows commenting. Every time a collaborator comments on an item, you send an e-mail to all interested parties. Using the incoming e-mail feature, you can allow them to reply directly from their e-mail clients, process the message, and create a new comment transparently in your app.

Task Queues

One of the most crucial aspects of the behavior of many applications is performance—in particular, the rapidness with which your app responds to requests. In an ecosystem where computers and systems develop and progress very quickly, it is important to keep up with this pace and make sure your app is responsive enough that it does not affect the overall user experience. Nowadays this means most regular requests should return a result in less than 200 milliseconds.

Tasks queues help with that by providing a way for you to schedule and execute tasks outside of the scope of the request. These tasks are useful when a given request needs to trigger a longer-running operation in order to fulfill its needs—currently the deadline of task queue requests is 10 minutes. Suppose, for example, that when a user asks to join a meeting in LunchMates, you may want to show suggestions of people that the users likely want to invite to their meetings. One way to achieve this is to access a social API to check if the requester and the event owner share any acquaintances. But you do not want to make the user wait while you do that. Instead, you return a response to the user as soon as the request to join the meeting is created and schedule a new task that takes care of accessing the third-party API and persisting volatile information about friends until the event takes place.

Task queues can be either of two types:

- In *push queues*, App Engine is in charge of handling the management of the queue based on its configuration. When you enqueue a task, App Engine attempts to start executing it as soon as it can. Push queues are a great option if you prefer the system to take care of the job of handling tasks, and the operations you need to perform affect content that also lives in your application in App Engine.
- *Pull queues* reduce App Engine's responsibility to holding tasks that need to be executed. Therefore a pull queue needs a consumer to process the tasks in it. This consumer can live in any part of your application in App Engine or in any other system or back end. Note that this approach also requires the consumer (you) to take care of task management in the context of scaling the system and deleting executed tasks from the queue. Pull queues are a good option if you have application functionality scattered across systems, infrastructures, and providers, or you simply need to have control over the processing of tasks.

You specify queues for your application with their respective configuration in the `queue.yaml` (or `queue.xml` if you are using Java) file. Like other configuration files, `queue.yaml` is placed in the root folder of your application. Depending on your application's requirements, you can either use one queue or group tasks in different queues based on the nature of the tasks. For example, a task to send an e-mail to newly registered users may have more priority (e.g.: a higher execution rate) than a task that crunches numbers to measure KPIs used in internal reports.

■ **Note** The system comes with a default push queue that you can use to start scheduling tasks right away. If the default queue meets your needs, you do not need to create a `queue.yaml` file to define other queues.

Push Queues

This is how you create a push queue in queue.yaml:

```
total_storage_limit: 300M

queue:
- name: email_queue
  rate: 10/s
  bucket_size: 20
  max_concurrent_requests: 10
  retry_parameters:
    task_retry_limit: 10
    task_age_limit: 1d
    min_backoff_seconds: 10
    max_backoff_seconds: 200
    max_doublings: 3
```

Push queues have two types of parameters. In the first group, `rate`, `bucket_size`, and `max_concurrent_requests` determine how tasks are consumed over time:

- `rate` defines the number of times per second that a batch of tasks attempts to execute.
- `bucket_size` determines the number of tasks to process on each attempt.
- `max_concurrent_requests` limits the number of requests that can be executed simultaneously.

The configuration in `retry_parameters` describes how tasks that fail are retried.

`task_retry_limit` and `task_age_limit` specify the maximum number of retries and the time that can pass since the task was first executed, respectively, before a task is considered to fail permanently. If the two parameters are specified, the task will keep retrying until both conditions are met.

Task queues in App Engine follow an exponential backoff-based strategy for retries. This means each time a task fails, the time interval until the next attempt grows either linearly or exponentially. In push queues, tasks are considered completed if the handler in charge of processing them responds with a success HTTP status code (within the range of 200-299). You can configure the details of this behavior using the following parameters:

- `min_backoff_seconds` is the initial waiting time in seconds before reattempting to execute a task.
- `max_doublings` limits the number of times the interval is doubled between attempts.
- `max_backoff_seconds` determines the maximum waiting time before reattempting to execute a task. Subsequent failures always have the same waiting time, which matches the specified value in this parameter.

Let's use an example to illustrate this. Suppose you have the following configuration for a push queue:

```
- name: email_queue
  rate: 2/s
  bucket_size: 10
  max_concurrent_requests: 10
  retry_parameters:
    task_retry_limit: 9
    task_age_limit: 10m
    min_backoff_seconds: 10
    max_backoff_seconds: 600
    max_doublings: 5
```

This queue attempts to process tasks twice a second, in batches of 10, only if no more than 10 tasks are running at the same time. Tasks are retried until the limit of 10 attempts and the age of 10 minutes are reached. The first time, the task fails; the next attempt is not run for 10 seconds. On the next 5 failures, the time interval is doubled until it reaches 600 seconds.

Suppose that a bug in your code causes the task to fail permanently. The result is as follows:

Attempt #	Current Age, at Least (secs)	# of Retries	Waiting Time until Next Attempt (secs)
1	0	0	10
2	10	1	20
3	30	2	40
4	70	3	80
5	150	4	160
6	310	5	**320** *max number of doublings (5)
7	**630 *age limit reached**	6	480
8	1110	7	**600** *max backoff seconds (600)
9	1710	8	600
10	2310	**9 *retry limit**	600

`task_age_limit` and `task_retry_limit` are met in the tenth retry, so the task is considered to fail permanently. If neither of these two parameters is specified, the task is retried indefinitely.

Pull Queues

Here is the pull version of a queue similar to the previous one:

```
- name: email_queue
  mode: pull
  acl:
    - user_email: <admin_email>
    - writer_email: <admin_email>
    - writer_email: <writer_email>
  retry_parameters:
    task_retry_limit: 9
```

Notice how this queue has a parameter called `acl`. The values specified are used to construct the access control list needed to authorize access to task queues from systems that operate outside of App Engine. These external applications need to operate through the Task Queue REST API. Only e-mails that belong to Google accounts are accepted as valid parameters. E-mails specified under `user_email` are allowed to list, get, lease, delete, and update tasks, whereas those specified under `writer_email` are intended to be used only for enqueuing new tasks.

■ **Pro Tip** In order for an e-mail address to access all the functions from the REST API, it needs to be set as both a `user_email` and a `writer_email`.

Tasks in pull queues are deleted after the consumer has tried to retrieve them for execution as many times as specified in the parameter `task_retry_limit`. If this parameter is not set, tasks are never deleted automatically; the consumer is the only agent responsible—and entitled—to do this.

Handling Tasks

From this point on, the operational focus is on push queues. This mode, given its managed nature and simplicity compared to using pull queues, is more appropriate, according to the principles for building your next big thing used throughout this book. To read more about pull queues, check the document "Using Pull Queues" for Python,[8] Java,[9] and Go.[10]

In push queues, a handler is the responsible for processing tasks. Thus, when you add a task to the queue, you must specify the URL of the handler that controls its execution.

To see how push queues work, let's take the operation that creates a request to join a meeting as an example. This operation creates a new record in Cloud Datastore with information about the person who is trying to join a meeting and the state of the operation. After the record is added successfully, an e-mail is sent to notify the owner of the meeting. In our first naïve implementation, the operation does not return until the e-mail is sent. You can use a task queue to send this e-mail so that you can return a response to the user immediately, while the e-mail nessage is processed and sent in the background.

The updated logic that enqueues a new task after the join request has been created looks like this:

```
from google.appengine.api import taskqueue
....
def post(self, meeting_id): # Posts a request to join a meeting

    # Creation of the request to join a meeting
    meeting = Meeting.get_by_id(int(meeting_id))
    join_request = MeetingRequest(parent=self.user_key, meeting=meeting.key)
    join_request.put()

    # Notify meeting owner
    params = {'owner_id': meeting.owner.id()}
    taskqueue.add(queue_name='email', url='/tasks/email', params=params)

    self.response.status = 201
    self.response.write(json.dumps(join_request, cls = JsonSerializer))
```

This time, instead of sending the e-mail right away, a task is added to the `email` queue, executed by the handler under the URL `/tasks/email` with the specified parameters.

---

[8]"Using Pull Queues in Python," Google Inc., 2015, `https://cloud.google.com/appengine/docs/python/taskqueue/overview-pull`.
[9]"Using Pull Queues in Java," Google Inc., 2015, `https://cloud.google.com/appengine/docs/java/taskqueue/overview-pull`.
[10]"Using Pull Queues in Go," Google Inc., 2015, `https://cloud.google.com/appengine/docs/go/taskqueue/overview-pull`.

Here are some additional arguments that `google.appengine.api.taskqueue.add` accepts:

- `name` is the task name. Task names cannot be longer than 500 characters and must be composed of one or more digits, letters, underscores, and/or dashes. Tasks names are unique at the queue level, and attempts to create tasks with the same name will fail. You can use the name of a task to manually delete it from the queue. Note that task-deletion acknowledgement can take up to 7 days. A name for a task cannot be reused until the system is aware that the first task added with this name was completely removed.
- `headers` holds a dictionary with the headers sent to the handler of the request.
- `transactional` accepts `True` or `False` and determines whether the task is added to the queue if the associated transaction is committed successfully. Transactional tasks are considered to be part of the transaction in question. These tasks must not be given a custom name.

Now you need to write the handler that takes care of task execution. You are going to create a separate web app application to host handlers for tasks. It is recommended that you protect access to these internal handlers by limiting access to administrators. You do that by setting the `login` parameter of the handler to `admin`. Start by adding the new task handler to `app.yaml`:

```
....
handlers:
- url: /tasks/.*
  script: main.tasks
  login: admin
....
```

Now, in `main.py`, create the application `tasks`. This application is responsible for directing task-related requests to the appropriate handler:

```
....
from tasks.emails import *
....
TASK_ROUTES = [
    DomainRoute(config.subdomain, [ # Allowed domains

        routes.PathPrefixRoute(r'/tasks', [

            # Emails
            Route(r'/email', handler=EmailTaskHandler)
        ])
    ])
]
tasks = webapp2.WSGIApplication(TASK_ROUTES, debug=True)
```

Finally, you need to create the handler. To conveniently separate different parts of the application, you can create a new folder called `tasks` and place `emails.py` in it. Do not forget to add an empty `__init__.py` file to the newly created folder; otherwise it will not be inspected when looking for packages and classes.

In your new e-mail handler, you only need to implement logic for the POST method, which is the HTTP method used by push queues by default:

```
#!/usr/bin/env python

import webapp2
from google.appengine.api import mail

from model.model import UserData

class EmailTaskHandler(webapp2.RequestHandler):

    def post(self):

        owner_id = self.request.get('owner_id')
        owner_email = UserData.get_by_id(owner_id).email

        if mail.is_email_valid(owner_email):

            sender_address = 'LunchMates <lunchmates@appid.appspotmail.com>'
            subject = 'Request to join your meeting'
            body = 'Somebody requested to join your meeting. Check it out!'

            mail.send_mail(sender_address, owner_email, subject, body)
```

The first action performed extracts the owner ID sent as a parameter when enqueuing the task. The way you access this information is identical to how you do it in regular requests. The rest of the logic to send the e-mail should not be a surprise at this point. As previously mentioned, the request is run until the task succeeds or all retry conditions are met.

Later in this chapter, you see how to deploy your application to the cloud, to upload the latest changes of the application. If you only need to update the configuration of your queues (in queue.yaml), you can run the command update_queues from appcfg.py:

```
appcfg.py -A <project-id> update_queues <path-to-root-folder>
```

Here, path-to-root-folder is the path to the folder containing your project (the path where your app.yaml or queue.yaml lives). The <project-id> is the unique identifier for your application. This identifier is the same as the one assigned to your application in Google Developers Console when you create the project for the first time.

■ **Note** You can delete a queue by uploading a new queue.yaml excluding the queue to delete. If a queue that has tasks still to process is deleted, the execution is paused and is not restored until a new queue.yaml containing the queue in question is uploaded again.

Task Queues in the Administration Console

You can explore the state of your queues and tasks both from the console operating locally in your development server and in Google Developers Console. In both cases, you can see the list of queues and their respective configuration, the tasks that are currently enqueued, and options to delete queues and tasks.

To access this panel, do the following:

1. Navigate to Google Developers Console: `https://console.developers.google.com`.
2. Select your project, or create a new one.
3. On the left menu, expand Compute and then App Engine, and click Task Queues.

Deleting Tasks

Tasks can also be deleted programmatically. To purge the entire content of a queue or a single task, you do the following:

```
from google.appengine.api import taskqueue

# Purge entire queue
queue = taskqueue.Queue(queue_name)
queue.purge()

# Delete a task inside of a queue
queue = taskqueue.Queue(queue_name)
queue.delete_tasks(taskqueue.Task(name=task_name))
```

`queue_name` and `task_name` are the names given to the queue and the task, respectively.

Deferred Tasks

App Engine provides an alternative way to use task queues without the need to deal with the configuration details. `google.appengine.ext.deferred` is a useful built-in library for small tasks that need to be executed in the background without other requirement, such as creating your own task handler.

The `defer()` method takes a callable object as the first parameter—that is, any object that implements the `__call__()` method, such as a function. From the second parameter on, you specify the arguments that you need to pass to the callable when the work is executed.

To use this utility, you need to enable this library in the `builtins` section of `app.yaml`:

```
builtins:
- deferred: on
```

Here is an example:

```
# email_sender.py
from google.appengine.api import mail

def notify_owner_new_meeting_request(owner_email):

    if mail.is_email_valid(owner_email):
```

```
    sender_address = 'LunchMates <lunchmates@appid.appspotmail.com>'
    subject = 'Request to join your meeting'
    body = 'Somebody requested to join your meeting. Check it out!'

    mail.send_mail(sender_address, owner_email, subject, body)
```

■ **Note** The callable executed using `defer()` has to be accessible by name, because the scope from which `defer()` is called is not preserved. For example, you must not define the callable object in the request-handler module. Instead, you can place it in a separate module, as in the previous example.

To send the e-mail, all you need to do is call `defer()` with the previously defined function and the owner's e-mail address:

```
from google.appengine.ext import deferred
from email_sender import notify_owner_new_meeting_request
....
# Notify meeting owner
deferred.defer(notify_owner_new_meeting_request, owner_email)
....
```

As mentioned earlier, the deferred library uses task queues to operate, but it does so transparently by using the default queue and a previously defined handler.

You can pass specific parameters of the task as arguments of the `defer()` utility by prepending them with an underscore so they are not read as parameters of the callable. For example, you can specify the queue where you want your logic to be executed:

```
deferred.defer(notify_owner_new_meeting_request, owner_email, _queue='email')
```

■ **Pro Tip** Keep your data small. Data associated with push task queues is limited to 100KB. Technically, the same limitation applies to deferred tasks. However, if the data is larger than that, the deferred library stores it temporarily in Cloud Datastore, which increases the limit to 1MB, but has implications for performance when you store and retrieve information to and from disk.

Deferred tasks are retried on failure, just like regular tasks. Sometimes, though, a task may fail permanently. If you do not want a task to be retried, you can return before the error happens so that the task is considered to have succeeded or raise a `deferred.PermanentTaskFailure` exception. This special exception is treated as a permanent failure that is logged in the system. When you raise this exception, the task is flushed from the queue and never retried again.

Scheduled Tasks

Scheduled tasks, also commonly known as cron jobs, are executed at defined times or regular intervals. This type of task is useful when you need logic to be executed at specific points in time, like when the generating reports, analytics, performing clean-up tasks, and so on. Scheduled tasks share many similarities with tasks in Task Queues from an operational standpoint. However, scheduled tasks are not retried in case of failure.

You can configure scheduled tasks in your `cron.yaml` file, located in the root folder of your application (along with the other YAML files). Each entry in this file defines a new scheduled task:

```
cron:
- description: delete meetings without activity for one year
  url: /tasks/meeting-cleanup
  schedule: every 30 days

- description: remind users about pending requests longer than 10 days
  url: /tasks/request-summary
  schedule: every monday 07:00
  timezone: Europe/Amsterdam

- description: weekly report
  url: /tasks/weekly-report
  schedule: every 7 days
```

The accepted parameters for each job are as follows:

- `url` (required): The target URL for the job. Just as for other tasks, this URL needs to point to a handler in your App Engine application that takes care of processing the task.
- `description`: Use this field to help you understand the duties of a given task. This text is also shown in the development and production consoles.
- `timezone`: The time zone applied to the schedule rules. The expected format is the name of a standard `zoneinfo` time zone name.[11] If this parameter is not specified, UTC is used.
- `target`: Determines which module or version of your application is used. The value specified here is prepended to the host of your URL. This can be either a module or a version of your application.
- `schedule` (required): Determines when is the task executed. The syntax is based on a readable, English-like combination of keywords that determines the time and/or periodicity of the schedule.

Schedule Format

You can use two types of format to define a schedule: periodic and specific.

[11]"List of tz Database Time Zones" (in their standard form), `https://en.wikipedia.org/wiki/List_of_tz_database_time_zones`.

Periodic Format

This format has the following structure:

```
every N (hours|mins|minutes) ["from" (time) "to" (time)]
```

N is a number indicating the number of hours or minutes. The time range is optional. If it is specified, the task will only run in this range. Here are a couple of examples:

```
every 12 hours : runs every 12 hours.
every 5 minutes from 10:00 to 14:00 : runs every five minutes from 10:00 to 14:00.
```

The first three times the request runs happen at 10:00, 10:05 and 10:10 respectively. Similarly, the last three times happen at 13:50, 13:55 and 14:00.

Specific Timing Format

Use this format if you need tasks to be executed at specific times on specific days of the week or the month:

```
("every"|ordinal) (days) ["of" (monthspec)] (time)
```

- `ordinal` determines the position of a day in the month (such as `first monday` or `third tuesday` in the month).
- `days` are the days of the week either in long (`monday`) or short (`mon`) mode.
- `monthspec` is an optional part in which you can use a list of one or more months to constrain the schedule, or `every month` if the part is omitted.
- `time` defines the exact time of day when the cron should be triggered.

Here are some examples for this format:

```
second,third mon,wed,thu of march 17:00 : runs the second and third Mondays, Wednesdays and
Thursdays of March at 17:00.
every monday 09:00 : Gets triggered every Monday of the month at 09:00.
1st monday of sep,oct,nov 17:00 : runs every first monday of September, October and November
at 17:00.
every day 00:00 : runs every day at midnight.
```

If you are unsure about your cron configuration, you can obtain a readable version of it and check that the rules specified satisfy your needs. You do that with the `cron_info` command:

```
appcfg.py -A <project-id> update_cron <path-to-root-folder>
```

Updating Cron Information

Just as is the case for tasks queues and indexes, `appcfg.py` provides a command to update your cron configuration in production:

```
appcfg.py update_cron <path-to-root-folder>
```

`path-to-root-folder` is once again the folder where your application is located in your file system.

Logs

Logging helps you troubleshoot, analyze, and, ideally, reconstruct unwanted application states based on events that took place in the past. App Engine generates logs for deployed applications with information about incoming requests and the returned responses, including detailed information about errors if there were any during the lifetime of the request. To see these logs, go to the Developers Console (https://console.developers.google.com), select a project, and navigate to Logs in the Monitoring section.

The Python SDK in App Engine uses Python's standard logging library to work with logs. This library defines five levels of severity: debug, info, warning, error, and critical. Use them based on the type of event you are reporting. For instance, use debug for events that are useful when developing your application locally, warning to inform you about something that is unexpected but does not disrupt the user, and critical to report an undesired and damaging scenario.

For example, returning to a previous example, the operation of adding information to your memory cache can fail. If that occurs in a production environment, you do not want to interrupt users, because the outcome for them is the same. Still, you want to make sure you are aware of such thing so you can react later:

```
import logging
....
for meeting in query:
    results.append(meeting)

if not memcache.set(TOP_MEETINGS_KEY, results, 30):
    logging.error('Query results %s failed to be cached in memory' % TOP_MEETINGS_KEY)
```

Deploying

So far, you have been introduced to the building blocks of App Engine. You are now ready to show the world the application you have been working on in this chapter. If you have not done so yet, it is time to let Google know about your project. To create a project, do the following:

1. Navigate to Google Developers Console (https://console.developers.google.com).
2. Click Create Project.
3. Fill in the Project Name and Project ID fields. Remember that the project ID is unique across the entire Google Cloud.
4. Choose a billing account, or create a new one.
5. Under Advanced Options, choose USA or EU for the location of your data center based on where you expect to have the majority of the users accessing your application. These settings can only be set on project creation.
6. Click Create. You are finished!

Deploying your application is as easy as executing one command in your terminal or command-line console:

```
appcfg.py -A <project-id> update <path-to-root-folder>
```

path-to-root-folder is the path to the folder containing your project (the path where app.yaml lives), and project-id is the identifier for your application in Google Developers Console. Let's assume the path to the application is ./Development/lunchmates and your project identifier is lunch--mates. You then run

```
appcfg.py -A lunch--mates update ./Development/lunchmates
```

And boom! Your application is deployed and live to the world. You can access it with the following URL http://<application-id>.appspot.com/. For this example, the application ID is lunch–mates, so the final URL is http://lunch--mates.appspot.com/.

The appcfg.py command includes a complete set of functions to help you manage your application directly from the command line. They include utilities to update or delete indexes; update the configuration for tasks queues, cron jobs, DoS protection, and downloading; and so on. To read more about this, check the official documentation for appcfg.py at https://cloud.google.com/appengine/docs/python/tools/uploadinganapp.

■ **Note** You can also deploy your application using Google App Engine Launcher. As mentioned previously, this tool helps you organize and manage projects locally. To deploy an application, simply select it in the list and click Deploy.

■ **Pro Tip** Be patient! It is possible that the first time you run requests that access Cloud Datastore, you may get NeedIndexError exceptions for indexes that are not present in the application. Indexes can take a bit of time to be generated; so if you see this error, try the request again a few minutes later. If the problem persists, check your index configuration under index.yaml.

Summary

You now have the tools you need to develop your own application and let App Engine take care of devOps (development operations) tasks like scaling, managing instances, load balancing, and so on. You have also experienced the power of App Engine reflected in one of its main strengths: the ability to build something operational that scales with your users in only a few lines of code, using the platform and the set of services and libraries that come with it. But many features did not make it into this chapter like Search API, multitenancy, or sockets. Resources are available online and offline on these topics. Sites like Stack Overflow[12] and the documentation at Google[13] do a very good job of staying up to date with the rapid evolution of the platform. In addition, a very complete book[14] by Dan Sanderson dives deep into the guts and features of App Engine and contains all you need to know about it, both in Java and Python.

[12]Stack Overflow is the leading question-and-answer site for professional programmers: http://stackoverflow.com/questions/tagged/google-app-engine.

[13]"Google App Engine: Platform as a Service," official documentation, https://cloud.google.com/appengine/docs.

[14]Dan Sanderson, *Programming Google App Engine*, 2nd ed, O'Reilly Media, 2012.

Finally, it is important to remember that we live in a lucky époque for technology. We have tools to build things that work seamlessly without much effort from the development side. App Engine is not the only PaaS out there, which illustrates the increasing trend of simplifying things that were difficult before so that you can focus on what makes a difference. For example, you can build a simple application with a real-time schedule for public transportation in your city, or a service that tracks the trends of the deadliest diseases in the world to help find indicators that flatten the path for doctors and researchers; and deploy them without worrying about infrastructure hassles.

It is sensible to think that this direction will continue and be pursued by the principal companies and agents involved with the development of these platforms, so that we do not have to solve the same problems over again. We live in a fortunate era. Show the world what you can do!

CHAPTER 6

Next Generation DevOps Initiatives

In Chapters 4 and 5, you learned about two important technologies in Google Cloud Platform: Google Compute Engine and Google App Engine. Compute Engine, being an infrastructure as a service (IaaS) product, is targeted at system and network administrators. App Engine, being a platform as a service (PaaS) product, is targeted at application developers. Each of these products mirrors the industry trend of building public cloud services along the lines of IaaS and PaaS; they occupy the two ends of the compute spectrum.

Although this broad but disconnected product cluster has made it easier for organizations and individuals to embrace the public cloud, the true power of the public cloud is created by a continuous spectrum (imagine a rainbow) of services that are connected to one another and morph into each other in its product offerings. Google, along with other large public cloud players, is leading the charge in defining these transformations.

In this chapter, you begin by learning about the advantages and shortcomings of traditional IaaS and PaaS models that define the need for new types of computing products. Following this, we introduce you to two new Cloud Platform initiatives: Google Container Engine and Google App Engine based Managed Virtual Machines. Let's start with Compute Engine.

Compute Engine manages the hardware lifecycle—procurement, setup, maintenance, and retiring—and provides system administrators and network administrators with maximum control over architecture and system design. Compute Engine users are expected to know how to set up the operating system and application framework and install and configure applications. This level of control is useful when you are migrating proprietary and legacy applications to the public cloud. However, once applications become popular with users, it takes significant time, resources, and expertise to make them scale in sync with the workload. In addition, the types and sizes of resources offered by the public cloud infrastructure are likely to be more up to date than the options that were available during application development, leaving the applications in a non-optimized state.

App Engine, on the other hand, due to its unique and modularized high-performance architecture and system design, is suitable for new, scalable web applications that are built from scratch. Adapting proprietary and legacy applications remains a challenge on the App Engine platform because existing applications need to be reworked extensively to be adapted to the App Engine architecture. Even new applications require workarounds for capabilities that are disabled in the App Engine custom application runtimes, such as writing to local file system.

Based on this description of the capabilities and challenges of IaaS and PaaS offerings from Cloud Platform, an ideal application-hosting solution should have the following characteristics.

- *Application encapsulation and abstraction*: The application should be encapsulated in a resource container that is disconnected from the underlying computational platform. The resource requirements should be specified in abstract terms, such as amount of CPU and RAM, and not be linked to a specific type of virtual or physical machine.
- *Standard application runtimes*: The underlying application runtime should be an instance of the standard runtime that is made available by the runtime producer. It should not be modified in any way. In particular, it should not introduce any constraints on the application design and architecture.
- *Platform management*: The cloud service provider should manage the underlying operating system platform, but the application developer should have full administrative access as well.
- *Automatic scaling*: The application-hosting platform should enable automatic scaling of the application, and the unit of scaling should be in terms of modules rather than the underlying physical or virtual machine (VM) specifications.
- *Legacy application support*: Legacy applications should be supported and scaled on par with new applications that are designed using modern design patterns.

An ideal hosting platform is built with all of these characteristics and is able to support both legacy and modern applications. The following sections describe a new approach to software development and IT operations that has taken the world of computing by storm—literally. We begin by sharing the fundamentals of this new approach and then describe two budding products from Cloud Platform.

Containers

In order to appreciate the new container-based software development and distribution model and the excitement surrounding it, you need to know about some of the inefficiencies bundled with the previous-generation computing model (generally known as *virtualization*). Virtualization solved real-world problems faced by IT operations staff, including consolidation of underutilized physical servers as VMs on a single physical host. Although virtualization helped to reduce the physical footprint and enabled VM migration during physical host maintenance, virtualization technology introduced additional computational overhead. Let's consider an example to help you understand this situation more clearly.

Let's say that a system administrator previously hosted two applications on two physical hosts. Application A was running on operating system A using physical host A, and application B was running on operating system B using physical host B. The system administrator observed that the physical machines were being underutilized and decided to consolidate the two applications (and their operating systems) using a single physical host A. The new setup will use a single host operating system A that supports two VMs powered by a software hypervisor. VM 1 will host operating system A, enabling application A, and VM 2 will host operating system B, enabling application B. Figure 6-1 illustrates this virtualized architecture.

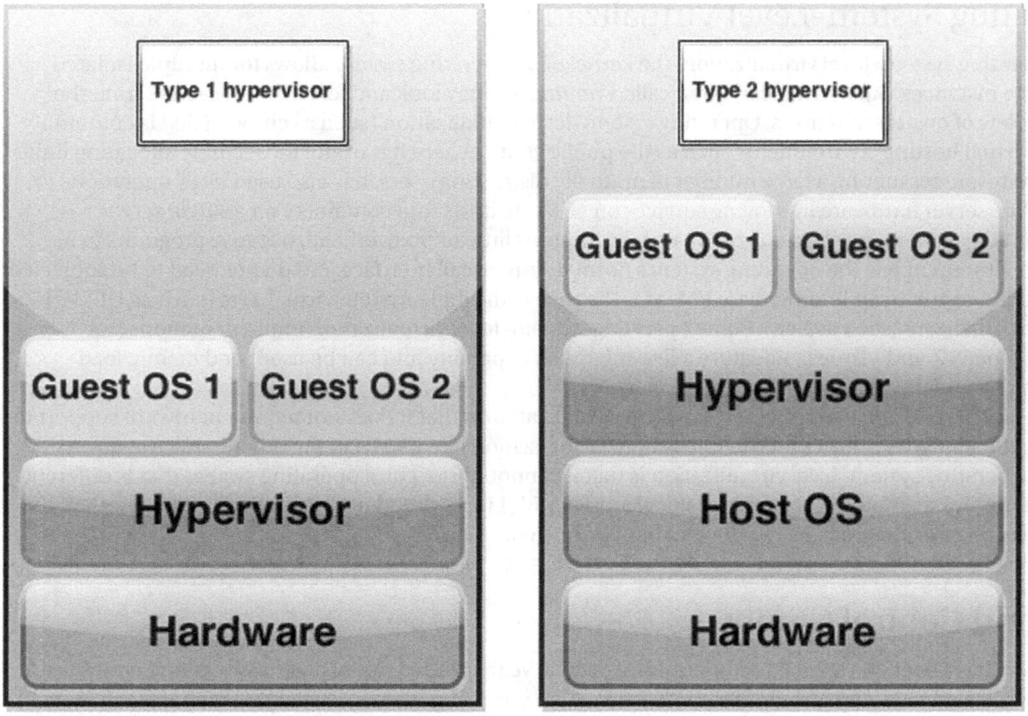

Figure 6-1. *Hypervisor models, type 1 and type 2*

Virtualization has fulfilled its promise of resource consolidation. However, it has introduced inefficiency in the delivery model, because applications are the end-user visible components in a software stack, and everything else supporting it is typically seen as an overhead. Hence, fewer additional layers mean better software execution and more efficient hardware resource utilization. Unfortunately, in the example virtualization model, software A faces the prospect of double emulation first by the guest operating system and second by the host operating system. These additional software translations mean application software A runs much less efficiently than it would on a physical server.

You may point out that type 1 virtualization (where the host operating system is not present) incurs lesser overhead. Although this is true, inefficiencies are also incurred when multiple instances of the operating system, whether the same or different, are executed in different VMs, and the hypervisor schedules an entire operating system whenever any part of the application needs to be executed. Scheduling an entire operating system is considered heavyweight from a computational perspective. Another inefficiency is the resources required for the operating system, especially when either the same user or several customers on a single physical host use multiple instances of the same operating system.

The ideal application-hosting environment provides the required computational resources—CPU, system RAM, disk I/O, and network I/O—on a supported operating system while guaranteeing that applications are completely isolated from one another from a security and privacy perspective. In addition to isolated, guaranteed system resources, applications also need specific versions of certain libraries. If these requirements can be satisfied, then you no longer need to run a complete operating system in a VM when it is only required to support an application, and you can attain a new level of efficiency that matches and surpasses (when several applications are consolidated) what was achieved with a pre-virtualized setup (using independent physical servers). This is the promise and technical model of containers.

Operating System-Level Virtualization

With operating system-level virtualization, the kernel of an operating system allows for multiple isolated user space instances. Such instances, often called *containers*, may look and feel like real servers from the point of view of owners and users. Operating system-level virtualization (such as chroot, jails) is commonly used in virtual hosting environments such as the public cloud, where it is useful for securely allocating finite hardware resources among a large number of mutually distrusting users. It is also used by IT operations to consolidate server hardware by moving services on separate hosts into containers on a single server.

Operating system-level virtualization usually imposes little or no overhead, because programs in a virtual environment use the operating system's normal system-call interface and do not need to be subjected to emulation or run in an intermediate VM, as is the case with whole-system virtualizers (such as QEMU) and paravirtualizers (such as Xen). Some operating-system-level virtualization implementations (for example OpenVZ and Virtuozzo) feature a live-migration capability and can be used for dynamic load-balancing of containers between nodes in a cluster.

The upside of using operating system-level virtualization is that it does not require hardware support to perform efficiently, as is the case with full-system virtualization like KVM. On the other hand, the downside of using operating system-level virtualization is that it cannot host a guest operating system that is different from the host, or a different guest kernel. For example, with Linux, different distributions can be hosted, but alien operating systems such as Windows cannot be hosted.

LXC and Control Groups

Containers have been part of the Linux kernel for several years. Due to this historic association, containers are often referred to as *Linux containers (LXC)*. LXC is an operating system-level virtualization environment for running multiple isolated Linux systems (containers) on a single Linux host. LXC relies on control groups (cgroups) and namespaces support present in the Linux kernel to provide an isolated virtual environment for applications that has its own process and network space.

Google invented the cgroups functionality and contributed it to the open source Linux kernel project. The cgroups functionality has been part of the mainline Linux kernel since version 2.6.24, which was released on January 24, 2008. At its core, cgroups adds new capabilities to the Linux kernel that limit, isolate, and account for system resources (CPU, memory, and network and disk I/O) consumed by a single process or a collection of processes. Control groups can be hierarchical, where a group inherits limits from its parent group. Control groups also add the ability to measure how many resources one or a group of processes has consumed. This accounting capability is essential for billing purposes in a shared service or public cloud model. Control groups can be frozen, check-pointed, and restarted on the same or a different system running a compatible operating system, paving the way for hardware independence.

The key difference between containers and VMs is that whereas the hypervisor emulates entire server hardware, containers just abstract the operating system kernel. This means, in many cases, that your overhead is reduced by 99.9%, with the application encapsulated in a neat, tiny capsule. On the other hand, hypervisors can support different operating systems or kernels on a single physical machine. Containers are also in an early stage of deployment and as of this writing are conspicuously absent from the Mac OS X and Windows kernels. But Microsoft has promised to support Docker in a future Windows server release (`http://news.microsoft.com/2014/10/15/DockerPR`).

Namespaces

A Linux kernel technology called *namespaces* is essential to provide the container's isolated workspace. When you run a container, a set of namespaces is created for that container. Each aspect of a container runs in its own namespace and does not have access outside it.

Following are some of the namespaces types:

- `pid`: Used for process isolation (PID = process ID)
- `net`: Used for managing network interfaces (NET = networking)
- `ipc`: Used for managing access to IPC resources (IPC = interprocess communication)
- `mnt`: Used for managing mount points (MNT = mount)
- `uts`: Used for isolating kernel and version identifiers. (UTS = Unix timesharing system)

Docker

Docker is an open platform for developing, shipping, and running containerized applications. At its core, Docker provides a way to run an application that is securely isolated in a container. Isolation and security allow you to run many containers, potentially owned by different users, simultaneously on your host. The lightweight nature of containers, which run without the extra load of a hypervisor, means you can get more out of your hardware. The entire Docker container platform has been released as open source at `https://github.com/docker`.

Docker is written in the Go programming language and uses several capabilities available in the Linux kernel. In addition, Docker brings several new things to the container world. First, Docker makes containers easier and safer to deploy and use than previous approaches. Second, Docker has helped to build an industry-wide consensus and brought much-needed standardization to the container format and interface definition through its work on `libcontainer`. Docker also supports traditional Linux containers using LXC.

Docker uses client-server architecture and has three main entities: client, daemon, and hub. The Docker client communicates with the Docker daemon via sockets or through a RESTful API. The communication channel depends on whether the client and daemon run on the same system or on different systems. The Docker daemon manages the complete container lifecycle from building, running, and distributing through terminating your Docker containers.

The Docker hub is the official repository for sharing and managing Docker images and is offered as a software-as-a-service (SaaS) model. Hosting of public images is free, but Docker Inc. charges a fee for hosting private images. In addition, Docker Inc. sells a Docker Hub Enterprise version that enables (large) organizations to have a Docker repository behind their enterprise firewall.

From a system design perspective, Docker consists of two components: Docker images and Docker containers.

Docker Images

A Docker image is a read-only template listing all components of an application software stack. An image typically specifies an operating system, an application server, and the application itself. For example, a Wordpress image could specify the Debian OS, Apache web server, and Wordpress application. You can use public images as-is, update existing images, and build new images. Docker images are the build component of Docker and are used to create Docker containers.

Each Docker image consists of a series of layers. Docker uses union file systems to combine these layers into a single image. Union file systems let you transparently overlay files and directories of separate file systems, known as *branches*, forming a single coherent virtual file system. These layers are one of the reasons Docker is so lightweight. When you change a Docker image—for example, by updating an application to a new version—a new layer is built. Thus, rather than replacing the entire image or rebuilding, as you might with a VM, only that layer is added or updated. You don't need to distribute an entire new image—just the update. This makes distributing Docker images faster and simpler than distributing complete virtual machine images or even applications.

Every image starts from a base image. You can use base images from the Docker Hub public repository or use your own base image. Docker images are then built from these base images using a simple, descriptive set of steps called *instructions*. Each instruction creates a new layer in the Docker image. Instructions include actions like these:

- Run a command.
- Add a file or directory.
- Create an environment variable.
- Run applications on container boot up.

These instructions are stored in a file called a Dockerfile. Docker reads this Dockerfile when you request a build of an image, executes the instructions, and returns a final image. A Docker image is read-only. When Docker creates a container from an image, it adds a read-write layer on top of the image (using a union file system), in which your application runs.

Docker Containers

A Docker container is created from a Docker image. Docker containers are similar to Unix directories and hold everything needed for an application to run. Docker containers can be started, stopped, moved, and deleted. They are the run component of Docker. Let's look at an example of a launching a simple `docker` command.

In the following `docker` command invocation, the `docker` client binary is used to launch a new container from an image—Ubuntu, in this case—using the `run` option. Once the container is launched, the application `/bin/bash` will be executed in the container, giving you a bash shell that you can use to interact with the container:

```
$ sudo docker run -i -t Ubuntu /bin/bash
```

We will now explain to you the various parts of this command:

- The "*docker run*" command starts a new container from a docker image and optionally runs a command within it. In this case, you are starting an *Ubuntu* image and running the "*/bin/bash*" command within it.
- The "*-i*" option, which can also be represented as "*--interactive=false*". instructs Docker to keep STDIN (i.e., standard input) open even if not input source is attached.
- The "*-t*" option, which can also be represented as "*--tty=false*". instructs Docker to allot a pseudo-TTY
- In general, the Docker run command syntax follows the format "`docker run [OPTIONS] IMAGE [COMMAND] [ARG..]`".
- For more options of this run command, you can execute "`docker run --help`" from your terminal window.

In order to create a virtual environment, Docker performs the following actions in the background:

1. *Acquires the image*: If the specified image does not exist locally, Docker pulls it down from Docker Hub and uses it for the new container.
2. *Creates a new container*: Once Docker has the image; it uses it to create a container.

3. *Creates a directory and mounts a read-write layer*: The container is created in the file system, and a read-write layer is added.
4. *Adds a network interface*: Docker creates a network bridge interface that allows the Docker container to talk to the local host.
5. *Assigns an IP address*: Docker attaches an available IP address from a pool.
6. *Executes a command*: Docker runs an application that you specify.
7. *Sets up IO redirection*: Docker connects and logs standard input, outputs, and errors from the container.

Congratulations—you have your first running container! From here, you can manage your container, interact with your application, and then, when you are finished, stop and remove your container.

Kubernetes

Kubernetes is an orchestration system for managing containerized applications across multiple hosts in a cluster. Kubernetes handles scheduling application containers onto nodes in a compute cluster. It provides mechanisms for application deployment, scheduling, updating, maintenance, and scaling. A key feature of Kubernetes is that it actively manages containers to ensure that the state of the cluster continually matches the user's intentions. Kubernetes supports Docker containers and has been released as open source at `https://github.com/GoogleCloudPlatform/kubernetes`. The system consists of several concepts: pods, nodes, volumes, labels, and annotations. It groups the containers that make up an application into logical units for easy management and discovery. This section guides you through each of these core concepts and components.

A Kubernetes cluster is managed using the Kubernetes cluster manager. The Kubernetes cluster manager can be accessed using an API, a GUI, or a command-line interface. `kubectl` is the client-side CLI tool that you can use to control the Kubernetes cluster manager.

Pods

In Kubernetes, all application containers such as Docker containers run in pods. A pod can host a single container or multiple containers, making pods the smallest deployable units that can be created, scheduled, and managed, rather than individual application containers. When a pod contains multiple containers, Kubernetes guarantees that all the containers in the pod are co-located on the same machine and can share resources. From this perspective, a pod models an application-specific logical host in a containerized environment. It may contain one or more applications that are relatively tightly coupled—in a pre-container world, they would have executed on the same physical or virtual host. Each pod gets its own IP address that is separate from the host. This makes it far easier to manage containers and port legacy applications i.e., there will be no software port conflicts. You will learn more about this in the networking section below. Applications in a pod also have access to shared volumes, which are defined at the pod level and made available in each application's file system.

The context of the pod can be defined as the conjunction of several Linux namespaces:

- *PID namespace:* Applications in the pod can see each other's processes.
- *Network namespace:* Applications in the pod have access to the same IP and port space and they can use 'localhost' when communicating with other containers in the pod.
- *IPC namespace:* Applications in the pod can use System V IPC or POSIX message queues to communicate.
- *UTS namespace:* Applications in the pod share a hostname.

For each pod you create, the system finds a machine that is healthy and that has sufficient available capacity, and starts up the corresponding container(s) there. If a container fails, Kubernetes' node agent, called the Kubelet, automatically restarts it. However, if the pod or its machine fails, it is not automatically moved or restarted unless the user also defines a *replication controller*, explained in the next section.

Replication Controllers

Although you can create and manage pods yourself, it is recommended that you use Kubernetes' replication controller. This is because a replication controller ensures that a specified number of pod *replicas* are running at any one time. A replication controller accomplishes this by replacing pods that are deleted or terminated for any reason, as in the case of node failure or disruptive node maintenance, such as a kernel upgrade. For this reason, we recommend that you use a replication controller even if your application requires only a single pod. In this context, a replication controller is similar to a process supervisor, but it supervises multiple pods across multiple nodes instead of individual processes on a single node. The replication controller delegates local container restarts to an agent on the node (such as Kubelet or Docker).

The replication controller creates a pod from a pod template. The replicated set of pods may constitute an entire application, a micro-service, or one layer in a multitier application. Multiple pods from the same or different applications can share the same machine as well. But a replication controller is not a pod configuration-monitoring service. Instead, a replication controller acts like a cookie cutter: once a cookie has been cut, it has no relationship to the cutter. Subsequent changes to the pod template or even switching to a new pod template has no direct effect on the pods already created. Similarly, pods created by a replication controller may subsequently be updated directly. This is a deliberate design choice and is in contrast to a pod, which specifies the current desired state of all containers belonging to the pod.

Volumes

A pod can also contain zero or more *volumes*, which are directories that are private to a container or shared across containers in a pod. A pod specifies which volumes its containers need in its `ContainerManifest` property. A process in a container sees a file system view composed from two sources: a single Docker image and zero or more volumes. A Docker image is at the root of the file hierarchy. Any volumes are mounted at points on the Docker image; volumes do not mount on other volumes and do not have hard links to other volumes. Each container in the pod independently specifies where on its image to mount each volume. This is specified as a `VolumeMounts` property.

At the time of this writing, Kubernetes supports multiple types of volumes, for example: EmptyDir, HostDir, GCEPersistentDisk, and NFS.

> *EmptyDir*: An EmptyDir volume is created when a pod is bound to a node. It is initially empty, when the first container command starts. Containers in the same pod can all read and write the same files in the EmptyDir. When a pod is unbound, the data in the EmptyDir is deleted forever. An EmptyDir is typically used as scratch space.
>
> *HostDir*: A HostDir allows access to files on the current node. Some uses for a HostDir are running a container that needs access to Docker internals and running cAdvisor in a container.
>
> *GCEPersistentDisk*: Compute Engine Persistent Disk is a network-hosted persistent disk available to applications hosted on Compute Engine IaaS. Persistent Disk is either based on magnetic disk or solid-state disk technology. A volume with a `GCEPersistentDisk` property allows access to files on a GCEPersistentDisk.

- At the time of this writing, you must create a PD using `gcloud` or the Compute Engine API before you can use it. There are some restrictions when using a GCEPersistentDisk:
    - The nodes (what the Kubelet runs on) need to be Compute Engine VMs.
    - The Compute Engine VMs need to be in the same Compute Engine project and zone as the PD.
    - Compute Engine PDs can either be mounted as read/write by a single pod or as read-only by multiple pods.
- *NFS*: Kubernetes NFS volumes allow an existing NFS share to be made available to containers in a pod.

Kubernetes is in very active development. Refer to the project documentation at `http://kubernetes.io` for additional Volume types.

Labels and Annotations

Labels are key/value pairs that are attached to objects such as pods. Each object can have a set of key/value labels defined. Each key must be unique for a given object. Labels can be attached to objects at creation time and subsequently added and modified at any time. The following is a JSON-formatted label for an object:

```
"labels":
{
  "key1" : "value1",
  "key2" : "value2"
}
```

Labels can be used to organize and select subsets of objects. For example, labels are useful to refer to a set of pods—say, to limit the set of pods on which a mutating operation should be performed or that should be queried for status. You can use equality-based (`=`, `==`, `!=`) operators and set-based (`in`, `notin`) operators to shortlist pods that match certain criteria. Labels enable architects to map their application architecture onto system objects in a loosely coupled fashion, without requiring clients to store these mappings.

Although Kubernetes can use labels add metadata to identify objects, you may need to attach arbitrary non-identifying metadata that can be used by client programs. This facility is provided by annotations and can be used for retrieval by API clients such as tools, libraries, and so on. The information may be large, may be structured or unstructured, may include characters that are not permitted by labels, and so forth. Such information is not used for object selection and therefore doesn't belong in labels.

Like labels, annotations are key-value maps:

```
"annotations":
{
  "key1" : "value1",
  "key2" : "value2"
}
```

Networking

In this section, you will learn about the networking fabric present in Kubernetes. Our objective is to explain the concepts of networking in Kubernetes and distinguish it from the Docker model. Hence, we will first start with the Docker model.

Docker Model

Docker follows the "normal" way of networking that is suitable for single host deployments. By default, Docker uses host-private networking. It creates a virtual bridge, called `docker0` by default, and allocates a subnet from one of the private address blocks defined in RFC1918 (`http://en.wikipedia.org/wiki/Private_network`) for that bridge. For each container that Docker creates, it allocates a virtual Ethernet device (called `veth`) that is attached to the bridge. The `veth` is mapped to appear as `eth0` in the container, using Linux namespaces. The in-container `eth0` interface is given an IP address from the bridge's address range.

The result is that Docker containers can talk to other containers only if they are on the same machine (and thus the same virtual bridge). Containers on different machines cannot reach each other—in fact, they may end up with the exact same network ranges and IP addresses. In order for Docker containers to communicate across nodes, they must be allocated ports on the machine's own IP address, which are then forwarded or proxied to the containers. This obviously means containers must either coordinate which ports they use very carefully or else be allocated ports dynamically.

Kubernetes approaches networking somewhat differently than Docker's defaults. It assigns every pod its own IP address allocated from an internal network, so you do not need to explicitly create links between communicating pods. However, it is not recommended that you connect to pods using their IP addresses. This is because pods can fail and be replaced by new pods with different IP addresses on different nodes. Instead, if a pod, or a collection of pods, provides a service, then you should create a service object spanning those pods, and clients should connect to the IP of the service object.

Kubernetes Model

Coordinating ports across multiple developers is very difficult to do at scale and exposes users to cluster-level issues outside of their control. Dynamic port allocation brings a lot of complications to the system. Rather than deal with this, Kubernetes takes a different approach.

Kubernetes encourages a flat address space and does not dynamically allocate ports, instead allowing users to select whichever ports are convenient for them. To achieve this, it allocates an IP address for each pod—containers in a pod share their network namespaces—including their IP address. This means containers in a pod can all reach each other's ports on `localhost`. This does imply that containers in a pod must coordinate port usage, but this is no different than processes in a VM. The Kubernetes team calls this the *IP-per-pod* model.

Kubernetes imposes the following fundamental requirements on networking implementations (barring any intentional network-segmentation policies):

- All containers can communicate with all other containers without NAT.
- All nodes can communicate with all containers (and vice versa) without NAT.
- The IP that a container sees itself as is the same IP that others see it as.

The above Kubernetes requirements makes the case for a flat IP network whereas traditional networking uses multiple hierarchies and address translations. These requirements are usually satisfied by having a Software Defined Networking based network fabric, advanced routing support provided by a cloud platform, an API into your routers, or a software overlay network such as Flannel, etc.

Services

A Kubernetes service is an abstraction that defines a logical set of pods and a policy by which to access them. A label selector determines the set of pods targeted by a service. Every service is also assigned a virtual IP address. Kubernetes calls the tuple of the service IP and the service port the *portal*.

A local agent (called the *kube-proxy*) runs on the source machine and forwards the request from a container running in a Kubernetes pod to one of the corresponding back-end containers. The kube-proxy takes care of tracking the dynamic set of back ends as new pods on new hosts replace purged pods, so that the service IP address (and DNS name) never changes.

Every node in a Kubernetes cluster runs a kube proxy. This application watches the Kubernetes master for the addition and removal of service and `Endpoints` objects. For each service, it opens an arbitrary port on the local node. Any connections made to that port are proxied to one of the corresponding back-end pods. Which back end to use is decided based on the `AffinityPolicy` of the service.

Kubernetes supports two primary modes of finding a service: environment variables and DNS. When a pod is run on a node, the kubelet adds a set of environment variables for each active service. This implies that any service that a pod wants to access must be created before the pod itself. This is not a practical solution, and DNS does not have this restriction. The DNS server watches the Kubernetes API for new services and creates a set of DNS records for each. With DNS active cluster-wide, all pods should be able to do name resolution of services automatically.

A service in Kubernetes is a REST object, similar to a pod. Like all the REST objects, a service definition can be POSTed to the API Server to create a new instance. For example, suppose you have a set of pods, each of which exposes port 8088 and carries the label `app=MyIndicator`:

```
{
  "kind": "Service",
  "apiVersion": "v1beta3",
  "id": "indicator",
  "selector": {
    "app": "MyIndicator"
  },
  "containerPort": 8088,
  "protocol": "TCP",
  "port": 80
}
```

This specification creates a new service object named `indicator` that targets TCP port 8088 on any pod with the `app=MyIndicator` label. The service's selector is evaluated continuously, and the results are posted in an `Endpoints` object also named `indicator`. For Kubernetes-native applications, Kubernetes offers a simple Endpoints API that is updated whenever the set of pods in a service changes. For non-native applications, Kubernetes offers a virtual-IP-based bridge to services that redirects to the back-end pods.

Services, in addition to providing abstractions to access pods, can also abstract any kind of back end such as external database cluster, independent databases, other services, and non-Kubernetes controller back ends.

Namespace

Every resource in Kubernetes, such as a pod, is identified by a URI and has a UID. Important components of the URI are the kind of object (such as a pod), the object's name, and the object's namespace. Every name is unique in its namespace; and in contexts where an object name is provided without a namespace, it is assumed to be in the default namespace. The UID is unique across time and space.

DNS

DNS is offered as a cluster add-on. If enabled, a DNS pod and service are scheduled on the cluster, and the kubelets are configured to tell individual containers to use the DNS service's IP.

Every service defined in the cluster (including the DNS server itself) is assigned a DNS name. By default, a client pod's DNS search list includes the pod's own namespace and the cluster's default domain.

The cluster DNS server (SkyDNS) supports forward lookups (A records) and service lookups (SRV records).

The DNS pod that runs holds three containers: skydns, etcd (which SkyDNS uses), and a Kubernetes-to-SkyDNS bridge called kube2sky. The kube2sky process watches the Kubernetes master for changes in services and then writes the information to etcd, which skydns reads. This etcd instance is not linked to any other etcd clusters that might exist, including the Kubernetes master.

Google Container Engine

Container Engine is Cloud Platform's service for hosting containerized applications. Container Engine is built using Docker containerization technology and the Kubernetes container-orchestration platform. Container Engine is built using Compute Engine resources; specifically VMs. Container Engine introduces two additional entity types—clusters and nodes—that map the Compute Engine resources to Container Engine terminologies.

A Container Engine *cluster* is a centrally managed group of Compute Engine resources running Kubernetes. A cluster includes a master node and worker nodes, which are Compute Engine VMs and are all provisioned on a configured IP private network. The master becomes the entry point for creating and controlling the compute resources, reached through the cluster's API endpoint. The master runs the Kubernetes API server, which services REST requests, schedules pod creation and deletion on worker nodes, and synchronizes pod information (such as open ports and location) with service information.

A node in the cluster provides processor and memory resources. A node belongs to only one cluster and is provisioned and turned on during cluster creation. The number of nodes created is based on the total amount of Compute Engine resources expected. The cluster master schedules work on each node. Each node runs the Docker runtime and hosts a kubelet agent, which manages the Docker containers scheduled on the host. Each node also runs a simple network proxy.

Let's walk step by step through the process of setting up a containerized application using Docker and Kubernetes. In the following example, you use a Docker image for Wordpress (https://registry.hub.docker.com/u/tutum/wordpress) to create a publicly accessible Wordpress web site backed by a MySQL database, running in a Container Engine pod.

The first step is to create your cluster. A cluster consists of a single master instance and a set of worker nodes. The master and each worker node is a Compute Engine VM. The number of worker nodes is specified at the time of cluster creation. In this example, you create a cluster with a single VM of class n1-standard-1, as shown in Listing 6-1.

Listing 6-1. Container Engine Command to Create a Single Node Cluster

```
$ gcloud alpha container clusters create hello-wordpress --num-nodes 1 \
--machine-type n1-standard-1
Waiting for cluster creation...done.
Create cluster succeeded!

Using gcloud compute copy-files to fetch ssl certs from cluster master...
Updated [https://www.googleapis.com/compute/v1/projects/cloud-platform-book].
Warning: Permanently added '104.154.71.171' (RSA) to the list of known hosts.
Warning: Permanently added '104.154.71.171' (RSA) to the list of known hosts.
```

```
kubecfg.key  100%  1704  1.7KB/s  00:00
Warning: Permanently added '104.154.71.171' (RSA) to the list of known hosts.
kubecfg.crt  100%  4429  4.3KB/s  00:01
Warning: Permanently added '104.154.71.171' (RSA) to the list of known hosts.
ca.crt  100%  1229  1.2KB/s  00:00
kubeconfig entry generated for hello-wordpress. To use standalone kubectl with
this cluster, run

$ export KUBECONFIG=/Users/cloudplatformbook/.config/gcloud/kubernetes/kubeconfig
$ gcloud alpha container kubectl config use-context gke_cloud-platform-book_us-
central1-a_hello-wordpress

clusterApiVersion: 0.15.0
containerIpv4Cidr: 10.140.0.0/14
creationTimestamp: '2015-04-20T08:51:05+00:00'
enableCloudLogging: true
endpoint: 104.154.71.171
masterAuth:
  password: hPECW5tsXQtUkJei
  user: admin
name: hello-wordpress
network: default
nodeConfig:
  machineType: n1-standard-1
  serviceAccounts:
  - email: default
    scopes:
    - https://www.googleapis.com/auth/compute
    - https://www.googleapis.com/auth/devstorage.read_only
    - https://www.googleapis.com/auth/logging.write
  sourceImage: https://www.googleapis.com/compute/v1/projects/google-containers/global/
images/
container-vm-v20150317
nodeRoutingPrefixSize: 24
numNodes: 1
selfLink: https://www.googleapis.com/container/v1beta3/projects/261451503272/zones/
us-central1-a/clusters/hello-wordpress
servicesIpv4Cidr: 10.143.240.0/20
status: running
zone: us-central1-a
```

You now have two instances in this project: the worker node that you specified, and the master (see Listing 6-2). The master takes care of pod scheduling and runs the Kubernetes API server.

Listing 6-2. Listing the Nodes in the Cluster

```
$ gcloud compute instances list
NAME    ZONE    MACHINE_TYPE  INTERNAL_IP  EXTERNAL_IP  STATUS
k8s-hello-wordpress-master us-central1-a n1-standard-1 10.240.58.160 104.154.71.171
RUNNING
k8s-hello-wordpress-node-1 us-central1-a n1-standard-1 10.240.104.209 130.211.160.118
RUNNING
```

Now let's create a pod to host the Wordpress container. Recall from the previous section that a pod is a group of containers, tied together for the purposes of administration and networking. It can contain a single container or many. In this example you need only one container, built with the `tutum/wordpress` image. To make the Wordpress installation accessible from outside the pod, you open port 80 on the cluster and expose it to the pod. Thereafter, clients (such as other pods or a browser) can connect to the container over port 80. Using your favorite text editor, create a configuration file called `wordpress.json` with the following contents:

```
{
  "id": "wordpress",
  "kind": "Pod",
  "apiVersion": "v1beta3",
  "desiredState": {
    "manifest": {
      "version": "v1beta3",
      "containers": [{
        "name": "wordpress",
        "image": "tutum/wordpress",
        "ports": [{
          "containerPort": 80,
          "hostPort": 80
        }]
      }]
    }
  }
}
```

Use this file and the `container kubectl create` command to create your pod as shown in Listing 6-3.

Listing 6-3. Creating a Kubernetes Pod Using the `gcloud kubectl` command

```
$ gcloud alpha container kubectl create -f wordpress.json
pods/wordpress
```

You can also list all the Kubernetes clusters in your current project using the command shown in Listing 6-4.

Listing 6-4. `Listing` All the Kubernetes Clusters in the Current Project

```
$ gcloud alpha container clusters list
clusters:
- clusterApiVersion: 0.15.0
  containerIpv4Cidr: 10.140.0.0/14
  creationTimestamp: '2015-04-22T07:23:35+00:00'
  enableCloudLogging: true
  endpoint: 130.211.160.118
  masterAuth:
    password: G9eeMmqewKHdOG8m
    user: admin
  name: hello-wordpress
  network: default
  nodeConfig:
    machineType: n1-standard-1
```

```
    serviceAccounts:
    - email: default
      scopes:
      - https://www.googleapis.com/auth/compute
      - https://www.googleapis.com/auth/devstorage.read_only
      - https://www.googleapis.com/auth/logging.write
    sourceImage: https://www.googleapis.com/compute/v1/projects/google-containers/
global/images/
container-vm-v20150317
  nodeRoutingPrefixSize: 24
  numNodes: 1
  selfLink: https://www.googleapis.com/container/v1beta3/projects/261451503272/zones/
us-central1-a/clusters/hello-wordpress
  servicesIpv4Cidr: 10.143.240.0/20
  status: running
  zone: us-central1-a
```

Let's list the pods running in this application. To do so, use the command shown in Listing 6-5.

Listing 6-5. gcloud command line to describe a single pod in Container Engine

```
$ gcloud alpha container kubectl get pod wordpress
POD  IP  CONTAINER(S)  IMAGE(S)  HOST  LABELS  STATUS  CREATED
wordpress   10.140.1.4   wordpress      tutum/wordpress
k8s-hello-wordpress-node-1.c.cloud-platform-book.internal/ <none> Running 35 seconds
```

You can also use the command `gcloud alpha container kubectl get pods` to list all the pods that you have created in the Container Engine application associated with your current project.

Now that your Wordpress pod is running, the last step is to expose it to the Internet so that you and your visitors can access it. You do so by creating a firewall rule to allow incoming traffic to your Compute Engine firewall. The console command and output in Listing 6-6 show the successful configuration of the Compute Engine firewall.

Listing 6-6. Creating a Firewall Rule that Allows Incoming HTTP Traffic in Port 80

```
$ gcloud compute firewall-rules create hello-wordpress-node-80 --allow tcp:80 \
--target-tags k8s-hello-wordpress-node
Created [https://www.googleapis.com/compute/v1/projects/cloud-platform-book/global/
firewalls/
hello-wordpress-node-80].
NAME                    NETWORK SRC_RANGES RULES  SRC_TAGS TARGET_TAGS
hello-wordpress-node-80 default 0.0.0.0/0  tcp:80          k8s-hello-wordpress-node
```

`--target-tags k8s-hello-world-node` opens port 80 only for nodes whose names contain the specified tag. In this case, it means your worker node can accept external traffic, but the master cannot.

That's it! You now have a working Kubernetes cluster consisting of a single node built using a Compute Engine VM that is running a single container, using the `tutum/wordpress` image. That Docker image includes the Wordpress installation files and a MySQL database. The Docker container serves the Wordpress launch page and is accessible over port 80 at the pod's IP address. You can visit the pod host's IP address in your browser. The IP address is listed in the External IP column of the worker node in the response to the command `gcloud compute instances list`. In this example, the IP address is 130.211.160.118. Figure 6-2 shows the Wordpress setup page that appears after Wordpress is installed and configured.

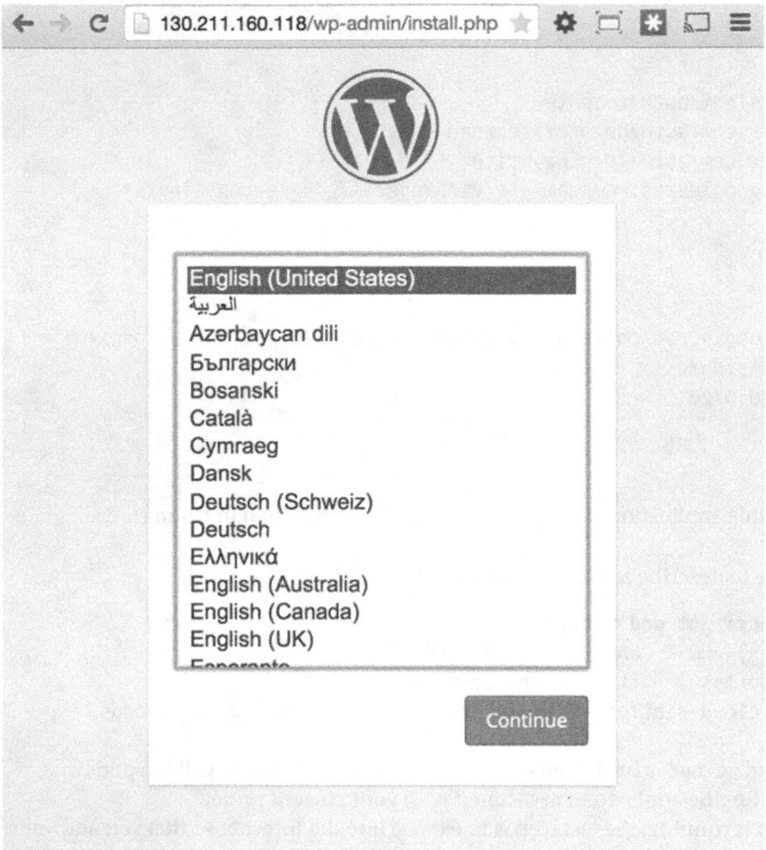

Figure 6-2. *Wordpress installation wizard: running in a Docker container and managed by Kubernetes*

This completes the setup of a Docker container with a Kubernetes container-orchestration system using Container Engine. You can proceed with the setup of the Wordpress content-management system. After you have done some experimentation, you may want to remove the allotted resources to save money. Listing 6-7 and Listing 6-8 show the cleanup commands and the corresponding output that delete the Kubernetes cluster and the associated firewall rules.

Listing 6-7. Deleting a Kubernetes Container Cluster

```
$ gcloud alpha container clusters delete hello-wordpress
Waiting for cluster deletion...done.
name: operation-1429686019822-854293f1
operationType: deleteCluster
selfLink: https://www.googleapis.com/container/v1beta3/projects/261451503272/zones/
us-central1-a/operations/operation-1429686019822-854293f1
status: done
target: /projects/2614515032s72/zones/us-central1-a/clusters/hello-wordpress
targetLink: https://www.googleapis.com/container/v1beta3/projects/261451503272/zones/
us-central1-a/clusters/hello-wordpress
zone: us-central1-a
```

Listing 6-8. Deleting the Firewall Rule that Allows HTTP 80 Bound Traffic

```
$ gcloud compute firewall-rules delete hello-wordpress-node-80
The following firewalls will be deleted:
 - [hello-wordpress-node-80]

Do you want to continue (Y/n)?  Y

Deleted [https://www.googleapis.com/compute/v1/projects/cloud-platform-book/global/
firewalls/
hello-wordpress-node-80].
```

App Engine Managed Virtual Machines

App Engine is the PaaS product from Cloud Platform. App Engine supports four programming languages: Python, PHP, Go, and Java. Its design philosophy made it necessary to modify the application runtimes, which resulted in some language features being disabled—such as access to the file system—on App Engine as compared to the runtimes' standard counterparts. The classic application-hosting environment is known as the *sandbox environment* and contains your code, a web server, and a language runtime. Other than the application code, the components in the App Engine hosting environment are immutable and managed by Google.

App Engine now offers a second hosting option: Managed virtual machines (VMs). The Managed VM hosting environment lets you run App Engine applications on configurable Compute Engine VMs. The VM hosting environment offers more flexibility and provides more CPU and memory options. Importantly, App Engine applications that run in a Managed VMs hosting environment are not subject to the restrictions imposed on the sandboxed runtimes (Java, Python, PHP, and Go).

Having two application runtimes doesn't mean you have to go all-in with either of them. Google has made it easy and allows you to choose the hosting environment (sandboxed or Managed VM) separately for each module in your application. This means an application can contain a mix of modules that use different hosting environments. For instance, you might use the sandbox environment for your client-facing front end and use a module running in a Managed VM for back-end processing. At the same time, it is not possible to have both runtimes for a single module, and every instance of any specific module runs in the same type of environment.

The following list highlights some of the new features of the Managed VMs hosting environment in App Engine:

- *Background processes and threads*: Applications can launch child processes and monitor them. Applications can also create threads without any restrictions.
- *Secure shell access*: You can access live instances of your application's modules using the SSH protocol.
- *Writable local disk*: Applications can write scratch data to an ephemeral disk that is initialized as part of the VM startup.
- *Extending applications*: You can install and use third-party applications and libraries.
- *Legacy applications*: You can install binary versions of any legacy software and invoke it from your App Engine application.

Google manages the underlying VM hosting environment and ensures that the VMs are health-checked, healed, and co-located in the same geographical region with other instances in the project. In addition, Google automatically applies critical, backward-compatible updates to the underlying operating system. This is done on a weekly basis, during which the VMs are automatically restarted. SSH access to Managed

VMs is disabled by default, and you can enable access to individual VMs that host your application runtimes from the Developers Console. At this time, the status of the VM is changed from `Google-managed` to `user-managed`. This status change disables the periodic health checks and automatic operating system updates. However, the VM remains attached to the App Engine load balancer and continue to receive incoming web traffic. Once you have finished debugging, you can change the status back to `Google-managed`. At this point, App Engine discards the VM and launches a new VM from the template.

Managed VMs use software containers to run multiple user spaces in one Compute Engine instance. Managed VMs build and run Docker container images, which are specified by a Dockerfile. As explained in a previous section, a Dockerfile includes all the system and application software necessary to run your app, along with dependency rules that keep everything up to date. Docker containers are portable and ensure that the production runtime environment is identical to the environment in the development machine. You use Google Cloud SDK commands to run this container on your local machine or deploy it to the production App Engine.

A Managed VMs environment supports two types of application runtimes: standard and custom runtimes. Google has preconfigured and created the standard runtime: a Docker image, which contains a complete language implementation with no sandbox constraints. A standard runtime has also built-in support for the Managed VM life cycle and health-checking requests and includes APIs that support popular App Engine services: Datastore, Memcache, Task Queues, Logging, and Users. As of this writing, as mentioned earlier, standard runtimes are available for Python, Java, and Go. You only need to add a few lines to your app's configuration file that refer to and use a standard runtime. You can extend and enhance a standard runtime by adding new Docker commands to the standard runtime's Dockerfile, which is supplied by the Google Cloud SDK.

Custom runtimes allow you to define new runtime environments. New runtime environments include alternative implementations of languages in standard runtimes, new language runtimes, or additional components on standard runtimes such as application interpreters or application servers. To create a custom runtime, you create a Dockerfile with a base image of your choice and add other Docker commands as needed to build the desired runtime environment. A custom runtime should handle the Managed VM life cycle and respond to health-checking HTTP requests.

Getting Started

App Engine Managed VMs use Docker containerization technology to power one or more user spaces on Managed Compute Engine VMs. Hence, you need to install the Docker software on your developmental system to package your application as Docker containers. Docker installation differs based on the operating system on your development system and is also dependent on the version and flavor of the operating system, such as different distributions and versions of the Linux OS. We have not included installation instructions here, because this information may become stale quickly. Follow the installation instruction at `https://docs.docker.com/installation` to set up Docker on your operating system.

We are using Ubuntu Linux version 14.04 in a VirtualBox VM on OS X Yosemite for the examples in this section. If your installation of Docker is successful, you should see output similar to Listing 6-9 for the commands shown.

Listing 6-9. Listing Docker Processes: Because No Containers Are Active, the List Is Empty

```
VM$ docker ps
CONTAINER ID  IMAGE  COMMAND  CREATED  STATUS  PORTS  NAMES
```

Now, test your Docker installation by running the hello-world container as shown in Listing 6-10.

Listing 6-10. Running the Docker Container hello-world

```
VM$ docker run hello-world
<..snip..>
Hello from Docker.
This message shows that your installation appears to be working correctly.
<..snip..>
To try something more ambitious, you can run an Ubuntu container with:
 $ docker run -it ubuntu bash
```

As suggested by the hello-world container, launch the Ubuntu Docker container. In both of these cases, if the Docker image is not available locally, it is automatically pulled from the public Docker registry https://hub.docker.com. Listing 6-11, Listing 6-12, and Listing 6-13 show the commands and associated output.

Listing 6-11. Listing the Kernel Details of the Ubuntu VM

```
VM$ uname -a
Linux VirtualBox 3.16.0-34-generic #47~14.04.1-Ubuntu SMP Fri Apr 10 17:49:16 UTC 2015
x86_64 x86_64 x86_64 GNU/Linux
```

Listing 6-12. Launching the Latest Version of the Ubuntu OS in a Container on the Ubuntu VM

```
VM$ docker run -it Ubuntu bash
```

Listing 6-13. Listing the Kernel Details of the Ubuntu Container (Remember to Execute This Command in the Container)

```
root@1f09c91919bf:/# uname -a
Linux 1f09c91919bf 3.16.0-34-generic #47~14.04.1-Ubuntu SMP Fri Apr 10 17:49:16 UTC 2015
x86_64 x86_64 x86_64 GNU/Linux
```

As you can see, the Linux kernel versions of the host and the container are exactly the same. Yet the execution environment is completely isolated, providing the benefits of virtualization at a very low computational cost. It is also possible to execute another version of the Ubuntu OS or a different Linux distribution as well, at a lower computational cost than with full-system virtualization. While the container is running, list the Docker processes again from a new terminal window, and observe that the running Docker container is listed, as shown in Listing 6-14.

Listing 6-14. Listing the Running Docker Containers

```
$ docker ps
CONTAINER ID  IMAGE  COMMAND  CREATED  STATUS  PORTS  NAMES
1f09c91919bf  ubuntu:latest  "bash"  7 seconds ago  Up 7 seconds  cocky_bartik
```

In addition to Docker images available from Docker hub, Google also makes available public Docker images at Google Container Registry. The Container Registry is accessible from gcr.io (see Listing 6-15); in addition to public Docker images, it enables you to upload, share, and download private Docker images. Let's see how to download and install the standard Python runtime for Managed VMs.

Listing 6-15. Downloading the Docker Container from Google Container Registry

```
VM$ docker pull gcr.io/google_appengine/python-compat
Pulling repository gcr.io/google_appengine/python-compat
<..snip..>
Status: Downloaded newer image for gcr.io/google_appengine/python-compat:latest
```

At this stage you should have three Docker images in your local system. You can list them using the command in Listing 6-16.

Listing 6-16. Listing Local Docker Images

```
VM$ docker images
REPOSITORY  TAG  IMAGE ID  CREATED  VIRTUAL SIZE
ubuntu  latest  b7cf8f0d9e82  39 hours ago  188.3 MB
hello-world  latest  91c95931e552  5 days ago  910 B
gcr.io/google_appengine/python-compat  latest  b0cf89be3a06  3 weeks ago  280.7 MB
```

Now, let's examine the Dockerfile of the Python runtime that you download from `gcr.io`. First, you need to locate the Dockerfile. It is in the Google Cloud SDK, which depends on your location. The easy way to find it is to use the `find` command (see Listing 6-17).

Listing 6-17. Bash Shell Commands to Locate the Dockerfile

```
$ sudo -s
# find / -type f -print | grep -i Dockerfile
```

This locates all instances of Dockerfile in your system, from which you can shortlist the Dockerfile for the Python runtime. The Dockerfile is a text document, and you can list its contents using a text editor or a command-line tool. Listing 6-18 uses the Linux command `cat` to show the file's contents.

Listing 6-18. Listing the Contents of a Dockerfile

```
VM# cat Dockerfile
FROM ubuntu:12.10
MAINTAINER Joffrey F <joffrey@dotcloud.com>
RUN apt-get update
RUN yes | apt-get install python-pip
ADD . /home/docker-py
RUN cd /home/docker-py && pip install .
```

As you can see, the Dockerfile is very easy to understand. It starts with a base image and builds layers on top of it. The RUN Docker command executes the associated command line. This is like the Unix exec command, except that it is cross-platform; Docker uses appropriate system-level commands depending on the OS and version it is running.

In this example, you use the `gcloud` command-line tool to package Docker images, test the Docker images locally, and upload it to the production App Engine Managed VMs platform. You need to install some additional components for the `gcloud` command-line tool to work with Managed VMs: run the command `gcloud components update app` from a bash shell to enable the App Engine components.

Deploying Docker Containers

This section uses two code examples to show the core differences between a sandboxed App Engine application and a Managed VM App Engine application and to show how easy it is switch a sandboxed App Engine application to a Managed VM App Engine application. Let's start with a simple sandboxed Python application.

The sample application consists of two files: `app.yaml` and `main.py`. Listing 6-19 lists the contents of the `app.yaml` configuration file, and Listing 6-20 lists the contents of `main.py`. Then we explain their major sections.

Listing 6-19. `app.yaml` File for a Sandboxed Runtime

```
1 module: default
2 version: 1
3 runtime: python27
4 api_version: 1
5 threadsafe: yes
6
7 instance:class: B1
8 manual_scaling:
9   instances: 1
10
11 handlers:
12 - url: .*
13   script: main.app
```

Listing 6-20. `main.py`

```
import webapp2

class HelloHandler(webapp2.RequestHandler):
  def get(self):
    msg = 'hello %s!\n' % self.request.headers.get('X-AppEngine-Country', 'world')
    self.response.headers['Content-Type'] = 'text/plain'
    self.response.out.write(msg)

app = webapp2.WSGIApplication([('/', HelloHandler)],
                              debug=True)
```

Most parts of these files are self-explanatory, and Chapter 5 describes them in detail as well. For now, let's focus on some key elements.

Following are the important points in `app.yaml`:

- *Line 3* declares that this is a Python application and states the required language version.
- *Line 7* declares the required App Engine instance class to be `B1`. `https://cloud.google.com/appengine/docs/python/config/backends` lists the specs.
- *Lines 8 and 9* disable the default App Engine auto scaling and instead declare that manual scaling should be used.
- *Lines 12 and 13* state that for all URLs, App Engine should invoke the `main.py` file.

And here are the primary points in `main.py`:

- *Line 1* indicates that this Python program uses the webapp2 Python framework (`https://webapp-improved.appspot.com`).
- *Lines 3-7* declare a Python class that returns a `"hello $country_name"` string.
- *Lines 9 and 10* are the entry point for this Python App Engine application.

Follow these steps to run this application in your local system:

8. Create a new directory.
9. Create two text files: `app.yaml` and `main.py`.
10. Copy the contents from Listing 6-19 and Listing 6-20 (excluding the line numbers), or download the files from the Github repository at `https://github.com/GoogleCloudPlatform/appengine-vm-fortunespeak-Python`.
11. Execute the program using the command `$ gcloud preview app run ./app.yaml`.

The first time you launch the dev server, it takes some time to download the resources necessary to provision your local VM. If you've preloaded the standard runtime images, the command may run more quickly. You'll know the process is complete when the terminal output shows the `_ah/start` request. The program listens to port 8080, and you can access it either using your web browser or using the `curl` program. Listing 6-21 and Listing 6-22 show the command lines and corresponding output of running the App Engine application.

Listing 6-21. Executing a Sandboxed App Engine Application Using the Sandbox Environment

```
VM:~/Projects/AppEngine/Sandbox/fortunespeak$ gcloud preview app run ./app.yaml
Module [default] found in file [~/Projects/AppEngine/Sandbox/fortunespeak/app.yaml]
INFO     2015-04-24 02:24:59,279 devappserver2.py:726] Skipping SDK update check.
WARNING  2015-04-24 02:24:59,441 simple_search_stub.py:1126] Could not read search indexes
from /tmp/appengine.cloud-platform-book.cloudplatformbook/search_indexes
INFO  2015-04-24 02:24:59,443 api_server.py:172] Starting API server at:
http://localhost:53153
INFO  2015-04-24 02:24:59,446 dispatcher.py:186] Starting module "default" running at:
http://localhost:8080
INFO  2015-04-24 02:24:59,446 admin_server.py:118] Starting admin server at:
http://localhost:8000
INFO  2015-04-24 02:25:00,331 module.py:1692] New instance for module "default" serving on:
http://localhost:8080

INFO     2015-04-24 02:25:00,865 module.py:737] default: "GET /_ah/start HTTP/1.1" 404 52
INFO     2015-04-24 02:25:33,670 module.py:737] default: "GET / HTTP/1.1" 200 10
INFO     2015-04-24 02:25:34,060 module.py:737] default: "GET /favicon.ico HTTP/1.1" 404 154
INFO     2015-04-24 02:25:38,150 module.py:737] default: "GET / HTTP/1.1" 200 10
```

Listing 6-22. Accessing the App Engine Application Using the Command Line

```
VM:~/Projects/AppEngine/Sandbox/fortunespeak$ curl http://localhost:8080
hello ZZ!
```

Let's now convert this sandboxed application and upgrade it to use the standard Python runtime that is part of the Managed VMs environment. You will be happy to note that no code changes are required for this transition; `main.py` remains the same. You just need to make some minor updates to the `app.yaml` file, as shown in Listing 6-23.

Listing 6-23. `app.yaml` File for Managed VMs

```
 1 module: default
 2 version: 1
 3 runtime: python27
 4 vm: true
 5
 6 api_version: 1
 7 threadsafe: yes
 8
 9 resources:
10   cpu: .5
11   memory_gb: 1.3
12
13 manual_scaling:
14   instances: 1
15
16 handlers:
17 - url: .*
18   script: main.app
```

The following are the only two changes required to switch from the sandboxed environment to Managed VMs:

- *Line 4* adds `vm: true`.
- *Lines 9-11* replace the `instance:class` key with a `resources` section.

This example specifically uses CPU and memory configurations that are not a standard-instances class in the sandbox VM. Upon execution, App Engine assigns an appropriate Compute Engine machine type that can provide at least the requested resources.

Let's execute this version of the application. In your test system, make a new directory, copy the `main.py` file, and re-create the `app.yaml` file. Listing 6-24 shows the gcloud command line and the corresponding output.

Listing 6-24. Running the App Engine Managed VM in the Local Developmental Server

```
VM:~/Projects/AppEngine/ManagedVM/fortunespeak$ gcloud preview app run ./app.yaml
Module [default] found in file [/home/cloudplatformbook/Projects/AppEngine/ManagedVM/
fortunespeak/app.yaml]
INFO: Refreshing access_token
INFO: Refreshing access_token
INFO: Looking for the Dockerfile in /home/cloudplatformbook/Projects/AppEngine/
ManagedVM/fortunespeak
```

```
INFO: Looking for the default Dockerfile for runtime [python27]
INFO: Dockerfile for runtime [python27] is found in /home/cloudplatformbook/Applications/
google-cloud-sdk/lib/googlecloudsdk/appengine/dockerfiles. Copying it into application
directory.
INFO  2015-04-24 03:12:29,837 devappserver2.py:726] Skipping SDK update check.
INFO  2015-04-24 03:12:29,883 api_server.py:172] Starting API server at: http://localhost:36382
INFO  2015-04-24 03:12:29,912 dispatcher.py:186] Starting module "default" running at:
http://localhost:8080
INFO  2015-04-24 03:12:29,913 admin_server.py:118] Starting admin server at:
http://localhost:8000
INFO  2015-04-24 03:12:29,913 containers.py:259] Building docker image cloud-platform-book.
default.1 from /home/cloudplatformbook/Projects/AppEngine/ManagedVM/fortunespeak/Dockerfile:
INFO  2015-04-24 03:12:29,913 containers.py:261] -------------------- DOCKER BUILD ------
--------------
INFO  2015-04-24 03:12:29,940 containers.py:280] Step 0 : FROM gcr.io/google_appengine/
python-compat
INFO  2015-04-24 03:12:30,457 containers.py:280] ---> b0cf89be3a06
INFO  2015-04-24 03:12:30,463 containers.py:280] Step 1 : ADD . /app
INFO  2015-04-24 03:12:30,535 containers.py:280] ---> 96e72471bd4c
INFO  2015-04-24 03:12:30,541 containers.py:280] Removing intermediate container
522c51b81714
INFO  2015-04-24 03:12:30,541 containers.py:280] Successfully built 96e72471bd4c
INFO  2015-04-24 03:12:30,542 containers.py:292] ------------------------------------------
--------------
INFO  2015-04-24 03:12:30,542 containers.py:304] Image cloud-platform-book.default.1 built,
id = 96e72471bd4c
INFO  2015-04-24 03:12:30,543 containers.py:534] Creating container...
INFO  2015-04-24 03:12:30,591 containers.py:560] Container
8d7bc660a8f532fc6bc8621cfe2320e1c918ee1354cb054f37742ea65dcc2c3c created.
INFO  2015-04-24 03:12:30,795 module.py:1692] New instance for module "default" serving on:
http://localhost:8080

INFO  2015-04-24 03:12:30,800 module.py:737] default: "GET /_ah/start HTTP/1.1" 500 48
INFO  2015-04-24 03:12:30,804 health_check_service.py:101] Health checks starting for
instance 0.
```

When you execute this command, gcloud creates a new Dockerfile and uses it to create the Docker container. You can look in this file and, if required, extend it further. The commands in Listings Listing 6-25 to 6-27 show the gcloud command line and corresponding output.

Listing 6-25. Listing the Contents of the ManagedVM Application Directory

```
VM:~/Projects/AppEngine/ManagedVM/fortunespeak$ ls -l
total 12
-rw-rw-r-- 1 cloudplatformbook cloudplatformbook 197 Apr 24 10:52 app.yaml
-rwxr-xr-x 1 cloudplatformbook cloudplatformbook 154 Apr 24 11:12 Dockerfile
-rw-rw-r-- 1 cloudplatformbook cloudplatformbook 347 Apr 24 10:51 main.py
```

Listing 6-26. Listing the Dockerfile Type Using a Linux Bash Shell Command

```
VM:~/Projects/AppEngine/ManagedVM/fortunespeak$ file Dockerfile
Dockerfile: ASCII text
```

Listing 6-27. Listing the Contents of the Dockerfile

```
VM:~/Projects/AppEngine/ManagedVM/fortunespeak$ cat Dockerfile
# Dockerfile extending the generic Python image with application files for a
# single application.
FROM gcr.io/google_appengine/python-compat

ADD . /app
```

The last step is to deploy the app to the production App Engine Managed VMs environment. This is accomplished using the command `gcloud preview app deploy ./app.yaml`. Listing 6-28 shows the command and corresponding output.

Listing 6-28. Deploying the App Engine Managed VMs App to the Production Environment

```
VM:~/Projects/AppEngine/ManagedVM/fortunespeak$ gcloud preview app deploy ./app.yaml
You are about to deploy the following modules:
 - cloud-platform-book/default/20150424t113250  From:
 [/home/cloudplatformbook/Projects/AppEngine/ManagedVM/fortunespeak/app.yaml]
Do you want to continue (Y/n)?  Y

Updating module [default] from file
 [/home/cloudplatformbook/Projects/AppEngine/ManagedVM/fortunespeak/app.yaml]
Pushing image to Google Container Registry...
/home/cloudplatformbook/Applications/google-cloud-sdk/./lib/requests/packages/urllib3/util/
ssl_.py:79:
InsecurePlatformWarning: A true SSLContext object is not available. This prevents urllib3 from
configuring SSL appropriately and may cause certain SSL connections to fail. For more
information, see
https://urllib3.readthedocs.org/en/latest/security.html#insecureplatformwarning.
  InsecurePlatformWarning
The push refers to a repository [gcr.io/_m_sdk/cloud-platform-book.default.20150424t113250] (len: 1)
Sending image list
Pushing repository gcr.io/_m_sdk/cloud-platform-book.default.20150424t113250 (1 tags)
Image 511136ea3c5a already pushed, skipping
<..snip..>
Pushing
Buffering to disk: 6.656 kB
Image successfully pushed=====================================>] 6.656 kB/6.656 kB
Pushing tag for rev [9c48b26f6861] on {https://gcr.io/v1/repositories/_m_sdk/
cloud-platform-book.default.20150424t113250/tags/latest}
11:34 AM Host: appengine.google.com
11:34 AM Application: cloud-platform-book (was: None); version: 20150424t113250 (was: None)
11:34 AM
Starting update of app: cloud-platform-book, version: 20150424t113250
11:34 AM Getting current resource limits.
11:34 AM Scanning files on local disk.
```

```
11:34 AM WARNING: Performance settings included in this update are being ignored because your
application is not using the Modules feature. See the Modules documentation for more information.
Python: https://developers.google.com/appengine/docs/python/modules/
Java: https://developers.google.com/appengine/docs/java/modules/
Go: https://developers.google.com/appengine/docs/go/modules/
PHP: https://developers.google.com/appengine/docs/php/modules/.
11:34 AM Cloning 4 application files.
11:34 AM Starting deployment.
11:34 AM Checking if deployment succeeded.
11:34 AM Deployment successful.
11:34 AM Checking if updated app version is serving.
11:34 AM Will check again in 5 seconds.
<..snip..>
11:36 AM Checking if updated app version is serving.
11:36 AM Enough VMs ready (1/1 ready).
11:36 AM Completed update of app: cloud-platform-book, version: 20150424t113250
```

After this step is complete, your application is live on the Internet, and you can access it using the URL `https://cloud-platform-book.appspot.com`. Listing 6-29 shows the invocation and return value. Note that the live instance of your application can determine the origin country of the request, as expected.

Listing 6-29. Accessing the Live Managed VMs Application Using the `curl` Command-Line Tool

```
VM:~$ curl http://cloud-platform-book.appspot.com
hello SG!
```

Let's list the Compute Engine instances in your project and verify that App Engine has created an appropriate Compute Engine instance for your container. To do so, us the command `gcloud compute instances list`, as shown in Listing 6-30.

Listing 6-30. Listing the Compute Engine Instances in Your Project Using the `gcloud` Command-Line Tool

```
VM:~$ gcloud compute instances list
NAME  ZONE  MACHINE_TYPE  INTERNAL_IP  EXTERNAL_IP  STATUS
k8s-hello-wordpress-master  us-central1-a n1-standard-1 10.240.178.145 130.211.160.118
RUNNING
k8s-hello-wordpress-node-1  us-central1-a n1-standard-1 10.240.70.213  104.154.71.171
RUNNING
cloudplatformbook  us-central1-f n1-standard-2 10.240.203.206 146.148.64.211  RUNNING
gae-default-20150424t113250-n1n2 us-central1-f g1-small  10.240.155.213 104.197.63.204
RUNNING
```

From this output, you can see that App Engine has created a `g1-small` instance that is appropriate to accommodate your Docker container. At this stage, you have successfully completed deploying a Python program as a containerized application in the App Engine Managed VMs runtime. You can extend the Dockerfile that was automatically generated by the Google Cloud SDK and include other third-party applications, system components, and so on. You can also update the Python program to use Managed VMs-specific features, such as writing to ephemeral local storage.

Live Debugging

Another important capability added by the App Engine Managed VMs environment is the ability to connect to the container running your application and perform live debugging over SSH. It is possible to connect to both containers running in your development machine and also to the production App Engine environment. This section guides you through these possibilities.

The following are the high-level steps to enable SSH debugging in the local development system. Then, Listings 6-31 to 6-34 show the actual command line and output:

1. Find the container ID.
2. Start a shell in the container.
3. Connect to the container.
4. Exit.

Listing 6-31. Listing the Running Containers (Note the `CONTAINER ID` of Your Instance)

```
VM:~/Projects/AppEngine/Sandbox/fortunespeak$ docker ps
CONTAINER ID  IMAGE  COMMAND  CREATED  STATUS  PORTS  NAMES
8599f8004dd1  a0a4d3826611:latest  "/usr/bin/python2.7  6 seconds ago  Up 6 seconds
0.0.0.0:32774->8080/tcp  google.appengine.cloud-platform-book.default.20150424t063335.0.
2015-04-24T063335.930784Z
```

Listing 6-32. Executing a Shell in the Container that Is Running Your Application

```
cloudplatformbook@VirtualBox:~/Projects/AppEngine/Sandbox/fortunespeak$ docker exec -it
 8599f8004dd1 /bin/bash
```

Listing 6-33. Executing a Simple Command in the Container

```
root@8599f8004dd1:/home/vmagent/app# uname -a
Linux 8599f8004dd1 3.16.0-34-generic #47~14.04.1-Ubuntu SMP Fri Apr 10 17:49:16 UTC 2015
x86_64 GNU/Linux
```

Listing 6-34. Exiting the Shell

```
root@8599f8004dd1:/home/vmagent/app# exit
exit
```

Before you can access a Managed VM in production, you need to unlock your Managed VMs environment—that is, switch it to `user-managed`. You can do so using either the web-based Developers Console or the `gcloud` command-line tool.

Perform the following steps in Developers Console to switch your VM from `Google-managed` to `user-managed`:

1. Go to Developers Console, select your project, and navigate to the Compute Engine VM instances page.
2. From there, select a particular instance.
3. At the top of the console page that displays your instance details, click the SSH button. This unlocks the instance and opens a terminal window where you are SSH'd into your machine.

Now that you are in the machine, you need to install the `container_exec` tool. Use the following commands, as shown in Listings 6-35 to 6-38:

1. `$ sudo -s`
2. `$ curl http://storage.googleapis.com/vmruntime-images/container_exec.tar.gz | tar xzv`
3. `$ mv nsenter /usr/bin/nsenter`
4. `$ mv container_exec.sh /usr/bin/container_exec`

The following listings 6-35 to 6-38 show the output from executing the previous commands in your Managed VM. We first connect to the VM using SSH. Making a connection is similar to connecting to a Compute Engine. The command template is "`gcloud compute ssh <vm-name>`"

```
Connected, host fingerprint: ssh-rsa 2048 28:16:9B:DB:3E:D1:C6:88:D0:53:CF:06:CF:B6:9B:2F
Linux gae-default-20150424t113250-n1n2 3.16.0-0.bpo.4-amd64 #1 SMP Debian 3.16.7-ckt4-3~bpo70+1
(2015-02-12) x86_64
The programs included with the Debian GNU/Linux system are free software;
the exact distribution terms for each program are described in the
individual files in /usr/share/doc/*/copyright.
Debian GNU/Linux comes with ABSOLUTELY NO WARRANTY, to the extent
permitted by applicable law.
```

Listing 6-35. Switching to the Root User so It Is Easier to Execute the Next Few Commands

```
cloudplatformbook_gmail_com@gae-default-20150424t113250-n1n2:~$ sudo -s
```

Listing 6-36. Downloading the `container_exec` Bundle from the Official Channel

```
root@gae-default-20150424t113250-n1n2:/home/cloudplatformbook_gmail_com# curl
 http://storage.googleapis.com/vmruntime-images/container_exec.tar.gz | tar xzv
  % Total    % Received % Xferd  Average Speed   Time    Time     Time  Current
                                 Dload  Upload   Total   Spent    Left  Speed
100 26430  100 26430    0     0  48789      0 --:--:-- --:--:-- --:--:-- 49494
./container_exec.sh
./nsenter
```

Listing 6-37. Moving the Binary `nsenter` to the `/usr/bin` Directory Because It Is Present in the `$PATH` Variable

```
root@gae-default-20150424t113250-n1n2:/home/cloudplatformbook_gmail_com#
mv nsenter /usr/bin/nsenter
```

Listing 6-38. Moving the Shell Script `container_exec` to the `/usr/bin` Directory Because It Is Present in the `$PATH` Variable

```
root@gae-default-20150424t113250-n1n2:/home/cloudplatformbook_gmail_com#
mv container_exec.sh /usr/bin/container_exec
```

After these required steps, the remaining steps are the same as for accessing the container in the development system: list the Docker processes, note the container ID, and connect to the container, debug, and exit. Listing 6-39 shows the command line and corresponding output in the Managed VM.

Listing 6-39. Listing the Docker Containers (or Processes) in the Live App Engine Environment

```
cloudplatformbook_gmail_com@gae-default-20150424t113250-n1n2:~$ sudo docker ps
CONTAINER ID  IMAGE  COMMAND  CREATED  STATUS  PORTS  NAMES
6ea42a4a608e  gcr.io/_m_383821482475384888/cloud-platform-book.default.
20150424t113250:latest   "/usr/bin/python2.7    3 hours ago         Up 3 hours
0.0.0.0:8080->8080/tcp   gaeapp

5c0bd2d9c78c  127.0.0.1:5000/google/appengine-fluentd-logger:1919c  "/opt/google-fluentd
3 hours ago
Up 3 hours  evil_sammet

29bc7b1dc60d  google/docker-registry:latest  "./run.sh"  3 hours ago
Up 3 hours  k8s_docker-registry.9e1bd80b_1.default.http  7b602a49

429f70421e42  google/cadvisor:0.7.1  "/usr/bin/cadvisor"  3 hours ago  Up 3 hours  k8s_
cadvisor.da4ae36d_
cadvisormanifes12uqn2ohido76855gdecd9roadm7l0.default.file_
cadvisormanifes12uqn2ohido76855gdecd9roadm7l0_80bb9a23

be5ea1d2c497  kubernetes/pause:go  "/pause"  3 hours ago  Up 3 hours
0.0.0.0:5000->5000/tcp   k8s_net.28539020_1.default.http_a022020d

030a5b5a0239  kubernetes/pause:go  "/pause"  3 hours ago  Up 3 hours
0.0.0.0:4194->8080/tcp  k8s_net.a0f18f6e_cadvisormanifes12uqn2ohido76855gdecd9roadm7l0.
default.file_
cadvisormanifes12uqn2ohido76855gdecd9roadm7l0_36f49bf1
```

This output shows six containers running in the Managed VM. Two observations can be made from this output: the Python application runs in the first container in the list, and the last two containers have the prefix `kubernetes`. This proves that App Engine Managed VMs are essentially a `Google`-managed, Kubernetes-orchestrated container cluster; whereas Container Engine is `user`-managed Kubernetes cluster. Let's connect to the live container and execute a few commands as shown in Listing 6-40 and Listing 6-41.

Listing 6-40. SSHing to the Application Container

```
cloudplatformbook_gmail_com@gae-default-20150424t113250-n1n2:~$ container_exec
6ea42a4a608e /bin/bash
Entering 6ea42a4a608e, pid 3259
```

Listing 6-41. Executing a Simple Command to List All Kernel Options

```
root@6ea42a4a608e:/# uname -a
Linux 6ea42a4a608e 3.16.0-0.bpo.4-amd64 #1 SMP Debian 3.16.7-ckt4-3~bpo70+1 (2015-02-12)
x86_64 GNU/Linux
```

Now that you have finished debugging the live VM, let's switch it back to being `Google`-managed so that the health checks can resume. This time, you use the `gcloud` command-line tool to switch the status, as shown in Listing 6-42 and Listing 6-43.

Listing 6-42. Listing the Modules in Your Application

```
VM:~/Projects/AppEngine/Sandbox/fortunespeak$ gcloud preview app modules list
MODULE   VERSION          IS_DEFAULT
default  20150424t113250  *
```

Listing 6-43. Switching the Module to google-managed

```
cloudplatformbook@VirtualBox:~/Projects/AppEngine/Sandbox/fortunespeak$ gcloud preview
app modules set-managed-by --version 20150424t113250 default --google
Changing state in progress.  Will try again in 1 seconds.
```

When this command is executed, App Engine discards the debugged VM and replaces it with a new VM. Hence, should you again switch the status of the VM to be `user-managed`, you have to reinstall the `container_exec` tool and redo the other modifications you performed earlier. For this reason, we recommend that that you keep the VM set to `user-managed` until you finish all the required debugging and then switch management back to App Engine. Finally, if you would like to switch the module to `user-managed` from the command line, replace the `--google` flag with `--self`.

Configuring a Managed VM

The Managed VMs runtime allows you to configure the runtime in several ways. These configuration options can be provided as part the configuration file—`app.yaml`, for example. The following list shows the major categories, after which we describe them:

- Runtime (standard vs. custom)
- Scaling (manual vs. automatic)
- Network setting
- Resource setting
- Health checking

The `vm` and `runtime` keywords together define the choice of the runtime: standard or custom. The following are the configuration key:value pairs:

```
runtime: <standard-runtime>
vm: true
```

or

```
runtime: custom
vm: true
```

As of this writing, the only valid `<standard-runtime>` options are python27 and go. You can also create a custom runtime, based off a standard runtime. Creating a custom runtime is an advanced topic and you may refer to the URL `https://cloud.google.com/appengine/docs/managed-vms/appengine/managed-vms/custom-runtimes` for more details.

Managed VMs support manual and automatic scaling. You can specify the scaling type, along with accompanying settings, in your module's configuration file. If you do not specify any scaling type in the configuration file, automatic scaling is used with the default settings of a minimum of two instances and 50% target CPU utilization. You can activate manual scaling using the following configuration stanza. Replace 2 with the desired number of instances:

```
manual_scaling:
  instances: 2
```

Automatic scaling has two required configuration parameters and two optional parameters. The required parameters are the minimum and maximum number of instances. The optional parameters are the cool-down period and target CPU utilization. Here's an example:

```
automatic_scaling:
  min_num_instances: 2
  max_num_instances: 20
  cool_down_period_sec: 60
  cpu_utilization:
    target_utilization: 0.5
```

In this case, the minimum number of instances is 2 and the maximum is 20. This means on deployment, the Managed VMs environment creates 2 containerized instances and, depending on the load, will scale up to a maximum of 20 instances. The technology behind the autoscaling technology used in Managed VMs is the same technology present in Compute Engine autoscaler. Note that the minimum number of instances in a Managed VM is 1, not 0 as in sandboxed environment. The cool-down period is the time interval between autoscaling checks; it must be greater than or equal to 60 seconds (the default value). This minimum value requirement means scaling changes may occur less frequently in a Managed VM versus a sandboxed hosting environment. Target CPU utilization is the CPU use averaged across all running instances and is used to decide when to reduce or increase the number of instances. This metric has a default value of 0.5.

The network configuration is in essence a firewall configuration for your application containers. You can specify that certain ports should forward from the Managed VM to your container. Forwarded ports can use the same port number on the Managed VM and the container or use different port numbers. You can add tags to all the container instances the system launches for this module—for example, during an autoscaling scale-out operation. The tags can be used to refer to this group of instances, such as during a firewall rule update. You can also apply these rules to a particular network by specifying its name in the configuration. The following is an example network-configuration stanza:

```
network:
  forwarded_ports:
  - 8081
  - 8082:8083
  instance:tag: <tag-name>
  name: <network-name>
```

In this example, two ports are forwarded: port 8081 is forwarded from the Managed VM to the container, and port 8082 is forwarded from the Managed VM to port 8083 in the container. If you do not specify a network name, VMs are assigned to the project's default network (which has the name `default`).

Resource settings control the computing resources for the instances of a module. The settings consist of three values: CPU, main memory size, and secondary storage size. CPU is a multiple of cores and can be less than 1 with a default value of 0.5. Main memory (aka RAM) and secondary storage (aka hard disk) are specified in gigabytes. The default value of RAM is 1.3GB, and the default for hard disk is 10GB. The hard disk size also has an upper bound of 10TB. App Engine assigns a machine type based on the amount of CPU and memory you've specified. The machine is guaranteed to have at least the level of resources you've specified; it might have more. The following is an example resource setting stanza:

```
resources:
  cpu: .5
  memory_gb: 1.3
  disk_size_gb: 10
```

The App Engine Managed VMs runtime sends periodic health-check requests to your VMs. Health checks are used to confirm that a VM instance has been successfully deployed and has a healthy status. Each health check must be answered in a specified time interval. An instance is unhealthy when it fails to respond to a specified number of consecutive health-check requests. An unhealthy instance does not receive any client requests, but health checks are still sent. If an unhealthy instance continues to fail to respond to a predetermined number of consecutive health checks, it is restarted. Health checks are enabled by default and use sensible default values. You can manually disable health checks, although we highly recommend that you don't. Recall that health checks also are automatically disabled when you switch the VM from `Google-managed` to `user-managed`.

You can customize VM health checking by adding an optional `health_check` section to your configuration file. Here is an example stanza:

```
health_check:
  enable_health_check: True
  check_interval_sec: 5
  timeout_sec: 4
  unhealthy_threshold: 2
  healthy_threshold: 2
  restart_threshold: 60
```

The elements of this configuration stanza are as follows:

- `enable_health_check`: Enables or disables the health check. The default value is `True`. To disable health checking, set it to `False`.
- `check_interval_sec`: Controls the time interval between checks. The default value is 5 seconds.
- `timeout_sec`: Controls the health-check timeout interval. The default value is 4 seconds.
- `unhealthy_threshold`: An instance is unhealthy after failing this number of consecutive checks. The default value is 2 checks.
- `healthy_threshold`: An unhealthy instance becomes healthy again after successfully responding to this number of consecutive checks. The default value is 2 checks.
- `restart_threshold`: Specifies the number of consecutive check failures that trigger a VM restart. The default value is 60 checks.

Summary

In this chapter, you learned about an important DevOps method—application containers—that is revolutionizing the entire software industry, not just Google. Application containers are seen as an important step forward in software engineering. Containers eliminate the inefficiencies associated with virtualization when used to host multiple operating systems on a single machine while at the same achieving the same end goal. Although containers, like virtualization, were invented decades ago, they were not easy to use until recently. Just as hardware-virtualization technologies in CPUs enabled the rapid adoption of virtualization, the standardization and easy-of-use provided by Docker have been the primary boost for the current excitement about application containers. Google, along with other tier-1 cloud providers, is making it easy for developers to package applications and deploy them at scale in the industry-leading Cloud platform.

This chapter began by describing the technology behind application containers, some of which were invented by Google and contributed back to the community as open source. Following this, you were introduced to the Docker product that is at the forefront of application containers. You learned about a shared container-orchestration technology called Kubernetes that was invented by Google and contributed to the community as open source. And you learned about two products from Cloud Platform called Container Engine and App Engine Managed VMs. Container Engine is the productization of the open source Kubernetes project and is the easiest way to build an orchestrated application that comprises several layers of containers interacting with each other. Managed VMs, on the other hand, provides a management layer on top of Compute Engine and lets you run App Engine applications. The App Engine applications are packaged as Docker containers. Managed VMs also uses the open source Kubernetes container-orchestration platform. In a nutshell, Container Engine provides an unmanaged container-orchestration platform that you can use to architect web-scale applications, whereas Managed VMs provides a managed container platform.

PART III

Google Cloud Platform - Storage Products

CHAPTER 7

Google Cloud SQL

Google Cloud SQL is a MySQL database service that is hosted on the Google Cloud Platform and fully managed by Google Inc. MySQL databases that are hosted on Cloud SQL can be accessed by applications hosted on Google Compute Engine, Google App Engine apps, and external applications and users outside of the Google Cloud Platform.

Cloud SQL offers top-of-the-line features required by large enterprise, small businesses, and startups alike. This list summarizes these features, and the following sections look at them in detail:

- Automatically encrypts stored Cloud SQL data
- Automatically encrypts in-transit Cloud SQL data inside Google's network
- Supports encrypted connections from external sources
- Requires explicit authorization of clients, and enforces deny-all-by-default
- Automatically performs synchronous/asynchronous replication of data to multiple Cloud Platform zones, to provide greater data durability
- Automatically fails over to slave instances to ensure greater availability of the database service
- Performs automated scheduled backups by default at no additional cost
- Easily restores from backups with point-in-time capability
- Supports databases up to 500GB in size
- Provides innovative on-demand availability of DB instances, resulting in reduced cost
- Guarantees 99.95% uptime SLA for Cloud SQL
- Provides a fully managed database server, including patch management and new version rollouts
- Hosts MySQL databases in US, Europe, or Asia
- Supports connections over IPv4 and IPv6
- ISO/IEC 27001 compliant

This chapter examines Cloud SQL—the managed MySQL database service from the Google Cloud Platform—in detail using an example-based approach. In the example, you deploy the Wordpress blogging software. You use all the salient features of Cloud SQL, such as secure network access to database instances, database replicas to other Cloud SQL instances, and external MySQL instances, to highlight some best practices in designing a scalable and reliable relational-database-based back end for your (web) applications.

Building a Reliable MySQL Back End with Cloud SQL

In this section, you configure and create a Cloud SQL instance and access the MySQL database using a MySQL client from both inside and outside of the Google Cloud Platform. You exclusively use the Google Cloud SDK and associated gcloud command-line interface (CLI) tool and learn all the commands progressively. The examples have been tested using the Google Cloud SDK installed on a Mac and should work identically on other Cloud SDK–supported platforms. If you have not done so, install the Google Cloud SDK from https://cloud.google.com/sdk. Refer to chapter 2 for more details.

All the Cloud SQL commands in the Cloud SDK CLI tool use the following structure:

```
$ gcloud sql <...>
```

You can use the --help option at any level to learn about the options at that level:

```
$ gcloud sql [<...>] --help
```

Creating a Cloud SQL Instance

Before you begin creating the instance, let's determine whether any Cloud SQL instances have already been launched. To do so, you use the instances list option as follows:

```
$ gcloud sql instances list
NAME  REGION  TIER  ADDRESS  STATUS
Listed 0 items.
```

Let's create a Cloud SQL instance using the CLI tool. For this, you add the instances create suffix option to the gcloud sql base command prefix (see Listing 7-1) and declare the essential details as shown in Listing 7-2. Leave all the options at their default values. This command takes a few moments to configure, create, and launch the database instance. While the database is being created, you may see a spinning cursor; this is due to the synchronous nature of the gcloud CLI tool.

Listing 7-1. Command Template to Create an Instance

```
$ gcloud sql instances create YOUR_INSTANCE_NAME
```

■ **Note** Some of "gcloud" command-line tool argument list and output string is longer than what fits a single line. We have manually split such long lines into two or more lines for ease of reading throughout this chapter. For input argument list we have added a " \" at the end of list just like with traditional bash shell inputs. You can ignore these two characters and input the two lines as a single continuous line in your console. For return values we have split them at ".../cloud-platform-book/" part (if applicable) or at another white space of the output.

Listing 7-2. Actual Execution to Create an Instance with Default Values

```
$ gcloud sql instances create us-wordpress
Creating Cloud SQL instance...done.
Created [https://www.googleapis.com/sql/v1beta3/projects/cloud-platform-book/
instances/us-wordpress].
NAME          REGION      TIER  ADDRESS  STATUS
us-wordpress  us-central  D1    -        RUNNABLE
```

The instance name that you provide is automatically prefixed with the project name and the Google Apps domain name (if applicable), as shown here:

```
Non-domain: YOUR_PROJECT_NAME:YOUR_INSTANCE_NAME
Domain-specific: YOUR_DOMAIN:YOUR_PROJECT_NAME:YOUR_INSTANCE_NAME
```

In this command, you provided the name for the Cloud SQL instance, and the gcloud utility intelligently filled in the details for other essential parameters. Specifically, it chose the size of the database and the region where the database was created. If you wanted the database instance to be located elsewhere or to be a different size, then you can specify them during the instance creation. In order to specify the values, you need to know all the permissible values. You can also find the values using the gcloud CLI tool, as shown in Listing 7-3.

Listing 7-3. Listing the Database Sizes Available from Cloud SQL

```
$ gcloud sql tiers list
TIER  AVAILABLE_REGIONS                          RAM     DISK
D0    us-central, europe-west1, asia-east1  128 MB  250 GB
D1    us-central, europe-west1, asia-east1  512 MB  250 GB
D2    us-central, europe-west1, asia-east1  1 GB    250 GB
D4    us-central, europe-west1, asia-east1  2 GB    250 GB
D8    us-central, europe-west1, asia-east1  4 GB    250 GB
D16   us-central, europe-west1, asia-east1  8 GB    250 GB
D32   us-central, europe-west1, asia-east1  16 GB   250 GB
```

Note that Google constantly adds new products to the Cloud Platform and upgrades existing ones. Hence, when you run this command, your output may look different.

Using these this values, you can now create a D2 instance in the Asian region using the following command:

```
$ gcloud sql instances create asia-wordpress --tier D2 --region asia-east1
Creating Cloud SQL instance...done.
Created [https://www.googleapis.com/sql/v1beta3/projects/cloud-platform-book/
instances/asia-wordpress].
NAME            REGION      TIER  ADDRESS  STATUS
asia-wordpress  asia-east1  D2    -        RUNNABLE

$ gcloud sql instances list
NAME            REGION      TIER  ADDRESS  STATUS
asia-wordpress  asia-east1  D2    -        RUNNABLE
us-wordpress    us-central  D1    -        RUNNABLE
```

The instance-creation command has additional options that you can use to further customize the Cloud SQL instance. You can view all the possible options and their permitted values by using the following command:

```
$ gcloud sql instances create --help
```

At this stage, you have created a Cloud SQL instance of your desired size and in your desired region. However, you can't connect to it yet. This is because you need to perform three requisite steps for external connectivity: assigned an IP address to the instance, set a root password, and add the IP address to the authorized list. Listing 7-4 performs these steps using the corresponding options in the `gcloud sql` CLI tool and then connects to the instance using the MySQL client tool. Using the Cloud SQL `instances patch` command, you can modify an existing instance.

Setting Up Access to Cloud SQL Instance

Listing 7-4. Assigning an IPv4 Address to the Cloud SQL Instance

```
$ gcloud sql instances patch asia-wordpress --assign-ip
The following message will be used for the patch API method.
{"project": "cloud-platform-book", "instance": "asia-wordpress", "settings":
{"ipConfiguration":
{"enabled": true}}}
Patching Cloud SQL instance...done.
Updated [https://www.googleapis.com/sql/v1beta3/projects/cloud-platform-book/
instances/asia-wordpress].

$ gcloud sql instances list
NAME            REGION       TIER  ADDRESS          STATUS
asia-wordpress  asia-east1   D2    173.194.240.58   RUNNABLE
us-wordpress    us-central   D1    -                RUNNABLE
```

From this output, you can see that you have successfully assigned an IPv4 address to your Cloud SQL instance. Note that it currently is not possible to reserve a static IP address and assign it to a Cloud SQL database. Also, you have to explicitly state whether you need an IPv4 address; every Cloud SQL instance gets an IPv6 address free of charge, whereas you will be charged for an unused IPv4 IP address. You can see the IPv6 address assigned to your instance by using the `describe` option and filtering the output to extract the required detail:

```
$ gcloud sql instances describe asia-wordpress | grep ipv6Address
ipv6Address: 2001:4860:4864:1:d7e1:541b:e80a:43fe
```

The next step is to assign the IP address to the authorized list of IP addresses for your Cloud SQL instance. You need to determine your current externally visible IP address for this purpose. There are many ways to do this, such as visiting a web site like `www.whatismyip.com`. (This requires a graphical environment that may not always be available.) Listing 7-5 and Listing 7-6 use the free online service to determine your externally visible IP address and add it to the authorized list for your Cloud SQL instance in the Asian region.

Listing 7-5. Finding Your Current IP Address in a Unix/Linux Environment

```
$ curl bot.whatismyipaddress.com
103.224.116.114 <snip>
```

Listing 7-6. Updating the Instance and Granting Access to Your IP Address

```
$ gcloud sql instances patch asia-wordpress --authorized-networks 103.224.116.114
The following message will be used for the patch API method.
{"project": "cloud-platform-book", "instance": "asia-wordpress",
"settings": {"ipConfiguration": {"authorizedNetworks": ["103.224.116.114"]}}}
Patching Cloud SQL instance...done.
Updated [https://www.googleapis.com/sql/v1beta3/projects/cloud-platform-book/
instances/asia-wordpress].
```

In this case, it is possible to specify a range of IP addresses using CIDR notation. For example, you could add all of your organization's possible external-visible IP addresses, in case the next connection to the Cloud Platform was routed through a different IP address.

Cloud SQL can also be used as the relational database back end for applications running on Google App Engine. Because the App Engine platform is a platform-as-a-service, there is no specific Internet-visible IP address for each application. Hence, you cannot use the `--add-authorized-network` option to whitelist an App Engine application. Instead, Cloud SQL provides a dedicated option to whitelist an App Engine application. You can use the `patch` command to grant access to each App Engine application `gae-app-name` that needs to access the Cloud SQL instance. Here is the command template:

```
$ gcloud sql instances patch YOUR_INSTANCE_NAME --authorized-gae-apps GAE_APP_NAME
```

One final and essential step is to set the root password of the Cloud SQL instance. This can be done using the `set-root-password` option to the master `gcloud` command. There are two variations to this command. In the first variation, you provide the password as part of the command invocation, as follows:

```
$ gcloud sql instances set-root-password asia-wordpress --password 'password'
Setting Cloud SQL instance password...done.
Set password for [https://www.googleapis.com/sql/v1beta3/projects/cloud-platform-book/
instances/asia-wordpress].
```

For two major reasons, both Google and the authors of this book discourage this method. First, the password is visible on the screen, which may lead to password theft via shoulder surfing. Second, at least on Linux and Unix systems, all commands entered in a shell are automatically stored in a history archive file. This history file can be accessed by other system users, such as super users, resulting in possible divulgence of the password.

For this chapter's example, use the second variation of the command, where you provide the password stored in a local file:

```
$ gcloud sql instances set-root-password asia-wordpress --password-file password.txt
Setting Cloud SQL instance password...done.
Set password for [https://www.googleapis.com/sql/v1beta3/projects/cloud-platform-book/
instances/asia-wordpress].
```

After setting the root password of the Cloud SQL instance, you should consider deleting the local password file to increase the confidentiality of the root password. One option that is not available for this command is interactive prompting for a password at the command line. This option is not present because the gcloud CLI tool is a non-interactive tool by design. There are some minor exceptions where the tool is interactive, but it does not accept arbitrary input even in those cases.

Connecting to your Cloud SQL Instance

Next, let's connect to the Cloud SQL instance using the standard MySQL client. Depending on the platform you are on, you may need to follow a different process to install the MySQL client. Listing 7-7 and Listing 7-8 provide examples of how to install the MySQL client on a Debian or Debian-based system like Ubuntu, or Mac OS X, respectively. Visit www.mysql.com for details on other platforms. Listing 7-9 connects to the Cloud SQL instance.

Listing 7-7. Installing MySQL on Debian or Debian-Based Systems

```
$ sudo apt-get get update
$ sudo apt-get install mysql-client
```

Listing 7-8. Installing MySQL on Mac OS X (Yosemite) Using MacPorts

```
$ sudo port install mysql56
$ PATH=$PATH:/opt/local/lib/mysql56/bin
```

Listing 7-9. Connecting to the Cloud SQL Instance Using the MySQL CLI

```
$ mysql -h 173.194.240.58 -u root -p
Enter password:
Welcome to the MySQL monitor.  Commands end with ; or \g.
Your MySQL connection id is 41
Server version: 5.5.38 (Google)
<snip>
Type 'help;' or '\h' for help. Type '\c' to clear the current input statement.

mysql> show databases;
+--------------------+
| Database           |
+--------------------+
| information_schema |
| mysql              |
| performance:schema |
+--------------------+
3 rows in set (0.11 sec)

mysql>
```

With the completion of these steps, you have a functioning and accessible Cloud SQL–hosted MySQL database instance. This is the minimum configuration required in order for applications to access databases. If an application is hosted within Google Cloud, such as on Compute Engine or App Engine, then this setup is sufficient. However, if the database instance is accessed from the public Internet, then you need to address a security shortcoming. The shortcoming is in the communication stream between client and server, which is unencrypted although authenticated. In the previous example, if the user was using an eavesdrop-able network, such as an open Wi-Fi network, a malicious man-in-the-middle could learn the root password that was set.

Securing Access to your Cloud SQL Instance

Let's look at how to turn on secure communication for Cloud SQL and use it to communicate from your MySQL client to the Cloud SQL–hosted MySQL database. The following are the major steps in sequential order to create a SSL connection to Cloud SQL:

1. Create a cryptographic key pair.
2. Download the public key certificate.
3. Download the CA signing certificate.

The command shown in Listing 7-10 generates a cryptographic key pair comprising private and public keys. Here is the generic version of the command:

```
$ gcloud sql ssl-certs --instance YOUR_INSTANCE_NAME create CERT_NAME CERT_FILE
```

Listing 7-10. Creating an SSL Certificate Using the `gcloud` CLI Tool

```
$ gcloud sql ssl-certs --instance asia-wordpress create asia-wordpress-cert \
asia-wordpress-client-key.pem
```

The private key is stored in the `CERT_FILE` in the local system and is never uploaded to Cloud SQL. Hence, if you lose this private key, you have to create a new certificate. The public key is automatically uploaded to Cloud SQL. A private certification authority (CA) that is internal to the Google Cloud Platform then signs the public key and generates a public key certificate. You can retrieve the server public key certificate you just created with the `ssl-certs describe` command:

```
$ gcloud sql ssl-certs --instance asia-wordpress describe asia-wordpress-cert
cert: |-
  -----BEGIN CERTIFICATE-----
  MIIDPzCCAiegAwIBAgIEWSZxFzANBgkqhkiG9w0BAQUFADBcMTcwNQYDVQQDEy5H
  b29nbGUgQ2xvdWQgU1FMIENsaWVudCBDQSBhc2lhLXdvcmRwcmVzcy1jZXJ0MRQw
  EgYDVQQKEwtHb29nbGUsIEluYzELMAkGA1UEBhMCVVMwHhcNMTUwMjE3MDA0MDQ4
  WhcNMTcwMjE2MDA0MDQ4WjBBMRwwGgYDVQQDExNhc2lhLXdvcmRwcmVzcy1jZXJ0
  MRQwEgYDVQQKEwtHb29nbGUsIEluYzELMAkGA1UEBhMCVVMwggEiMA0GCSqGSIb3
  DQEBAQUAA4IBDwAwggEKAoIBAQDGuNlOGDbZe81QImeAaGbtqGF1Mno5C9Vqe5uJ
  qhLN9vCFlzior9nhN7yiYyyGqDK3RAmybuHFh812CCYKEJ6gayoyssJdzTIY35ne
  u3ibKamMns+/bfxz7JNuWQRJIzXpI2R5xtVZdBmfum+N2JIimhjTUOLJO3nplfq1
  6TetVw28XJDRBBxngoCvkn6W4oE1gqTnisOgefyJVgCb8deTzGKmOjYogQ/SGUFc
  tHewFD6ylzWsa8vtEaNu2emJnZY+yQAtdHHCFcSuPSvnOU82TfPVQK8ghp5KTdkS
  D4jFTgkLH+b6skdaOxh5jYpuCOyuasGPiNgxst7m2RnAaOfDAgMBAAGjJDAiMCAG
  A1UdEQQZMBeBFXNwdGtyaXNobmFuQGdtYWlsLmNvbTANBgkqhkiG9w0BAQUFAAOC
  AQEARI5NTmkiO/L932rvxemhPmuZwWRzRSMTOFVfDKDpgYgwuCMlIj4G3eoAaYyc
  KdERstJrnzcy9rYwx1CAIRC3Q2ViZ47WCsfB4+NEzxjBmqJJ5Uulj/flDd75G59r
  zmO6OTBM8wwEn3z9e6oLtbulWvXx1d9CvjnT3NvFq2Gc4P6hH2Gb8z+9CPzi7OoV
  eOv/IP/w1fN4jLVO+oF8j5HaXJAV9+MzR32xJtHIwJJWUJj+JjOnuXik7sIMWWbO
  KiKJSwwZMJkoao7q1ctHjGLkc1W6kH9fTr8rO8ZmG/SDdlHu5WlS4VAicU57BTeO
  SsFk1C3SUqjgATkF31Pdg23g3Q==
  -----END CERTIFICATE-----
certSerialNumber: '1495691543'
commonName: asia-wordpress-cert
createTime: '2015-02-17T00:40:48.646000+00:00'
```

```
expirationTime: '2017-02-16T00:40:48.646000+00:00'
instance: asia-wordpress
kind: sql#sslCert
sha1Fingerprint: dfc029254af708477e8477e200afb9f18827c395
```

From this console output, save the contents between the comments `-----BEGIN CERTIFICATE-----` and `-----END CERTIFICATE-----`, including the comments, into a file named `asia-wordpress-client-cert.pem`. The generic version of this command is as follows:

```
$ gcloud sql ssl-certs --instance YOUR_INSTANCE_NAME describe CERT_NAME
```

The final step in the securing process is to download the Cloud SQL Server CA signing certificate. You extract the Server CA certificate from the console output of the `describe` command for the Cloud SQL instance. The following example extracts the Server CA certificate for the `asia-wordpress` instance using the bash shell command grep and the Unix pipe. The option `-A NUM` extracts `NUM` number of lines following the matching line. Here, 27 is an invocation-specific number that extracts all the details about the certificate:

```
$ gcloud sql instances describe asia-wordpress | grep -A 27 serverCaCert
serverCaCert:
  cert: |-
    -----BEGIN CERTIFICATE-----
```

```
    MIIDITCCAgmgAwIBAgIBADANBgkqhkiG9w0BAQUFADBIMSMwIQYDVQQDExpHb29n
    bGUgQ2xvdWQgU1FMIFNlcnZlciBDQTEUMBIGA1UEChMLR29vZ2xlLCBJbmMxCzAJ
    BgNVBAYTAlVTMB4XDTE1MDIxNjA5NDgyNFoXDTE3MDIxNTA5NDgyNFowSDEjMCEG
    A1UEAxMaR29vZ2xlIENsb3VkIFNRTCBTZXJ2ZXIgQ0ExFDASBgNVBAoTC0dvb2ds
    ZSwgSW5jMQswCQYDVQQGEwJVUzCCASIwDQYJKoZIhvcNAQEBBQADggEPADCCAQoC
    ggEBAInjqsXrTe6ASnf+8lWgQCuIA4A6PlP4xHGUJO4CZRq0ECOotCnjwZfrEMOb
    28dP9EZE63yVbFEiPdAmuLeOElwcEU/Lga9FMOFl+mitTqdDm1Ygpc3iPXIacvNB
    vuTkSTeESwn2XSusMhjKBgbZa+zpTbf34ALZgBWwQc/3dJe3Qe24x7AgRjXWge8v
    okWOJIpd5vx9aEDHBUvPgFz/IhJUmzO9GNqyUx+ZoDU/Pw3DlGuoW7gHEEHepLZM
    IVq+N5jwl9vsOOyDXl/r9LHMPRkIOuzVQuw7rIvs5yn4pjw6J+6XUa2U1FxHzHQc
    rLcFOf7+pbNm7dKCNeiDfC68EC8CAwEAAaMWMBQwEgYDVR0TAQH/BAgwBgEB/wIB
    ADANBgkqhkiG9w0BAQUFAAOCAQEAYw5XOLWc1maEX9tz/kSkHWtFBXJPWDGu9XSL
    +1Nt4kOnKJdMbuvN5Oovf+p5NWnjvcEMRWKrKoBBtUWAcPrVOe3Ob6hz6geqmqzZ
    tpoZ9/nrv4ctmz1EOgAr8zP3ehKytB3veRp656l54Pp6S7y7sxpKa5TXVYdzhae1
    zlt8cTVmthdCafMyWiHbp53OPM4FeNLNtTKP/puF1yjQvWFG1PfLzNvu6XAxm9JP
    33zb/xxw5GxrvCMqria9eGh/ilSsi1SCzFeOKYDy8rGh7EQzTXYsb69g3GwEhfgJ
    AMq/2fpixWdGijt/RBgrapyVCjeMwg58zGxuhFDOxt2OOlmnQA==
```

```
    -----END CERTIFICATE-----
  certSerialNumber: '0'
  commonName: C=US,O=Google\, Inc,CN=Google Cloud SQL Server CA
  createTime: '2015-02-16T09:48:24.777000+00:00'
  expirationTime: '2017-02-15T09:48:24.777000+00:00'
  instance: asia-wordpress
  kind: sql#sslCert
  sha1Fingerprint: 198761169f1a0b07fb6bd4b53086a15eb4a54950
```

From this console output, save the contents between `-----BEGIN CERTIFICATE-----` and `-----END CERTIFICATE-----`, including these two lines, in a file named `asia-wordpress-ca-cert.pem`. You can choose any filenames for the three files as long as you can remember which file contains what information. As a rule of thumb, we suggest the following convention for naming the three files created in this step: `INSTANCE_NAME-{client/ca}-{key/cert}.pem`.

Finally, you need to restart the Cloud SQL instance to enable the certificate and to start using encrypted communication between the database instance and clients:

```
$ gcloud sql instances restart asia-wordpress
Restarting Cloud SQL instance...done.
Restarted [https://www.googleapis.com/sql/v1beta3/projects/cloud-platform-book/
instances/asia-wordpress].
```

Now let's use the MySQL CLI client tool and connect to the Cloud SQL instance securely. Listing 7-11 gives the command template, and Listing 7-12 provides an example linked to the `asia-wordpress` Cloud SQL instance to show the interaction.

Listing 7-11. Command Template to Connect Securely to a MySQL Server Instance

```
$ mysql --ssl-ca=ca-cert.pem --ssl-cert=client-cert.pem --ssl-key=client-key.pem \
--host=instance-IP --user=user-name --password
```

Listing 7-12. Example Using the Template in Listing 7-11

```
$ mysql --ssl-ca=asia-wordpress-ca-cert.pem --ssl-cert=asia-wordpress-client-cert.pem \
--ssl-key=asia-wordpress-client-key.pem --host=173.194.240.58 --user=root --password
Enter password:
Welcome to the MySQL monitor.  Commands end with ; or \g.
Your MySQL connection id is 14
Server version: 5.5.38 (Google)

Copyright (c) 2000, 2015, Oracle and/or its affiliates. All rights reserved.

Oracle is a registered trademark of Oracle Corporation and/or its
affiliates. Other names may be trademarks of their respective
owners.

Type 'help;' or '\h' for help. Type '\c' to clear the current input statement.

mysql> show databases;
+--------------------+
| Database           |
+--------------------+
| information_schema |
| mysql              |
| performance:schema |
+--------------------+
3 rows in set (0.06 sec)

mysql> quit
 Bye
```

If you are using another SQL client, check its documentation to see whether it supports SQL communication over SSL. The following tools are known to support SQL over SSL:

- MySQL workbench (www.mysql.com/products/workbench)
- Toad for MySQL (http://software.dell.com/products/toad-for-mysql)
- Squirrel SQL (http://squirrel-sql.sourceforge.net)

We would also like to highlight here that connections between Cloud SQL and App Engine are always encrypted. Therefore you do not need to create client certificates for them.

You have now met the objective of this section: you have configured and deployed a Cloud SQL database instance and accessed it securely over the network. However, before concluding the section, we want to emphasize that many of the commands you have learned can be consolidated into a single command. Listing 7-13 shows the template for this amalgamated approach, and Listing 7-14 deploys a Cloud SQL instance in Europe.

Listing 7-13. Amalgamated Template for Creating a Cloud SQL Instance

```
$ gcloud sql instances create YOUR_INSTANCE_NAME \
--tier TIER \
--region REGION \
--pricing-plan PRICING_PLAN \
--assign-ip \
--authorised-networks SOURCE_IPs
```

Listing 7-14. One-Step Command to Create a Cloud SQL Instance in the European Union

```
$ gcloud sql instances create europe-wordpress --tier D4 --region europe-west1 \
--pricing-plan PACKAGE --assign-ip --authorized-networks 103.224.116.114
Charges will begin accruing immediately. Really create Cloud SQL
instance?

Do you want to continue (Y/n)?  Y

Creating Cloud SQL instance...done.
Created [https://www.googleapis.com/sql/v1beta3/projects/cloud-platform-book/
instances/europe-wordpress].
NAME              REGION        TIER  ADDRESS        STATUS
europe-wordpress  europe-west1  D4    173.194.81.27  RUNNABLE
```

The rest of the steps for creating a root password and setting up a secure communication channel is the same as described earlier and is not repeated here.

Building a Scalable MySQL Cluster with Cloud SQL

The objective of this section is to scale out your database setup and to add read capacity in the process. This is achieved by creating what is called a *read replica* in database server terminology. In simple words, you create a read-only copy of the master database, referred to as *slave database*. The master and slave databases are synchronized on every write update. Applications that are read-heavy on databases can read from either master or slave databases. If the databases are replicated in sync mode, the response will be the same; however, there may be a very short delay if the databases are replicated using an async method.

In Cloud SQL, both the master database instance and the read replica (the slave database) should reside in the same geographical zone. This requirement ensures that the (synchronous) replication is in the sub-millisecond range and that thus the state of the databases is always the same.

In this section, you create a read replica of a master MySQL database and host it in Cloud SQL. You use the popular Wordpress web application and link it to the Cloud SQL database. Following are the high-level steps required to set up a MySQL database read replica in Cloud SQL:

1. Enable database backups.
2. Enable binary logs in the master instance.
3. Wait for at least one backup to complete.
4. Create a Cloud SQL read replica.

Let's try these steps. In each case, we show the command template followed by an example usage.

Step 1: Checking and Enabling (If Required) Database Backups

Step 1 begins by listing the Cloud SQL instance properties, as shown in Listing 7-15 and Listing 7-16.

Listing 7-15. gcloud Command Template to List SQL Instance Properties

```
$ gcloud sql instances describe YOUR_INSTANCE_NAME
```

Listing 7-16. Actual Command Execution to List SQL Instance Properties

```
$ gcloud sql instances describe asia-wordpress | grep -A 5 'backupConfiguration:'
backupConfiguration:
  - binaryLogEnabled: false
    enabled: false
    id: 75bd1d5d-1a04-4ee7-8ae7-e409c9e8a212
    kind: sql#backupConfiguration
    startTime: 00:00
```

From this console output, you can see that backups are currently disabled. Let's proceed to enable backups; see Listing 7-17 and Listing 7-18. Simply setting the backup start time enables Cloud SQL backups. Once this is done, you list the property again and confirm that backups are indeed enabled.

Listing 7-17. gcloud Command Template to Enable Database Backups

```
$ gcloud sql instances patch YOUR_INSTANCE_NAME --backup-start-time HH:MM
```

Listing 7-18. Actual Command Execution to Enable Database Backups for the Instance

```
$ gcloud sql instances patch asia-wordpress --backup-start-time 13:00
The following message will be used for the patch API method.
{"project": "cloud-platform-book", "instance": "asia-wordpress", "settings":
{"backupConfiguration": [{"kind": "sql#backupConfiguration", "enabled": true,
"id": "75bd1d5d-1a04-4ee7-8ae7-e409c9e8a212", "startTime": "13:00", "binaryLogEnabled": false}]}}
Patching Cloud SQL instance...done.
Updated [https://www.googleapis.com/sql/v1beta3/projects/cloud-platform-book/
instances/asia-wordpress].
```

Rerun the query to list the SQL instance properties. From the following console output, you can see that backups have indeed been enabled and are scheduled to start at 13:00 in the GMT time zone:

```
$ gcloud sql instances describe asia-wordpress | grep -A 5 'backupConfiguration:'
backupConfiguration:
  - binaryLogEnabled: false
    enabled: true
    id: 75bd1d5d-1a04-4ee7-8ae7-e409c9e8a212
    kind: sql#backupConfiguration
    startTime: '13:00'
```

Step 2: Checking and Enabling (If Required) Binary Logs in the Master Instance

The console output in Listing 7-19 shows that binary logs are disabled.

Listing 7-19. Checking Binary Logs in the Master Instance

```
$ gcloud sql instances describe asia-wordpress | grep binaryLogEnabled
- binaryLogEnabled: false
```

Enable the binary log for this instance, and verify that it has been enabled:

```
$ gcloud sql instances patch --enable-bin-log asia-wordpress
The following message will be used for the patch API method.
{"project": "cloud-platform-book", "instance": "asia-wordpress", "settings":
{"backupConfiguration": [{"kind": "sql#backupConfiguration", "enabled": true,
"id": "75bd1d5d-1a04-4ee7-8ae7-e409c9e8a212", "startTime": "13:00", "binaryLogEnabled": true}]}}
Patching Cloud SQL instance...done.
Updated [https://www.googleapis.com/sql/v1beta3/projects/cloud-platform-book/
instances/asia-wordpress].
$ gcloud sql instances describe asia-wordpress | grep binaryLogEnabled
- binaryLogEnabled: true
```

Step 3: Waiting for a Database Backup to Be Available

Next, check whether at least one backup has been completed since the creation of the Cloud SQL database instance; see Listing 7-20. After enabling database backups, you may have to wait up to 24 hours for a backup to be created by Cloud SQL. You can shorten this time period by selecting the closest 4-hour time window to your time zone. Remember, the time zone is always listed in local time; you may have to convert to a central time zone if you have Cloud SQL instances in multiple zones.

Listing 7-20. Checking for a Database Backup

```
$ gcloud sql backups --instance asia-wordpress list
DUE_TIME                          ERROR  STATUS
2015-02-17T13:00:00.198000+00:00  -      SUCCESSFUL
```

You can see more details about the backup by using the `describe` option as shown in Listing 7-21 and Listing 7-22.

Listing 7-21. gcloud Command Template to Describe a Database Backup

```
$ gcloud sql backups --instance YOUR_INSTANCE_NAME describe DUE_TIME
```

Listing 7-22. Actual Execution of the Command to Describe a Database Backup

```
$ gcloud sql backups --instance asia-wordpress describe 2015-02-17T13:00:00.198000+00:00
backupConfiguration: 75bd1d5d-1a04-4ee7-8ae7-e409c9e8a212
dueTime: '2015-02-17T13:00:00.198000+00:00'
endTime: '2015-02-17T15:03:25.315000+00:00'
enqueuedTime: '2015-02-17T15:03:03.655000+00:00'
instance: asia-wordpress
kind: sql#backupRun
startTime: '2015-02-17T15:03:03.656000+00:00'
status: SUCCESSFUL
```

Because there is at least one backup, you can move to the next step of creating a read replica.

Step 4: Creating a Cloud SQL Read Replica

Having satisfied all the prerequisite steps, you can create a read replica of your master Cloud SQL database instance. Listing 7-23 gives the command template, and Listing 7-24 instantiates the command and executes it for the asia-wordpress Cloud SQL instance.

Listing 7-23. gcloud Command Template to Create a Read Replica of a Cloud SQL MySQL Database

```
$ gcloud sql instances create READ_REPLICA_NAME --master-instance-name MASTER_INSTANCE_NAME
```

Listing 7-24. Actual Execution of the Command to Create a Read Replica

```
$ gcloud sql instances create asia-wordpress-replica --master-instance-name asia-wordpress \
--region asia-east1
Creating Cloud SQL instance...done.
Created [https://www.googleapis.com/sql/v1beta3/projects/cloud-platform-book/
instances/asia-wordpress-replica].
NAME                    REGION      TIER  ADDRESS  STATUS
asia-wordpress-replica  asia-east1  D1    -        RUNNABLE
```

Listing 7-25 and Listing 7-26 list the relevant properties of both the master and replica Cloud SQL instances to ensure that replication has been set up as desired.

Listing 7-25. Relevant Properties of the Read Replica Instance

```
$ gcloud sql instances describe asia-wordpress-replica | grep databaseReplicationEnabled
databaseReplicationEnabled: true
$ gcloud sql instances describe asia-wordpress-replica | grep masterInstanceName
masterInstanceName: cloud-platform-book:asia-wordpress
```

Listing 7-26. Relevant Properties of the Master Instance

```
$ gcloud sql instances describe asia-wordpress | grep -A 1 replicaNames
replicaNames:
- asia-wordpress-replica
```

This console output shows that the database replication succeeded. More important, the command syntax for creating a read replica is the same as that for creating a regular Cloud SQL instance, with the minor addition of specifying an additional option: `--master-instance-name`. This shows the ease with which you can set up a read replica in Cloud SQL.

Setting Up WordPress CMS with Cloud SQL as Backend

Next, let's set up the popular Wordpress web application, which uses Cloud SQL as its MySQL database back end. To do this, you set up two Linux instances and install Wordpress in each of them. One Wordpress installation will be linked to the master MySQL database hosted in Cloud SQL, and the second Wordpress installation will be linked to the Cloud SQL hosted read replica. Your objective is to focus on configuring connectivity between the application and the database.

This example uses Google Compute Engine—the infrastructure-as-a-service from the Google Cloud Platform—to create two Linux-based instances. Both Compute Engine instances are installed with the Debian distribution of Linux. You can use any Linux distribution and host the servers anywhere on Internet; just make sure you add the Internet-visible IP address of the Linux instance to the Cloud SQL instance's authorized network. Call these instances `master` and `slave`. We leave out the Compute Engine–specific details for brevity and ask you to refer to chapter 4 "Google Compute Engine" in this book for a detailed introduction to the topic.

Let's assume that you have created two Compute Engine instances, using either the `gcloud` CLI tool or the Developers Console. Following are the Compute Engine instances we created for this example:

```
$ gcloud compute instances list
NAME                  ZONE          MACHINE_TYPE  INTERNAL_IP    EXTERNAL_IP     STATUS
asia-wordpress-slave  asia-east1-b n1-standard-1 10.240.224.131 130.211.246.208 RUNNING
asia-wordpress-master asia-east1-b n1-standard-1 10.240.101.162 107.167.191.27  RUNNING
```

Log in via SSH to the master instance, and update the system software (see Listing 7-27) and Apache web server (see Listing 7-28). $ refers to shell commands executed on the client workstation, and `VM$` refers to shell commands executed on the remote Compute Engine VMs:

```
$ gcloud compute ssh asia-wordpress-master --zone asia-east1-b
```

Listing 7-27. Initialization Commands to Update the System Software Packages

```
VM$ sudo apt-get update
VM$ sudo apt-get upgrade
VM$ sudo reboot
```

Listing 7-28. Setting Up Apache Web Server and Associated Packages

```
VM$ sudo apt-get install apache2
VM$ sudo apt-get install php5 php-pear php5-mysql
```

Next, install the latest stable version of the Wordpress software directly from the `http://wordpress.org` SVN software repository (see Listing 7-29). In order to do this, you first need to install the subversion client software in your VM:

```
VM$ sudo apt-get install subversion
<snip>
```

Listing 7-29. Setting Up Wordpress on a Debian System

```
VM$ cd /var/www
VM$ sudo -s
VM$ sudo mkdir wordpresss
VM# chown www-data:www-data ./wordpress
VM# su - www-data
VM$ bash
VM$ cd /var/www/wordpress
VM$ svn co https://core.svn.wordpress.org/tags/4.1 .
<snip>
```

You now have Wordpress installed under the `/var/www/wordpress` directory on the master VM. Wordpress is not configured, though—specifically, it is not linked to Cloud SQL. Do that next, as shown in Listing 7-30. Alternatively, you can create the database using the `gcloud` console tool or the Developers Console.

Listing 7-30. Creating a Database Using the MySQL Client in the Cloud SQL Instance

```
$ mysql --ssl-ca=asia-wordpress-ca-cert.pem --ssl-cert=asia-wordpress-client-cert.pem \
--ssl-key=asia-wordpress-client-key.pem --host=173.194.240.58 --user=root --password
Enter password:
<snip>

mysql> CREATE DATABASE wordpress;
Query OK, 1 row affected (0.19 sec)

mysql> CREATE USER 'wordpress'@'%' IDENTIFIED BY 'lk8skdks';
Query OK, 0 rows affected (0.09 sec)

mysql> GRANT ALL ON wordpress.* TO 'wordpress'@'%';
Query OK, 0 rows affected (0.13 sec)
```

Use your favorite editor to edit the `wp-config.php` file and update the essential information: host, username, password, and database. Listing 7-31 and Listing 7-32 show the relevant sections of the file before and after the changes required.

Listing 7-31. Relevant Part of `wp-config.php` Before Changes in the Master Compute Engine Instance

```
// ** MySQL settings - You can get this info from your web host ** //
/** The name of the database for WordPress */
define('DB_NAME', 'database_name_here');

/** MySQL database username */
define('DB_USER', 'username_here');
```

```
/** MySQL database password */
define('DB_PASSWORD', 'password_here');

/** MySQL hostname */
define('DB_HOST', 'localhost');
```

Listing 7-32. Relevant Part of `wp-config.php` After Changes in the Master Compute Engine Instance

```
// ** MySQL settings - You can get this info from your web host ** //
/** The name of the database for WordPress */
define('DB_NAME', 'wordpress');

/** MySQL database username */
define('DB_USER', 'wordpress');

/** MySQL database password */
define('DB_PASSWORD', 'lk8skdks');

/** MySQL hostname */
define('DB_HOST', '173.194.240.58');
```

The instructions in this example are tailored for our instances—we used example-specific IP addresses for the Compute Engine instance and Cloud SQL instance. Be careful when you substitute the information from your deployment.

The last step to have a working Wordpress installation is to open a web browser, point to the URL (made up of the IP address and the Wordpress directory), and complete the 5-minute installation. The URL to the master instance in our case is `http://107.167.191.27/wordpress`.

You can repeat this process to install Wordpress and other prerequisites in the slave Compute Engine instance and link to the Cloud SQL read replica. The purpose is to show that if you update the master Wordpress instance—say, by writing a new blog post—the slave Wordpress instance is automatically updated because Cloud SQL automatically syncs the databases. In this example case, because the databases are synchronized already, you don't need to create them and can skip this step. Go ahead and update the `wp-config.php` file and point to the read replica Cloud SQL database. If all permissions are set up correctly, then Wordpress will not run the installation again and will simply display the blog. The URL to the slave instance in our case is `http://130.211.246.208/wordpress`.

Expanding the Cloud SQL MySQL Cluster with External Nodes

This section shows you how to set up an externally hosted read replica of a master MySQL database server hosted in Cloud SQL. The required actions are split between those that need to be taken on the master Cloud SQL instance and those that you take on the replica externally hosted MySQL server instance.

Here are the high-level configuration steps on the master Cloud SQL instance:

1. Add the replica instance IP to authorized networks.
2. Enable the binary log.
3. Create a database backup.
4. Start replication.

And these are the high-level configuration steps on the read replica externally hosted MySQL instance:

1. Download the database dump from the master Cloud SQL instance.
2. Set the `server-id`.
3. Set the master information.
4. Start the slave.

The example scenario is similar to the Wordpress setup in the previous section, with some minor differences. The master Compute Engine instance links to Cloud SQL, whereas the slave Virtual Machine (VM) instance links to a MySQL server installed in the VM itself. The Wordpress database in this slave MySQL server is a read replica of the Wordpress database hosted in Cloud SQL. After you complete the setup in the following sections, you should have a master Cloud SQL instance and two read replicas: one hosted in Cloud SQL and another hosted externally. You can continue to use the two Compute Engine VM instances that you set up in the previous section; we only describe new instructions and refer you to the previous section for repeated commands.

Setting Up a MySQL Server External to Cloud Platform

In this section, you set up a MySQL server instance external to Google Cloud Platform and use it to mirror a Cloud SQL instance. You assemble a hypervisor-powered VM on a workstation and install the suitable version of MySQL server software. We guide you through the process of installation and configuration from scratch, providing direct instructions or pointing to appropriate online sources. Let's begin by setting up the VM.

For this example, we used the free hypervisor software VirtualBox from Oracle Inc. (`www.virtualbox.org`) on a Mac Book Pro running OS X Yosemite edition. You can use any hypervisor software as long as it can power an OS that is supported by the MySQL server software. We used Ubuntu 14.04 LTS version as the OS; again, you can use any OS as long as it supports the MySQL server software. Finally, we used MySQL server version 5.5, because it's currently the supported version for replication in Cloud SQL. See `https://cloud.google.com/sql/docs/replication` for an updated list of supported versions.

Following are the three recommended steps for setting up MySQL server software on a workstation:

1. Install the hypervisor software.
2. Install a suitable OS.
3. Install supported MySQL client and server software.

For reasons of brevity and due to the abundance of online documentation, we don't describe steps 1 and 2. Refer to the following links to set up the VirtualBox hypervisor and install the Ubuntu OS in a VM:

- WiKiHow blog post (with pictures), "How to install Ubuntu on VirtualBox," `www.wikihow.com/Install-Ubuntu-on-VirtualBox`
- Cloud Network YouTube video, "How to Install Ubuntu 14.04 on Oracle VirtualBox," `www.youtube.com/watch?v=QkJmahizwO4`
- Official guide for installing Ubuntu on VirtualBox, `https://help.ubuntu.com/community/VirtualBox`

Let's proceed to step 3: setting up the MySQL server software on the VirtualBox-powered VM. The bash shell commands you execute in the VM are prefixed with `VM$` to distinguish them from commands to execute on the host workstation. You install MySQL version 5.5 because this is the version supported for replication in Cloud SQL. To do so, use the following command-line commands on an Ubuntu 14.04 system.

First you install the MySQL client software to connect to both local and remote MySQL server instances:

```
$ sudo apt-get install mysql-client
<..snip..>
```

Next you install the specific version of the MySQL server software (if you use `sudo apt-get install mysql-server`, it may install the default version, which for Ubuntu 14.04 is MySQL 5.6):

```
$ sudo apt-get install mysql-server-5.5
<..snip> set a root password (not used for Cloud SQL instance) when prompted <snip..>
```

Log in to the local MySQL server to ensure that you have access and to verify that the correct version has been installed:

```
$ mysql -h localhost -u root -p
Enter password:
Welcome to the MySQL monitor.  Commands end with ; or \g.
Your MySQL connection id is 14
Server version: 5.5.41-0ubuntu0.14.04.1 (Ubuntu)
<..snip..>
mysql> exit
Bye
```

After executing these instructions, you have fully functional MySQL server software hosted in a VM on your workstation. As an exercise, we suggest that you set up a different root password for this instance than for your Cloud SQL. This way, when you turn on replication shortly, you will be able to observe that your local configuration (including the root password) has been overwritten by your Cloud SQL configuration.

Next you need to make sure you can connect to the Cloud SQL instance from this VM; this is essential for enabling replication. The required steps are covered earlier in this chapter; see Listing 7-5 and Listing 7-6 for details. Repeat the process, adding your VM's publicly visible IP address as an authorized IP address on Cloud SQL. Once this setup is finished, you should be able to connect to the Cloud SQL instance from the VM:

```
VM$ mysql -h 173.194.242.117 -u root -p
Enter password:
Welcome to the MySQL monitor.  Commands end with ; or \g.
Your MySQL connection id is 363
Server version: 5.5.38-log (Google)
<..snip..>
mysql> quit
Bye
```

You should now enable binary logs and Cloud SQL backups and have Cloud SQL generate at least one backup. This process is similar to setting up read replicas in Cloud SQL; see Listing 7-15 through Listing 7-22 for details. After you've done that, you can set up the master Cloud SQL instance to honor external read replicas.

The configuration process in the master Cloud SQL instance is to create a new Cloud SQL user account and assign required permissions to allow replication by an external slave server. *External*, in this context, refers to a MySQL server instance outside of the Cloud SQL platform. Hence, it is also possible to use a Compute Engine VM with MySQL server and make it a slave to a master Cloud SQL instance. The slave MySQL database server will use this account to log in to the master Cloud SQL database server.

The console commands and corresponding output in Listings 8-33 through 8-36 show the process of creating the user account and assigning the required permissions.

Listing 7-33. Logging In Securely to the Master Cloud SQL Instance

```
$ mysql --ssl-ca=asia-wordpress-ca-cert.pem --ssl-cert=asia-wordpress-client-cert.pem \
--ssl-key=asia-wordpress-client-key.pem --host=173.194.242.117 --user=root --password
Enter password:
<..snip..>
```

Listing 7-34. Creating a New User Account in the Master Cloud SQL Instance

```
mysql> CREATE USER 'replication-user'@'%' IDENTIFIED BY 'replica-password';
Query OK, 0 rows affected (0.10 sec)
```

Listing 7-35. Granting the Replication Slave Permission to Enable Replication by a User Account

```
mysql> GRANT REPLICATION SLAVE ON *.* TO 'replication-user'@'%';
Query OK, 0 rows affected (0.10 sec)
```

Listing 7-36. Flushing Privileges to Apply the Changes and Quit

```
mysql> flush privileges;
Query OK, 0 rows affected (0.00 sec)

mysql> quit
Bye
```

These steps complete the configuration on the master Cloud SQL instance and make it ready to accept replication requests from a slave MySQL server instance. Now, let's configure the slave MySQL server instance.

You need to perform these high-level steps in the externally hosted slave VM instance:

1. Perform a SQL dump of the master Cloud SQL instance.
2. Import the SQL dump into the slave MySQL server.
3. Configure the master information in the slave MySQL server.

There are three ways to perform a MySQL data dump from the master Cloud SQL server. You can use the web-based Developers Console, the `mysqldump` command-line utility, or the Cloud SQL API. This example uses `mysqldump`; see `https://dev.mysql.com/doc/refman/5.5/en/mysqldump.html` for more information on this tool. Listings 8-37 through 8-39 show the command-line options, arguments, and corresponding output.

Listing 7-37. Use `mysqldump` tool to Download All the Databases; Settings from the Master CloudSQL Instance

```
VM$  mysqldump -h 173.194.242.117 -u root -p --all-databases --master-data=2 --events \
> master.sql
Enter password:
```

Listing 7-38. Listing the `mysqldump` File

```
VM$ ls -l
total 440
-rw-rw-r-- 1 cloudplatformbook cloudplatformbook 447741 Apr 15 22:11 master.sql
```

Listing 7-39. Importing the .sql File into the Slave MySQL Server Instance

```
VM$ mysql -u root -p < master.sql
```

■ **Tip** The previous database-import operation specifically ignores the -h (host) option. This is because Cloud SQL creates a NULL user attached to localhost, and using -h localhost interferes with the import process. If you are keen on specifying the host option, you can use -h 127.0.0.1 instead. To clarify, Listing 7-40 lists the MySQL users in the Cloud SQL instance.

Listing 7-40. Listing MySQL Users in a MySQL Server

```
mysql> select Host, User from mysql.user;
+-----------+------------------+
| Host      | User             |
+-----------+------------------+
| %         | replication-user |
| %         | root             |
| %         | wordpress        |
| 127.0.0.1 | root             |
| ::1       | root             |
| localhost |                  |
| localhost | root             |
+-----------+------------------+
7 rows in set (0.00 sec)
```

Configuring the MySQL server in the VM to be a slave of the master Cloud SQL server requires changing three settings:

1. Set the server ID.
2. Set the master information.
3. Start replication.

The server ID is a MySQL system variable (server-id) and is used by the server and the slave to identify each other. It is an integer and should be unique among all of the master's slaves. The server ID is defined in a configuration file, usually my.cnf. Here is the location of the MySQL configuration file in Ubuntu 14.04:

```
VM$ ls -l /etc/mysql/my.cnf
-rw-r--r-- 1 root root 3516 Apr 15 22:22 /etc/mysql/my.cnf
```

The following command extracts the default definition of the server-id variable

```
VM$ cat /etc/mysql/my.cnf | grep server-id
#server-id              = 1
```

As you can see, the my.cnf file contains a system variable called server-id, but it is disabled by default. You can use your favorite text editor to uncomment the line and assign the variable a unique value. Alternatively, you can add a new entry and leave the default untouched:

```
VM$ cat /etc/mysql/my.cnf | grep server-id
#server-id              = 1
server-id=8
```

The mysqldump file you created earlier includes a CHANGE MASTER TO MASTER_LOG_FILE comment specifying the log coordinates. Search for this string, and copy and paste the entire line into the MySQL command line without the initial - (the MySQL comment marker). Complete the CHANGE MASTER TO command by specifying the rest of the information for connecting to the master, including MASTER_HOST, MASTER_USER, and MASTER_PASSWORD. Listing 7-41 and Listing 7-42 show you the process along with the information specific to our installation. Note that you need to log in to your local MySQL before issuing the commands in Listing 7-42.

Listing 7-41. Extracting the Log Coordinates from the mysqldump File

```
VM$ cat master.sql | grep -i "CHANGE MASTER"
-- CHANGE MASTER TO MASTER_LOG_FILE='mysql-bin.000031', MASTER_LOG_POS=753;
```

Listing 7-42. Changing the Status of the Local MySQL Server to Be a Slave of the Master Cloud SQL Server

```
mysql> CHANGE MASTER TO MASTER_LOG_FILE='mysql-bin.000031', \
MASTER_LOG_POS=753, MASTER_HOST='173.194.242.117', \
MASTER_USER='replication-user', MASTER_PASSWORD='replica-password';
Query OK, 0 rows affected (0.01 sec)
```

The final step in configuring the slave MySQL server is to start the slave. You do so using the start slave MySQL command:

```
mysql> start slave;
Query OK, 0 rows affected (0.00 sec)
```

You can verify whether the slave MySQL server is configured correctly by showing its status. To do so, use SHOW SLAVE STATUS as shown in Listing 7-43. In the output, if the value for the variable Slave_IO_State is “Waiting for master to send event”, then the setup is complete and the slave server is waiting for the master to send events.

Listing 7-43. Showing the MySQL Slave Status

```
mysql> SHOW SLAVE STATUS\G;
*************************** 1. row ***************************
               Slave_IO_State: Waiting for master to send event
                  Master_Host: 173.194.242.117
                  Master_User: replication-user
                  Master_Port: 3306
                Connect_Retry: 60
              Master_Log_File: mysql-bin.000031
          Read_Master_Log_Pos: 930
               Relay_Log_File: mysqld-relay-bin.000002
                Relay_Log_Pos: 430
```

```
      Relay_Master_Log_File: mysql-bin.000031
           Slave_IO_Running: Yes
          Slave_SQL_Running: Yes
            Replicate_Do_DB:
        Replicate_Ignore_DB:
         Replicate_Do_Table:
     Replicate_Ignore_Table:
    Replicate_Wild_Do_Table:
Replicate_Wild_Ignore_Table:
                 Last_Errno: 0
                 Last_Error:
               Skip_Counter: 0
        Exec_Master_Log_Pos: 930
            Relay_Log_Space: 587
            Until_Condition: None
             Until_Log_File:
              Until_Log_Pos: 0
         Master_SSL_Allowed: No
         Master_SSL_CA_File:
         Master_SSL_CA_Path:
            Master_SSL_Cert:
          Master_SSL_Cipher:
             Master_SSL_Key:
      Seconds_Behind_Master: 0
Master_SSL_Verify_Server_Cert: No
              Last_IO_Errno: 0
              Last_IO_Error:
             Last_SQL_Errno: 0
             Last_SQL_Error:
Replicate_Ignore_Server_Ids:
           Master_Server_Id: 881423946
1 row in set (0.00 sec)

ERROR:
No query specified
```

Congratulations! You have completed the setup of an external MySQL slave server. After working through this example and the one in the previous section, you know how to build a synchronized read-only replica database hosted either in the Google Cloud Platform or elsewhere on the Internet.

You can now install Wordpress in the VM and connect it to the local MySQL server. The contents of both Wordpress installations will be synchronized in real time, although there may be minor synchronization latency.

Measuring the Performance of Cloud SQL

This final section of the chapter shows you how to measure the performance of a Cloud SQL instance. The objective is *not* to compare the performance of the Cloud SQL service with other services but rather to characterize the different instance sizes and the maximum number of concurrent connections they can support. This approach will help you select the right Cloud SQL instance size. Again, we urge you not to use the literal numbers shown in this section (because Google constantly improves the Cloud SQL platform) but to run the tests when you deploy.

Many performance-measuring tools are available in MySQL. This section uses a diagnostic tool that has been prepackaged with MySQL since version 5, because it saves you the hassle of installing a new tool. The tool is called MySQLslap, and database administrators and developers use it alike to load-test and benchmark their database servers.

MySQLslap can emulate a large number of simultaneous users and load a database. The tool is highly configurable, and you can use the various test results to select the right instance size for your application. Our objective is not explain the entire tool and its options but to show you a recommended option and how to measure the performance of your Cloud SQL instance.

MySQLslap is automatically installed as part of MySQL installation. In this example, you install the MySQL packages in a Compute Engine VM and use MySQLslap to benchmark the Cloud SQL instance. Using a Compute Engine VM instead of a system elsewhere has the advantage that you don't need to worry about network latencies between MySQLslap and Cloud SQL. Here is how you get the MySQLslap tool:

```
$ gcloud compute ssh asia-wordpress-master

VM$ sudo apt-get install mysql-client mysql-server
<snip>

VM$ which mysqlslap
/usr/bin/mysqlslap
```

MySQLslap supports both auto-generated and custom queries. We recommend that you start with auto-generated queries and, if required, move on to custom queries if the auto-generated queries do not model your application closely enough. Begin by emulating a single connection, and look at the response:

```
$ sudo mysqlslap --user=root --password --host=173.194.240.58 --auto-generate-sql --verbose
Enter password:
Benchmark
        Average number of seconds to run all queries: 0.416 seconds
        Minimum number of seconds to run all queries: 0.416 seconds
        Maximum number of seconds to run all queries: 0.416 seconds
        Number of clients running queries: 1
        Average number of queries per client: 0
```

This output shows the time it takes one client to execute its queries in a single iteration. As with any benchmarking experiment, it is advised that you do several iterations and use the average response time. Let's do 100 concurrent connections with the auto-generated queries running 10 times:

```
$ sudo mysqlslap --user=root --password --host=173.194.240.58 --concurrency=50 \
--iterations=10 --auto-generate-sql --verbose
Enter password:
Benchmark
        Average number of seconds to run all queries: 14.658 seconds
        Minimum number of seconds to run all queries: 12.191 seconds
        Maximum number of seconds to run all queries: 16.948 seconds
        Number of clients running queries: 50
        Average number of queries per client: 0
```

Notice that you provide root credentials for MySQLslap to run these tests. You may be uncomfortable with this. This example shows that MySQLslap creates its own database to run these tests and does not touch other databases in the server. But if you still are not satisfied, you can instantiate a temporary instance in the same Cloud SQL zone to run these tests and delete it after the tests. Following is the console output showing that MySQLslap creates its own database during the tests, which it drops at the end of the tests:

```
$ mysql --ssl-ca=asia-wordpress-ca-cert.pem --ssl-cert=asia-wordpress-client-cert.pem \
--ssl-key=asia-wordpress-client-key.pem --host=173.194.240.58 --user=root --password
<snip>

mysql> show databases;
+--------------------+
| Database           |
+--------------------+
| information_schema |
| mysql              |
| mysqlslap          |
| performance:schema |
| wordpress          |
+--------------------+
5 rows in set (0.23 sec)
```

MySQLslap's auto-generated SQL creates a table with two fields. Most real-life and production databases have more fields. You can configure MySQLslap to emulate this by adding fields to the table. Two parameters (`--number-char-cols` and `--number-int-cols`) make this customization possible. These parameters specify the number of varchar and int types of columns to add to the table.

The following example tests with an auto-generated SQL query with 10 numeric columns and 10-character type columns. You emulate 100 client connections, and you repeat the test 100 times:

```
VM$ sudo mysqlslap --user=root --password --host=173.194.240.58 --concurrency=100 \
--iterations=100 --number-int-cols=10 --number-char-cols=10 --auto-generate-sql --verbose
Enter password:

Benchmark
        Average number of seconds to run all queries: 27.764 seconds
        Minimum number of seconds to run all queries: 23.906 seconds
        Maximum number of seconds to run all queries: 34.737 seconds
        Number of clients running queries: 100
        Average number of queries per client: 0
```

■ **Note** we want to state that the current generation of Cloud SQL is built for the low- to medium-traffic market segment. This means the number of queries per second is limited. Hence, it shouldn't come as a shock to you if the number of queries doesn't scale up beyond a certain value. Future generations of Cloud SQL are likely to position the cloud service for the high-traffic market.

Summary

In this chapter, you learned about Cloud SQL, the relational database hosting service from the Google Cloud Platform. Relational databases are the mainstay data back ends for legacy applications. As more and more legacy applications move to the public cloud to take advantage of better infrastructure, uptime, and economies of scale, it is important that you know how to use this relational database hosting service from a leading public cloud provider.

The chapter began by providing an introduction to Cloud SQL and explaining the various access methods. Following this, you saw examples of how to configure a single Cloud SQL database instance for a web application. You extended this setup to build a MySQL cluster by adding a read replica that was also hosted on Cloud SQL. You further upgraded the MySQL cluster by adding read replicas hosted outside of the Cloud SQL platform. Finally, you learned to measure the performance of a Cloud SQL–hosted database using standard database-benchmarking tools. You should now have sufficient information to kick-start your Cloud SQL journey!

CHAPTER 8

Cloud Storage

Google Cloud Storage is Google's proposal for storing data in the cloud by using its own infrastructure. It brings some of the features that power the entire Google Cloud Platform, such as high availability, scalability, and performance. If you are familiar with other data-storage systems like Amazon S3, OpenStack Swift, and storage in Azure, you can consider Cloud Storage in the same family.

Typical applications of such services involve storing medium- to large-sized data that is served to clients across the globe and does not need to be processed in the cloud. Examples are online backups, avatars, internal logs, media files, web sites (or part of them), and so on. Data is organized in buckets that contain objects. Unlike a usual file structure, buckets cannot be nested within each other.

This service is conveniently exposed to developers through two RESTful APIs: XML and JSON. In addition, client libraries targeting most relevant programming language nowadays use these two. Google also provides a command-line tool that allows you to perform many of the most common operations very quickly, such as managing buckets and objects and editing access control lists.

Your First File Upload

To get a feel for what you can do with Cloud Storage, in this section you install the `gsutil` tool, create a bucket, and upload files for a newly created project.

Installing gsutil

On Windows, download Python (`https://www.python.org/downloads`) and `gsutil` (`https://storage.googleapis.com/pub/gsutil.zip`) and install them using a default configuration. It is recommended that you unzip `gsutil` in a folder of the same name placed in the root of your hard drive: `C:\gsutil`.

If you are using Unix, install pip first. Here are the commands on Debian and Ubuntu:

```
$ sudo apt-get install gcc python-dev python-setuptools libffi-dev
$ sudo apt-get install python-pip
```

And this is the command on Mac OS X:

```
$ sudo easy_install -U pip
```

Also get `gsutil` from pip:

```
$ sudo pip install gsutil
```

Enabling Cloud Storage

Access Google Developers Console (`https://console.developers.google.com`) with your Google account, and enable Cloud Storage under APIs & Auth in the left panel as shown in Figure 8-1.

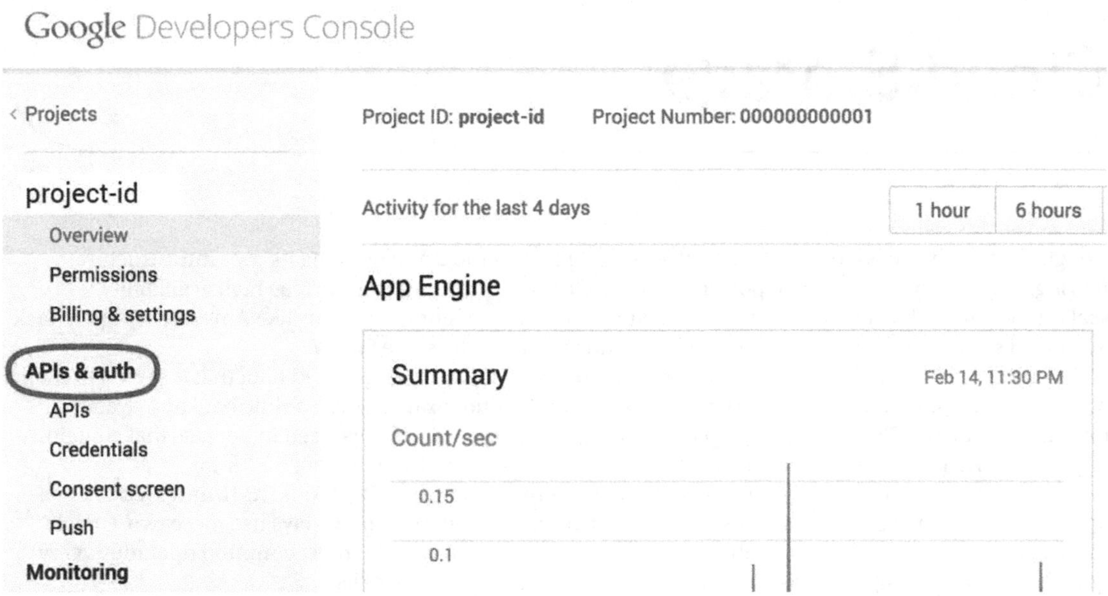

***Figure 8-1.** Accessing APIs in Google Developers Console*

Enabling Billing

In order to start using Cloud Storage, you need to enable billing. You can do that by choosing Settings ➤ Enable Billing.

Now it is time for some fun: creating a bucket under one of your projects and adding a couple of files to it. You delete the content later.

Authorizing Your Google Account at the Command Line

Use the following command from `gcloud` to authenticate your Google account and use it as the default for future operations:

```
$ gcloud auth login
```

■ **Note** `gcloud` is a command-line tool that grants you quick access to development operations and services in Google Cloud. This tool is installed automatically with the Google Cloud SDK. If you do not have that installed by now, your investment in this book could be seriously questioned. However, everybody deserves a second chance: you can download it from `https://cloud.google.com/sdk/#Quick_Start`.

This command opens a new browser and prompts you with a login screen. After you successfully enter your credentials, `gcloud` adds the given account to the list of authenticated users and selects it as the currently active one. You can access this list through `gcloud auth list` or revoke access with `gcloud auth revoke`.

■ **Tip** Explore the help section for each command (`-h`) for more usage details. For example, `gcloud auth -h`, `gcloud auth list -h`, `gcloud auth revoke -h`, and so on.

Running Commands with gsutil

Let's start with something simple and list all the buckets using the `ls` command:

```
$ gsutil ls
```

Commands executed from `gsutil` and other command-line tools in Google Cloud return results for the currently active project. To change that, use the following command:

```
$ gcloud config set project <project-id>
```

Here, `project-id` represents the project identifier of the current project. Take this chance to explore the rest of the configuration with `gcloud config list`, and use `gcloud config [set|unset] <property-name> <new-value>` to edit its contents.

Creating a New Bucket

Creating a bucket with `gsutil` is very straightforward. Use the `mb` command as follows:

```
$ gsutil mb gs://<bucket-name>
```

■ **Note** Bucket names are global across the entire repository of projects in Google Cloud Storage. So, if you try to use a name like `hello`, you will most likely receive a `ServiceException: 409 Bucket hello already exists`. Prefixing buckets with your project name, project ID, or bucket hierarchy is a great way to avoid duplicates.

Uploading Your First File

Uploading files is very similar to using the Unix command `cp` to copy files from a source to a destination location:

```
$ gsutil cp file1.txt gs://<bucket-name>
```

Good engineers always like to double-check that machines do not get the message wrong. If you are one of these, you can list all the files again to be sure your new file was properly uploaded. This time, show the size and upload date for each file with the `-l` option:

```
$ gsutil ls -l gs://<bucket-name>
```

■ **Tip** To download objects from Cloud Storage to your machine, simply reverse the arguments you use with the `cp` command, like this: `gsutil cp gs://<bucket-name>/file1.txt file1.txt`. If you do not specify a name for the file locally, it will be kept the same.

Cleaning Up

Enough testing. It is time to clean up and delete what you just created:

```
$ gsutil rm gs://<bucket-name>/*
$ gsutil rb gs://<bucket-name>
```

■ **Note** Only buckets with no content can be removed. This command cannot be undone. The bucket name is made available to other users immediately after deletion.

Why Use Cloud Storage?

In addition to the benefits mentioned earlier, Cloud Storage benefits from features targeted to improve speed and availability. The following are some of the most relevant:

- *Edge-caching*: Google data centers and other nodes are distributed across the globe, and data is delivered to users from the closest place on Earth.
- *Specific bucket locations*: These can help you reduce latency and therefore increase perceived performance for the entire system.
- *Strong consistency for files:* Data is available as soon as it is successfully uploaded to Cloud Storage.
- *Server-side encryption*: Data is transparently encrypted before it is written to disk on Google's side.
- *Resumable uploads:* These allow you to upload files without consuming the extra resources of restarting the upload process from the beginning in case of error.
- *Controlled lifespan:* The lifespan of the objects in a bucket is based on one or more defined conditions.
- *Access control lists (ACLs):* You can define permissions for users or groups, down to the level of discrete actions (read and write). These rules apply to buckets and objects in conjunction or independently.

Google's philosophy regarding sustained discounts and pricing reductions based on the economics and evolution of computing costs ensures a bright path for services like Cloud Storage. In addition, more affordable prices mean more storage and potential benefits in terms of bandwidth, I/O, flexibility regarding the type of storage, and so on.

Strong Consistency in Cloud Storage

Before diving deeper into some of the features of Cloud Storage and beginning to configure, upload, categorize, and automate tasks for a project, you need to understand what *strong consistency* means in this context. When you create, update, or delete new objects, they are not available for read operations until they are successfully uploaded. This applies to both the object's data and its metadata. This means if an error occurs during one of the previously mentioned operations, these objects will never be available. Despite its benefits, strong consistency comes at a price: slightly higher latency. In order to ensure read access, Cloud Storage waits until a given object is replicated in multiple data centers before returning a successful response.

This does not apply to list operations, which behave in an eventually consistent fashion: that is, requesting a list of objects or buckets may return stale information. However, accessing the objects directly only returns up-to-date information.

Additionally, consistency on deletions of objects that are publicly available depends on the caching strategy you define, because changes on these operations are not reflected until the specified lifetime of the cache expires. For example, if you delete an object whose cache was previously set to expire after an hour, subsequent reads to that object will return a valid resource until that hour has passed. You can control this by setting the `Cache-Control` header at upload time (see RFC2616).

Applications of Cloud Storage

This chapter's examples use two interesting applications of this technology: DevOps and application development. You see in greater depth some of Cloud Storage's most relevant features, you learn about their practical use in order to get the most out of them in your current projects, and you are introduced to their associated challenges.

On the back-end/application development side, this chapter's example uses the geolocalized LunchMates app, which helps find individuals who share common interests meet and chat about them over lunch or a drink. You develop a feature that lets users upload documents and attach them to specific discussions or meetings so that other lunchmates can access them. This example dives deep into resumable uploads and signed URLs.

On the DevOps side, you take advantage of the flexibility of `gsutil` to use your file repository in the cloud. You control ACLs, and perform tasks in batches that you can automate in systems such as continuous integration, internal scripts or cron-jobs, and so on.

■ **Note** As with products on the Google Cloud Platform, accessing and using Cloud Storage is not limited to hosting your entire infrastructure with Google. APIs and command-line tools are conveniently exposed so that you can be as free and creative as you like to shape your back-end infrastructure based on your needs. Nevertheless, as you may expect, having your services operate in the same network delivers better-performing connections and interoperability among different services.

Access Control

Like many of the greatest technological achievements of the past, this example starts by creating a new blank folder or file. Creating a bucket with `gsutil` is as straightforward as typing and executing a single command. It is no more difficult through the Developers Console (`https://console.developers.google.com`). To create a new bucket, do the following:

1. Authenticate with your Google account.
2. From the list, select the project you are working on.
3. Navigate to Storage ➤ Cloud Storage ➤ Storage Browser through the panel on the left.
4. Click Create a Bucket, as shown in Figure 8-2.

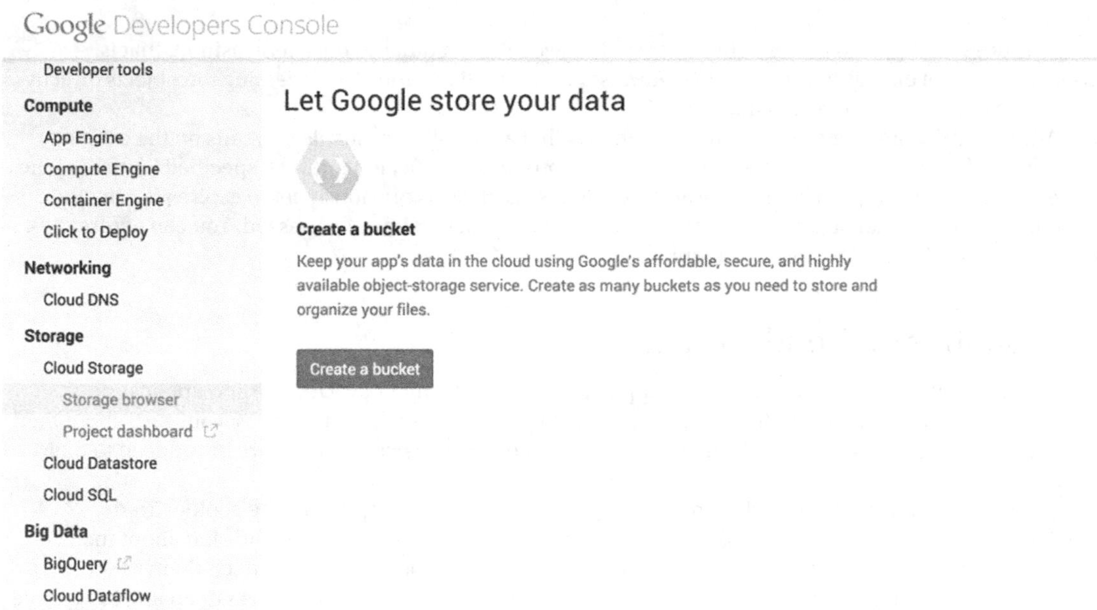

Figure 8-2. *Accessing Cloud Storage's file browser from Google Developers Console*

5. Give the bucket a name, and you are good to go (see Figure 8-3). What about `lunchmates_document_dropbox`?

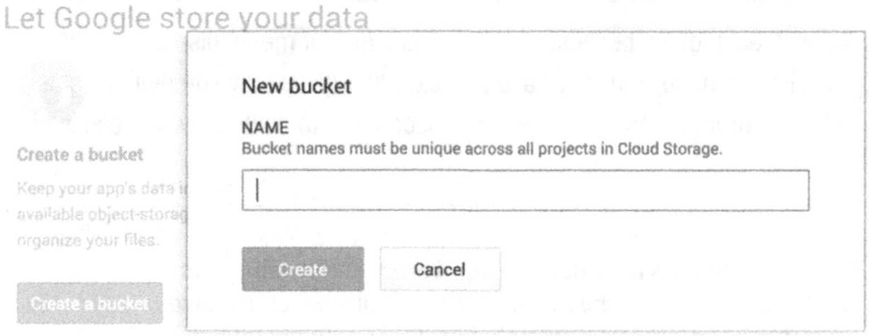

Figure 8-3. *Creating a new bucket from Google Developers Console*

■ **Note** Remember that bucket names are global—they are shared across all Google projects and accounts, and thus they have to be unique at that level. You can test the existence of a bucket name externally by performing a request to Cloud Storage and watching the responses. If the contents of your buckets require protection, make sure to use not-obvious bucket names.

Now, let's define in more detail what you want to build. Users of the LunchMates app can create lunch entries or meetings that propose a topic and a place and time to meet. As an example, Maria is very interested in horizontal scalability strategies. She has a free slot for lunch today and decides to create an entry about this topic in the app that suggests meeting at 13.00 at a restaurant called Scale 101. She also decides that the meeting has a maximum of five possible mates.

As soon as the entry for the meeting is created, the creator and the potential attendees are allowed to attach documents to it. To make that possible, you decide to create one bucket to host all documents for your users. You obviously do not want to provide permanent access rights to all users who register on your app and create a meeting, but you need a way to acknowledge that a given user is entitled to upload one or more files at a certain point in time.

There are two main ways to control access to documents in Cloud Storage and a third alternative that is convenient in certain cases:

- *ACLs*: Access control lists represent the most complete option to distribute access rights among users. ACLs are granted on a bucket or object level and apply to a user or group of users identified directly through Google—storage ID, Gmail, or corporate accounts in Google—or are alternatively open to any user on the Internet. Each object can have up to 100 ACL entries. When an object is requested, ACLs are checked and grant access if at least one entry is satisfied or return `403 Forbidden` otherwise.

- *Signed URLs:* This is an alternative strategy to ACLs to provide access to objects in cloud storage without the need for a Google account. Signed URLs are created on request and allow those with access to read, upload, or delete a given resource in your file system for a limited amount of time. For this example, especially given that you do not want to require users to have a Google account, signed URLs appear to be the right path to take. A signed URLs is required to have an expiration date after which the URL is no longer valid. This helps make the system a bit more robust and secure if the signed URL is handled properly: keeping it safe and always transmitting it through protected channels.

Note These methods can coexist with each other, because they provide different mechanisms to grant access to an object or group of objects. For example, you may have a bucket that gives only you owner rights, for which you have created a signed URL in order to make this resource accessible to anybody with access to the link.

- *Resumable uploads:* This mechanism is provided by Cloud Storage to enable users to resume uploads from a certain position in the file and with an optional chunk size. This is useful in scenarios involving large files, unstable or poor connectivity (such as mobile networks), limited resources, or high traffic. Note that when a regular upload fails and is retried, redundant traffic is transmitted, because the upload restarts from byte 0. In contrast to ACLs, resumable uploads do not require users to have a Google account or expose URLs that could be compromised due to incorrect handling. Instead, authentication happens on the server side and under your control. For example, you can use the same authentication system that is already in place for the rest of your application to successfully authenticate a user and then provide the user with a resumable upload link. Resumable uploads are an appropriate approach for any user to tackle authenticated and flexible uploads to cloud storage.

The upload portion of the example uses resumable uploads, and the read operations—when users view documents for an upcoming meeting—use signed URLs. In order to maintain flexibility with different systems, the example uses Cloud Storage's JSON API. Although the logic is written in Python to provide a realistic system scenario, the relevant part with respect to storage can be easily replicated in other languages and systems.

Note The connection and authorization process of your server logic against Cloud Storage happens on a server-to-server basis. This is referred as *service accounts* in the documentation for Cloud Storage, which is consistent with the nomenclature used in the OAuth section. The OAuth2 authentication process is not included in this and other chapters—this topic requires a dedicated explanation in order for you to understand the different types of access as well as how and when to apply them. For details see Chapter 3. By now, we assume that you have an API token or use of one of Google's client libraries to authenticate your requests.

Resumable Uploads

Yes, it is finally time to use your fingers and keys to make some noise. Remember Maria? She is the creator of the meeting used in this example, and she is ready to attach a document to it. Figure 8-4 illustrates the complete upload process.

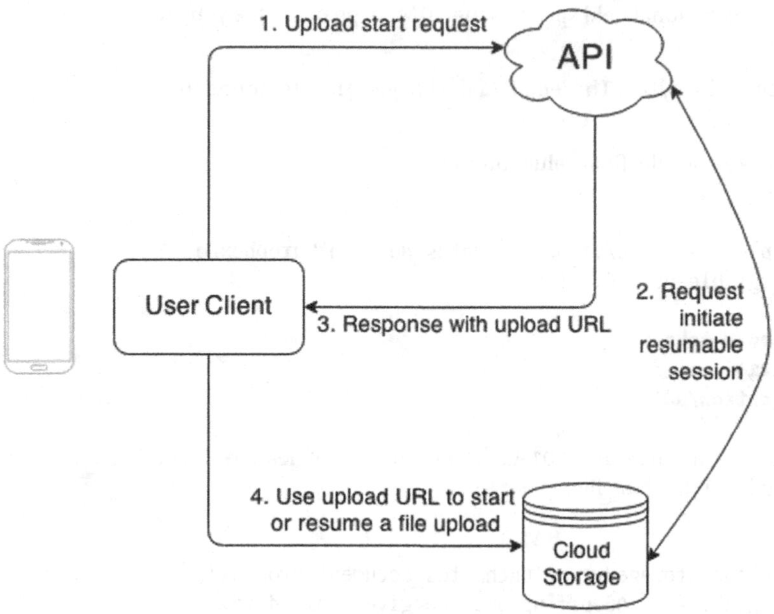

Figure 8-4. *Steps to initiate a resumable upload*

After the user selects a file to upload, a request is sent to the API to start the upload process. Once Maria is authenticated in the system, you can ask Cloud Storage for the final URL location where Maria will upload her file (step 2 in Figure 8-4). You do that as follows:

```
POST
https://www.googleapis.com/upload/storage/v1/b/<bucket_name>/o
?uploadType=resumable&name=<file_name>

Authorization: Bearer <your_auth_token>
X-Upload-Content-Length: <length_of_the_content_in_bytes>
X-Upload-Content-Type: <content_mime_type>
```

This request simply informs Cloud Storage that you are attempting to start a resumable upload to a given bucket, with the metadata specified. Let's fill in the gaps:

- `bucket_name`: Specifies the bucket to which the file is uploaded. Previously in this chapter, you created a bucket for this purpose and named it `lunchmates_document_dropbox`.
- `file_name`: The name of the file to upload. You already know the name of the file—you can use the value Maria sent in the initial request to your API or choose it on your own. For example, you can generate the file name internally, including identifiers, timestamps, or any hash that facilitates administration.
- `your_auth_token`: The token returned from the OAuth process against Cloud Storage API. Remember that in this case, you are using server-to-server authentication. To be able to upload files, you have to at least authenticate for `read_write` scope: `https://www.googleapis.com/auth/devstorage.read_write`. We discuss the other two possible scopes (`read_only` and `full_control`) later in this chapter.

- `content_mime_type`: This optional field specifies the MIME type of the file you are about to upload.
- `length_of_the_content_in_bytes`: The length of the file you are attempting to upload.

This is how the request looks like once the final values are set:

```
POST
https://www.googleapis.com/upload/storage/v1/b/lunchmates_document_dropbox/o
?uploadType=resumable&name=bigtable-osdi06.pdf

Authorization: Bearer <your_auth_token>
X-Upload-Content-Length: 221214
X-Upload-Content-Type: application/pdf
```

If this request is executed successfully, it returns `201 Created` with a set of headers, including one holding the URL to which you need to upload the file:

```
Location:
https://www.googleapis.com/upload/storage/v1/b/lunchmates_document_dropbox/o
?uploadType=resumable&name=bigtable-osdi06.pdf&upload_id=<given_upload_id>
```

This URL contains an `upload_id` parameter that uniquely defines the upload session. It is required to persist this URL during the entire upload process, because you will reuse it whenever there is an attempt to write bytes on this file into Cloud Storage—whether because the upload needs to be resumed or because the file is uploaded in chunks.

■ **Note** Upload URIs expire within a day or so if not used at all, or a bit longer period if it is being actively used to upload chunks of content. Therefore, it is recommended to start the upload process as soon as you obtain the upload URI as well as resume interrupted uploads as quickly as possible. If the upload URI expires, the upload request will respond with a `404 Not Found`. In that case you must request a new upload URI and use the new location to start the upload process from the beginning.

Now, directly from your client, you can use the URL to upload the file into Cloud Storage. You do that with a PUT request to the upload URL, a `Content-Length` header specifying the size of the file in bytes, and the binary data to upload in the body of the request.

■ **Note** If you are uploading the file in chunks, they must be a size that is a multiple of 256KB (262, 144 bytes). That does not apply to the last chunk, which is always smaller than 256KB.

This is how the upload request looks:

```
PUT
https://www.googleapis.com/upload/storage/v1/b/lunchmates_document_dropbox/o
?uploadType=resumable&name=bigtable-osdi06.pdf&upload_id=<given_upload_id>

Content-Length: 221214
Content-Type: application/pdf

<contents_of_file>
```

If the file is uploaded successfully, the request returns a `200 OK` response. If it does not, whether due to the connection being unexpectedly interrupted or the request responding with an error code that shows a problem on the server side, you expose this all the way to the client to tell Maria that something failed during the process.

Suppose the upload fails. Maria really wants to get that file into the cloud so her lunchmates can read it before they meet, so she retries the upload. When she does, the client knows this is not a new upload request because you previously stored the `upload_id` for that request. As mentioned before, this is useful for avoiding consuming extra resources by starting a new upload process. Instead, you upload only what is still missing.

It is hard to guess how many bytes made it to the servers at Google. To find out, you perform the following request:

■ **Note** The following process applies any time you intend to resume an interrupted upload.

```
PUT
https://www.googleapis.com/upload/storage/v1/b/lunchmates_document_dropbox/o
?uploadType=resumable&name=bigtable-osdi06.pdf&upload_id=<given_upload_id>

Content-Length: 0
Content-Range: bytes */221214
```

As you can see, you need to perform a `PUT` request to the same URL you used to try to upload the file, but with empty content—`Content-Length` is 0, and there is no body—and specifying the range of bytes for which you need the request to apply. In this case, given that you do not know that number, the value must be as shown, where 221214 is the number of bytes specified in the `Content-Length` header of the upload request (the total number of bytes of the content you are trying to upload).

The expected response for this request `308 Resume Incomplete`. It contains a set of headers, including `Range`. This header shows the number of bytes that Cloud Storage received previously. You use this value in the next request to let the system know the point at which to start sending the content of your file. Here is the header

```
Range: bytes=0-<number_of_bytes_received>
```

where `number_of_bytes_received` is the number of bytes that Cloud Storage knows about for the document you are uploading.

Finally, retry the PUT request you used to begin uploading this file, but this time add a header for the range of bytes to upload, making sure you only send the contents of the file from the necessary point:

```
PUT
https://www.googleapis.com/upload/storage/v1/b/lunchmates_document_dropbox/o
?uploadType=resumable&name=bigtable-osdi06.pdf&upload_id=<given_upload_id>

Content-Range:
bytes <position_of_first_byte_to send>-<position_of_last_byte_to_send>/<total_file_size>
Content-Length: <length_of_the_chunk>

<contents_of_file>
```

To illustrate, let's take the previous example and assume the initial upload request could only send 10 bytes of the PDF document successfully. This is the current scenario:

- Total size of file: 221214
- Number of bytes uploaded successfully: 10
- Position of first byte to send in the next resumable upload: 11
- Position of last byte to send in the next resumable upload = Total size of file - 1 = 221213[1]
- Length of the chunk = Total size of file - position of first byte to send = 221214 - 11 = 221203

Put these values into the request:

```
PUT
https://www.googleapis.com/upload/storage/v1/b/lunchmates_document_dropbox/o
?uploadType=resumable&name=bigtable-osdi06.pdf&upload_id=<given_upload_id>

Content-Range: bytes 11-221213/221214
Content-Length: 221203

<contents_of_file>
```

Just like before, `200 OK` is returned if everything went fine and the file was fully uploaded into the specified bucket. This file is not public, because you do not want the content you just uploaded to be seen by anybody else on the Internet. Attempts to access it will result on a `403 Forbidden` response code.

Signed URLs

A meeting has been created in your app and has a file attached to it. After waiting a while, Maria has her first lunchmate join the meeting. Alejandro is also very interested in back-end infrastructure and decides to take this chance to discuss it over lunch with Maria. He happens to have never heard of any service from a company called Google, so he does not have a user/e-mail account there. Therefore he cannot get long-term access to the document in the meeting or any document in Cloud Storage, unless access for that document is set to public. But that would make the document available to everybody with Internet access, which definitely is not acceptable in this case.

---

[1]Byte chunks are zero based.

Instead, you create a signed URL to access that document on behalf of your service, granting access to the requester for a limited amount of time. Once again, by following this approach, your system is in charge of acknowledging whether a user is entitled to see the contents/documents of a meeting and go ahead and generate a signed URL for it.

You can generate signed URLs by using the Cloud Storage `gsutil` command-line tool like so:

```
gsutil signurl -d 10m path/to/privatekey.p12 gs://bucket/object
```

The `-d` option determines the duration until the link expires. For more information, check the command's help section:

```
gsutil signurl --help
```

Given that you are approaching the problem from a server-side perspective, this part of the chapter explores how a signed URL is constructed, signed, and encoded for use. Remember that as soon as Alejandro gets access to the meeting and discovers the document that Maria attached previously, he will attempt to open it. Therefore, in order to avoid annoying users, you need to generate the signed URL that grants access to the document as soon as it is created, and cache it in your system. For example, you can store the signed URL associated with a file in the memory cache and set the same expiration time for the entry as that in the signed URL; then, whenever a user requests access to the document, you can look for the entry in memory and return the link if it exists or generate a new one if it has already expired.

URL Structure

Here is how the final URL looks:

```
<base_url>
?GoogleAccessId=<google_access_storage_id>
&Expires=<expiration_timestamp_seconds>
&Signature=<url_encoded_signature>
```

From right to left, it is as follows:

- `base_url` is the URL corresponding to a resource in Cloud Storage. You are referring to the file that was uploaded previously, so it is `https://lunchmates_document_dropbox.storage.googleapis.com/bigtable-osdi06.pdf`.
- `google_access_storage_id` identifies the service authorizing the request. This is the client ID e-mail of your service account, and it has the following format:

  ```
  <identifier>@developer.gserviceaccount.com
  ```

■ **Note** You can check, create, and delete client IDs for any of your projects from the Developers Console, at APIs & Auth ➤ Credentials. For more information, see Chapter 3.

- `url_encoded_signature` is used to prove authenticity by matching whatever is sent under this query parameter with this same signature constructed on Google's side.

The final signed URL should be similar to this:

```
https://lunchmates_document_dropbox.storage.googleapis.com/bigtable-osdi06.pdf
?GoogleAccessId=1234567890123@developer.gserviceaccount.com
&Expires=1432927800000
&Signature=<url_encoded_signature>
```

Signature

The last piece of information missing from the URL is the signature. This is how it is formed:

```
<http_verb>\n
<content_md5>\n
<content_type>\n
<expiration>\n
<canonicalized_extension_headers><canonicalized_resource>
```

The parts are as follows:

- `http_verb` is the HTTP verb to be used in the resulting request. Signed URLs are restricted to `GET`, `PUT`, `HEAD`, and `DELETE`.
- `content_md5` is an *optional* part of the signature containing the MD5 digest of the content to be sent, encoded in base64. If specified, the same header needs to be added to the resulting request: for example, `Content-MD5: <content_md5>`. This part is not applicable for requests without content.
- `content_type` is an *optional* piece of the signature that tells the MIME type of the content. Similar to `content-MD5`, if this value is specified, the same header needs to be added to the resulting request.
- `expiration` is used to let the servers know when to stop accepting requests for this resource. The value has to be a timestamp in seconds since UTC January 1, 1970. This value must match what is sent in the request's `Expires` query parameter. In this example, it is 1432927800000.
- `canonicalized_extension_headers` is an *optional* portion of the signature used to specify extension headers that begin with `x-goog-`. The client emitting the request must provide the same headers along with it. These headers must be concatenated and lexicographically sorted in the following format:

  ```
  <header-1-name-lowercase>:<value-0>,<value-1>,...,<value-n>
  <header-2-name-lowercase>:<value-0>,<value-1>,...,<value-n>
  ...
  <zheader-3-name-lowercase>:<value-0>,<value-1>,...,<value-n>
  ```

  For example:

  ```
  x-goog-acl:public-read\nx-goog-meta-property:value1,value2\n
  ```

- `canonicalized_resource` is the path to the object being accessed with this request. In this case, it looks like `/lunchmates_document_dropbox/bigtable-osdi06.pdf`.

This is how the plain signature looks if you put all the pieces together:

```
GET\n\n\n1432927800000\n/lunchmates_document_dropbox/bigtable-osdi06.pdf
```

Here are a couple examples of signatures for other type of requests and resources. For clarity, new lines (\n) are shown as actual new lines:

```
GET


1432927800000
/lunchmates_document_dropbox/bigtable-osdi06.pdf

PUT
7Qdih1MuhjZehB6Sv8UNjA==
text/plain
1432927800000
x-goog-acl:private
/lunchmates_document_dropbox/hello_world.txt
```

The last step is to sign the resulting string using RSA signatures with an SHA256 digest and encode the result in base64. You do that by using PKCS keys generated under your client ID. There are various ways to perform this operation in different programming languages. For example, you can use OpenSSL in Python:

```
from OpenSSL.crypto import load_pkcs12, sign

key_text = open(PRIVATE_KEY_PATH, 'rb').read()
private_key = load_pkcs12(key_text, 'notasecret')
# 'notasecret' is the default password for Google-generated PKCS keys.

signed_signature = sign(private_key, signature_string, 'sha256')
encoded_signature = base64.b64encode(signed_signature)
```

■ **Note** To generate a new key, go to the Developers Console and navigate to APIs & Auth ➤ Credentials. If you have not created any client IDs, you can do so by clicking Create New Client ID. Click Generate a New P12 Key, and a fingerprint will be added for the new key, which will be downloaded to your computer. This key is meant to live somewhere safe in your production machines. Do not expose this or any configuration file containing the path of any key publicly or in version-control or source-code management systems.

A complete implementation is available of a test case written in Python that uploads and reads a file using signed URLs. You can find it in the `code-snippets` repository of this book under `cloud-storage/signed-urls.py`.

Once the signature is generated, you can put together the complete signed URL as specified. Taking the URL where you left it and adding the signature, you should end up with something similar to this:

```
https://lunchmates_document_dropbox.storage.googleapis.com/bigtable-osdi06.pdf
?GoogleAccessId=1234567890123@developer.gserviceaccount.com
&Expires=1432927800000
&Signature=eVANhCqwmVw8GSbWy94/2Xm2tZnLuPVQwFeSe2mNuOYlfcAKW48B08IooWtNgI25Ywvo56khIaqq
Nu19C6ZSIOgaqsyGlGHdQk593YeUx/D3namDPeAO1Tk3qBzQ29E/JFXK3JMiKYzWPFWXlrIhHM+CJ7C1lNlJ8
AOMt4LU+7k=
```

You can use this URL to access the resource in question without any further authorization. Remember that in order for Google to evaluate the signature, you need to add headers to the request with some of the fields you used to construct the signature, so that the same calculation can be done on the server side to be sure both signatures match. These include `Content-MD5`, `Content-Type`, and other `x-goog-` headers.

Be sure the resulting signed URL—especially the `Signature` query parameter—is not re-encoded or escaped, because that will cause the request to fail with a `403 Forbidden SignatureDoesNotMatch` error.

This is how your final GET request should look. Note that we have not added any body or `x-goog-` custom headers to the signature, so you do not need to add any extra headers to the request:

```
GET https://lunchmates_document_dropbox.storage.googleapis.com/bigtable-osdi06.pdf
?GoogleAccessId=1234567890123@developer.gserviceaccount.com
&Expires=1432927800000
&Signature=eVANhCqwmVw8GSbWy94/2Xm2tZnLuPVQwFeSe2mNuOYlfcAKW48B08IooWtNgI25Ywvo56khIaqqNu19
C6ZSIOgaqsyGlGHdQk593YeUx/D3namDPeAO1Tk3qBzQ29E/J FXK3JMiKYzWPFWXlrIhHM+CJ7C1lNlJ8AOMt4LU+7k=
```

You can send this URL back to Alejandro so that he can access documents that Maria—or any other participant in the meeting—uploads. When executing this request, he should receive a successful response with the file that Maria uploaded previously.

Handling Errors

As much as we wish it were so, the infrastructure supporting the Internet is not simple. It would not be surprising to find all sorts of hidden treasures and underworld civilizations along the way traveled by a single byte from the virtual location of a resource and its requester. Because of that, data transfers are sometimes slow and requests fail; and therefore it is important to be protected against potential errors that could affect the experience of your services.

It is always a good idea to retry network requests that fail due to an external cause before giving up the operation. These are the response codes to expect in such circumstances:

```
408 Request Timeout
500 Internal Server Error
502 Bad Gateway
503 Service Unavailable
504 Gateway Timeout
```

However, you do not want to keep retrying requests forever. A common approach is to adopt a strategy based on exponential back-off feedback—that is, decreasing the rate of subsequent attempts based on the result of the previous request. The simplest version of this is, for example, to retry the unsuccessful request at gradually increasing time intervals up to a certain limit, like so:

1. Send request . . . Failure . . . Wait for 2 seconds
2. Send request . . . Failure . . . Wait for 4 seconds
3. Send request . . . Failure . . . Wait for 8 seconds
4. . . .

Conversely, if your request is missing necessary parameters, is not encoded properly, or is malformed in any other manner, the server will respond with a `400 Bad Request` code. For example, upload IDs for resumable uploads expire after one week. If you attempt to use an expired upload ID, your request will fail with a `400 Bad Request`; hence it is necessary to process and understand the concrete error in the response in order to decide on the best action to take next.

Finally, it is highly recommended that you take advantage of integrity checks when uploading files to Cloud Storage. Just as in the examples used throughout the chapter, you can use the `Content-MD5` header to include the MD5 digest of the content being uploaded. Once the upload is finished, the object will be created only if the hash provided in the headers matches the value calculated on the server side.

ACLs (Access Control Lists)

By now, you know that Cloud Storage is a massive system of interconnected machines distributed across the globe that allows you to have binary information (your files) everywhere while making sure it is safe at the same time. Countless buckets and objects are stored in a tangle of contiguous nets. Such a system would not have an important number of current applications without long-term access control. After all, we live in the times of content generation and sharing. The latter, especially, needs to happen in a responsible manner.

ACLs suppose a very simple yet powerful approach to controlling how different users or groups of users access files or buckets. Thus ACLs apply to specific buckets or objects and define permissions and scopes for each entry. *Permissions* determine the actions that can be done against a bucket or object, whereas *scopes* specify the user or group of users to which the entry applies. Here is an example that grants read access to all users on the Internet for the object to which it is applied:

```
{
  "entity": "allUsers",
  "role": "READER"
}
```

■ **Note** The maximum number of ACL entries for a bucket or object is 100. You can give access to more than one user at once by using groups.

This chapter is approaching the examples from a system administrator or DevOps perspective. Because of this, you mainly use `gsutil` while learning the details of access control. Like other command-line routines, it is automatable in maintenance, supervision, deployment, and testing tasks, using, for example, cron jobs that run periodically or a continuous-integration tool like Jenkins or Travis.

Let's take an easy example: access logs. These files are present in every back end and help you troubleshoot the system and gather information about how users consume your APIs and apps. When these files grow bigger, they sometimes become hard to manage. This example addresses this issue by uploading access log files to Cloud Storage, specifying access control, and defining a policy for auto-deletion after a certain amount of time. That way, stale logs can be taken out of the way and stored safely for further consultation or analysis.

Permissions and Scopes

Before uploading your first access log, let's briefly discuss *permissions* (what users can do with objects or buckets) and *scopes* (who can see these permissions). Permissions—READER, WRITER, and OWNER—apply to bucket or objects and can be summarized as shown in Table 8-1.

Table 8-1. *Permission details in objects and buckets*

	READER	WRITER	OWNER
Objects	Allows users to download the object.	Not applicable.	In addition to granting READER permissions, allows users to read and write objects' metadata.
Buckets	Allows users to list the contents of the bucket.	Lets users list, create, overwrite, and delete objects in the bucket.	In addition to granting READER and WRITER permissions, enables users to read and write buckets' metadata.

These permission levels are also present in the OAuth scopes used when authenticating other services to act on your behalf in Cloud Storage (see Table 8-2).

Table 8-2. *OAuth scopes associated to the permissions available*

Permission	OAuth Scope	OAuth 2 URL
READER	devstorage.read_only	https://www.googleapis.com/auth/devstorage.read_only
WRITER	devstorage.read_write	https://www.googleapis.com/auth/devstorage.read_write
OWNER	devstorage.full_control	https://www.googleapis.com/auth/devstorage.full_control

■ **Note** Permissions in Cloud Storage are concentric; that is, when assigning a given permission, you are also granting all the other more restrictive permissions under it. For example, if you set WRITER permissions on a specific resource for Julian, one of your system administrators, he is also granted READER access on that same resource.

These are the allowed identifiers to define scopes on a given resource:

- *Google storage ID:* This string unequivocally identifies the Google account of a user or group. Storage IDs can be found in ACLs under the property `entityId`. To access ACLs for an object, you can run the following command in `gsutil`: `gsutil acl get gs://<path-to-object>`. You can also find the Google storage IDs of a project on the Developers Console at Storage ➤ Cloud Storage ➤ Storage Access.
- *E-mail address:* Similarly, you can use the e-mail addresses of regular Google accounts or groups (`..@googlegroups.com`) to specify the scope of an ACL.
- *Google Apps domain:* Another way to grant access to a group of individuals at once is to use a custom domain name associated with a Google Apps account. For example, if you have `my-cool-domain.com` associated with your Google Apps account, you can use `my-cool-domain.com` to specify a scope so that all users with an e-mail account in this domain can access a given resource.
- *Special identifiers:* `allAuthenticatedUsers` and `allUsers` are special identifiers that provide access to any user with a Google account and any user on the Internet, respectively.

To give all this theory some meaning, let's upload your first log file. For the purposes of this example, you use a file called `access.log` generated by Nginx. This file contains a record for each incoming request received during a certain period of time. Feel free to use your own values here as long as you maintain the constant of uploading a file with a journal of operations for any kind of system (a log file).

Start by creating the bucket that you are going to use to store these files:

```
$ gsutil mb -c NEARLINE gs://lunchmates_logs
```

You can specify three options to `mb`:

- `-p` determines the project to which the bucket will be added. It is recommended that you set your working project as the default before beginning to work on it. Here is a refresher of what you saw at the beginning of the chapter:

  ```
  $ gcloud config set project <project-id>
  ```

- Use `-l` to specify the location for the new bucket. Options are [ASIA | EU | US]. The default is US.
- You can also specify the class of storage to use with `-c`. You can choose among `DRA` (or `DURABLE_REDUCED_AVAILABILITY`), `NL` (or `NEARLINE`), and `S` (or `STANDARD`). The default is `STANDARD`.

Note that you are using the recently released Nearline storage. This storage class allows you to store content with a better compromise for *cold storage*, or infrequently accessed content. In this class, the price is reduced, but availability is slightly lower and latency higher. This is ideal for long-lived content without strict requirements in terms of access, which is precisely the case for log files.

Now you can perform the actual upload of your first log file:

```
$ gsutil cp access.log gs://lunchmates_logs
```

You made it—your log file is there. What are the implications in terms of access?

Default and Predefined ACLs

When you create or upload a new resource as you just did, Cloud Storage assigns a predefined set of permissions to it based on the default configuration. For buckets, a predefined ACL called `project-private` is assigned. Buckets can also specify a default ACL that is assigned to objects uploaded in this bucket. By default, `project-private` is also used for this purpose.

Predefined ACLs act as an alias for a group of permissions that you can use to quickly change many ACL entries for a given resource at once. Table 8-3 lists the predefined ACLs and their permissions.

Table 8-3. *List of built-in predefined ACLs*

Predefined ACL (ACL in JSON API)	Permissions
`project-private` (`projectPrivate`)	Grants `READER` permission to team members and `OWNER` permission to owners and editors.
`private`	Gives `OWNER` permission to the owner of the bucket or object.
`public-read` (`publicRead`)	Grants `OWNER` permission to the owner of the bucket or object. In addition, it allows `READER` access to any user on the Internet. When applied to a bucket, it allows any user on the Internet to list the contents of the bucket.
`public-read-write` (`publicReadWrite`)	This ACL is only applicable to buckets. It gives `OWNER` permission to the owner of the bucket and `READER` and `WRITER` permission to any user on the Internet. Therefore anyone can list, create, overwrite, and delete objects in this bucket without any authentication.
`authenticated-read` (`authenticatedRead`)	Grants `OWNER` access to the owner of the resource and `READER` permission to any user authenticated with a Google account.
`bucket-owner-read` (`bucketOwnerRead`)	This ACL is only applicable to objects. It gives `OWNER` permission to the owner of the object and `READER` permission to the owner of the bucket.
`bucket-owner-full-control` (`bucketOwnerFullControl`)	This ACL is only applicable to objects. It gives the bucket and object owners `OWNER` permission.

■ **Note** Editors, owners, and viewers are default roles on Google Cloud projects. These roles are shared across services on a global level. You can manage members and roles from the Developers Console, under Permissions.

To see the current ACL for a resource, run the following command:

```
$ gsutil acl get <path-to-resource>
```

So, here is the command for the newly created bucket:

```
$ gsutil acl get gs://lunchmates_logs/
```

The output is as follows:

```
[
  {
    "entity": "project-owners-<project-number>",
    "projectTeam": {
      "projectNumber": "<project-number>",
      "team": "owners"
    },
    "role": "OWNER"
  },
  {
    "entity": "project-editors-<project-number>",
    "projectTeam": {
      "projectNumber": "<project-number>",
      "team": "editors"
    },
    "role": "OWNER"
  },
  {
    "entity": "project-viewers-<project-number>",
    "projectTeam": {
      "projectNumber": "<project-number>,
      "team": "viewers"
    },
    "role": "READER"
  }
]
```

The result is very similar if you run the same command for the log file you just uploaded:

```
$ gsutil acl get gs://lunchmates_logs/access.log
```

Because you have not specified a default ACL for the bucket yet, uploaded objects are assigned the same predefined ACL: `project-private`. In addition to the three entries you saw earlier, there is another that grants `OWNER` permission to the user who uploaded the file. This entry cannot be changed unless the file is overwritten:

```
[
  <default bucket ACL entries>,
  {
    "entity": "user-<Google-Storage-ID>",
    "entityId": "<Google-Storage-ID>",
    "role": "OWNER"
  }
]
```

Coming back to the example, it is time to give all your system administrators read access to the bucket where the logs are uploaded so they can list the objects in the bucket. There are a couple of ways you can do that. The most straightforward is to add their e-mails to the `viewers` role of the project by going to the Developer Console and choosing <project> ➤ Permissions. But to make the example more illustrative, and given that your system administrators already have a Google group for internal communications, let's use the e-mail address for that group to scope this new permission:

```
$ gsutil acl ch -g lunchmates_sysadmins@googlegroups.com:R gs://lunchmates_logs
```

You can use two commands to change ACLs on resources:

- **set** replaces the entire ACL on a resource with the value provided either through a predefined ACL (such as `project-private`) or a file containing ACL entries. For example, the following command sets ACLs on your bucket to `private`:

  ```
  $ gsutil acl set private gs://lunchmates_logs
  ```

- Similarly, you can save the current ACL of a resource on a file, update the content manually, and reset it:

  ```
  $ gsutil acl get gs://lunchmates_logs > lunchmates_logs_acl.json
  ```

- Edit the contents of `lunchmates_logs_acl.json`:

  ```
  $ gsutil acl set lunchmates_logs_acl.json gs://lunchmates_logs
  ```

- `ch` adds or deletes ACL entries directly, just like its counterpart in Linux. The command allows batch operations.

Here's an example of `ch` that uses the earlier command:

```
$ gsutil acl ch -g lunchmates_sysadmins@googlegroups.com:R gs://lunchmates_logs
```

The first option (`-g`) defines the kind of scope you are trying to add. Valid values are

- `-u`, for single-user accounts like service accounts, user e-mails, and storage IDs.
- `-g`, for groups like group e-mails and custom domain names. You can also use special identifiers like `allUsers` and `allAuthenticatedUsers`. These are case insensitive and can be shortened to `all` and `allauth`, respectively.

Immediately after the identifier, the permission level is determined with a colon (`:`) followed by a single letter:

- `R` for `READER`
- `W` for `WRITER`
- `O` for `OWNER`

As mentioned previously, changes to ACL entries can be batched in a single command. Suppose, for example, that you wanted to do the following:

1. Delete the entry for the Google group you just created.
2. Add READER access to all authenticated users.
3. Add WRITER access to a specific e-mail.

The following command would do the job:

```
$ gsutil acl ch -d lunchmates_sysadmins@googlegroups.com -g AllAuthenticatedUsers:R -u
random_email@gmail.com:W gs://lunchmates_logs
```

Both set and ch also let you set or update ACLs on more than one resource at a time by using a wildcard expression at the object level:

```
$ gsutil acl [set|ch] <specific params> gs://lunchmates_logs/*.log
```

And you can operate recursively with the -r option:

```
$ gsutil acl [set|ch] -r <specific params> gs://lunchmates_logs
```

Back to the example. In addition to listing the contents of the bucket, you want your system administrators to be able to download any specific log they may be interested in. The best way to do that is to use a default ACL on buckets: that is, a set of ACL entries that is automatically assigned to every new object uploaded to the bucket in question.

The subcommand to read, replace, or change default ACLs is gsutil defacl. This command operates similarly to acl. Just as you did at the bucket level, you can run a very similar command to add the e-mail address of the system administrators' Google group to the current default ACL:

```
$ gsutil defacl ch -g lunchmates_sysadmins@googlegroups.com:R gs://lunchmates_logs
```

From now on, every time a file is uploaded to the logs bucket without specifying an ACL, it will be assigned whatever is on the default ACL of the bucket at this point in time. To test this new behavior, overwrite the same access log file by uploading it again:

```
$ gsutil cp access.log gs://lunchmates_logs
```

Checking the ACL for that object should include the entries of the bucket's default ACL in addition to the entry for the creator/owner of the file (the user who uploaded it):

```
$ gsutil acl get gs://lunchmates_logs/access.log
```

■ **Note** gsutil is a very powerful tool. To take full advantage of its potential, check the complete reference in the documentation for the Google Cloud Platform at https://cloud.google.com/storage/docs/gsutil.

Lifecycle Management

Log files can end up taking a lot of storage space, especially if you keep piling them up forever. However, performing a cleanup every once in a while is a task that is quick to do but must be done periodically forever. In order to avoid making somebody's work systematically boring, you can take advantage of object lifecycle configuration in Cloud Storage.

This feature is applied to buckets and acts at the object level. It allows you to define a set of rules or policies that, when met at the same time, trigger an action on specific objects in the bucket. At the time of this writing, the only action supported is `Delete`. This action deletes objects that meet the set of conditions you specify.

The conditions supported are as follows:

- Age: Satisfied after a specified amount of days after the date when an object was created, rounded to the next midnight in UTC. For example, if an object is created on 2029/11/10 01:00 UTC and the Age condition is set to 10, then the object expires on 2029/11/21 00:00 UTC.
- `CreatedBefore`: Met if an object was created before the specified date. The expected format for this date is `YYYY-mm-dd`.
- `NumberOfNewerVersions`: Applies only to versioned objects, and is met when there are `N` new versions for a given object.
- `IsLive`: Applies only to versioned objects. It matches live objects when set to `true` or archived ones if set to `false`.

■ **Note** Versions are a very powerful feature in Cloud Storage that lies outside the scope of this book. It allows you to enable versioning on objects, which is useful to track and keep changes on files (updates or deletions). To find out more, refer to the documentation at `https://cloud.google.com/storage/docs/object-versioning`.

Lifecycle configuration is described in a JSON file. Its structure is as follows:

```
{
   "rule":
   [
       {
           "action": {"type": "Delete"},
           "condition": {"age": <number_of_days>,
                         "CreatedBefore": <date_string YYYY-mm-dd>,
                         "NumberOfNewerVersions": <number_of_verisons>,
                         "isLive": [true|false]}
       },
       {
       ...
       },
       ...
   ]
}
```

Note that one rule can have many actions. When you define more than one condition for a given rule, all conditions must be met in order for the action to be applied.

Returning to the example, you can take advantage of lifecycle management to clean up logs that are older than one year so storage usage remains balanced. To do this, define the following rule and save it to a file called `one-year-rule.json`:

```
{
    "rule":
    [
        {
            "action": {"type": "Delete"},
            "condition": {"age": 365}
        }
    ]
}
```

To work with lifecycle configuration, you use the `gsutil lifecycle` command. Simply by using the `set` and `get` subcommands, you can check or assign lifecycle configurations in Cloud Storage.

Start by setting the new configuration to your logs bucket:

```
$ gsutil lifecycle set one-year-rule.json gs://lunchmates_logs
```

You can check the current lifecycle configuration of a bucket with the `get` subcommand:

```
$ gsutil lifecycle get gs://lunchmates_logs
```

To reset a bucket's lifecycle configuration, edit the JSON file to only include an empty JSON object, and reset it with the `set` command just as you did before:

```
$ gsutil lifecycle set one-year-rule.json gs://lunchmates_logs
```

Automation

Learning new things in tech should always lead to a reduction of repetitive tasks. Automation is a key part of system administration. It allows engineers—and, indirectly, anybody else—to stop worrying about things your brain does not do as well, in favor of other tasks for which a human brain is, at least so far, the best-suited machine in the world. Such tasks require abilities like creativity, contextual problem solving, and complex communication, among others. Machines "love" to perform low-load, repeating tasks while keeping their temperature and transistors in a relaxed state.

Having configured your logs bucket leaves you with only one task left to automate: uploading a log file as soon as it is ready. Whether you do that on periodic basis, based on the size of log files, or using a completely different approach, all you need to do is upload a file. That's it.

We are not expecting you to memorize all the commands used in the book, so here is a third reminder of how to do this using `gsutil`:

```
$ gsutil cp access.log gs://lunchmates_logs
```

You can also perform file uploads through the JSON API:

```
POST https://www.googleapis.com/upload/storage/v1/b/<bucket_name>/o?name=<file_name>
Authorization: Bearer <your_auth_token>
Content-Length: <content_length_in_bytes>
Content-Type: <content_mime_type> or application/octet-stream

<contents_of_file>
```

Remember that all new files uploaded to this bucket are assigned the default ACL in addition to the lifecycle configuration specified on the bucket level.

Summary

Cloud Storage is one of the cornerstones of Google Cloud Platform as it can be used to complement other services. For example, a typical use case for Compute Engine and App Engine is storing files that your users can access from your application. Or using Cloud Storage to persist system files that help you measure, organize and log the details of your business or project. Another example is Cloud Dataflow, a service that allows you to process and analyze large-scale information in the cloud to produce a set of results that are useful for you. Cloud Dataflow accepts using Cloud Storage as an input/output data source. Finally, the fact that Cloud Storage can operate and communicate with other systems outside of Google Cloud Platform, widens the possibilities that this service brings to almost any machine or device that can connect to the Internet.

In this chapter you have learned how to use Cloud Storage to store, protect and distribute files from both a system administrator and application development standpoint. You have also learned how to operate the command line tool `gsutil`, to perform maintenance and automated tasks; but also how to develop features for your application using the exposed JSON API.

Now it is time for you to tackle your own challenge or come up with better uses of this technology. After all, storage is not only an important building block of your application, system or project, but a foundation for the future of Internet and information.

CHAPTER 9

Google Cloud Datastore

Google Cloud Datastore[1] is a fully managed, schema-less database for storing nonrelational data. Cloud Datastore automatically scales with your users and supports ACID (atomic, consistent, isolated, durable) transactions, high availability of reads and writes, strong consistency for reads and ancestor queries, and eventual consistency for all other queries.

These features make Cloud Datastore a great option (fast, scalable, and available) in scenarios where there is no need for complex querying requirements. Due to its nature, this type of storage also has associated limitations that you must keep in mind. If some of these aspects are crucial to the success of your product or application, you may want to consider using a different alternative such as Cloud SQL, described in Chapter 7. But it is sensible to question these needs beforehand—in many cases, they may result from trying to solve problems using an inadequate solution. For example, if you are attempting to extract statistics or reports for your product from a very large table, you may be querying with `JOIN`s, filters, grouping, and so on. In the past, regular databases were used for this purpose; but today, you can take advantage of large-scale storage solutions like BigQuery, Redshift or Hadoop to tackle such challenges.

Often, managing Cloud Datastore's limitations properly leads to compromises that can help keep your data model and structure simple and fast. Some of the most relevant constraints are as follows:

- No `JOIN`s or subqueries are allowed.
- Entities that do not include a property named on the query do not appear in the results.
- Inequality filters are limited to a single property on each query.
- Properties used in inequality filters must be sorted before other properties.

Why Is Cloud Datastore Scalable?

Scalability is a big deal these days. Most companies offering backend as a service (BaaS) and platform as a service (PaaS) solutions place considerable focus on scalability. And those proposing better alternatives are the ones that needed to solve the issue for themselves in the first place, such as Google, Facebook (Parse), Microsoft (Azure), and Amazon Web Services.

To tackle this issue, Google bet on Bigtable, an internal effort to develop a database-like storage alternative with a prominent focus on scalability and high performance. It currently powers such widely used and relevant services as Google Maps, YouTube, and Gmail.

[1]"Google Cloud Cloud Datastore: A Fully Managed NoSQL Data Storage Service," Google Cloud Platform, 2014, `http://cloud.google.com/datastore/docs`.

Bigtable can be defined as a sparse map of keys and specific content associated with each of these keys in a multidimensional shape. Each cell is versioned with a timestamp, so multiple versions of the same cell are persisted for a limited amount of time. Bigtable splits its content into smaller units of information called *tablets*, which generally are no bigger than 100-200MB.[2] These tablets are unloaded and moved relatively fast across machines. As you may already have guessed, as data grows, the tablet dance becomes increasingly relevant. There is no good dance without choreography. And fortunately, Bigtable has its own choreographer: a load balancer especially designed for this purpose. Although it does not scale exactly linearly as tablets grow, it does a very good job and is one of the most interesting managed scaling alternatives available.

Why Is Cloud Datastore Highly Available?

Bigtable was also built to be distributed across machines and able to remain in sync. The goal is to keep the system consistent and functional through consensus, even if some of the machines that are hosting replicas become faulty. That's right: it uses machine consensus, with no master and no slaves. I know that sounds odd, so let us look at an example.

Suppose you need to persist a new entity, creating a new row with the content of the record. Assume that five replicas of your data live on different machines at the time of this write. Imagine that one of the replicas has a connectivity problem and another is unavailable because the tablet you're trying to write to is being moved. The write fails on these two and succeeds on the other three. Thus the overall result is successful, even though two of the replicas were not healthy, because the majority of the writes were achieved.

This architecture applies not only to writes and reads but also to the datacenters where your app lives and from which it is served. In the case of downtime due to planned or unplanned maintenance, your app can move itself to a different datacenter that is healthy. The result is a very low amount of unavailability or downtime.

Why Is Cloud Datastore Fast?

Operation speed was not necessarily the number-one priority for Cloud Datastore, but performance is a necessary building block. Cloud Datastore operates relatively fast not only because it was built to operate efficiently in challenging scenarios (large amounts of data, highly distributed systems) but also due to the compromises to be made from the developer perspective.

The Building Blocks of Cloud Datastore

From this point on, as usual in this book, you will learn about the fundamental parts of Cloud Datastore by following an example. Although Cloud Datastore was first integrated as part of App Engine, it is now conveniently available through the Node.js (with JSON) and ProtocolBuffer APIs. That means you can access it from pretty much any system that can host communications conforming the HTTP protocol.

This example mostly uses App Engine and the Python NDB Cloud Datastore API. If you're interested in how to access Cloud Datastore from Compute Engine or any other external infrastructure provider or service, see Chapter 4.

---

[2]F. Chang et al., "Bigtable: A Distributed Storage System for Structured Data," *ACM Transactions on Computer Systems* 26, no. 2 (2008):1–26.

You begin by creating the first part of the model for the LunchMate app. Here's the simplest version of model.py:

```
#!/usr/bin/env python

from google.appengine.ext import ndb

class Meeting(ndb.Model):
    created = ndb.DateTimeProperty(auto_now_add=True)
    venue_foursquare_id = ndb.StringProperty(required=True)
    location = ndb.GeoPtProperty()
    earliest_possible_start = ndb.DateTimeProperty(required=True)
    latest_possible_start = ndb.DateTimeProperty()
    topic = ndb.StringProperty(required=True)
    type = ndb.StringProperty(required=True, choices=['drink', 'lunch', 'brunch'])
    tags = ndb.StringProperty(repeated=True)
```

Properties

As you can see, each of the kinds that form the model is represented by a class that inherits from `ndb.Model` and defines the properties associated with it. Various types of properties are available in Cloud Datastore, from simple strings, numbers, and booleans to more specific containers such as blobs, keys, datetimes, and lists. In addition, different implementations may add other properties, made up of one or more of those just mentioned. For example, NDB includes `computed`, `json`, and `geo` properties. Each of them has a set of possible configurations to allow validation, specification of requirements and defaults, and so on.

For instance, in this example you add a property that is set automatically with the date when the meeting is created, a required string property for the ID of the venue where the meeting should take place, a property to store the location of the venue, the earliest and latest starting times for the meeting (represented by a `DateTimeProperty`) and three strings for the type, topic, and tags of the meeting. Note how for `type`, the possible values are constrained to those specified using `choices`. The `repeated` keyword in the `tags` property allows that property to hold and store a list of values of the defined type—strings, in this case.

Here is how you create and store an instance of a given meeting:

```
from datetime import datetime

dateformat_str = '%Y-%m-%dT%H:%M'

meeting = Meeting()
meeting.venue_foursquare_id = 'A9ABCD'
meeting.earliest_possible_start = datetime.strptime('2015-10-21T12:00', dateformat_str)
meeting.latest_possible_start = datetime.strptime('2015-10-21T13:00', dateformat_str)
meeting.topic = 'How to build your next big thing on Google Cloud Platform'
meeting.type = 'lunch'
meeting.tags = ['vegetarian', 'tech', 'programming', 'short']

meeting.put()
```

Now it is time to soothe your natural desire to learn about the rest of the property types:

■ **Note** Remember that, as mentioned earlier, different API implementations may add new properties or convenience wrappers around these basic types.

- *Integer*: 64-bit signed integer.
- *Floating-point number*: Double-precision floating-point number.
- *Boolean*: True or false.
- *Text string*: Unicode string; up to 500 characters when indexed, or 1MB otherwise.
- *Byte string*: Byte string; up to 500 bytes when indexed, or 1MB otherwise.
- *DateTime*: Specifies a point in time in UTC format. No time zone information is included. This property is consistent across other APIs in Cloud Datastore. As the name specifies, it holds a value for a specific day of the year and a certain point in time with microsecond precision.
- *Key*: A key path that unilaterally defines another entity in Cloud Datastore. That is, a key or group of keys containing its respective kind and identifier. This property is mainly used to reference other related entities in your model.
- *Embedded entity*: Holds the content of another generic object or structure. This type is useful when you need to store an unindexed group of keys and values that is not referenced or identified in your model.
- *List*: Contains an array of any of the values allowed in Cloud Datastore.

The `indexed` keyword defines whether the property is included in indexes. These indexes are used to return queries more quickly without any processing cost at read time, by creating records containing properties relevant to the index and a reference to the newly created entity at write time. Let us use an example to illustrate that.

Suppose you want to query for entities of the class you just created (`Meetings`), and you want to be able to retrieve them sorted by meeting type in ascending order. This requires an index on the `meeting.type` property. That way, when performing the query, Cloud Datastore retrieves results without the need for any post-processing.

Identifiers, Keys, and Ancestor Paths

Unlike other database systems, Cloud Datastore works similarly to a huge map or dictionary that holds keys and values. Each of the keys is used to represent an entity among all the records and is made up of the kind of entity and a unique string or numeric ID. Which one to choose depends on your concrete needs. For instance, if you want to create an instance of a given kind `User` with a string as an identifier, you can use the user's e-mail or username as the key. Conversely, if you do not specify a unique name for your key, Cloud Datastore assigns a unique numeric ID for you. Listings 9-1, 9-2, and 9-3 show how to use both approaches on the three different APIs.

Listing 9-1. App Engine Python NDB

```
# User specifying key name
new_user_key = ndb.Key(User, 'unique_username')
new_user = User(**args)
new_user.key = new_user_key

# User with automatically assigned identifier upon persisting
numeric_user = User(**args)  # gets a numeric id automatically assigned when stored
```

Listing 9-2. Node.js (JSON) API

```
// User specifying key name
var entity = {
   key: { path: [{ kind: 'User', name: 'unique_username'}] },
   ...
};
datastore.commit( {
   mutation: { insert: [entity] },
   mode: 'NON_TRANSACTIONAL'
}).execute(callback);

// User with automatically assigned identifier upon persisting
var numeric_entity = {
   key: { path: [{ kind: 'User'}] },
   ...
};
datastore.commit( {
   mutation: { insertAutoId: [numeric_entity] },
   mode: 'NON_TRANSACTIONAL'
}).execute(callback);
```

Listing 9-3. Protocol Buffers on Python

```
# User specifying key name
new_user = datastore.Entity()
path_element = new_user.key.path_element.add()
path_element.kind = 'User'
path_element.name = 'unique_username'

# User with automatically assigned identifier upon persisting
request = datastore.CommitRequest()
request.mode = datastore.CommitRequest.NON_TRANSACTIONAL
numeric_user = request.mutation.insert_auto_id.add()

path_element = numeric_user.key.path_element.add()
path_element.kind = 'User'
```

On the protocol buffer and Node.js APIs, the key is referred to as part of a property called `path`. This property has the form of a hierarchical group of keys, just like paths that specify the locations of files in the file system. That is a consequence of the fact that entities can have a certain number of parents, all of which together define their own ancestor path. Take as an example the following path, where the first element of each key is the kind and the other is the identifier:

```
Key(User, 'Parent') -> Key(User, 'Child') -> Key(Toy, 'Superman')
```

The following apply:

- The ancestor path of an entity is defined upon creation and cannot be changed.
- The root entity is defined by the first key in the path, in this case `Parent`.
- Two entities at the same hierarchical level never have the same identifier.
- Entities with a common parent belong to the same entity group.

Creating such ancestor paths is straightforward in all the APIs you've seen, as shown in Listings 9-4, 9-5, and 9-6.

Listing 9-4. App Engine Python NDB

```
parent_key = ndb.Key(User, 'Parent')
parent = User(**args)
parent.key = parent_key

child_key = ndb.Key(User, 'Child', parent=parent_key)
child = User(**args)
child.key = child_key

superman_key = ndb.Key(Toy, 'SuperMan', parent=child_key)
superman = Toy(**args)
superman.key = superman_key
```

Listing 9-5. Node.js (with JSON) API

```
// User specifying key name
var superman_key = { path: [{ kind: 'User', name: 'Parent' },
                            { kind: 'User', name: 'Child' },
                            { kind: 'Toy', name: 'SuperMan' }] };

var superman = {
   key: superman_key,
   ...
};
```

Listing 9-6. Protocol Buffers on Python

```
superman = datastore.Entity()
superman_key = superman.key

path_element = superman_key.path_element.add()
path_element.kind = 'User'
path_element.name = 'Parent'

path_element = superman_key.path_element.add()
path_element.kind = 'User'
path_element.name = 'Child'

path_element = superman_key.path_element.add()
path_element.kind = 'Toy'
path_element.name = 'SuperMan'
```

But why would you need to connect entities with each other this way? Entities that share the same parent on their ancestor path belong to the same entity group, including the parent. For instance, in the previous example, `Parent`, `Child`, and `Superman` belong to the same entity group. This turns out to be one of the most interesting parts of Cloud Datastore.

As mentioned earlier, Cloud Datastore is a nonrelational, highly available, distributed storage system, designed to cope with millions of operations in a short timeframe. Taking such an approach requires reconsidering long-accepted assumptions in the digital storage world, such as data replication and consistency. Unlike other relational solutions, Cloud Datastore assumes asynchronous replication across datacenters in order to increase performance at scale by reducing contention. That means every time you write to Cloud Datastore outside of an entity group, the operation returns before the new data has been fully applied and replicated. That not only is more performant but also allows many write operations to happen at the same time.

This methodology does not fit every scenario: in some situations, seeing the most up-to-date information is crucial for the proper functioning of your application. To achieve that, Cloud Datastore provides a mechanism that lets you to choose one approach or the other:

- *Strong consistency (more contention)*: Reads always return the most recent data, but there is a limit on how many writes can be processed in a given amount of time. This limit is one write per second per entity group.
- *Eventual consistency (higher throughput)*: Subsequent reads may return stale information, but you can handle more requests at the same time. Even though replication usually happens relatively quickly, there is no guarantee for that. In some cases, the entire process can take up to minutes.

Cloud Datastore has two ways to enforce strong consistency or, in other words, make sure that all pending operations from previous updates happen before the entity is queried. One of them is to retrieve an entity by its key, as shown in Listings 9-7, 9-8, and 9-9.

Listing 9-7. App Engine Python NDB

```
superman = superman_key.get()
```

Listing 9-8. Node.js API

```
datastore.lookup({ keys: [superman_key] }).execute(function(error, results) {
   if (!error) {
       var superman = null;
       if (result.found) {
           superman = result.found[0].entity;
       }
   });
```

Listing 9-9. Protocol Buffers on Python

```
request = datastore.LookupRequest()
request.key.extend([superman_key])

response = self.datastore.lookup(request)
if len(response.missing) is 1:
   raise Exception('entity not found')

superman = response.found[0].entity
```

The other approach is to operate in entity groups by using ancestor queries—that is, requesting entities that belong to a common ancestor. For example, if you query for all toys under the ancestor `Child`, you see the most recent version of the toys stored under that specific ancestor.

In addition to consistency, entity groups have two other very convenient features:

- *Locality*: Entities are stored in the same entity group on servers that are physically close to each other. This is because Cloud Datastore distributes data according to the lexicographical order of key names.
- *Transactionality*: Data changes in an entity group are applied as a single operational unit that either succeeds or fails as a whole. If it fails, no changes are applied to any of the entities involved. If more than one transaction tries to update the same entity or entities in the same entity group, the first one to commit succeeds, and all the rest fail. To minimize the effect of this limitation, make sure you execute every piece of code that does not directly affect the operation outside of the transaction.

■ **Note** If you actively define the key names of your entities, consider a mechanism that encourages uniform distribution. Keep in mind that a large amount of data that uses similar key names may result in a high occupation of servers that are physically close to each other, increasing the chances of negatively affecting performance.

TEST CASE

Assume that you're working on an application that processes pictures uploaded by users during live events. The application uses a slightly heavy algorithm that determines the score for a given picture, and you're using Cloud Datastore to collect the data. Every time a user adds a new picture, you need to create an entry with metadata for that picture and update the user's score; thus locality and transactionality are very helpful here. Strong consistency is also required, because the overall score is a weighted number calculated every time a picture is added. Thus this process must always see the most recent version of each picture's metadata.

Based on that, you decide to design your model as follows:

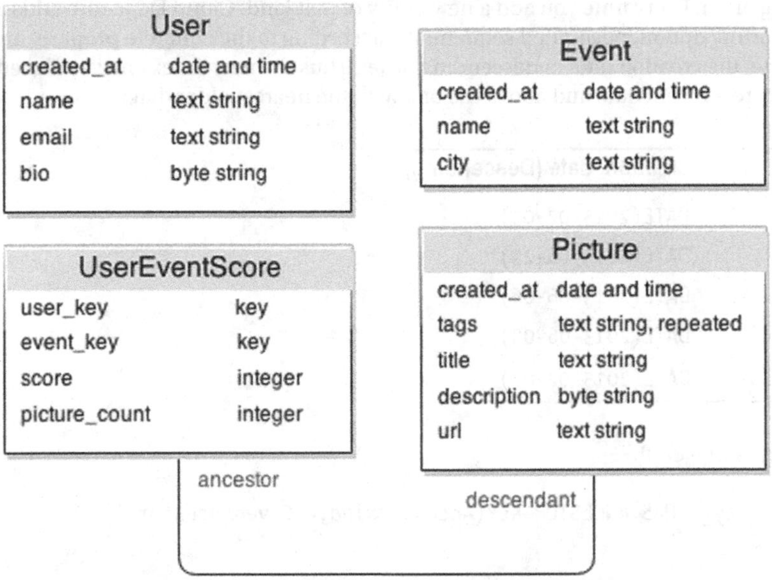

In this model, a given score and the pictures that affect it belong to the same entity group, so the previously mentioned limit of one write per second applies. In this case, it is a bearable limitation because it is unlikely that one user will upload more than one picture per second at a live event.

Cross-Group Transactions

You've seen how transactions apply to entity groups. In some cases, you may need transactionality without paying the extra price of organizing data under entity groups, whether due to their limited throughput or because doing so is inconvenient for your model from a structural standpoint.

If you need to perform an operation in a transaction involving entities that belong to different entity groups, you can do so using *cross-group* (XG) transactions. Cross-group transactions can operate over a maximum of five different entity groups and succeed only if no other transaction operates over any of the entity groups touched by the cross-group transaction.

Cloud Datastore Indexes

Indexes are a key part of Cloud Datastore. They're an important block in the foundation of how data is stored and queried, so a good understanding of them is crucial in order to properly optimize for performance and cost.

To start with, you need to forget all you know about indexes on other data-storage systems, or at least move that knowledge into a different part of your brain. The only conceptual resemblance between those other indexes and indexes in Cloud Datastore is that they all make queries somewhat faster. Full stop.

One of the reasons Bigtable can scale and yet remain performant is that queries do not need to do much processing when executed—records are already laid out in indexes the way they need to be output. Cloud Datastore makes this possible by adding as many entries as there are ways you need to arrange and sort the results of your query.

Let us look at a simple example. Suppose you need to query a specific kind with a given ancestor, sorted by creation date in descending order. Every time you add a new entity of that kind, Cloud Datastore adds an extra record for that specific sorting option, positioned sequentially according to the concrete property and ordering direction—in this case, the creation date in descending order. Thus the new index entry is placed below its neighbor with the nearest recent date and above the one with the nearest older date:

Kind	Ancestor Path	creation_date (Descending)
Post	User:alex	DATE(2015-02-05)
Post	User:alex	DATE(2014-06-25)
Post	User:alex	DATE(2013-06-06)
Post	User:alex	DATE(2013-06-05)
Post	User:bob	DATE(2015-02-03)

That way, when this query is triggered

```
SELECT * FROM Kind WHERE __key__ HAS ANCESTOR KEY(AncestorKind, 'GivenAncestor1')
ORDER BY creation_date DESC
```

Cloud Datastore will look for the first entity of that kind with that given ancestor in the part of the table where records are sorted by `creation_date` in descending order, returning all subsequent entities until the filtering conditions change or the end of the index or the maximum number of requested results is reached.

Indexes are described and constructed by specifying the properties of the kind they're targeted to act on, with the desired sorting direction (ascending or descending). Indexes that target ancestor queries must specify that by setting the `ancestor` property accordingly: `true` or `false`.

It is important to pay attention to the indexed nature of different properties. Previously in this chapter, you saw how some properties can be optionally indexed while others are unindexed by design. You have seen that queries over properties without an indexed value do not return results—but this statement can be misleading. Even though `indexed` is an argument that rules the behavior of a specific property of a kind, this does not mean it applies to all the entities that are already in the table.

TEST CASE

Suppose you're defining a model to track sales of cars. Thinking that you'll never need to filter based on wheel color, to save money, you decide to set this property to be unindexed. Later, an energetic businessperson who produces wheels seals an ambitious partnership with you; but in order to know which wheels work best, you both agree to start tracking sales according to wheel color. Accordingly, you make this property indexed and create an index for a new query that does the job.

When you first run the query, you see no results. You spend the entire day wondering why. The next day you add new cars to the system, run the same query again and surprisingly you see only the new cars you just added. This happens because entities with unindexed properties are not added to an index table that is interested in that specific property (wheel color, in this example). In order to see old records, you must rewrite the old entities so they're added to the newly created index table. Likewise, if you do not specify a value for a property in which an index is interested, it won't be added to the index.

It is crucial that you design your model carefully, paying attention to these features and, in some cases, thinking ahead about potential situations you may encounter over time. For instance, **using a default value to set properties that may be good candidates to be filtered or sorted in future queries** would prevent the unwanted scenario described here.

Cloud Datastore and the SDK do a good job on simplifying your experience with indexes. On one hand, Cloud Datastore creates default index tables so you do not need to worry about simple queries like the following:

- Kindless queries using only ancestor and key filters
- Queries using only ancestor and equality filters
- Queries using only inequality filters on a single property
- Queries using only ancestor filters, equality filters on properties, and inequality filters on keys
- Queries with no filters and only one sort order on a property

On the other hand, the development server attempts to create a fitting index if you run a query locally that has no associated index. That is, if you run every query in your application locally before you think about deploying, you begin with a promising set of indexes. Here's to the optimistic and the lazy—another powerful reason to fight in favor of local testing.

Indexes are specified in a configuration file called `datastore-indexes.xml` that only serves this purpose. It is by default an XML file stored in the `WEB-INF` folder, and it looks something like this:

```
<?xml version="1.0" encoding="utf-8"?>
<datastore-indexes autoGenerate="true">
   <datastore-index kind="User" ancestor="false">
       <property name="score" direction="desc" />
   </datastore-index>
   <datastore-index kind="Event" ancestor="false">
       <property name="date" direction="desc" />
       <property name="location" direction="asc" />
   </datastore-index>
</datastore-index>
```

Notice the `autoGenerate` property in the opening node of the indexes. When it is set to `true`, the development server creates another XML file called `datastore-indexes-auto.xml` located under `WEB-INF/appengine-generated` with autogenerated indexes based on the queries executed locally as explained earlier. Updating your indexes remotely with such a configuration combines the information in both files. Conversely, if `autoGenerated` is set to `false`, the content of autogenerated indexes is ignored, and both the local development server and your production environment throw exceptions when trying to execute a query for which no adequate indexes have been created. This configuration is helpful to test how queries and indexes behave locally.

This configuration file takes a different form on Python and Go in App Engine projects. It is a file called `index.yaml` that lives in the root of your project; and even though the syntax and organization are different, the concept remains the same:

```
indexes:
- kind: User
  properties:
  - name: score
    direction: desc

# AUTOGENERATED
- kind: Event
  ancestor: yes
  properties:
  - name: date
    direction: desc
  - name: location
```

You can obviate the `ancestor` property when it is false and the direction when it is ascending. In this case, autogenerated indexes are placed under the `# AUTOGENERATED` tag. If you want to manually add or adjust an index, simply place it above the tag.

Exploding Indexes

Indexes have a limit of writes per entity added. Currently this limit is 5,000—that is, no more than 5,000 records can be added to the index tables when you create and store a new entity to your model. This limit is risky especially when you're working with multivalued properties such as lists, given that Cloud Datastore adds a new record to the index for each different value in the list. Consider the following example:

```
SELECT * FROM Team WHERE shirt_color = 'red' AND shorts_color = 'white' ORDER BY name DESC
```

The shirt and shorts colors are multivalued properties. This sets the scenario for an exploding index

```
(shirt_color, shorts_color, -name)
```

that adds (shirt_color * shorts_color * name) number of entries to the index table per entity created by Cloud Datastore. For example, suppose you stored the following entity:

```
team = Team()
team.shirt_color = ['red', 'white', 'blue', 'green']
team.shorts_color = ['white', 'black', 'blue', 'green']
team.name = 'Guessed it already?'

team.put()
```

This creates 4 × 4 × 1 = 16 new records on the table for the index specified earlier—that is, any possible combination of the values for each property, so that further queries can locate a team by looking it up by any of the values in the lists on each property:

Kind	shirt_color	shorts_color	name
Team	red	white	Manchester United
Team	red	black	Manchester United
Team	red	blue	Manchester United
Team	red	green	Manchester United
Team	white	white	Manchester United
Team	white	black	Manchester United
Team	white	blue	Manchester United
Team	white	green	Manchester United
Team	blue	white	Manchester United
Team	blue	black	Manchester United
Team	blue	blue	Manchester United
Team	blue	green	Manchester United
Team	green	white	Manchester United
Team	green	black	Manchester United
Team	green	blue	Manchester United
Team	green	green	Manchester United

This is a concern not only due to the index limitation, but also because it affects billable costs assigned to your projects.

You can optimize this index by taking advantage of Cloud Datastore's ability to merge query results—done by using the zigzag merge join algorithm internally—which can merge results from scans to different indexes that are sorted by the same property. This allows for alternative approaches that avoid exploding indexes. Generally, the most optimized way to split these indexes is to avoid multivalued properties that coexist in a single index. Here is an example:

```
(ancestor, multi valued 1, [single valued properties], inequality or sort order)
(ancestor, multi valued 2, [single valued properties], inequality or sort order)
...
(ancestor, multi valued n, [single valued properties], inequality or sort order)
```

Coming back to the previously defined index,

```
(shirt_color, shorts_color, -name)
```

you can propose the following two indexes:

```
(shirt_color, -name)
(shorts_color, -name)
```

The writing costs of these new indexes are `(shirt_color * name) + (shorts_color * name)`, which equals 8 instead of 16 for the entity created in the previous example. Note that this approach takes part of the prewriting cost into the post-reading phase: you're writing fewer records into your index table, but Cloud Datastore now has to prescan and merge the results from the two indexes at read time.

With this in mind, there is a scenario where splitting the index to avoid its exploding nature can be less performant. Consider the query you just defined:

```
SELECT * FROM Team WHERE shirt_color = 'red' AND shorts_color = 'white' ORDER BY name DESC
```

There are lots of teams with either red shirts or white shorts, but only one that matches the combination of the two. Splitting the index as you just did would scan the first index table to find all teams with red shirts sorted by name in descending order, then scan the second index table to retrieve all teams with white shorts sorted by name in descending order, and merge the results from the two on the fly. Given the number of red shirts and white shorts, these two scans would find lots of false positives that would be discarded when the results are merged. This process incurs extra performance costs compared to using a single index.

It is crucial that you give your indexes some thought and test them in the field based on your general needs, data structure, and query requirements. This will determine to a great extent the performance, cost, and scaling fluidity of your application.

Queries

In this final section of the chapter, you apply the concepts learned so far and see the best side of Cloud Datastore. Despite the fact that Cloud Datastore is conceptually far different than relational databases, the possibilities and power of queries have evolved significantly while keeping Cloud Datastore performant and scalable—two of its flagship features.

As you've discovered in this chapter, Cloud Datastore gives you access to a variety of APIs that allow you to integrate it widely, from the managed App Engine to the lonely server in your home den. This section focuses on the Node.js and Protocol Buffer APIs and GQL—an SQL-like language that lets you operate against Cloud Datastore in a way familiar to most system and database administrators. If you're more interested in querying Cloud Datastore from App Engine using Python, you can find related content in Chapter 5.

■ **Warning** There are minor differences between GQL in the Python API in App Engine and Cloud Cloud Datastore GQL. Both are explained in other chapters of this book, but I do not explain the specific differences because they do not add value for the purpose of this book.

Queries let you retrieve data that has been previously persisted in Cloud Datastore. When defining queries, you can specify that you want to return specific properties or all of them, and the kind of objects you're looking for, filtered by any of their properties, keys, ancestor or descendants and sorted by one or more property values.

■ **Warning** Keep in mind that queries with filters over properties with no indexed values do not return any results.

Let us take the query from the previous section that retrieves teams with red shirts and white shorts, ordered alphabetically by their name, starting with its GQL representation:

```
SELECT name FROM Team WHERE shirt_color = 'red' AND shorts_color = 'white'
ORDER BY name DESC
```

Here is how you execute this (or any other) GQL query in the Node.js API:

```
function retrieveTeams(callback) {
   datastore.runQuery({
       gqlQuery: {
           allowLiteral: true,
           queryString: 'SELECT name FROM Team WHERE shirt_color = 'red'
                   AND shorts_color = 'white' ORDER BY name DESC',
       }
   }).execute(function(error, results) {
       if (!error) {
           entities = (results.batch.entityResults || []), map( function(result) {
               return result.entity;
          });
      }
      callback(error, entities);
   });
}
```

And similarly, here is the query using Protocol Buffers on Python:

```
request = datastore.RunQueryRequest()
gql_query = request.gql_query

gql_query.allow_literal = True
gql_query.query_string = 'SELECT name FROM Team WHERE shirt_color = "red"
                          AND shorts_color = "white" ORDER BY name DESC'

response = self.datastore.run_query(request)
results = [result.entity for result in response.batch.entity_result]
```

Let us concentrate on the bold text in each example where the query is being defined. The rest of the code remains the same: setting up the query, executing it, and processing the results.

After running your query and obtaining the results for the filters specified, you realize that it does not make much sense to only be able to select teams that meet the criteria of having a red-and-white clothing set. So, you decide to add a couple of options to the user-facing side of your application that allow you to specify the colors of the shirt and shorts at runtime.

In these circumstances, you can take advantage of argument binding and also protect your system against unwanted scenarios such as injection attacks. The arguments are preceded by an @ symbol and can be bound with keywords for each value (`@shirt_color_selection`, `@shorts_color_selection`) or numbers specifying the order in which the values are supplied (`@1`, `@2`).

Here is the updated GQL query property in the Node.js (JSON) API:

```
gqlQuery: {
   queryString: 'SELECT name FROM Team WHERE shirt_color = @shirt_color_selection
                 AND shorts_color = @shorts_color_selection
                 ORDER BY name DESC',
   nameArgs: [{ name: 'shirt_color_selection', value: {stringValue: 'red'} },
              { name: 'shorts_color_selection', value: {stringValue: 'blue'} }]
}
```

Alternatively, this query can be written this way:

```
gqlQuery: {
   queryString: 'SELECT name FROM Team WHERE shirt_color = @1
                 AND shorts_color = @2 ORDER BY name DESC',
   nameArgs: [{ value: {stringValue: 'red'} },
              { value: {stringValue: 'blue'} }]
```

Here is the query property in Protocol Buffers on Python:

```
gql_query.query_string = 'SELECT name FROM Team WHERE shirt_color = @shirt_color_selection
AND shorts_color = @shorts_color_selection ORDER BY name DESC'

query_argument = gql_query.name_arg.add()
query_argument.name = 'shirt_color_selection'
query_argument.value.string_value = 'red'

query_argument = gql_query.name_arg.add()
query_argument.name = 'shorts_color_selection'
query_argument.value.string_value = 'blue'
```

Once again, this is the same query using now numbered arguments:

```
gql_query.query_string = 'SELECT name FROM Team WHERE shirt_color = @1
AND shorts_color = @2 ORDER BY name DESC'

gql_query.number_arg.add().value.string_value = 'red'
gql_query.number_arg.add().value.string_value = 'blue'
```

Operating with Large datasets: OFFSET, LIMIT, and Cursors

This new feature in your app makes you so happy that you decide to look for data repositories and other sources to fill your database with as many teams as possible. After a couple of hours, you've found 250,000 teams. To satisfy your curiosity, you run the same query again, and it now takes significantly longer to deliver results. To avoid this undesired effect, Cloud Datastore provides a way to limit the number of query results. The following query returns the first 20 entities that meet the filtering criteria, sorted alphabetically:

```
SELECT name FROM Team WHERE shirt_color = 'red' AND shorts_color = 'white'
ORDER BY name DESC LIMIT 20
```

It is recommended that you limit the number of query results whenever possible in order to keep Cloud Datastore performing adequately, just as on most database systems.

LIMIT is often used in conjunction with OFFSET for pagination purposes—that is, to return a consistently limited number of results for a given large dataset. Suppose you want to show a list with all the teams you've collected. If you were to run that query without any limit on the number of results, you and your users would face unbearable waiting times. Paging—returning the list of teams in chunks of, for example, 20 results at a time—is a common way of tackling this common problem.

In GQL, this query returns the first 20 results of your dataset:

```
SELECT * FROM Team LIMIT 20
```

And this query returns the next 20 results after the position specified by the cursor:

```
SELECT * FROM Team LIMIT 20 OFFSET @startCursor
```

■ **Note** OFFSET accepts a number, a cursor, or both as parameters. All options let you specify the point from which you want to begin seeing results. Using a cursor jumps directly to a given record, whereas specifying a number makes your query start from the beginning of your collection (or cursor) and skip as many records as you determine, with the associated performance implications. For example, querying with an offset of 10,000 has a similar preprocessing impact similar to querying for those records.

Cursors can be extracted from queries after they're executed, represented as opaque strings that mark the position of the last result returned. Even though they're encoded before being given to you, exposing them could result in compromising information about your data structure and content. If that is not acceptable according to your design, consider encrypting your cursors. The example in Listings 9-10 and 9-11 fetches the first 20 teams from the list and extracts a cursor to use when requesting the next batch of 20.

Listing 9-10. Protocol Buffers on Python

```
request = datastore.RunQueryRequest()
gql_query = request.gql_query

gql_query.allow_literal = True
gql_query.query_string = 'SELECT * FROM Team LIMIT 20'
```

```
response = self.datastore.run_query(request)
results = [result.entity for result in response.batch.entity_result]

if response.batch.more_results == datastore.QueryResultBatch.NOT_FINISHED:
  end_cursor = response.batch.end_cursor
...

request = datastore.RunQueryRequest()
gql_query = request.gql_query

gql_query.allow_literal = True
gql_query.query_string = 'SELECT * FROM Team LIMIT 20 OFFSET @startCursor'

query_argument = gql_query.name_arg.add()
query_argument.name = 'startCursor'
query_argument.cursor = end_cursor
...
```

Listing 9-11. Node.js (JSON) API

```
function retrieveTeams(callback) {
   datastore.runQuery({
       gqlQuery: {
           allowLiteral: true,
           queryString: 'SELECT * FROM Team LIMIT 20',
       }
   }).execute(function(error, results) {
       if (!error) {
           entities = (results.batch.entityResults || []), map( function(result) {
               return result.entity;
           });
           if (results.batch.moreResults == 'NOT_FINISHED') {
               var last_end_cursor = results.batch.endCursor;
           }
          callback(error, results);
       }
   });
}
...
function retrieveTeams(callback, last_end_cursor) {
   datastore.runQuery({
       gqlQuery: {
           allowLiteral: true,
           queryString: 'SELECT * FROM Team LIMIT 20 OFFSET @startCursor',
           nameArgs: [{ name: startCursor, cursor: last_end_cursor }]
       }
   }).execute(function(error, results) {
       ...
   });
}
```

Filtering

Up to now, you've seen how to filter query results using property filters. You can also filter by key and ancestor. This gives you some new possibilities for how to query your immense list of teams:

```
SELECT * FROM Team WHERE foundation_date > 1910 ORDER BY foundation_date, name DESC LIMIT 20
```

This query returns a list of the youngest teams founded after 1910, sorted by foundation date and name.

Note that, as mentioned previously, when you're using inequality filters and sort orders, the property used in the inequality filter must be sorted first.

Let us now take the following query:

```
SELECT * FROM Team WHERE __key__ = KEY(League, 5125)
```

Filtering by key can be useful when you're looking for a specific record or fetching entries after or before a certain entity. Because of that, filters on keys also accept inequality operators. When you use inequality filters on keys, they're ordered according to their ancestor path and kind first and then by their key name or numeric ID. The key path and name are strings, ordered by byte value. Numeric IDs are sorted numerically. When a given set of results contains keys that have the same parent and kind, with a mix of key names and numeric IDs, the latter come first. Let us assume a hypothetical list of sorted keys for that purpose:

```
KEY(League, 1)
KEY(League, 3)
KEY(League, 134)
KEY(League, 'la_liga')
KEY(League, 'mls')
KEY(League, 'premier')
...
```

```
SELECT * FROM Team WHERE __key__ HAS ANCESTOR KEY(League, 'Premier')
```

This query returns all teams that have a key of the kind `League` with a key name `Premier` as a parent, independent of the position in the ancestor path for the given entity. Remember that ancestor queries grant strong consistency—results always see the most up-to-date version of the information, as opposed to eventually consistent results.

Optimizing for Costs: Keys-Only and Projection Queries

There are two types of queries in Cloud Datastore that can help you reduce latency and costs. Unsurprisingly, both act on the projection of the query by returning only entity keys or the properties that are necessary for a given purpose.

Suppose a kind is stored with eventual consistency—it does not belong to any entity group in your model. This kind is updated frequently, and you want users to see fresh results whenever possible; so, as soon as queries run, you decide to add some of the entities to a memory cache like Memcache or Redis. That way, every time a new user requests a list of this kind, you can check whether there is a record for each entity already in the memory cache and return it from there (because you know it will be the most up-to-date version) or go to Cloud Datastore otherwise.

To do so, you perform a so-called *keys-only query*:

```
SELECT __key__ FROM Team WHERE foundation_date > 1910 DESC LIMIT 20
```

This returns the keys only for the matching entities. You can later use them to check and retrieve the full entities from the memory cache or Cloud Datastore.

Similarly, you can limit the number of properties returned in a query on Cloud Datastore. As you've done previously, say you're only interested in the names of teams that match certain criteria:

```
SELECT name FROM Team WHERE shirt_color = 'red' AND shorts_color = 'white'
ORDER BY name DESC
```

This, again, helps you optimize for costs and performance.

Cloud Datastore uses indexes to serve projection queries, so the same advantages and limitations discussed earlier in this chapter apply here. For example, unindexed properties are not projected, and querying for more than one multivalued property causes an exploding index. Additionally, properties used in equality or using the `IN` clause filter cannot be projected.

Also remember that an index record is added for each value given to a multivalued property—or each combination of values, when you have more than one multivalued property on the same index. That could cause your projection query to return duplicated values, one per index record stored. To avoid that, you can group your results by using a `GROUP BY` clause on the property you're interested in:

```
SELECT name FROM Team WHERE shirt_color = 'red' AND shorts_color = 'white' GROUP BY name
```

Sorting

In Cloud Datastore, query results can be sorted by one or more properties in either ascending or descending order. If you do not specify sorting, results are returned in the same order as they were added to Cloud Datastore. Conversely, if you add one or more sorting properties, they're applied sequentially: results are sorted first by the first specified property in the query, and so on. Here are a couple of self-explanatory examples that have been used throughout the chapter:

```
SELECT * FROM Team WHERE shirt_color = 'red' AND shorts_color = 'white'
ORDER BY name DESC

SELECT * FROM Team WHERE foundation_date > 1910
ORDER BY foundation_date, name DESC LIMIT 20
```

If queries include properties with values of mixed types, Cloud Datastore orders them as follows:

1. Null values
2. Fixed-point numbers
    a. Integers
    b. Dates and times
3. Boolean values
4. Byte strings (short)
5. Unicode strings
6. Floating-point numbers
7. Cloud Datastore keys

Pricing

The amount billed to you depends on two factors. The first is the time that has passed since this book was written. This is because Google is consistently lowering the price of its services as technology makes it cheaper for the company to have you up and running in the cloud. That affects not only disk storage but also other areas like data transfer.

The other factor is, as you'd expect, usage: read and write operations, together with stored data, are the most relevant drivers of the final amount on your bill. Nevertheless, there is a convenient distinction between operations. For example, you are not charged for the so-called small operations like ID allocations and keys-only queries. Additionally, and as is common across other Google services, Cloud Datastore has a generous free quota that is reset daily. Naturally, this quota cannot deal with thousands of requests per second, but it is enough to support tests, prototypes, beta phases, or even live products if the requirements are not high and growth does not occur suddenly.

Summary

In this chapter, you've learned about the inner workings of Cloud Datastore, its strengths and drawbacks, and how to operate it through the available APIs and libraries. You also explored the features that make Cloud Datastore different from other data storage systems and how to take advantage of them to achieve greater performance and scalability.

If this is not enough to satisfy your curiosity, there is much more to learn about this topic. Here are some recommended resources:

- "Google App Engine Articles," Google Cloud Platform, 2015, `https://cloud.google.com/appengine/articles`
- F. Chang et al., "Bigtable: A Distributed Storage System for Structured Data," *ACM Transactions on Computer Systems* 26, no. 2 (2008):1–26
- Jason Baker et al., "Megastore: Providing Scalable, Highly Available Storage for Interactive Services," *Proceedings of the Conference on Innovative Data System Research* (CIDR) (2011): 223-234

Remember that even though books are relatively static in terms of content and knowledge, your world is anything but. Keep the communication flowing in user forums, question-and-answer sites like StackOverflow (`http://stackoverflow.com`), blogs, and anywhere else that helps you exchange information. The more exchange, the better for all of us, and ultimately for your apps, backend, systems, web sites and dreams.

PART IV

Google Cloud Platform - Big Data Products

CHAPTER 10

Google BigQuery

Big data is a widely used term that refers broadly to huge (and growing) datasets that no traditional data-processing application is able to capture, store, curate, analyze, and visualize in real time. Simply put, the data's rate of growth is so high that the tools cannot process incoming data, and the gap between processed and unprocessed data keeps increasing forever.

Several characteristics define big data. Here are the top three characteristics:

- *Volume*: This is the most important characteristic and probably the one that makes data *big data*. On-premises data-storage facilities cannot cater to true big data, because sooner or later you run out of either storage capacity or real estate. Using the public cloud is the right choice from day one.
- *Variety*: This describes the different types of data, including many formats within each type that cannot be stored efficiently using traditional data-storage systems such as structured relational database systems. Data can also be semi-structured or unstructured. Examples of variety include images, audio, video, documents, emails, RFID tags, cell phone GPS signals, and so on.
- *Velocity*: As the name suggests, this characteristic states the speed at which data needs to be captured, processed, and accessed. For example, during development, a web app may be tested with 10 data sources; but after deployment, the number of input sources may be 100,000 or more. Hence, the system should be able to scale without pre-warming. Also, once the data is available, it is important to have a fast channel to process it and generate value before the window of opportunity closes. Think about algorithmic trading to make buy/sell/hold decisions about equity in real time.

Big data is a natural fit for Google, which has a mission to organize the world's information and make it universally accessible and useful. To tackle this internal corporate problem, Google has built an arsenal of big-data tools that it uses across its product line, from search to Gmail. In Google Cloud Platform, Google makes some of these tools available so that external developers can use and process their own big data; meanwhile, Google uses its big-data technologies as the foundation for its other products. This chapter looks at Google BigQuery, and Chapter 11 discusses Google Cloud Dataflow.

The chapter presents BigQuery via a practice-oriented approach, using a real-life use case that analyzes the trends of visitors to a web site. You achieve this by analyzing the web server access log files: specifically, Apache web server, the most popular web server on the Internet today. You follow the entire data analysis extract, transform, load (ETL) lifecycle to load and query data using BigQuery.

Building Blocks and Fundamentals

BigQuery is the product of a research technology called Dremel, developed at Google Research (`http://research.google.com/pubs/pub36632.html`). BigQuery is a scalable, interactive, ad hoc query system for analysis of read-only nested data that is petabytes in size. These salient features make BigQuery a useful and unique hosted big data analytics platform. Let us now understand these characteristics in more detail.

- *Scalable*: Every data query in BigQuery may potentially run on thousands of CPUs across thousands of nodes. BigQuery dynamically selects the number of nodes and CPUs based on the size of the data in the tables. Because BigQuery is a hosted product, it costs the same if *x* CPUs work for *y* amount of time or if one CPU works for *x.y* amount of time. Of source, the former scenario returns results quickly, thereby saving you a precious resource—time—and thus BigQuery adopts this approach.
- *Interactive*: The key characteristic of an interactive system is speed. Every BigQuery query gets a tiny time-slice of a huge BigQuery cluster. This architecture means that you get your answers fast and don't need to wait to bring up a cluster just to run your jobs. Another collateral benefit is that you don't need to feed it work constantly to make it worth your while.
- *Ad-hoc*: The key characteristic of an ad-hoc system is the ability to support queries in all the stored data. BigQuery achieves this by doing a full-table scan on each query, without requiring indexes or pre-aggregation. Many other data analysis tools require you to design your data ingestion according to the types of questions you want to ask. BigQuery eliminates this burden and allows you to ask any question you want, after the data is already gathered.

When you use BigQuery, that combines the previous three characteristics, what you achieve is that instead of having to devote days to writing MapReduce code, or waiting hours between queries in order to refine or drill down into your data, you can get answers in seconds and dig into your data in real time.

BigQuery achieves the above goals through a shared multi-tenant architecture and by using distributed storage, columnar data layout, multilevel execution trees and is capable of running aggregation queries over trillion-row tables in seconds. Let us now understand few of the important implementation details.

- *Tree architecture*: BigQuery uses a multilevel hierarchical serving tree and execution engines to handle all incoming queries. The tree architecture comprises a root server, intermediate servers, and leaf servers. In this execution model, each incoming query is rewritten to increase execution efficiency. For example, the root server extract table metadata, partitions the query space, and rewrites the query before handing it over to the intermediate servers. Eventually, the root server is responsible for querying the data from the storage layer or from the local disk. Individual results are aggregated at each layer and passed back to the root server before being returned to the client.
- *Columnar layout & Distributed Storage*: In a relational data storage system such as a MySQL database, records are stored sequentially using a row-based storage engine. However, it is common for a query to extract only certain columns and not the entire record. This means the storage engine has to skip unwanted fields in a record to extract the required fields, resulting in higher computational costs and the use of more clock time. For the larger datasets typically associated with big data, this difference is obvious even if the database engine uses multiple query engines and uses horizontal data slicing. BigQuery uses columnar storage and stores the various columns separately. This enables the system to return only the queried columns,

resulting in lower computational cost and less time required. BigQuery uses a distributed storage backend to store your data. Distributed storage also helps make column storage more effective because each column can be read from a different spindle.

- *Shared Multi-tenant Architecture*: BigQuery is a shared, multi-tenant system that allows each query to get a tiny slice of time on thousands of dedicated nodes. So instead of having to bring up your own cluster and keep it busy to get your money's worth, you can get a tiny time-slice of a huge number of workers, in order to get your answer fast. Of course, you pay for only the compute and storage resources that your query actually uses and not leasing the entire cluster.

BigQuery stores data using a hierarchy of containers called *projects*, *datasets*, and *tables*. The associated actions of loading data, running queries, and exporting information are called BigQuery *jobs*:

- *Projects*: Projects are top-level containers in Google Cloud Platform. In addition to holding computing resources and user data, projects store information such as billing data and authorized users. Each Google Cloud Platform project is referred to by three identifiers:
    - *Project number*: Auto-assigned by Google Cloud Platform for the project's lifetime. The user cannot influence the project number.
    - *Project ID*: A string of three English words delimited by two hyphens. The user can choose a unique string at project-creation time, but once chosen, the ID cannot be changed later. The project ID is also used by the `gcloud` command-line tool and APIs to refer to the project.
    - *Project name*: A friendly description of the project for developer reference, consisting of a phrase. This description can be changed any number of times after the project is created.
- *Datasets*: Datasets are BigQuery-specific data containers and are one level lower in the hierarchy than projects. As the name suggests, a datasets is a collection of data that helps you organize and cluster data into groups. However, datasets do not contain any data themselves; the data is stored in tables. A dataset is simply a group of tables; every table must live inside a dataset. A dataset is assigned to a single project. In addition, datasets let you control access to tables by using access control lists (ACLs).
- *Tables*: Tables contain the data in BigQuery, along with a corresponding table schema that describes field names, types, and whether certain fields are mandatory or optional. Tables are required in various data import scenarios: when data is loaded into a new table name in a dataset, when an existing table is copied into a new table name, and when running queries. BigQuery also supports *views*, which are virtual tables defined by a SQL query.
- *Jobs*: Jobs are actions that are constructed by developers and executed by BigQuery on their behalf. Jobs include actions to load data, query data, export data, and copy data. Because BigQuery is typically used with large datasets, jobs may take a long time to execute. Hence, all jobs are executed asynchronously by BigQuery and can be polled for their status. BigQuery saves a history of all jobs associated with a project, and this list is accessible via all the three access methods: web-based Google Developers Console, gcloud command line tool and BigQuery API.

BigQuery officially supports the following data types. Each field in a table should be one of these types:

- `STRING`: 64KB UTF-8 encoded string.
- `INTEGER`: 64-bit signed integer.
- `FLOAT`: Double-precision floating-point format.
- `BOOLEAN`: True or false (case insensitive), or 1 or 0.
- `TIMESTAMP`: One of two formats—Unix timestamps or calendar date/times. BigQuery stores `TIMESTAMP` data internally as a Unix timestamp with microsecond precision.

UNIX TIMESTAMPS

A Unix timestamp is either a positive or a negative decimal number. A positive number specifies the number of seconds since the epoch (1970-01-01 00:00:00 UTC), and a negative number specifies the number of seconds before the epoch. The timestamp preserves up to six decimal places (microsecond precision).

DATE/TIME STRINGS

A date/time string is in the format YYYY-MM-DD HH:MM:SS. The `UTC` and `Z` attributes are supported. You can supply a time zone offset in date/time strings, but BigQuery doesn't preserve the offset after converting the value to its internal format. If you need to preserve the original time-zone data, store the time zone offset in a separate column. Date/time strings must be quoted when using JSON format.

Importing Data

As you learned in the previous section, you need a dataset in a project in order to load data. Listing 10-1, Listing 10-2, and Listing 10-3 use the `gcloud bq` command-line tool to list current projects and datasets and create a new dataset.

Listing 10-1. `gcloud bq` Command to List All Projects

```
$ bq ls -p
     projectId               friendlyName
 -------------------- -----------------------------
  cloud-platform-book   Google Cloud Platform Book
  cloud-3rdpartyweb      cloud-3rdpartyweb
  cloud-sotp             cloud-sotp
  new-cloud             New Cloud
  new-cloud-taiwan      New Taiwan
  mythical-sky-823      Cloud VPN Platform
```

Listing 10-2. `gcloud bq` Command to List All Datasets in a Single Project

```
$ bq ls cloud-platform-book:
  datasetId
 -----------
  logs
```

Listing 10-3. `gcloud bq` Command to Create a New Dataset

```
$ bq mk apache_logs
Dataset 'cloud-platform-book:apache_logs' successfully created.
$ bq ls
   datasetId
 -------------
  apache_logs
  logs
```

Let's begin the journey of analyzing Apache web server log files using BigQuery. First you need to load the data into BigQuery and follow the ETL process. You start by extracting the log files from the web server `logs` directory. Following this, you transform the data into a BigQuery-supported file format. Finally, you load the data using the `bq` BigQuery command-line tool.

In the ETL process, transformation is the challenging part; this requires you to understand both the source and target data formats. The data formats may depend on the versions of the software and whether any customizations have been made as part of the installation process. The test setup uses Apache web server version 2.2.22 running on Ubuntu Linux LTS version 12.04. If you use a different web server or different version of the Apache web server, then the log format may be different. However, it should contain all the basic information required in a web server access log.

Transform Apache Access Log Files

In an Apache web server configuration (version 2.2.22 specifically), the file format of the access log entries is controlled by `CustomLog` directives in the main server configuration file located at `/etc/apache2/apache2.conf`. The `CustomLog` directives are then referred to from virtual host definitions written as individual files in the `/etc/apache2/sites-available/` directory. Listing 10-4, Listing 10-5, and 11-6 show the relevant sections of the configuration files to help you understand the format of the access log.

Listing 10-4. `CustomLog` Directives in `/etc/apache2/apache2.conf`

```
# The following directives define some format nicknames for use with
# a CustomLog directive (see below).
# If you are behind a reverse proxy, you might want to change %h into %{X-Forwarded-For}i
#
LogFormat "%v:%p %h %l %u %t \"%r\" %>s %O \"%{Referer}i\" \"%{User-Agent}i\""
vhost_combined
LogFormat "%h %l %u %t \"%r\" %>s %O \"%{Referer}i\" \"%{User-Agent}i\"" combined
LogFormat "%h %l %u %t \"%r\" %>s %O" common
LogFormat "%{Referer}i -> %U" referer
LogFormat "%{User-agent}i" agent
```

Listing 10-5. Environment Variable Declaration in `/etc/apache2/envvars`

```
export APACHE_LOG_DIR=/var/log/apache2$SUFFIX
```

Listing 10-6. `AccessLog` declaration of `/etc/apache2/sites-available/default`

```
CustomLog ${APACHE_LOG_DIR}/access.log combined
```

This configuration writes log entries in a format known as the Combined Log Format (CLF), which is a superset of the Common Log Format. This is a standard format used by many different web servers and read by many log-analysis programs.

You can see that each access-log entry uses the format `"%h %l %u %t \"%r\" %>s %O \"%{Referer}i\" \"%{User-Agent}i\"" from the previous extracts`. The format is specified using a format string that looks like a C programming language–style `printf` format string and that can be configured. The following entry shows an example log-file entry produced in CLF:

```
127.0.0.1 - kris [01/Apr/2015:15:44:00 +0800] "GET /fire_dragon.jpg HTTP/1.1" 200 2025
 "http://www.example.com/start.html" (\"%{Referer}i\") "Mozilla/5.0 (Macintosh; Intel Mac
 OS X 10_10_2)
 AppleWebKit/537.36 (KHTML, like Gecko) Chrome/41.0.2272.104 Safari/537.36"
```

The parts of this log entry are as follows:

- `127.0.0.1 (%h)`: The IP address of the client (remote host) that made the request to the server. The default configuration is to store the IP address and not do a reverse lookup of the hostname. The IP address reported here is not necessarily the address of the client machine. If a proxy server exists between the user and the server, this address is the address of the proxy, rather than the originating machine.
- `- (%l)`: The RFC 1413 identity of the client, determined by `identd` on the client's machine. The hyphen in the output indicates that the requested piece of information is not available.
- `kris (%u)`: The user ID of the person requesting the URL, as determined by HTTP authentication. This field is - if the URL is not password protected or if the user is not yet authenticated, just as in the previous field.
- `[01/Apr/2015:15:44:00 +0800] (%t)`: The time at which the request was received. The format is [*day/month/year:hour:minute:second zone*]:
  - *Day*: 2 digits
  - *Month*: 3 letters
  - *Year*: 4 digits
  - *Hour*: 2 digits
  - *Minute*: 2 digits
  - *Second*: 2 digits
  - *Zone*: (`` `+' | `-' ``), 4 digits

- "GET /fire_dragon.jpg HTTP/1.1" (\"%r\"): The request line from the client, stored in double quotes. The request line contains a great deal of useful information. First, the method used by the client is GET. Second, the client requested the resource /fire_dragon.jpg. And third, the client used the protocol HTTP/1.1.
- 200 (%>s): The status code that the server sends back to the client. This information is very valuable, because it reveals whether the request resulted in a successful response (codes beginning with 2), a redirection (codes beginning with 3), an error caused by the client (codes beginning with 4), or an error in the server (codes beginning with 5). You can find the full list of possible status codes in the HTTP specification (RFC 2616, section 10) at www.w3.org/Protocols/rfc2616/rfc2616.txt.
- 2025 (%b): The size of the object returned to the client, not including the response headers. If no content was returned to the client, this value is -. Two alternate format strings exist for this field: %B logs 0 instead of - for no content; and %O logs total bytes sent, including headers, in which case it is never zero in value.
- "http://www.example.com/start.html" (\"%{Referer}i\"): The Referer (sic) HTTP request header. This field provides the web site from which the client reports having been referred. In this example, this should be the page that links to or includes the image file /fire_dragon.jpg. In cases where there is no referral, the value is simply -.
- "Mozilla/5.0 (Macintosh; Intel Mac OS X 10_10_2) AppleWebKit/537.36 (KHTML, like Gecko) Chrome/41.0.2272.104 Safari/537.36" (\"%{User-agent}i\"): The User-Agent HTTP request header. This is the identifying information that the client browser reports about itself to the web site and content. The format differs across browsers and in the same browser on different operating systems.

In an Ubuntu Linux system, Apache web server log files are stored in the /var/log/apache2/ directory. In its default configuration, Apache web server archives its log files every week. Hence, if you run a web server for more than a year, you are likely to see up to 52 log files. The output in Listing 10-7 shows the location and log files in the test setup.

Listing 10-7. Location of Apache Web Server Access Log Files in an Ubuntu Linux System

```
$ pwd
/var/log/apache2

$ ls -l access.log*
-rw-r----- 1 root adm  4602633 Apr  1 10:46 access.log
-rw-r----- 1 root adm 25051247 Mar 29 06:28 access.log.1
-rw-r----- 1 root adm  1470908 Jan 25 06:39 access.log.2.gz
<snip>
-rw-r----- 1 root adm  1470908 Jan 25 06:39 access.log.52.gz
```

The amount of data in each of these files is of trivial size in BigQuery scale, so we decided to combine the data from all 52 log files into a single file in chronological order. You can use several tools to achieve this outcome. In this case, we used the Linux command cat.

You now need to transform the data in CLF into either a comma-separated values (CSV) or JSON-encoded text file for import into BigQuery. This example uses CSV format because the data is not nested and does not require normalization. Given that you know the record format of the entries in the log file, all you need is a regular expression that is able to parse the access log file and write a CSV file.

In order to make it easy for you, we researched and found online two simple scripts written in the Perl and PHP programming languages. We used both scripts to transform the data with equivalent results. These scripts are hosted on the Github code-hosting platform, at the following URLs:

- **https://github.com/woonsan/accesslog2csv** (Perl script)
- **https://github.com/mboynes/Apache-Access-Log-to-CSV-Converter** (PHP script)

We made a few changes to the Perl script. Let's examine the key parts, highlighting the old and new methods and the rationale behind them. The updated script is available in the source repository accompanying this book.

The first change we made to the transformation script was to change the field delimiter in the output CSV file from a comma (`,`) to a `\t` (tab) character. This is required because the new user-agent strings of client browsers, especially on mobile devices, use commas, as shown in the earlier access log field description. Listing 10-8 and Listing 10-9 show the original and updated sections of the Perl script.

Listing 10-8. Original: Uses Commas as Delimiters

```
print STDOUT "\"Host\",\"Log Name\",\"Date Time\",\"Time Zone\",\"Method\",\"URL\",
\"Response Code\",\"Bytes Sent\",\"Referer\",\"User Agent\"\n";
```

Listing 10-9. New: Uses Tab Characters as Delimiters

```
print STDOUT "\"Host\"\t\"Log Name\"\t\"Date Time\"\t\"Time Zone\"\t\"Method\"\t\"URL\"\t
\"Response Code\"\t\"Bytes Sent\"\t\"Referer\"\t\"User Agent\"\n";
```

In BigQuery, the table schema accompanying the table lists the number of fields in each record. BigQuery is very strict about the number of fields because it uses a columnar storage backend. This is the primary reason to make sure the field delimiter is not present in the any of the fields, which will unintentionally increase the number of fields. Although the tab character is not expected to be present in the incoming HTTP request, you want to make sure it doesn't exist either. Toward this end, we added a new section in the Perl script to search and replace any tab characters, as shown in Listing 10-10.

Listing 10-10. Replacing Tabs with the String `TAB` in Field Values

```
$host =~ s/\t/TAB/g;
$logname =~ s/\t/TAB/g;
$year =~ s/\t/TAB/g;
$month =~ s/\t/TAB/g;
$day =~ s/\t/TAB/g;
$hour =~ s/\t/TAB/g;
$min =~ s/\t/TAB/g;
$sec =~ s/\t/TAB/g;
$tz =~ s/\t/TAB/g;
$method =~ s/\t/TAB/g;
$url =~ s/\t/TAB/g;
$code =~ s/\t/TAB/g;
$bytesd =~ s/\t/TAB/g;
$referer =~ s/\t/TAB/g;
$ua =~ s/\t/TAB/g;
```

Once the transformation to CSV file format is complete, you need to load the file into BigQuery before you can query the data. There are two options to load the data to BigQuery. First, you can load the data to Cloud Storage and then import it into BigQuery. Or, second, you can load the data directly to BigQuery. We recommend the first option—loading through Cloud Storage—because we found it to be more reliable and faster.

Loading data through Cloud Storage takes three steps: loading to a Cloud Storage bucket, making an empty BigQuery dataset, and transferring data from Cloud Storage to BigQuery. The console output in Listing 10-11, Listing 10-12, and Listing 10-13 shows these three steps using the command-line tools and the corresponding output. We used the Linux `time` system utility to measure the time taken for each step.

Loading Transformed Data to BigQuery via Cloud Storage

Listing 10-11. Step 1: Copying the Consolidated Apache Access Logs to Google Cloud Storage

```
$ time gsutil cp apache-access-log.csv gs://cloud-platform-book/
Copying file://apache-access-log.csv [Content-Type=text/csv]...
==> NOTE: <snip>
Uploading   gs://cloud-platform-book/apache-access-log.csv:        1.38 GiB/1.38 GiB

real    0m50.816s
user    0m8.071s
sys    0m5.819s
```

Listing 10-12. Step 2: Making a New BigQuery Dataset in the Current Project

```
$ time bq mk logs_gs
Dataset 'cloud-platform-book:logs_gs' successfully created.

real    0m3.830s
user    0m0.269s
sys    0m0.083s
```

Listing 10-13. Step 3: Loading the Data from Cloud Storage into BigQuery

```
$ time bq load --source:format=CSV logs_gs.access gs://cloud-platform-book/
apache-access-log.csv apache-access-logs-table-schema.txt
Waiting on bqjob_r4ffba7ac3eee8771_0000014c680a39c3_1 ... (42s) Current status: DONE

real    0m48.706s
user    0m0.371s
sys    0m0.095s
```

Step 3 uses a file-based approach to declare the table schema for the new table being created in BigQuery. This is the recommended approach for tables that contain a large number of columns. The file describes each field by providing its name, its type, and whether it is a recommended filed. The contents of this file are as follows:

```
[
  {"name": "IP", "type": "string", "mode": "required"},
  {"name": "Time", "type": "timestamp", "mode": "required"},
  {"name": "Request_Type", "type": "string", "mode": "required"},
  {"name": "Path", "type": "string", "mode": "required"},
  {"name": "Response", "type": "integer", "mode": "required"},
  {"name": "Referral_Domain", "type": "string", "mode": "required"},
  {"name": "Referral_Path", "type": "string", "mode": "required"},
  {"name": "User_Agent", "type": "string", "mode": "required"}
]
```

From this output, you can see that the process took 102 seconds of clock time to load a 1.38GB log file. Listing 10-14 shows the BigQuery command to load data from the console and the corresponding console output. You can see that the route for loading data through Cloud Storage is not only more reliable but also much faster. Note that we performed both approaches on the same day using the same system and network, one after another.

Listing 10-14. Directly loading Data into BigQuery

```
$ time bq load --source:format=CSV logs.access ./apache-access-log.csv
./apache-access-logs-table-schema.txt
Waiting on bqjob_r47465a3df1f3e23c_0000014c67ef3a35_1 ... (145s) Current status: DONE

real    147m31.160s
user    0m10.358s
sys    0m4.804s
```

In this command, the table schema is supplied in a text file. It is also possible to supply the table schema as part of the command line, as shown in Listing 10-15.

Listing 10-15. gcloud bq Command with the Table Schema on the Command Line

```
$ time bq load --source:format=CSV apache_logs.access_logs
gs://cloud-platform-book/apache-access-log.csv  Host:string,LogName:string,Time:timestamp,
TimeZone:string,Method:string,URL:string,
ResponseCode:integer,BytesSent:integer,Referer:string,UserAgent:string
Waiting on bqjob_r60bbcaa2cd7d8fc9_0000014c7fd0a597_1 ... (16s) Current status: DONE

real    0m42.363s
user    0m0.349s
sys    0m0.093s
```

The following bq command and corresponding console output show the table schema, number of rows, and total size of the data in the table:

```
$ bq show cloud-platform-book:logs_gs.apache_access_logs
Table cloud-platform-book:logs_gs.apache_access_logs

   Last modified              Schema              Total Rows   Total Bytes   Expiration
 ----------------- -------------------------- ------------ ------------- ------------
  30 Mar 12:07:45    |- Host: string            7028137      1112270720
                     |- LogName: string
                     |- Time: timestamp
                     |- TimeZone: string
                     |- Method: string
                     |- URL: string
                     |- ResponseCode: integer
                     |- BytesSent: integer
                     |- Referer: string
                     |- UserAgent: string
```

You are now ready to query the data!

Querying Data

In this section, you query the Apache web server access logs that you loaded to BigQuery in the previous section. You exclusively use the gcloud command-line tool to construct and execute the queries. The objective is to showcase the strengths and diversities of the SQL dialect supported by BigQuery, not to extract every possible statistics from the dataset. We ask a set of questions, discuss the answers, construct the query while explaining the syntax, execute the query, and finally interpret the results.

Here is Q1:

```
Legend: Objective = O, Query = Q, Response = R, Analysis = A

O1: List selected fields - Host, Time, URL, ResponseCode, BytesSent - of the first 5 records
in the data

Q1: SELECT Host, Time, URL, ResponseCode, BytesSent FROM [logs_gs.apache_access_logs] LIMIT 5

R1:
$ bq shell
Welcome to BigQuery! (Type help for more information.)
cloud-platform-book> SELECT Host, Time, URL, ResponseCode, BytesSent FROM
[logs_gs.apache_access_logs] LIMIT 5
```

```
Waiting on bqjob_r7af302e211713989_0000014c7e228796_1 ... (0s) Current status: DONE
+-----------+---------------------+-----+--------------+-----------+
|   Host    |        Time         | URL | ResponseCode | BytesSent |
+-----------+---------------------+-----+--------------+-----------+
| 127.0.0.1 | 2015-03-27 07:32:04 | *   |          200 |       126 |
| 127.0.0.1 | 2015-03-27 07:32:05 | *   |          200 |       126 |
| 127.0.0.1 | 2015-03-27 07:32:06 | *   |          200 |       126 |
| 127.0.0.1 | 2015-03-27 07:32:07 | *   |          200 |       126 |
| 127.0.0.1 | 2015-03-27 07:32:08 | *   |          200 |       126 |
+-----------+---------------------+-----+--------------+-----------+
cloud-platform-book> quit
Goodbye.
```

A1: We used the BigQuery shell to run an interactive query to meet this objective. The BigQuery shell is available as part of the Google Cloud SDK and can be easily started using the commands `bq shell`. Once inside the shell, you can type SQL queries just as you would in a regular SQL shell. When you are finished using the BigQuery shell, you can exit by using the `quit` command.

Let's move on to Q2:

```
O2: What are the top 10 traffic-generating client IPs to our website?

Q2: SELECT Host, Count(Host) As Hits FROM [logs_gs.apache_access_logs]
Group by Host Order by Hits DESC LIMIT 10

R2:
Waiting on bqjob_r38c3621dab252a3c_0000014c7d08d446_1 ... (0s) Current status: DONE
+----------------+---------+
|      Host      |  Hits   |
+----------------+---------+
| 127.0.0.1      | 2127406 |
| 10.128.215.151 | 1609667 |
| 10.142.45.129  | 1400049 |
| 10.130.86.213  | 1094896 |
| 10.138.25.97   |  620975 |
| 204.246.166.52 |    9072 |
| 54.240.148.108 |    7847 |
| 54.240.148.78  |    6397 |
| 54.239.129.82  |    4636 |
| 204.246.166.16 |    4371 |
+----------------+---------+
```

A2: The `Host` field from the table schema contains the IP address. The query requests that BigQuery count the number of times each IP address appears in the entire dataset and label the total `Hits`. The output is then grouped by IP address so that each IP address appears only once, and the results are sorted by the value of the `Hits` column and in descending order. This query shows that temporary columns in results can be named and referred to later in the query.

PRIVATE IP ADDRESSES

In the Internet addressing architecture, a *private IP network* is a network that uses private IP addresses. This private IP address is defined by RFC 1918 for Internet Protocol Version 4 (IPv4) and RFC 4193 for Internet Protocol Version 6 (IPv6). The purpose of defining a private IP range is to enable local networking among IP-enabled systems whose traffic need not be routed globally over the public Internet. Public routers will drop such traffic. As such, private IP ranges are not allotted to organizations globally.

Private IP ranges are used extensively in home and office networks. A network address translation (NAT) router or a proxy server is required if the source traffic from a system with a private IP address must be routed over the public Internet.

The following are the private addresses in the IPv4 address range:

```
10.0.0.0 - 10.255.255.255: Class A IP range
172.16.0.0 - 172.31.255.255: Class B IP range
192.168.0.0 - 192.168.255.255: Class C IP range
```

From the Q2 results, you can see that the top five IP addresses that generate traffic to the web site are in the private IP address range. Because private IP addresses are not routable on the public Internet, this traffic is from private networks where the virtual machine (VM) is hosted. Let's query all the traffic from the private IP address range.

The `Host` field is defined as type `string` in the table schema. To accommodate all possible private IPs from the private IP range, you need to convert this into a numeric value so that you can apply range operators to filter them from the dataset. Fortunately, BigQuery offers a function called `PARSE_IP` that converts an IPv4 address into an unsigned number. The URL `https://cloud.google.com/bigquery/query-reference` defines `PARSE_IP` as follows:

> *PARSE_IP(readable_ip): Converts a string representing IPv4 address to unsigned integer value. For example, PARSE_IP('0.0.0.1') will return 1. If string is not a valid IPv4 address, PARSE_IP will return NULL.*

The `PARSE_IP` function breaks the IPv4 address into four octets and uses the base value of 256 along with a digit placeholder value to arrive at the unsigned integer number. Here is an example, to make this process easier to follow.

Let's convent 10.0.0.0 into an unsigned number:

```
= (first octet * 2563) + (second octet * 2562) + (third octet * 256) + (fourth octet)
= (first octet * 16777216) + (second octet * 65536) + (third octet * 256) + (fourth octet)
= (10 * 16777216) + (0 * 65536) + (0 * 256) + (0)
= 167772160
```

The following are the unsigned numbers of the border IP address in each of the private IP ranges:

```
10.0.0.0 - 10.255.255.255 : 167772160 - 184549375
172.16.0.0 - 172.31.255.255 : 2886729728 - 2887778303
192.168.0.0 - 192.168.255.255 : 3232235520 - 3232301055
```

Let's use this function along with logic OR operator to construct a BigQuery query and filter all the internal traffic from private IP addresses to the web site:

Q3: What are the top 10 traffic-generating private IP clients to our website?

```
$ bq query "Select Host, PARSE_IP(Host) as IPvalue, count(Host) as Hits
from [logs_gs.apache_access_logs] where PARSE_IP(Host) >= 167772160 AND
PARSE_IP(Host) <= 184549375 group by Host, IPvalue"
Waiting on bqjob_r517ed70cd5f77b7e_0000014c7f175436_1 ... (0s) Current status: DONE
+----------------+-----------+---------+
|      Host      |  IPvalue  |  Hits   |
+----------------+-----------+---------+
| 10.142.45.129  | 177089921 | 1400049 |
| 10.138.25.97   | 176822625 |  620975 |
| 10.130.86.213  | 176314069 | 1094896 |
| 10.128.215.151 | 176215959 | 1609667 |
+----------------+-----------+---------+
```

Here is the second part of Q3:

Q3-2: Find hosts with IP address between 172.16.0.0 - 172.31.255.255

```
$ bq query "Select Host, PARSE_IP(Host) as IPvalue, count(Host) as Hits from
 [logs_gs.apache_access_logs] where PARSE_IP(Host) >= 2886729728 AND
PARSE_IP(Host) <= 2887778303 group by Host, IPvalue"
Waiting on bqjob_r2f39df990fdbdb4_0000014c7f1a1cdb_1 ... (0s) Current status: DONE
```

The third part of Q3 is as follows:

Q3-3: Find hosts with IP address between 192.168.0.0 - 192.168.255.255

```
$ bq query "Select Host, PARSE_IP(Host) as IPvalue, count(Host) as Hits from
 [logs_gs.apache_access_logs] where PARSE_IP(Host) >= 3232235520 AND
PARSE_IP(Host) <= 3232301055 group by Host, IPvalue"
Waiting on bqjob_r64e5a0007cd9de80_0000014c7f1aeacf_1 ... (0s) Current status: DONE
```

The fourth part of Q3 is as follows:

```
Q3-4: Find hosts with IP address in all private IP address range

$ bq query "Select Host, PARSE_IP(Host) as IPvalue, count(Host) as Hits
from [logs_gs.apache_access_logs] where \
PARSE_IP(Host) >= 167772160 AND PARSE_IP(Host) <= 184549375 OR \
PARSE_IP(Host) >= 2886729728 AND PARSE_IP(Host) <= 2887778303 OR \
PARSE_IP(Host) >= 3232235520 AND PARSE_IP(Host) <= 3232301055 \
group by Host, IPvalue order by hits desc limit 10"
Waiting on bqjob_r75b709c83f874113_0000014c7f237be7_1 ... (2s) Current status: DONE
+----------------+----------+---------+
|      Host      | IPvalue  |  Hits   |
+----------------+----------+---------+
| 10.128.215.151 | 176215959 | 1609667 |
| 10.142.45.129  | 177089921 | 1400049 |
| 10.130.86.213  | 176314069 | 1094896 |
| 10.138.25.97   | 176822625 |  620975 |
+----------------+----------+---------+
```

And here is the last part of Q3:

```
Q3-5: Count the total traffic from private IP

$ bq query "Select count(Host) as Total from [logs_gs.apache_access_logs] where \
> PARSE_IP(Host) >= 167772160 AND PARSE_IP(Host) <= 184549375 OR \
> PARSE_IP(Host) >= 2886729728 AND PARSE_IP(Host) <= 2887778303 OR \
> PARSE_IP(Host) >= 3232235520 AND PARSE_IP(Host) <= 3232301055"
Waiting on bqjob_r7507383b330c328c_0000014c7f39bedd_1 ... (0s) Current status: DONE
+---------+
| Total   |
+---------+
| 4725587 |
+---------+
```

In addition to the traffic from the private IP address range, which is presumably generated by infrastructure-monitoring services, there is also traffic from localhost or IP address 127.0.0.1. Human beings generated this traffic. Let's use a different query to discover the real traffic from public IP addresses only:

```
Q4. What is the top 10 public IP that are generating traffic to our website? What is the
total traffic to our website?
Q4.
# BigQuery query to discover top 10 public IP traffic generators to your web site

$ bq query "Select Host, count(Host) as Hits from [logs_gs.apache_access_logs] where \
Host != '127.0.0.1' AND (PARSE_IP(Host) < 167772160 OR PARSE_IP(Host) > 184549375) \
group by Host order by Hits DESC LIMIT 10"
```

```
Waiting on bqjob_r595bf414cb7bc939_0000014c7f648bed_1 ... (0s) Current status: DONE
+----------------+------+
|      Host      | Hits |
+----------------+------+
| 204.246.166.52 | 9072 |
| 54.240.148.108 | 7847 |
| 54.240.148.78  | 6397 |
| 54.239.129.82  | 4636 |
| 204.246.166.16 | 4371 |
| 54.240.148.85  | 3464 |
| 54.239.196.108 | 3448 |
| 54.251.52.153  | 2958 |
| 216.137.42.83  | 2909 |
| 54.240.158.56  | 2743 |
+----------------+------+

# BigQuery query to find out the total traffic to your web site

$ bq query "Select count(Host) as Total from [logs_gs.apache_access_logs] where \
> Host != '127.0.0.1' AND (PARSE_IP(Host) < 167772160 OR PARSE_IP(Host) > 184549375)"
Waiting on bqjob_r79f024b87cbba095_0000014c7f745729_1 ... (0s) Current status: DONE
+--------+
| Total  |
+--------+
| 175144 |
+--------+
```

A4: This query inverts the operators associated with the private IP range and includes the localhost IP address. You also compute the total traffic from public IP addresses using the `count` operation.

We hope the examples in this section have shown you the query variety and possibilities available when using BigQuery. See `https://cloud.google.com/bigquery/query-reference` for all the SQL functions you can use in BigQuery SQL queries.

Exporting Data and Creating Views

After you have imported and queried a massive dataset using BigQuery, you may need to export part of the data from BigQuery to be processed by another system, such as visualization, or to present it as part of a management report. You can do this easily with BigQuery, which supports data export to Google Cloud Storage.

The most common use case of the export feature is to export the results of a query. Let's export two pieces of useful information from the raw dataset: a list of unique IPs that have generated traffic to the web site, and a list of unique URLs in the web site that are accessed by client and their corresponding hit counts. You use this information in next section when you visualize it. You can use the `--destination_table` feature in BigQuery to export the results of queries and save the filtered result in two new tables, as shown in Listing 10-16 and Listing 10-17.

Listing 10-16. BigQuery Query to Save the List of Public IPs to a New Table

```
$ bq query --destination_table logs_gs.unique_ip_hits_table "Select Host, count(Host) as Hits
from [logs_gs.apache_access_logs] where \
> Host != '127.0.0.1' AND (PARSE_IP(Host) < 167772160 OR PARSE_IP(Host) > 184549375) \
> group by Host order by Hits DESC"
Waiting on bqjob_rb85945d06b195d6_0000014c8340f6bc_1 ... (0s) Current status: DONE
+----------------+------+
|      Host      | Hits |
+----------------+------+
| 204.246.166.52 | 9072 |
| 54.240.148.108 | 7847 |
| 54.240.148.78  | 6397 |
| 54.239.129.82  | 4636 |
| 204.246.166.16 | 4371 |
| 54.240.148.85  | 3464 |
| 54.239.196.108 | 3448 |
| 54.251.52.153  | 2958 |
| 216.137.42.83  | 2909 |
| 54.240.158.56  | 2743 |
| <snip>         |      |
+----------------+------+
```

Listing 10-17. BiqQuery Query to Save the List of Unique URLs to a New Table

```
$ ls -l query.bash
-rwxr-xr-x  1 sptkrishnan  staff  305 Apr  4 18:26 query.bash

$ cat query.bash
#!/bin/bash
bq query --destination_table logs_gs.unique_urls "select REGEXP_REPLACE(URL,
r'(\?[a-zA-Z0-9-=._&/,+?();%:#*!@^~<>]*)','') as BASE_URL, count(URL) as Hits from
 logs_gs.apache_access_logs where NOT REGEXP_MATCH(URL,
r'\.[a-zA-Z0-9-=._&/,+?();%:#*!@^~<>]+') group by BASE_URL order by Hits DESC"

$ ./query.bash
Waiting on bqjob_r12c153c56cc766c3_0000014c83f78ac5_1 ... (1s) Current status: DONE
+------------------------------------------------------+---------+
|                       BASE_URL                       |  Hits   |
+------------------------------------------------------+---------+
| *                                                    | 2127408 |
| /                                                    |  153184 |
| <snip>                                               |  <snip> |
+------------------------------------------------------+---------+
```

This query also uses BigQuery's regular-expressions capabilities. You now export this information from BigQuery to Cloud Storage and then to the local system, as shown in Listings 10-18 through 10-23.

Listing 10-18. BiqQuery Command to Copy a Unique IP Table as a CSV File to Cloud Storage

```
$ bq extract logs_gs.unique_ip_hits_table gs://cloud-platform-book/public-ip-hits.csv
Waiting on bqjob_r62f2820390d0cc7d_0000014c8424a54a_1 ... (42s) Current status: DONE
```

Listing 10-19. Cloud Storage Command to Copy the `public-ip-hits.csv` File to the Local System

```
$ gsutil cp gs://cloud-platform-book/public-ip-hits.csv public-ip-hits.csv
Copying gs://cloud-platform-book/public-ip-hits.csv...
Downloading file://public-ip-hits.csv:                          31.9 KiB/31.9 KiB
```

Listing 10-20. Listing the File Contents to Make Sure They Are the Same as the BigQuery Table

```
$ head -n 6 public-ip-hits.csv
Host,Hits
204.246.166.52,9072
54.240.148.108,7847
54.240.148.78,6397
54.239.129.82,4636
204.246.166.16,4371
```

Listing 10-21. BiqQuery Command to Copy a Unique URL Table as a CSV File to Cloud Storage

```
$ bq extract logs_gs.unique_urls gs://cloud-platform-book/unique_urls.csv
Waiting on bqjob_r195f68e14729f204_0000014c842bff76_1 ... (42s) Current status: DONE
```

Listing 10-22. Cloud Storage Command to Copy the `unique_urls.csv` File to the Local System

```
$ gsutil cp gs://cloud-platform-book/unique_urls.csv unique_urls.csv
Copying gs://cloud-platform-book/unique_urls.csv...
Downloading file://unique_urls.csv:                              120.9 KiB/120.9 KiB
```

Listing 10-23. Listing the File Contents to Make Sure They Are the Same as the BiqQuery Table

```
$ head -n 3 unique_urls.csv
BASE_URL,Hits
*,2127408
/,153184
```

In addition to exporting a table's contents as a CSV file, BigQuery can also export the contents into JSON and Apache AVRO format (`http://avro.apache.org`).

BigQuery also supports the creation of a SQL view, which is defined as a virtual table that stores the results of a query. Listing 10-24 gives the command template for defining a new view.

Listing 10-24. BigQuery bq Console Command Template to Create a View

```
$ bq mk --view="<query>" <dataset>.<view name>
```

Listing 10-25 and Listing 10-26 use this template to create a virtual table that stores all the unique public IPs and the number of hits from each of them.

Listing 10-25. Creating a BigQuery View that Extracts All Public IPs and Hits

```
$ bq mk --view "Select Host, count(Host) as Hits from [logs_gs.apache_access_logs] where \
Host != '127.0.0.1' AND (PARSE_IP(Host) < 167772160 OR PARSE_IP(Host) > 184549375) \
group by Host order by Hits DESC" logs_gs.unique_ip_hits_view
View 'cloud-platform-book:logs_gs.unique_ip_hits_view' successfully created.
```

Listing 10-26. Query BigQuery View to Find the Total Number of Public IPs.

```
$ bq query "select count(Host) as Total from logs_gs.unique_ip_hits_view"
Waiting on bqjob_r22c7d94650ebca23_0000014c82949925_1 ... (0s) Current status: DONE
+-------+
| Total |
+-------+
|  1964 |
+-------+
```

You can neither export the results from a view nor copy them into a real table. Hence, you should use views where you may want to rerun the underlying query transparently without retrying it again and again. This is useful when the original table has new data appended either through a load job or via data streaming.

Summary

This chapter introduced BigQuery, the big data–analysis tool from Google Cloud Platform. BigQuery, like other Google Cloud Platform products, does not charge up front for using or reserving resources. BigQuery makes it easy for individuals and organizations of any size to start using it while paying a low usage fee via a true pay-per-use model.

We guided you step by step through preparing data (using the ETL process), loading the data, running queries, and exporting filtered results. The exported results can be visualized using a variety of software such as Google Charts. We hope this example-based chapter has helped you to understand how to put BigQuery to work.

CHAPTER 11

Google Cloud Dataflow

A few times in this book, we have introduced chapters by reflecting on how much technology has changed over the past few years and how that has shaped our understanding of concepts like security, information channels, mobility, and social exchange. But possibly one of the most groundbreaking advances in recent years is related to how we understand, analyze, and process large subsets of information. The advances in processing power have set the perfect stage for giant amounts of information to be generated. Regrettably, in the early days, this information generally was not compatible or accessible; and when it was, the computational needs required to work with it were out of reach for most individuals and entities.

Cloud computing has not only opened the door to providing sufficient power to process large subsets of data but also contributed to raising awareness of the potential of cross-connecting different sources of information. Take the example of sequencing your own genome. As recently as ten years ago, this was only within reach for a handful of people in the world. Today, you can do this for a couple thousand dollars; and in a few years, almost every living human will be able to know their inner source code and use it to help prevent future illnesses before they manifest.

Google Cloud Dataflow was conceived by Google to simplify the construction of batch or streaming data processing pipelines simply by providing SDKs and a fully managed and elastic infrastructure optimized for parallel execution of pipelines. To do that, it makes the best possible use of Google Cloud Platform internally, outsourcing computing power to Google Compute Engine or using Google BigQuery and Google Cloud Storage as two of the options for data sources and sinks. Cloud Dataflow can also use streaming data channels like Google Cloud Pub/Sub to communicate with other services in a real time fashion.

As you see in this chapter, one of the main strengths of this technology resides on its unified programming model, which enables you to work with bounded and unbounded sets of information using the same pipeline by simply exchanging the steps that define where the information is taken from and put once processed. Also, its modularity allows for more effective testing, as well as flexibility in the replacement of different parts of your pipeline.

A unit of work in Cloud Dataflow is referred to as a *pipeline*. This is a group of tasks, including operations like reading, extraction, transformation, and writing of information. You can construct pipelines using the SDKs provided (an SDK is only available for Java as of this writing). Once your pipeline is ready, you can run it locally or directly in the cloud. In the latter case, your pipeline is analyzed and optimized before creating a job representation of it. During the execution of this job, you can monitor its status and progress and access the logs generated from Google Developers Console.

In the following sections, you see how to set up, design, and execute a job using Cloud Dataflow.

Setup

It all starts with your project in Google Developers Console: `https://console.developers.google.com`. If you do not have a project yet, go ahead and create it.

As mentioned earlier, Cloud Dataflow uses other services from Cloud Platform. You need to enable the APIs for Cloud Dataflow and the associated services. You do that by accessing APIs & Auth ➤ APIs from the left side panel in your newly created project in Developers Console. These are the APIs that you need to enable in order to work with Cloud Dataflow:

- Google Cloud Dataflow API
- Google Compute Engine
- Google Cloud Logging API
- Google Cloud Storage
- Google Cloud Storage JSON API
- BigQuery API
- Google Cloud Pub/Sub
- Google Cloud Datastore API

You can use the search box at the top of the page to find APIs quickly. To enable an API, access its detail page and click Enable API.

■ **Note** As mentioned earlier, Cloud Dataflow can use other services in Google Cloud Platform like Compute Engine and Cloud Storage. Some of these services are capped to a certain quota in the free trial mode. To go beyond these quotas you must enable billing. To do so, click the Preferences icon next to your profile at upper right on screen. If a project is selected, you see a Project Billing Settings options. From there, you can see the details of the billing account associated with that project. To see all the billing accounts you have registered, click Billing Accounts on the same Preferences menu.

If you have not done so yet, install the Google Cloud SDK: `https://cloud.google.com/sdk/#Quick_Start`.

This SDK comes with a command-line tool (`gcloud`) that you can use to operate services in Cloud Platform like Compute Engine, Cloud DNS, Cloud SQL, Cloud Storage, and others. You can also use Cloud Dataflow, in alpha phase as of this writing. Once the SDK is installed, you can log in using the command `gcloud auth login` and explore the possibilities of this tool by listing the associated components (`gcloud components list`) and checking the help section (`gcloud -h`).

In the example used in this chapter, you use Cloud Storage as a data source and sink. Therefore, you need to create a bucket that you later reference from your task in Cloud Dataflow. You can create a new bucket in your project using the Developers Console: go to Storage ➤ Cloud Storage ➤ Storage Browser. Click Create Bucket, give it a name, and choose the standard storage class and the region that fits your location. You also need to create a bucket in Cloud Storage to persist the files that your pipeline uses when executed. Remember that every bucket name must be globally unique. To read more about Cloud Storage and the specifics of creating buckets, see Chapter 8.

■ **Note** Thanks to the way Cloud Dataflow is designed, exchanging your data sources and is very simple. To see different examples using Cloud Storage to Cloud Pub/Sub or BigQuery, check the examples in the Cloud Dataflow SDK for Java under `https://github.com/GoogleCloudPlatform/DataflowJavaSDK`.

You are now ready to begin designing and coding your pipeline using the Java SDK. Java is the only option available as of this writing, but alternatives for other programming languages are planned. The first step is to create a Java project with a class in charge of defining your pipeline, with the source and target storage and the transformations to apply to the data set.

■ **Note** To run the examples in this chapter and those included in the Cloud Dataflow SDK, you need at least version 1.7 of the Java Development Kit. You can download and install this version from the Java downloads page at `www.oracle.com/technetwork/java/javase/downloads/index.html`.

Conveniently, the Cloud Dataflow Java SDK is available in Maven Central—a repository of libraries and other dependencies that are publicly available in the Internet so that applications can reference them transparently without needing to download and set them up manually. If you are using Maven as your build system, you can reference the SDK in your Java project by adding the following dependency to your `pom.xml` file:

```
<dependency>
    <groupId>com.google.cloud.dataflow</groupId>
        <artifactId>google-cloud-dataflow-java-sdk-all</artifactId>
    <version>LATEST</version>
</dependency>
```

In the examples used in this chapter, you use Gradle to build your application. This approach brings independence to your code because Gradle[1] provides the option to embed the build system in your project in the form of a wrapper.[2] You can see the files that make up this wrapper in the repository for the chapter examples.[3] The `gradlew` command takes care of the execution; the contents of the wrapper are located under `gradle/`.

This is how you add a dependency for the Cloud Dataflow Java SDK in Gradle:

```
dependencies {
    compile 'com.google.cloud.dataflow:google-cloud-dataflow-java-sdk-all:0.3.+'
}
```

---

[1]"Installing Gradle": `http://gradle.org/docs/current/userguide/installation.html`.
[2]"The Gradle Wrapper": `http://gradle.org/docs/current/userguide/gradle_wrapper.html`.
[3]The Gradle wrapper is in the repository of the example used in this chapter at `https://github.com/GoogleCloudPlatformBook/code-snippets/tree/master/cloud-dataflow`.

■ **Note** In both examples, the targeted version of the dependency is not strictly specified. In Maven, setting the version to `LATEST` fetches the latest available version of the SDK. Similarly, in Gradle, the targeted version is the latest minor update available. For example, if versions 0.3.150109, 0.3.150606 and 0.4 are available, the dependency in Maven fetches version 0.4 and the alternative in Gradle chooses 0.3.15.0606. This is useful during development so that you always use the most up-to-date snapshot of your dependencies; but it is strongly discouraged in production scenarios, because an update in one of your dependencies could break your business logic, affecting your users. The code in this book is written using version 0.3.150109 of the Cloud Dataflow SDK for Java.

From this point on, you can use your favorite IDE or text editor to write your code. If you ask us, IntelliJ IDEA features a great integration with Gradle, and Sublime Text is a fantastic text editor. For the sake of simplicity, in this chapter the Java code is built and executed using Gradle directly through the command line.

The Building Blocks of Cloud Dataflow

The idea behind Cloud Dataflow is to help you abstract the details of the system that you use to perform processing operations, taking it to a level that resembles the way your brain operates when thinking about a specific problem. For example, data from source A is transformed into states 1, 2, and 3 and stored in data sink B.

Four main concepts will help you construct your jobs and understand the way Cloud Dataflow operates: pipelines, `PCollections`, transforms, and data sources and sinks.

In the following sections you get an introduction to these concepts. To dive into the details of each of them, check the reference for the SDK in Java - `https://cloud.google.com/dataflow/release-notes/java`.

■ **Note** As of this writing this service is in beta phase, thus it is possible that backward-incompatible changes are introduced. Because of that, it is important to keep an eye on the development of the service if you have bigger plans using Cloud Dataflow.

Pipelines

A pipeline represents a single unit of processing in Cloud Dataflow. Pipelines are constructed by writing logic on top of the Cloud Dataflow SDK and generally define where to read the data from and where to write the results back, as well as all the intermediate steps applied to the data, referred to as *transforms*. Pipelines are designed to run on independent services or runners, and the Cloud Dataflow service is one of them. The steps in your pipeline are executed as a single unit of work that cannot share information with other jobs.

This is an example of a dummy pipeline written in Java:

```
public class MyFirstPipeline{

    public static interface Options extends PipelineOptions {
        ...
    }

    public static void main(String[] args) {

        // Creates the options with the arguments coming from the command line
        Options options = PipelineOptionsFactory.fromArgs(args)
                                                .withValidation().as(Options.class);

        Pipeline pipeline = Pipeline.create(options);

        // Reads from source and writes to sink using SDK provided PTransforms
        pipeline.apply(TextIO.Read.named("Read Input")
                                  .from("gs://lunchmates_logs/access.log"))
                .apply(TextIO.Write.named("WriteOutput")
                                  .to("gs://lunchmates_logs/output/results.txt"));

        pipeline.run();
    }
}
```

This is the one most basic versions of a pipeline possible. All it does is read content from the input and then write it to the output. Normally you would add other transformations between these two steps. The names specified using the method `.named()` are used by the system to describe the steps involved in the process.

PCollection

A `PCollection` is the canonical representation of your data in a pipeline. Every step involved in the process takes and/or returns a `PCollection` object on its own or contained in another collection or container object. `PCollections` can hold any type of object—from integers or strings to composite objects like key-value pairs or `TableRows` from BigQuery—without any size restrictions. It is more appropriate to think of `PCollections` as data containers than regular collections, because they differ from collections substantially. For example, `PCollections` are immutable and only allow sequential access to their content.

PCollections can be classified according to their boundaries:

- Bounded PCollections hold datasets of a limited and known size that do not change. Data sources and sinks for the classes TextIO, BigQueryIO, and DatastoreIO, and those created using the custom source/sink API, operate with bounded PCollections.
- Unbounded PCollections represent information that is being added continuously, such as real-time or streaming information. This type of PCollection does not have known boundaries. The class PubSubIO works with unbounded PCollections on both the source and sink sides. BigQueryIO accepts unbounded PCollection objects as sink information: that is, you can write the resulting unbounded PCollections in BigQuery using BigQueryIO.

Unbounded PCollections are virtually unlimited; therefore, you need to define interruption points that allow Cloud Dataflow to work with chunks of transformed information coming from this type of PCollection. Attempting to apply grouping transformations—for example, GroupByKey—to unbounded PCollections will cause your pipeline to fail to construct, making the job fail. In other words, it is impossible to retrieve the values for all possible keys in a collection that is continually growing.

You can tune the factors that determine this division of information by using *windowing*—that is, setting the boundaries of originally unbounded collections based on a set of parameters or functions that you determine. This decision can be made based on data size, fixed or dynamic time intervals, or discrete conditions. For more information about windows[4] and triggers,[5] check the Google Cloud Platform documentation.

In addition to the aforementioned, other data sources and sinks may be added in the near future.

Transforms

Transforms represent each of the steps you use to mutate your data from the original to a modified state, operating with PCollections directly (taking and returning PCollection objects, or a list of them). PTransform objects must implement the apply method, which is where transformations are defined. In this method, you can add any logic necessary to obtain the desired results for your data.

If many steps are involved in a single transformation, it is recommended that you break the operation into smaller versions that you can group together. This not only improves readability and possibilities for testability, but also helps you visualize your pipeline when in action. The transformations applied are represented in hierarchically organized boxes that you can graphically interact with from the Developers Console by expanding and collapsing them to dive into the details.

Figure 11-1 shows an example pipeline in the Cloud Dataflow section in Developers Console when it's executed.

[4]Windows in Cloud Dataflow: https://cloud.google.com/dataflow/model/windowing.
[5]Triggers in Cloud Dataflow: https://cloud.google.com/dataflow/model/triggers.

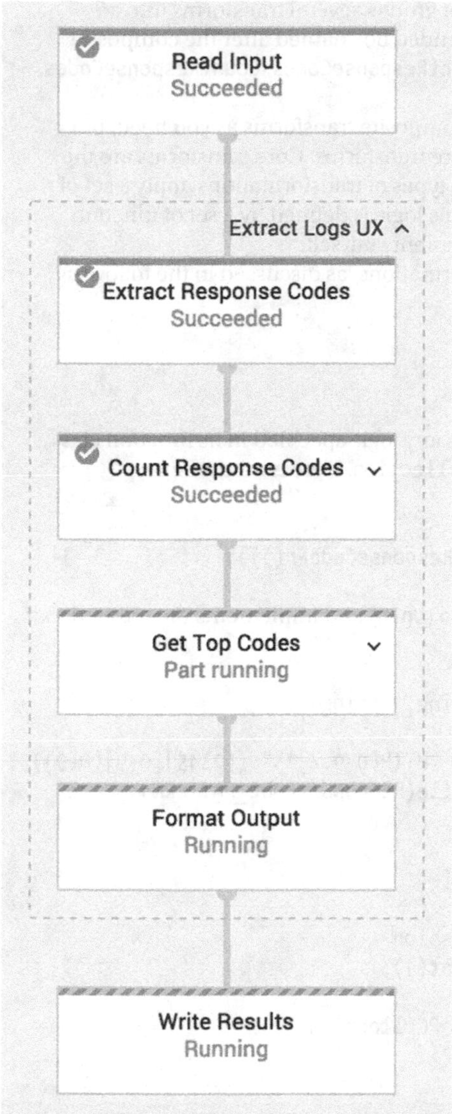

Figure 11-1. *Graphical representation of your pipeline in the Developers Console*

Using the example pipeline, here is how you apply a single transformation between the input read and the output write:

```
// Reads from source and writes to sink using SDK provided PTransforms
pipeline.apply(TextIO.Read.named("Read Input").from(options.getInput()))
        .apply(new ExtractLogExperience().withName("Extract Logs UX"))
        .apply(TextIO.Write.named("Write Output").to(options.getOutput()));
```

ExtractLogExperience is a custom composite transform that groups several transforms into a single unit. You can see that in Figure 11-1, where there is an expanded box named after the composite transformation class that groups four other subtransforms: ExtractResponseCodes, CountResponseCodes, GetTopCodes, and FormatOutput.

You can group functionality using as many levels of nested composite transforms as you need, but in the end, the core of your composite transforms is formed by core transforms. Core transforms are the foundation of Cloud Dataflow's parallel-processing model. These types of transformations apply a set of rules that complement the logic specific to the transformation. This logic is defined by a set of function classes that are either defined by the system or that you can implement yourself.

Cloud Dataflow SDK provides four fundamental core transformations, as discussed in the following sections.

ParDo: Processing Data in Parallel

ParDo is a core transformation for parallel operation that executes any logic specified in its function class (DoFn) and applies it to each of the elements in the associated PCollection. Here is an example:

```
PCollection<String> responseCodes = linesCollection
.apply(ParDo.named("Extract Response Codes").of(new GetResponseCodeFn()));
```

GetResponseCodeFn inherits from the class expected by ParDo (DoFn) and implements the method that processes each of the elements, processElement:

```
private static class GetResponseCodeFn extends DoFn<String, String> {

    private static final String RESPONSE_CODE_PATTERN = "HTTP[0-9./]*\" ([2345][0-9][0-9])";
    private static final Pattern pattern = Pattern.compile(RESPONSE_CODE_PATTERN);

    @Override
    public void processElement(ProcessContext context) {

        // Find matches for the specified regular expression
        Matcher matcher = pattern.matcher(context.element());

        // Output each response code into the resulting PCollection
        if (matcher.find()) {
            context.output(matcher.group(1));
        }
    }
}
```

The logic in processElement is scoped to the processing of a single object because the execution of the transformation may happen in parallel across different instances. That is, the collection may be split into subcollections that are processed by different machines at the same time.

ParDo(s) can take multiple input data through side inputs. These inputs are represented by PCollectionViews, computed by earlier steps in the pipeline that add information on how to process the main input PCollection. Similarly, ParDo(s) can return multiple output PCollections using PCollectionList if all the collections in the list contain the same data type or PCollectionTuple otherwise.

GroupByKey

This transformation allows you to group key-value pair collections in parallel using their key. GroupByKey is useful in collections containing a set of pairs with duplicated keys holding different values. The resulting dataset is a collection of pairs with unique keys holding multiple values each.

Combine

This transformation allows you to aggregate a collection of values into a single value—Combine.globally—or key-value pairs into key grouped collections—Combine.perKey. In addition to the aggregation type, this transformation accepts an Fn class referencing a function that is used to aggregate the items in the collection. For example, the following snippet calculates the mean of all the elements in a PCollection into a single result:

```
PCollection<Integer> collection = ...;
PCollection<Double> mean = collection.apply(Combine.globally(new Mean.MeanFn<Integer>()));
```

The classes that hold these mathematical operations also contain helper methods that you can use to reference the same operations with much cleaner syntax. For example, the previous method can be replaced with

```
PCollection<Integer> collection = ...;
PCollection<Double> mean = collection.apply(Mean.<Integer>globally());
```

Now, suppose you have a set of key-value pairs in which each element holds a list of values. This can happen, for example, after a GroupByKey transformation:

```
book, 4,2,4
song, 1,2
movie, 8,3
```

As in the previous snippet, you can extract the maximum value of the list of elements for each of the keys in a set of key-value pairs:

```
PCollection<Integer> collection = ...;
PCollection<KV<String, Long>> max = collection
.apply(Combine.<String, Long>perKey(new Max.MaxLongFn()));
```

Just like before, there is a helper method to generate the same Combine directive:

```
PCollection<Integer> collection = ...;
PCollection<KV<String, Long>> max = collection.apply(Max.<String>longsPerKey());
```

This function returns the same pairs, including only the maximum value for each entry:

```
book, 4
song, 2
movie, 8
```

Flatten: Merging Data Collections

Flatten helps you merge a list of PCollection-holding objects of the same type into a single PCollection:

```
PCollection<String> collection1 = ...
PCollection<String> collection2 = ...

PCollectionList<String> collections = PCollectionList.of(collection1).and(collection2);
PCollection<String> mergedResults = collections.apply(Flatten.<String>pCollections());
```

When you use unbounded PCollections with windows, all collections must have equal windowing functions—WindowingFn—to ensure that all elements have the same window strategy and sizing.

Data Sources and Sinks

Data sources define where your data is read from, whereas sinks specify where the data is written after the processing is done. Reading and writing the information you're working with are usually the first and last steps of a processing job, respectively. Cloud Dataflow makes it simple to treat different sources and sinks in a similar way by providing you with a set of interfaces, each representing different types of storage systems and services. That way, you can flexibly decide where your information comes from and where it goes.

Data sources and sinks work with PCollection objects; sources generate them, and sinks accept them as input when performing the final write operation. As of this writing, the Cloud Dataflow Java SDK includes the following transforms to operate with data sources and sinks.

Text Files

The class TextIO works with files stored in your local file system or in Google Cloud Storage. To reference files in Cloud Storage, you need to specify the appropriate gs scheme: gs://<bucket>/<filepath>.

This is how you read a file from Cloud Storage:

```
PipelineOptions options = PipelineOptionsFactory.create();
Pipeline pipeline = Pipeline.create(options);

PCollection<String> lines = pipeline.apply(TextIO.Read.named("ReadMyInputLogs")
                                        .from("gs://path-to-your-file/file.ext"));
```

Similarly, here is how you write the contents of a PCollection object into a file in Cloud Storage:

```
lines.apply(TextIO.Write.named("WriteMyInputLogs")
      .to("gs://path-to-your-file/file.ext"));
```

Note that Cloud Dataflow shards the execution of your job by default; because of that, output files can be generated with suffixes specifying shard numbers. If you want to control the final part of the file name, you can append a suffix using the method .withSuffix(".icontrolmyownextensions").

Avro Files

The class AvroIO operates similarly to TextIO, with the main difference being that AvroIO operates with Avro files with an associated schema instead of regular text files. Here is an example of reading Avro files as the input of your pipeline:

```
PipelineOptions options = PipelineOptionsFactory.create();
Pipeline pipeline = Pipeline.create(options);

PCollection<AvroType> lines = pipeline.apply(AvroIO.Read.named("ReadAvroFromGCS")
                                      .from("gs://path-to-your-file/file.avro")
                                      .withSchema(AvroType.class);
```

BigQuery Tables

You can use the class BigQueryIO to operate with tables in BigQuery as a means of reading and writing data. To do that, you need to specify the fully qualified name of the table you want to work with. This consists of three parts, concatenated together as follows: `<project-id>:<dataset-id>.<table-id>`.

If you obviate the project ID, the default project specified in PipelineOptions is used. You can access this value through the PipelineOptions.getProject method. In this instance, the table name is as follows: `<dataset-id>.<table-id>`.

Here is an example of a pipeline that reads information from a table in BigQuery:

```
PipelineOptions options = PipelineOptionsFactory.create();
Pipeline pipeline = Pipeline.create(options);

PCollection<TableRow> habitablePlanets = pipeline.apply(BigQueryIO.Read
                  .named("ReadPlanetInformation")
                          .from("earth-is-a-strange-place:planets.habitable-planets"));
```

Cloud Pub/Sub Messages

You can read from and write data to Cloud Pub/Sub messages using the class PubSubIO. You do that by specifying either a subscription that has already been created in Cloud Pub/Sub or the topic you are interested in.

■ **Note** Due to the nature of Cloud Pub/Sub messages, this data source can only be used in streaming pipelines. Therefore, you need to enable the streaming flag in PipelineOptions. For the same reason, PubSubIO operates with unbounded collections; thus you must specify a window strategy for the resulting PCollection before applying transformations that expect data with defined boundaries, such as GroupByKey and Combine.

The following snippet uses a topic called `projects/earth-is-a-strange-place/topics/habitable-planets` in Cloud Pub/Sub as a data source:

```
PipelineOptions options = PipelineOptionsFactory.create();
Pipeline pipeline = Pipeline.create(options);

String topicName = "projects/earth-is-a-strange-place/topics/habitable-planets";
PCollection<String> dataFromTopic = pipeline.apply(PubsubIO.Read
                                               .named("ReadFromPubsub")
                                               .topic(topicName));
```

Similarly, you can write `PCollections` into Cloud Pub/Sub channels by doing the following:

```
PCollection<String> dataFromTopic = ...;
dataFromTopic.apply(PubsubIO.Write.named("WriteToPubsub").topic(topicName));
```

To learn more about Cloud Pub/Sub, see Chapter 13.

Constructing and Executing Jobs in Cloud Dataflow

Now you have a basic idea of how Cloud Dataflow operates and how to model the blocks that construct a job or pipeline using the SDK in Java. In this section, you apply these concepts to a practical example that you program and execute using the service in the cloud.

MAKING USERS AS HAPPY AS A PIE

In this example, the idea is to make users of your service happy. Sure, that is obvious, but how do you do it? Access logs not only provide valuable information to system administrators and developers, but also give you an idea of what your clients—and thus your users—see when they exchange information with your service or API.

For example, if your logs show a significantly greater presence of any response codes other than 200–299, there may be a need to fix some things. In this example, you process the `access.log` file that you uploaded to Google Cloud Storage in Chapter 8 and generate an output file that lists the occurrences of each response code in the logs.

■ **Pro Tip** If you have not read Chapter 8 yet, don't worry. You can use any of the thousands of `access.log` files indexed by Internet search engines.

Before getting your hands on the keyboard, it is important to design your system. Doing so helps you to identify potential issues in your strategy and speeds up the developing part.

As mentioned, the goal is to measure the impact of response codes from incoming requests to your server. The starting point is an `access.log` file, and the result should be something like a list of response codes and the number of occurrences for each of them. One approach to get that result is the following:

1. Read the file from the input.
2. Extract the response codes from the log lines.
3. Count the number of occurrences for each response code.
4. Get a list with the five most common response codes, to discard noise.
5. Format the results in an appropriate way to output.
6. Write the results to the data sink.

■ **Note** Before executing your pipeline, Cloud Dataflow automatically optimizes the steps involved. Because of that, the steps you define may not be executed in the same order you specify in your code.

Now that you know how your system should operate, you can start the fun part. The first thing to do is create the pipeline with which you will operate. A pipeline holds all the necessary information about the processing job—for example, the origin and destination of the data, the location of staging files for execution, the number of workers to execute the job, the project identifier in Google Cloud, and so on—as well as the transformations applied to it.

To create your pipeline, you call the `create` method, passing `PipelineOptions` as a parameter:

```
PipelineOptions options = PipelineOptionsFactory.create();
Pipeline pipeline = Pipeline.create(options);
```

The `PipelineOptions` object holds the information about the environment that the pipeline needs. You can take this approach one step further by loading the parameters with the arguments provided directly from the command line:

```
PipelineOptions options = PipelineOptionsFactory.fromArgs(arguments);
Pipeline pipeline = Pipeline.create(options);
```

Finally, you can also extend the functionality of `PipelineOptions` using inheritance. Suppose you want to control the data source and sink locations as parameters in your pipeline options object. You can do that by creating a new object that inherits from `PipelineOptions` and defining new properties that you can add as arguments whenever you run your job from the command line. In this example, the class `AllowedOptions` adds two more parameters:

```
public static interface AllowedOptions extends PipelineOptions {

   @Description("Default path to logs file")
   @Default.String("gs://lunchmates_logs/access.log")
   String getInput();
   void setInput(String value);
```

```
    @Description("Path of the file to write the results to")
    @Default.String("gs://lunchmates_logs/output/results.txt")
    String getOutput();
    void setOutput(String value);
}

AllowedOptions options = PipelineOptionsFactory.fromArgs(args)
                                              .withValidation()
                                              .as(AllowedOptions.class);

Pipeline pipeline = Pipeline.create(options);
```

This new class allows you to include two more arguments in the running command: `--input` and `--output`. These names are extracted from the getters and setters specified in your class. Note that you can specify default options in case the arguments are not set. Finally, the creation of the `PipelineOptions` object now includes a validation method according to the target class you just created. This validates the arguments obtained, based on the annotations and methods configured in your class.

As mentioned, in addition to the default arguments, you can set values for input and output locations:

```
$ ./gradlew run -Pargs="--project=lunch--mates
                        --runner=BlockingDataflowPipelineRunner
                        --stagingLocation=gs://lunchmates_logs/staging
                        --input=gs://lunchmates_logs/access.log
                        --output=gs://lunchmates_logs/output/results.txt"
```

Later, when the pipeline is ready for execution, we discuss the possible values for the arguments in this command.

Now that your pipeline is configured, you need to get some data. In this case, the `access.log` file you want to process is located in Cloud Storage at the location specified in the `PipelineOptions` object: `gs://lunchmates_logs/access.log` by default. Because the content is plain text, you use `TextIO` to read it:

```
pipeline.apply(TextIO.Read.named("Read Input").from(options.getInput()));
```

The result is written back to Cloud Storage in a text file, placed in the output folder specified in the `PipelineOptions` object: `gs://lunchmates_logs/output/results.txt` by default. Your pipeline now has entry and exit points:

```
pipeline.apply(TextIO.Read.named("Read Input").from(options.getInput()))
          .apply(new ExtractLogExperience().withName("Extract Logs UX"))
          .apply(TextIO.Write.named("Write Results")
                              .to(options.getOutput())
                              .withSuffix(".txt"));
```

All the steps are named so that the entire flow is easier to understand when it is being executed and represented in Cloud Dataflow.

Notice that there is only one transformation in this pipeline, named `Extract Logs UX`. This is a custom composite transform that contains subtransforms. When defining your own composite transforms, the system uses that to represent the flow diagram and group modules—which are shown as boxes—based on this hierarchy.

As expected, the class ExtractLogExperience contains all the necessary steps according to the design of this flow:

```
public static class ExtractLogExperience
extends PTransform<PCollection<String>, PCollection<String>> {

    @Override
    public PCollection<String> apply(PCollection<String> lines) {

        //1. Filter log line to extract response code
        PCollection<String> responseCodes = lines.apply(ParDo.named("Extract Response Codes")
                                                    .of(new GetResponseCodeFn()));

        //2. Counts occurrences for each response code found
        PCollection<KV<String, Long>> responseCodeResults = responseCodes
                                    .apply(Count.<String>perElement()
                                                .withName("Count Response Codes"));

        //3. Get the top five response codes
        PCollection<List<KV<String, Long>>> topThreeResponseCodes = responseCodeResults
                                    .apply(new TopCodes().withName("Get Top Codes"));

        //4. Format response codes and counts into a printable string
        return topThreeResponseCodes.apply(ParDo.named("Format Output")
                                            .of(new FormatResultsFn()));
    }
}
```

When you create a class that inherits from PTransform. you specify the type of the input and output objects. As you can see in the definition of the class, this transform receives a PCollection<String> representing a collection with each of the lines of the log file and returns the same type of object; this time, each line represents the response code and the number of occurrences in the entire log.

1. Filter Log to Extract Response Code

Notice that because you are working with PCollections throughout the pipeline, the same apply method is used to add other transformations to it.

A filtering operation is a common task for ParDos. Remember that this is simply a container that executes some logic in parallel (you define the logic to execute in a class that inherits from DoFn). Other common tasks that fit parallel execution are formatting data and processing items in the collection in an independent fashion (for example, on a per-key basis). In this case, this is specified in the class GetResponseCodeFn:

```
private static class GetResponseCodeFn extends DoFn<String, String> {

    private static final String RESPONSE_CODE_PATTERN = "HTTP[0-9./]*\" ([2345][0-9][0-9])";
    private static final Pattern pattern = Pattern.compile(RESPONSE_CODE_PATTERN);
```

```
    @Override
    public void processElement(ProcessContext context) {

        // Find matches for the specified regular expression
        Matcher matcher = pattern.matcher(context.element());

        // Output each response code into the resulting PCollection
        if (matcher.find()) {
            context.output(matcher.group(1));
        }
    }
}
```

Similar to PTransforms, DoFn defines two types of arguments, corresponding to the input and output types, respectively.

The method processElement is called for every element in the collection. In this example, the regular expression looks for a common pattern in log files—HTTP/[version]" [response-code]. If the pattern is matched, the first group—the one containing the response code—is returned.

The output of this step should look something similar to the following (replacing new lines with bars "|"):

```
200 | 201 | 500 | 500 | 404 | 401 | 201 | 401 | 404 | 302 | 401 | 401 | 401 | 204 | 200 | ...
```

2. Count Occurrences for Each Response Code Found

In this step, the goal is to count the number of occurrences for each unique response code in the collection provided by the previous step. For this purpose, you can use the Count transform provided by the SDK, which does exactly what you are looking for:

```
PCollection<KV<String, Long>> responseCodeResults = responseCodes
                   .apply(Count.<String>perElement()
                                .withName("Count Response Codes"));
```

As you can see, the response object is a collection of key-value pairs of String and Long types, holding the unique response code and number result of the count transformation. The expected output is as follows:

```
[Response Code]: [# of occurrences]
200: 1248
201: 256
404: 512
401: 192
500: 64
503: 96
422: 1024
```

3. Get the Top Five Response Codes

In this step, you get the top five most common response codes. Similar to step 2, you use a transform provided by the Cloud Dataflow Java SDK, but in this instance the Top class requires a comparator that you need to define. For readability, modularity, and testability reasons, you create a custom PTransform class that simply applies the transformation from the Top class. As you can see, this new class is called TopCodes. Here is its definition:

```
private static class TopCodes
extends PTransform<PCollection<KV<String, Long>>, PCollection<List<KV<String, Long>>>> {

    @Override
    public PCollection<List<KV<String, Long>>>
    apply(PCollection<KV<String, Long>> responseCodes) {

        return responseCodes.apply(Top
        .of(5, new SerializableComparator<KV<String, Long>>() {

            @Override
            public int compare(KV<String, Long> o1, KV<String, Long> o2) {
                return Long.compare(o1.getValue(), o2.getValue());
            }
        }));
    }
}
```

Once again, this transform defines the input and output types. In this case, the output is a list of key-value pairs containing as many results as specified in the Top class.

In the apply method, you call the Top transform and specify the number of results you want to return, along with the anonymous inner comparator class. This class is used to let Top know how to determine which value is greater than the other.

Based on the result from the previous step, the output is as follows:

```
[Response Code]: [# of occurrences]
200: 1248
422: 1024
404: 512
201: 256
401: 192
```

4. Format Response Codes and Counts into a Printable String

In this step, you prepare and convert the processed content into the desired output format. For this example, you use the nomenclature <response-code>|<number-of-occurrences> so that you can read and parse the content quickly from other systems.

Just as in step 1, you perform this operation in parallel with a ParDo. In this case, the class defining the logic to execute is called FormatResultsFn, which once again inherits from DoFn:

```
private static class FormatResultsFn extends DoFn<List<KV<String, Long>>, String> {

    @Override
    public void processElement(ProcessContext context) {
        for (KV<String, Long> item : context.element()) {
            context.output(item.getKey() + "|" + item.getValue());
        }
    }
}
```

The final result of the processing job should look like this:

```
200|1266
302|99
404|75
301|31
304|20
```

This completes the pipeline job. As shown in the definition part, this content is now written into the desired output determined by the PipelineOptions configuration.

All that is left is running your pipeline. For reference purposes, here is the entire main method:

```
public static void main(String[] args) {

    AllowedOptions options = PipelineOptionsFactory.fromArgs(args)
                                                   .withValidation()
                                                   .as(AllowedOptions.class);
    Pipeline pipeline = Pipeline.create(options);

    pipeline.apply(TextIO.Read.named("Read Input").from(options.getInput()))
            .apply(new ExtractLogExperience().withName("Extract Logs UX"))
            .apply(TextIO.Write.named("Write Results").to(options.getOutput())
                                                        .withSuffix(".txt"));

    pipeline.run();
}
```

You can find the complete source for this pipeline in the code-snippets repository under the folder named cloud-dataflow —https://github.com/GoogleCloudPlatformBook/code-snippets/tree/master/cloud-dataflow.

Executing your pipeline

Your pipeline is now ready to run. Pipelines run in *runners* that execute your job locally, in Google's infrastructure or in third-party services.

To run the pipeline, you use the Gradle command that you saw earlier. Before getting into that, let's look at the contents of the `build.gradle` file. This file, located in the root folder of your project, is in charge of executing your code and determining the type of application, versions, and dependencies:

```
apply plugin: 'java'
apply plugin: 'application'

sourceCompatibility = JavaVersion.VERSION_1_7
targetCompatibility = JavaVersion.VERSION_1_7

mainClassName = 'com.lunchmates.LogAnalyzer'

repositories {
    mavenCentral()
}

dependencies {
    compile 'com.google.cloud.dataflow:google-cloud-dataflow-java-sdk-all:0.3.+'
    testCompile 'junit:junit:4.11'
}

task resources {
    def resourcesDir = new File('build/resources/main')
    resourcesDir.mkdirs()
}

run {
    if (project.hasProperty('args')) {
        args project.args.split('\\s')
    }
}

run.mustRunAfter 'resources'
```

This works as follows, from top to bottom:

- The `plugins` define the type of application to execute. This parameter allows Gradle to conveniently set up conventions and extensions.
- `sourceCompatibility` and `targetCompatibility` determine the target Java version to use for this application.
- The `mainClassName` specifies the class that is executed when you run the build script. This is always the class that contains the pipeline you intend to run.
- In the `repositories` section, you specify the different local and remote repositories from which you will fetch dependencies.
- `dependencies` is a list of libraries that your project needs to work. In this case, the Java SDK for Google Dataflow is added in this section. This makes dependency management simple and flexible.

The rest of the build script is specific to Google Dataflow. task `resources` creates the folder `/resources/main`, which Dataflow expects to find in the `directory` folder. Finally, the `run` method preprocesses the arguments string, turning it into a list that can be accessed in your code.

To run the pipeline, execute the `run` command in Gradle:

```
$ ./gradlew run -Pargs="--project=lunch--mates
                        --runner=DirectPipelineRunner
                        --stagingLocation=gs://lunchmates_logs/staging
                        --input=gs://lunchmates_logs/access.log
                        --output=gs://lunchmates_logs/output/results.txt"
```

The `runner` parameter determines whether your project runs using the Cloud Dataflow service or locally. To run your project locally, you can omit the `runner` parameter or use `DirectPipelineRunner`. Conversely, if you want to run it using Cloud Dataflow, you need to use `DataflowPipelineRunner` or `BlockingDataflowPipelineRunner`. The first value executes your pipeline asynchronously, whereas if you use `BlockingDataflowPipelineRunner`, the job is executed synchronously, so the console does not return until the work is done. During this time, the logs and execution information about the project are output in the console.

Here is a list of other relevant arguments for the configuration of your pipeline:

- `--project` selects the project in Google Cloud used to run your pipeline. The expected value is the identifier of your project.
- `--streaming` is a `boolean` value that determines whether streaming mode is enabled or disabled.
- `--stagingLocation` determines the location the service uses to store local binaries needed for distributed execution. It must be a valid Cloud Storage URL.
- `--tempLocation` specifies the location that the service uses to store temporary files. It must be a valid Cloud Storage URL.

In addition, you can specify the arguments of your custom `PipelineOptions` class if you specified one. In this example, remember that you added `input` and `output` to specify the data source and sink to operate with.

Running your project locally is encouraged before bumping instances. This way, you can troubleshoot and debug your code before using production resources. When you run your project locally, it is recommended that you work with a data set that fits in the computer's memory. Remember that you can use local files as data sources. And keep in mind that running your job locally also interacts with cloud services like Cloud Storage or BigQuery.

When you are ready to execute your job using the Cloud Dataflow service, you can specify one of the runners mentioned earlier. This creates a JSON representation of your module that is uploaded to Cloud Dataflow, optimized, and finally executed. Once your pipeline starts running, you can monitor its progress from the Cloud Dataflow panel in the Developers Console, in the Big Data section of the left bar. It shows you a list of the recently executed and in-progress jobs. Clicking one of them takes you to the detail page for that job. Cloud Dataflow features an intuitive representation of your pipeline, using collapsible, connected boxes, according to the structure of the steps involved in the process. This graph is updated in real time and shows information such as logs, summary of the task, and the number of records currently being processed. This is another great way to debug your pipeline logic, because you have an expectation about which steps reduce or increase the number of potential output records.

The following command runs your project synchronously using the Cloud Dataflow service for the project `lunch--mates`, places local and temporary files in the bucket `lunchmates_logs/staging` in Cloud Storage, takes the input data from the default input defined in `PipelineOptions` `gs://lunchmates_logs/access.log`, and writes the result into the default output `gs://lunchmates_logs/output/results.txt`:

```
$ ./gradlew run -Pargs="--project=lunch--mates
                        --runner=BlockingDataflowPipelineRunner
                        --stagingLocation=gs://lunchmates_logs/staging"
```

Showing Results

Choosing an appropriate data sink for your pipeline depends primarily on the purpose of the generated information. Here is a list of the options and their typical applications:

- BigQuery, if you intend to perform further analysis or aggregations with data from other sources.
- Cloud Storage, if the generated data is intended to be static and independent. For example, suppose you build an intelligent pipeline that extracts the essence of encyclopedias and reduces them to a few pages of text. You can store the result in Cloud Storage, because you do not need to further analyze or combine the outcome.
- Cloud Datastore, if you want to expose the data directly on an application you develop.
- Cloud Pub/Sub, is very powerful when your data is not constrained and changes continuously. For example real-time scenarios.

In this example, the ideal use of the results would be to show them in a simple web site that performs a very basic analysis of the top response codes and delivers a conclusion. Cloud Datastore and Cloud Storage are great data sinks for this purpose, because you can load information from these two sources easily from an application hosted in Google App Engine, for example.

Summary

In this chapter, you have been introduced to a service that makes processing big data a less cumbersome duty by abstracting the infrastructural details of the system away from you so that you can focus on the details of your problem. You learned about the building blocks of the system, constructed a pipeline using Cloud Dataflow components, and ran it locally and using Google Cloud's infrastructure.

Remember that as of this writing, this service is in beta phase, so there is a lot to look forward to in such areas as working with other programming languages, having more options to run pipelines in different providers, adding functions that help you process data, and so on. At the same time, some things may be subject to change, such as specific syntax or procedures. Because of that, if this service is crucial to you, we recommend that you keep an eye of the development of the platform and pair that with your learning process.

Independent of your final outcome and whether Cloud Dataflow is the right solution for it, Google and other companies are very interested in providing tools to help you handle and analyze big data in as quick and straightforward a manner as possible. This is a great time to catch the train with these technologies, which represent one of the biggest advances in computing in the last decade.

Finally, the Cloud Dataflow team is engaging in open source activities: the Java SDK for Cloud Dataflow is open and available in GitHub under the following repository: `https://github.com/GoogleCloudPlatform/DataflowJavaSDK`. This is a great opportunity for the technology itself and also for you to get a better understanding of how your logic operates and to learn and contribute as the technology evolves.

CHAPTER 12

Google Cloud Pub/Sub

Some of us still remember the days when it was exciting to open a browser and see how content was loaded and shown on the screen. You could not be sure what you were going to see or why you were receiving the information, but it was thrilling despite the amount you were paying for an hour of access to the Internet.

Nowadays, the Internet is part of our lives, as an increasing number of devices are interconnected in networks that represent our friends, private life, work, home, and more. Not only that, but the Internet is also part of the way we think. We expect Internet services to be fast and to provide the information we need, we have a better understanding about how it works as a whole, and we hold and wear devices that are connected to the Internet. You may even see children—who have been raised with the Internet—trying to execute swipe gestures or press buttons on printed paper media like magazines.

In such a demanding environment, from a technological standpoint, there is an increasing need for systems to act in a smart way while people do other things: to curate content for you while you are sleeping, to publish your picture to various social networks at the same time without having to wait for the spinner to disappear from your screen, or to automatically send e-mails to your friends who have not chosen their preferred dates to go camping next week while you prepare your tent. In summary, we want our systems to communicate with each other. If we need this functionality today, imagine how it will look like in ten years when your house speaks to your car, your fridge talks to the supermarket, or your calendar service directly sends a message to your friends.

Google Cloud Pub/Sub is a service that provides secure, durable, scalable messaging capabilities to connect independent systems in the cloud. Cloud Pub/Sub allows asynchronous exchanges of information in a many-to-many structured way that operates inside and outside of Google Cloud Platform. Currently, it features a very simple interface that is operable using HTTP and JSON through its API, which makes the system flexible and adaptable to almost any scenario. As with other APIs, you can use the client libraries provided by Google to simplify access to Cloud Pub/Sub.

This service addresses critical needs of a typical system that uses this technology, such as data encryption at rest and transfer time, data and delivery reliability using explicit acknowledgement notifications, custom delivery—using push or pull mechanisms—and high availability worldwide.

Simply put, Cloud Pub/Sub acts as a many-to-many independent bus for messages that can be published to a topic by any party who is granted access; the messages are queued, temporarily stored, and subsequently delivered to subscribers on that specific topic. Once a subscriber has finished processing the messages, they must respond, acknowledging their consumption. This removes the messages from the subscriber's queue. Figure 12-1 shows a typical setup with three topics, two of which have subscribers.

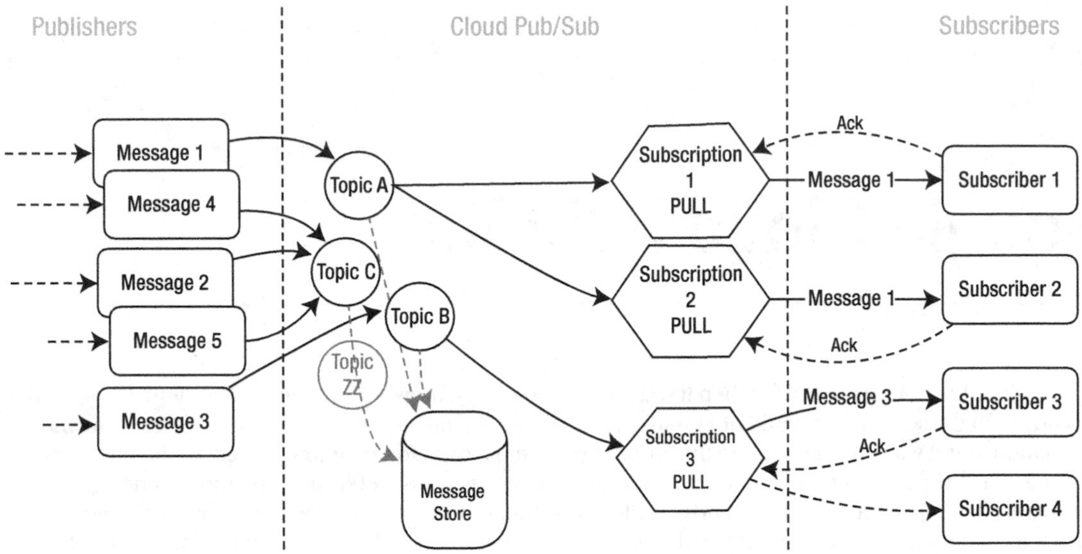

Figure 12-1. *Lifecycle of a message in Cloud Pub/Sub*

In this instance, five messages are published into three different topics. For topics with subscribers, the messages are added to the subscription queues. Subscribers with a push configuration are sent the messages as soon as possible. Conversely, for pull subscribers, messages are queued and stored, ready for the consumer to pull them on demand. Messages published on topics without a subscriber may be lost; in this example, that is true for messages 2, 4, and 5.

If a message is published to a topic with many subscriptions, a copy of the message is queued on each of them. If a subscription has more than one subscriber, the message is sent to only one of them and considered consumed as soon as this subscriber processes it and acknowledges consumption back to the subscription.

Setting Up Your System

Before publishing your first message, you need to enable the Cloud Pub/Sub API. To do that, go to Google Developers Console at `https://console.developers.google.com`. Select a project or create a new one, navigate to APIs & Auth, and click APIs. If you do not see Cloud Pub/Sub in the list, use the search box and look for "Pub/Sub API" to find it. In its section, click Enable API.

Now you can access Cloud Pub/Sub functions using the exposed HTTP JSON API or the client library for the programming language you are using. You can see the list of client libraries and the steps to install them at `https://developers.google.com/api-client-library`.

This API is restricted to authorized accounts; therefore, you need credentials to make calls to it. Note that publishers and subscribers are generally parts of your system that need to communicate with each other. Because of that, there is no need to authorize users to perform requests on their behalf; instead you authorize your application using a service account. Google App Engine and Google Compute Engine applications have associated default service accounts that you can use when you perform requests to the APIs through the client libraries. If you are calling a Google API from somewhere else, you can still use this functionality by creating a service account, downloading the key associated with it, and placing it somewhere private in your system. When you use the default credentials—`GoogleCredentials.get_application_default()`—the client libraries look for this key under the path set in the environment variable

GOOGLE_APPLICATION_CREDENTIALS. Set this variable to the path where you stored your key. To create a service account, go to APIs & Auth from one of your projects in Developers Console, and select Credentials. Click Create New Client ID, and choose Service Account for the type of your application. Select a JSON key, and create the account. This JSON file contains all the necessary information to obtain authorized access to Google APIs. Place this file somewhere in your server where it cannot be accessed publicly. To read more about OAuth2 and service accounts, see Chapter 3.

To obtain access to the Cloud Pub/Sub API using the Python client library, create the credentials to authorize your calls and build the client with them:

```
from oauth2client.client import GoogleCredentials
from apiclient import discovery

PUBSUB_API_SCOPE = 'https://www.googleapis.com/auth/pubsub'

credentials = GoogleCredentials.get_application_default()
if credentials.create_scoped_required():
    credentials = credentials.create_scoped(PUBSUB_API_SCOPE)

pubsub_client = discovery.build('pubsub', 'v1beta2', credentials=credentials)
```

If you need to use an access token for these credentials directly, you can force obtaining a new token with the following snippet:

```
from httplib2 import Http

credentials._refresh(Http().request)
credentials.access_token
```

At this point, your client is ready to begin exploring the API. To start with, you can list the topics in your projects:

```
pubsub_client.projects().topics().list(project='projects/<project-id>').execute()
```

Here, project-id is the identifier of your project in Developers Console. This is also referred to as app-id, application-id, or Project ID.

Topics

As you can see in Figure 12-1, messages are published to topics. Organizing content in topics allows you to create flexible systems in terms of how messages are published and distributed across subscribers. A topic is defined by its name, which is a combination of the project and topic identifiers in a URI path-like form:

```
projects/<project-id>/topics/<topic-id>
```

For example, to create a new topic called habitable-planets in your project earth-is-a-strange-place, the topic name would be the following:

```
projects/earth-is-a-strange-place/topics/habitable-planets
```

■ **Note** Topics, subscriptions, messages, and attributes are referred to as *resources*. In v1beta2, the current version of Cloud Pub/Sub API as of this writing, resource names must start with a lowercase letter; end with a lowercase letter or number; and contain only lowercase letters, numbers, dashes, underscores, or periods. A resource name must be longer than 2 and shorter than 256 characters and cannot begin with the string `goog`.

As one of the examples in this chapter, you are going to orchestrate the search for habitable planets.

TEST CASE: A NEW WORLD

Ten years from now, during his routine morning shower, Javier starts to think about how strange and unstable this world has become. He feels nostalgic about how things used to be. That thought leads to the realization that if things continue in the same direction, future generations may need another place to live, far from the only planet humanity has ever called home. The greatest acts in human history began with simple steps, he thinks, and so he decides to help observatories with their efforts to find habitable planets.

Many observatories have automated routines programmed into telescopes to look for patterns that may help find such planets. Therefore, Javier devises a very simple system in which telescopes notify a back-end application every time they find a potential match for a habitable planet. The telescopes publish a message to Cloud Pub/Sub that is delivered to subscriptions that, in turn, notify him and other interested parties as well as store information about the new discovery on a database. You are Javier, and you do not want to lose a single second.

The first thing you need to do before publishing messages is to create topics. To create a topic using the previously instantiated API client in Python, you do the following:

```
pubsub_client.projects().topics().create(
    name='projects/<project-id>/topics/<topic-id>', body={}).execute()
```

Assuming you create a project called `earth-is-a-strange-place` and come up with `habitable-planets` a topic identifier, the same command looks like this:

```
pubsub_client.projects().topics().create(
    name='projects/earth-is-a-strange-place/topics/habitable-planets',
    body={}).execute()
```

■ **Pro Tip** You can let the client library handle automatic retries to 500 error responses for you by specifying the argument `num_retries` as an argument in the `execute` method. Requests are retried with randomized exponential back-off that is, every retry is attempted after a longer waiting time. If all requests fail, the error returned is the one corresponding to the last attempt. The value you specify defines the number of times the client will attempt to access the resource, not including the initial request. For example, the following request is retried once after the original call fails: `client.methods()...execute(num_retries=1)`.

You can also access the API directly through HTTP and JSON. This is how you create the same topic as before, using the Python client library:

```
PUT https://pubsub.googleapis.com/v1beta2/
projects/earth-is-a-strange-place/topics/habitable-planets

Authorization: Bearer <your_auth_token>
```

Similarly, you can delete topics with the following request:

```
# Python
pubsub_client.projects().topics().delete(
    topic='projects/earth-is-a-strange-place/topics/<topic_to_delete>'
).execute()

# JSON API
DELETE https://pubsub.googleapis.com/v1beta2/
projects/earth-is-a-strange-place/topics/<topic_to_delete>

Authorization: Bearer <your_auth_token>
```

To retrieve the list of topics, you need to account for pagination. When the number of results exceeds a certain limit, Google APIs break the content into pages. If more results are available, you get a `nextPageToken` parameter in the response. Note that this applies to other endpoints and APIs:

```
# Python
def list_resource(resource:request, resource:name, page_token=None):

    response = resource:request.list(
        project='projects/earth-is-a-strange-place',
        pageToken=page_token).execute(num_retries=1)

    for resource in response[resource:name]:
        print resource

    new_page_token = response.get('nextPageToken')
    if new_page_token:
        list_resource(resource:request, resource:name, new_page_token)

list_resource(pubsub_client.projects().topics(), 'topics')

# JSON API
GET https://pubsub.googleapis.com/v1beta2/projects/earth-is-a-strange-place/topics
Authorization: Bearer <your_auth_token>
```

In this case, you define a method that takes care of obtaining and applying the page token to requests. This happens until this property is not returned any more—which means the last request corresponds to the last page of results.

■ **Note** CRUD operations look similar when applied to other resources, both using the Python client library and calling the JSON API directly. Therefore, not all requests are covered in this chapter. To see an updated snapshot of the API, endpoints, and methods, we recommend that you use Google API Explorer (`https://developers.google.com/apis-explorer`) and browse the API you are interested in.

Subscriptions

Before the first message is submitted, you need to configure your system on the consumer end so that potential subscribers can process and acknowledge consumption of messages. Subscriptions establish a connection between a topic and the consumer(s) of the messages. Once a subscription is created, messages published on the topic of interest are added to the subscription's queue.

To create a subscription, you call the `.subscriptions().create(...)` method, passing the URI of the new subscription and the body containing the topic to which to subscribe. Alternatively, you can specify the `pushConfiguration` and `ackDeadlineSeconds` parameters. You see them in action later in the chapter. For now, let's stick to the basics:

```
# Python
project_uri = 'projects/earth-is-a-strange-place'
topic_uri = '%s/topics/habitable-planets' % project_uri
subscription = project_uri +
'/subscriptions/new-habitable-planets-notifier'

body = {'topic': topic_uri}

pubsub_client.projects().subscriptions().create(
    name=subscription_uri, body=body).execute()

# JSON API
PUT https://pubsub.googleapis.com/v1beta2/
projects/earth-is-a-strange-place/subscriptions/new-habitable-planets-notifier

Authorization: Bearer <your_auth_token>
Content-Type: application/json

{
    "topic": "projects/earth-is-a-strange-place/topics/habitable-planets"
}
```

Listing and deleting subscriptions follows the same structure as for topics. For example, the URL to delete a subscription in the JSON API is

```
<host>/<version>/
projects/earth-is-a-strange-place/subscriptions/<subscription_to_delete>
```

Or, using the Python client library, it is as follows:

```
project_id = 'earth-is-a-strange-place'
subscription_id = '<subscription_to_delete>'
subscription = 'projects/%s/subscriptions/%s' % (project_id, subscription_id)

pubsub_client.projects().subscriptions().delete(
    subscription=subscription).execute()
```

Based on your system's nature and requirements, you can choose between pull and push subscriptions.

Push Subscriptions

Push subscriptions proactively send incoming messages to an endpoint in your system that takes care of processing the message and returning an HTTP status code to tell Cloud Pub/Sub whether the message completed successfully. In practice, this operation behaves similarly to an incoming request to the provided endpoint, with the message data and attributes coming as part of the body of the request. Returning a successful response (200, 201, 203, 204, 102) acknowledges the message, and it is deleted from the queue. Otherwise, the same message is redelivered for retrial.

This type of subscription is advantageous in scenarios where you do not want to manage message distribution, or when operating in near-to-real time is important. If you already have an application running in App Engine under the same project ID, it is recommended that you host your push endpoint there: doing so simplifies endpoint verification, and your system may benefit from potential intra-project optimizations, as is the case for other Google services working together.

To create a push subscription, you just need to define the pushConfig parameter by specifying a pushEndpoint:

```
body = {
    "topic": "projects/earth-is-a-strange-place/topics/habitable-planets",
    "pushConfig": {
        "pushEndpoint": "https://<verified-host>/<your-push-endpoint>"
    }
}
```

Alternatively, you can change the behavior of the subscription between push and pull by modifying its push configuration. Here is how you specify a push endpoint in the subscription's configuration, turning it into a push subscription:

```
# Python
project_id = 'earth-is-a-strange-place'
subscription_id = 'new-habitable-planets-notifier'
subscription = 'projects/%s/subscriptions/%s' % (project_id, subscription_id)

body = {
    'pushConfig': {
        'pushEndpoint': 'https://<verified-host>/<your-push-endpoint>'
    }}

pubsub_client.projects().subscriptions().modifyPushConfig(
    subscription=subscription, body=body).execute()
```

```
# JSON API
POST https://pubsub.googleapis.com/v1beta2/
projects/earth-is-a-strange-place/subscriptions/new-habitable-planets-notifier
:modifyPushConfig

Authorization: Bearer <your_auth_token>
Content-Type: application/json

{
    "pushConfig": {
        "pushEndpoint": "https://<verified-host>/<your-push-endpoint>"
    }
}
```

In push subscriptions, the selected endpoint is considered verified if it operates from an application in App Engine that is registered in the same Google Cloud project. If your push endpoint is hosted on a non-App Engine application or on an application other than the one from which you are operating Cloud Pub/Sub, you need to verify and register it manually in Developers Console. Push endpoints need to operate over secure connections (HTTPS), and thus servers must present a signed SSL certificate.

To register a domain on your project to be accepted as a trusted resource, you first need to verify that you own that domain. To do that, navigate to the Webmaster Tools (`https://www.google.com/webmasters/tools`), click Add a New Site, and enter the URL of the site in question. Follow the steps to complete the verification process.

Now you can register the domain as an allowed resource for your project. To do so, go to your project in Developers Console and navigate to APIs & Auth ➤ Push. Click Add Domain, and enter the previously verified URL for the trusted domain. If verification completed successfully, the new domain appears in the list of allowed push resources. You can now use endpoints for that domain as push targets in Cloud Pub/Sub subscriptions.

To switch the behavior of your subscription back to pull, simply change `pushConfiguration` to hold an empty object:

```
body = {
    "pushConfig": {}
}
```

Pull Subscriptions

Pull subscriptions do not deliver messages actively. Instead, the consumer must fetch messages by calling the `pull` method on a specific subscription. Messages are returned in JSON format in the response. In addition to the message information, an acknowledgement identifier is attached to each of the results. When the consumer processes a message gracefully, it must confirm consumption of it by calling the `acknowledge` method on the subscription in question before the deadline is reached. This method is able to acknowledge many messages at a time; hence, it accepts an array of acknowledgement identifiers:

```
# Python
project_id = 'earth-is-a-strange-place'
subscription_id = 'new-habitable-planets-notifier'
subscription = 'projects/%s/subscriptions/%s' % (project_id, subscription_id)
```

```
body = {'ackDeadlineSeconds': 600,
        'ackIds': [<list_of_ack_ids>]}

pubsub_client.projects().subscriptions().acknowledge(
    subscription=subscription, body=body).execute()

# JSON API
POST https://pubsub.googleapis.com/v1beta2/
projects/earth-is-a-strange-place/subscriptions/new-habitable-planets-notifier
:acknowledge

Authorization: Bearer <your_auth_token>
Content-Type: application/json

{
    "ackIds": [<list_of_ack_ids>]
}
```

Pull queues are useful when you need control over message processing or you need to operate flexibly from different systems that are independent from each other. Note that messages in pull subscriptions can be requested from any device or system that can send and process requests over HTTP.

To create a pull subscription, simply omit the pushConfig parameter in the request to create a new subscription.

Acknowledgement Deadline

When messages are sent or leased by consumers, there is a time limit before they can acknowledge consumption of the messages. If they fail to do that, the current processing effort is discarded and the message is made available again in the subscriber queues. This deadline is 60 seconds by default. You can change this value to up to 600 seconds by specifying the parameter ackDeadlineSeconds when creating your subscription. This is an example of a body used in previous requests:

```
body = {
    "topic": "projects/earth-is-a-strange-place/topics/habitable-planets",
    "pushConfig": {
        "pushEndpoint": "https://<verified-host>/<your-push-endpoint>"
    },
    "ackDeadlineSeconds":599
}
```

Alternatively, if you need to extend the deadline for a specific message, you can change the current value by specifying the acknowledgement identifier of the message along with the new deadline:

```
# Python
project_id = 'earth-is-a-strange-place'
subscription_id = 'new-habitable-planets-notifier'
subscription = 'projects/%s/subscriptions/%s' % (project_id, subscription_id)

body = {'ackDeadlineSeconds': 600,
        'ackId': '<message_ack_id>'}
```

```
pubsub_client.projects().subscriptions().modifyAckDeadline(
subscription=subscription, body=body).execute()

# JSON API
POST https://pubsub.googleapis.com/v1beta2/
projects/earth-is-a-strange-place/subscriptions/new-habitable-planets-notifier
:modifyAckDeadline

Authorization: Bearer <your_auth_token>
Content-Type: application/json

{
    "ackDeadlineSeconds": 600,
    "ackId": "<message_ack_id>"
}
```

Messages

At this point, your Cloud Pub/Sub system is ready to start operating. Messages can be published to the created topic. This causes the subscription associated with that topic to begin enqueueing messages for further processing—note that the current subscription does not have a push configuration. This means messages are added but not delivered until a consumer pulls them from the subscription.

Messages have the following structure:

```
{
    "data": "<base64-no-line-feeds-variant-representation-of-payload>",
    "attributes": {
        "attribute1": "<attribute1-value>",
        "attribute2": "<attribute2-value>",
       ...
    },
    "messageId": "<message-id-string>"
}
```

where:

- The content of the `data` property must be encoded in Base64 format.
- `messageId` is a string that is generated when the message is published and guaranteed to be unique in the scope of the topic.
- `attributes` is an optional property that you can use to set string key-value entries that are sent to the subscribers receiving the message.

When publishing a message, you specify the `data` and, optionally, the `attributes` property. The overall size of the message cannot be bigger than 10MB.

■ **Note** Messages are not guaranteed to be delivered in the same order they were created. If you need messages to maintain their original order, it is recommended that you add information in the `attributes` property to help you organize your messages; for example, you can use a timestamp to check which messages were published before. Similarly, even though messages are supposed to be delivered only once, this is not guaranteed. Therefore, it is recommended that operations performed by consumers of your messages are *idempotent*—that is, receiving the same message more than once does not affect the overall result of the operation. For instance, in the example in this chapter, you are tracking the search for potentially habitable planets. Because you are storing information about those planets in your database, if a message is delivered more than once, you can avoid duplication by querying your database for planets with the timestamp and coordinates generated by the telescope before storing the new candidate.

Returning to the example about the search of habitable planets, suppose that the registered telescopes have a routine to send the results of their findings every 12 hours. To each message, the telescope attaches its name, the timestamp of the planet registration, and the planet's celestial coordinates. The telescope also attaches a verbose message to give potential subscribers some context about the message's content.

Suppose that in the last 12 hours, the Kepler telescope found two candidates to be habitable planets. The process to publish the associated messages is as follows:

```
# Python
import base64
....

message_data = base64.b64encode('Add another habitable planet to my list!')
body = {
    'messages': [{
        'data': message_data,
        'attributes': {
            'timestamp': '1749099512',
            'candidate_name': 'KOI-3284.01',
            'right_ascension': '18h 46m 35s',
            'declination': '+41deg 57m 3.93s',
            'telescope': 'Kepler'
        }
    },
    { .... }]
}

topic_uri = 'projects/earth-is-a-strange-place/topics/habitable-planets'
pubsub_client.projects().topics().publish(
    topic=topic_uri, body=body).execute()

# JSON API
POST https://pubsub.googleapis.com/v1beta2/
projects/earth-is-a-strange-place/topics/habitable-planets:publish
```

```
Authorization: Bearer <your_auth_token>
Content-Type: application/json

(The body has the same content as the body variable in the Python example above)
```

If everything works as expected, you get a successful `200 OK` response and an array with the identifiers of the messages created in the body. These two messages are stored, waiting for a subscriber to consume them. Because the current subscription does not have a push configuration, it behaves as a pull subscription—messages are not be delivered to any endpoint or server and can only be consumed on demand.

Processing Messages

Messages are handled differently depending on the type of queue you work with. In push queues, Cloud Pub/Sub is in charge of delivering messages to the push endpoint you specify. To obtain the data of a message, you need to parse the body from the incoming request. Conversely, in pull queues you are responsible for leasing, processing and acknowledging messages. You request messages directly from the Cloud Pub/Sub API, obtaining the associated data by parsing the response.

Pull Subscriptions

To consume elements from your subscription queue, you use the `pull` method. This method accepts two parameters:

- `maxMessages` determines the maximum number of messages to return, based on the consumer's processing expectations.
- `returnImmediately` is a boolean value that, when set to `false`, keeps the request on hold until either enough messages are published to satisfy the maximum number of messages specified in the previous parameter or the request times out. If the value is set to `true`, the request returns the current messages in the queue immediately, up to the maximum specified.

This is how you call the `pull` method for the subscription of interest using the Python client library:

```
max_n_messages = 10
project_id = 'earth-is-a-strange-place'
subscription_id = 'new-habitable-planets-notifier'
subscription = 'projects/%s/subscriptions/%s' % (project_id, subscription_id)

body = {'returnImmediately': True,
        'maxMessages': max_n_messages}

messages_response = pubsub_client.projects().subscriptions().pull(
subscription=subscription, body=body).execute()

received_messages = messages_response.get('receivedMessages')
if received_messages is not None:

   # Prepare the list of successfully processed messages
   ack_ids = []
```

```
    for message in received_messages:
        pubsub_message = message.get('message')

        if pubsub_message:

            data = base64.b64decode(str(pubsub_message.get('data')))
            attributes = pubsub_message.get('attributes')
            if attributes is not None:
                print 'Processing habitable planet candidate: '
                + attributes['candidate_name']

                # Here you can do any kind of processing with your messages,
                # like checking for existence in your database or
                # storing it otherwise and notifying the interested parties via email

                # Append the ack id to the list for a batched ack request
                ack_ids.append(message.get('ackId'))

# An acknowledgement call is sent for messages processed successfully
ack_body = {'ackIds': ack_ids}
pubsub_client.projects().subscriptions().acknowledge(
    subscription=subscription_uri, body=ack_body).execute()
```

Similarly, you can request the pull method on your subscription using the JSON API in Cloud Pub/Sub:

```
POST https://pubsub.googleapis.com/v1beta2/
projects/earth-is-a-strange-place/subscriptions/new-habitable-planets-notifier
:pull

Authorization: Bearer <your_auth_token>
Content-Type: application/json

{
    "maxMessages":10,
    "returnImmediately":true
}
```

This request returns up to a maximum of 10 messages enqueued in your subscription. The response has the following structure:

```
{
    "receivedMessages": [
    {
        "ackId": "<message_ack_id>",
        "message": {
            "data": "<base64-no-line-feeds-variant-representation-of-payload>",
            "attributes": {
                "timestamp": "1749099512",
                "right_ascension": "18h 46m 35s",
                "candidate_name": "KOI-3284.01",
                "telescope": "Kepler",
```

```
                "declination": "+41deg 57m 3.93s"
            },
            "messageId": "80017642126"
        }
    },
    {....}]
}
```

After you process your messages, you can acknowledge them in a batch using the acknowledge method on the subscription:

```
POST https://pubsub.googleapis.com/v1beta2/
projects/earth-is-a-strange-place/subscriptions/new-habitable-planets-notifier
:acknowledge

Authorization: Bearer <your_auth_token>
Content-Type: application/json

{
   "ackIds": [ "<ack_id_1>", "<ack_id_2>", ...., "<ack_id_n>"]
}
```

■ **Note** To see a complete example of using the Python client library, involving creation and deletion of topics and subscriptions, and publication, processing, and acknowledgement of messages, check the folder `pub-sub` in the GitHub repository `code-snippets` at `https://github.com/GoogleCloudPlatformBook/code-snippets`.

Push Subscriptions

As explained previously, push subscriptions differ from pull subscriptions in the fundamental way they operate. When a message is published to a topic with a push subscription, the message is delivered immediately to the push endpoint specified in the configuration.

To illustrate this type of subscription, let's create a notification system for one of the sample applications used throughout the book. LunchMates helps users organize small meetups over lunches, drinks, coffees, and so on for people interested in a common topic. A crucial aspect of an application like this is the ability to rate attendees, topics, and places to meet, but it is hard to know when a mini-event has ended. You could assume that a meeting finished the day after it started, but it is always more effective to ask users right after they experience an event. Because of a partnership with a payments company, you know when a user of the application pays the bill at the end of a meeting, so you decide to integrate with the company's API to publish a Cloud Pub/Sub message in your application. The message is then delivered to the configured endpoint.

Remember that you can change the push configuration of your subscription by calling the `modifyPushConfig` method on a subscription:

```
POST https://pubsub.googleapis.com/v1beta2/
projects/lunch--mates/subscriptions/meeting_finish_subscription
:modifyPushConfig
```

```
Authorization: Bearer <your_auth_token>
Content-Type: application/json

{
    "pushConfig": {
        "pushEndpoint": "https://lunch--mates.appspot.com/tasks/meetings/finished_event"
    }
}
```

The new value of pushConfig includes the endpoint where you want your messages to be published for that subscription. This endpoint is hosted in App Engine. This is what the request handler looks like:

```
class MeetingsTaskHandler(webapp2.RequestHandler):

    def meetingFinished(self):

        # Email information
        sender_address = 'Lunch Mate <lunchmates@lunch--mates.appspotmail.com>'
        subject = 'How was your meeting'
        body = 'Rate your last meeting!'

        # Get the message from pub/sub
        message = json.loads(urllib.unquote(self.request.body).rstrip('='))
        message_data = base64.b64decode(str(message['message']['data']))

        attributes = message['message']['attributes']
        if len(attributes) == 0:
            return

        # Get all accepted meeting requests
        query = MeetingRequest.for_meeting(
            int(attributes['meeting_id']), 'accepted')

        for request in query:
            attendee = request.key.parent().get()

            if attendee is not None and mail.is_email_valid(attendee.email):
                mail.send_mail(sender_address, attendee.email, subject, body)
```

This method simply extracts the necessary information from the message to retrieve all the attendees of the meeting—accepted meeting requests—and sends each of them an e-mail asking them to rate their experience. If it is executed without any error, this handler responds with a `200 OK` response (the default response code in `webapp2.RequestHandler`). This response serves as a means of acknowledgement for Cloud Pub/Sub, which deletes the message from the queue.

■ **Note** To see the source for the entire App Engine application, check `repository lunchmates-api` at `https://github.com/GoogleCloudPlatformBook/lunchmates-api`. Pay special attention to the `app.yaml` file, the `main` module, and the request handler just shown, which is placed in `tasks/meetings.py`. These files determine the full path the request follows when it arrives at the App Engine servers.

Summary

In this chapter, you have learned how to communicate with different systems, infrastructures, and services regardless of their nature, using a publisher-subscriber approach. You also saw how to take advantage of such technology using Google Cloud's infrastructure and connect your application to other technologies such as App Engine.

We want to stress that this technology is meant to work independently and with as little supervision as possible. Remember that any technology that operates with queues and automatic retrial of requests is subject to generating artificial load due to recurring errors: when requests fail, they are added back to the queue for retrial (in this instance, Cloud Pub/Sub uses exponential back-off to alleviate the negative effects of this event). This affects not only your costs and maintenance efforts but also the user experience. Because of that, it is sensible to design your business logic using a defensive and resilient approach so that your system can recover from unwanted scenarios caused by unexpected events or human mistakes.

As of this writing, Cloud Pub/Sub is still in beta. If this service forms an important part of your application, make sure you stay up to date with the latest news. The documentation on Developers Console and API Explorer (`https://developers.google.com/apis-explorer`) is a crucial resource to work with in scenarios like this.

PART V

Google Cloud Platform - Networking and Services

CHAPTER 13

Google Cloud DNS

The domain name system (DNS) is a global hierarchical distributed database that stores the mapping between a domain name and an IP address or other associated details such as the hostname. This mapping is called a *DNS record*, and associated records are stored in a *DNS zone*. From this perspective, the DNS zone can be seen as a container for DNS records that have the same suffix in a domain name. For example, `db.cloudplatformbook.com` and `web.cloudplatformbook.com` are two DNS records in the `cloudplatformbook.com` DNS Zone.

Google Cloud DNS is a globally distributed, low-latency, high-performance, resilient, authoritative domain name service. As with other Google Cloud Platform products, Cloud DNS is also available via a REST API, the `gcloud` command-line tool, and the web-based graphical Developers Console.

Cloud DNS consists of managed zones and a resource record sets collection; these serve as a one-to-one mapping between DNS zones and records. All records in a managed zone are served by the same set of Cloud DNS servers. Cloud DNS uses anycast to serve the managed zones from many redundant locations around the world. The benefits of this architecture are high availability and low latency for applications and users alike.

Cloud DNS supports the following types of DNS records:

- *SOA:* Start of authority record, which specifies authoritative information on a DNS zone. Cloud DNS automatically creates an SOA resource record for every managed zone.
- *NS:* Name server record, which delegates a DNS zone to an authoritative DNS server.
- *A:* IPv4 address record, which maps host names to their IPv4 address.
- *AAAA:* IPv6 address record, which maps host names to their IPv6 address.
- *PTR:* Pointer record, used to create reverse DNS lookups—that is, to map IP addresses to host names.
- *CNAME:* Canonical name record, used to create alias names.
- *MX:* Mail exchange record, used to identify mail servers for the domain.
- *SPF:* Sender policy framework record, used to state the authoritative e-mail servers for a domain.
- *TXT:* Text records, which can be used to publish arbitrary human- and machine-readable information.
- *SRV:* Service location record, used by some VOIP and instant-messaging protocols and applications.
- *NAPTR:* Name authority pointer records, used in Internet telephony applications and often combined with SRV records in a chained fashion.

Each record can be seen as a key-value pair. A hostname, when used as the value of a record, should be a fully qualified DNS name (terminated with a period [.]). Cloud DNS supports wildcard records for all record types except NS.

Two entities play a key role in determining how long a change takes to reach a user: an authoritative DNS server and a DNS resolver. Cloud DNS is an authoritative DNS server and publishes the DNS zones and records. Change requests are usually applied within a minute and consist of two transparent steps:

1. Updates to the central control plane are applied synchronously (the client sends a write and then can read it back immediately in an API call).

2. Updates are replicated to the global serving plane asynchronously, normally in less than a minute.

The user is usually connected to a DNS resolver that caches the DNS zones and records of various domains. The cache validity is controlled by a parameter called time to live (TTL) that is associated with each DNS record.

TTL is a DNS record attribute that specifies how long a DNS record should be cached by the querying system, such as the end user system or intermediate DNS resolver. TTL is represented in seconds, and all systems outside of the authoritative name server should use it as a countdown timer. The DNS standard further states that a DNS resolver should discard an expired cached DNS record and retrieve it again from the DNS server. Setting a high TTL value means there is less traffic to the DNS server because the DNS resolver caches records longer. The negative aspect of a high TTL value is that an update to a DNS record takes much longer to propagate to the user. In addition, some DNS resolvers do not honor TTL values and use a fixed refresh interval or time to fetch updates. It is therefore recommended that during the system design and development stages, you keep TTL values low so that changes propagate faster (ideally). Once the system is in production, you can send a change request to Cloud DNS and set a high TTL value to reduce queries to the DNS server and save costs.

If you or your customers observe that the current DNS resolver is not following the standard and is fetching DNS records in an arbitrary fashion, you may want to consider using the DNS resolver from Google: Google Public DNS (`https://developers.google.com/speed/public-dns`). Google Public DNS is a fast, free, global DNS resolution service that can be used in place of your current DNS resolver (typically your ISP). The change is easy to make: all you have to do is set your primary and secondary DNS resolver IPs to 8.8.8.8 and 8.8.4.4. One downside of using the Google Public DNS resolver in an enterprise is that you may not be able to resolve some corporate web sites if they are served by an internal DNS server.

Publishing Your Internet Identity

This section walks through the complete process of setting up DNS for a web site using Cloud DNS. You use a real domain—the domain for this book, `cloudplatformbook.com`—in this walkthrough. The examples use the `gcloud` command-line tool.

The first step in setting up DNS for a domain using Cloud DNS is to create a managed zone for the DNS zone that you would like to host in Cloud DNS. The DNS zone in this case is `cloudplatformbook.com`. Listing 13-1 shows is the `gcloud` command to create this managed zone.

Listing 13-1. `gcloud` DNS Command to Create a Managed Zone

```
$ gcloud dns managed-zones create cloudplatformbook \
 --description='Managed Zone for Google Cloud Platform Book' --dns-name='cloudplatformbook.com'
Created [https://www.googleapis.com/dns/v1beta1/projects/cloud-platform-book/
managedZones/cloudplatformbook].
NAME               DNS_NAME                DESCRIPTION
cloudplatformbook  cloudplatformbook.com.  Managed Zone for Google Cloud Platform Book
```

Let's dissect this command and the response from Cloud DNS to understand the transaction. Just like other cloud platform products, Cloud DNS commands in `gcloud` are housed as subcommands under `gcloud dns <options>`. You can at any time use the `--help` option to get a list of the commands available at that hierarchy. For example, if you run the command `gcloud dns -help`, you get all the options available at the highest hierarchy level.

To create a managed zone, you must provide the following parameters:

- *DNS name:* The DNS zone suffix that this managed zone will publish on the Internet. You should own this domain or at least have administrative access to a domain registrar panel, because you make changes later to make Cloud DNS the official DNS server.
- *Description:* A Cloud DNS–specific field for your reference only. It is recommended that you provide meaningful data to help you remember what this managed zone is associated with.
- *Zone Name:* A Cloud DNS–specific field that must be unique within a project. The name cannot contain any spaces and is a required field in subsequent API requests. By convention, it usually matches the DNS zone name, as in this example.

Once the command in Listing 13-1 has been issued, Cloud DNS creates a managed-zone object for the DNS zone specified. It returns a formatted result, which restates parts of the creation request. You can retrieve the same information anytime by using the `list` command to list all the DNS zones managed by Cloud DNS in your project. Listing 13-2 shows the command and the corresponding result.

Listing 13-2. `gcloud` DNS Command to List Managed Zones

```
$ gcloud dns managed-zones list
NAME                 DNS_NAME                   DESCRIPTION
cloudplatformbook    cloudplatformbook.com.     Managed Zone for Google Cloud Platform Book
```

In addition to this overview information, you can get detailed information about a single managed zone by using the `describe` command. Listing 13-3 uses the `describe` command to get more details about the `cloudplatformbook` managed DNS zone.

Listing 13-3. `gcloud` DNS Command to Describe One Managed Zone

```
$ gcloud dns managed-zones describe cloudplatformbook
NAME                 DNS_NAME                   DESCRIPTION
creationTime: '2015-03-15T04:27:13.299Z'
description: Managed Zone for Google Cloud Platform Book
dnsName: cloudplatformbook.com.
id: '8730191890933023381'
kind: dns#managedZone
name: cloudplatformbook
nameServers:
- ns-cloud1.googledomains.com.
- ns-cloud2.googledomains.com.
- ns-cloud3.googledomains.com.
- ns-cloud4.googledomains.com.
```

Two items in the returned result merit special mention:

- id: Cloud DNS automatically assigns a numeric number as the identifier for this managed-zone object. This is how this managed zone is identified internally within Cloud DNS. You don't need to remember this or write it down, because you can always retrieve all the managed zones using the command `$ gcloud dns managed-zone list`.
- nameServers: For every managed zone, Cloud DNS automatically assigns multiple DNS servers that are located at different Google-operated data centers. You must delegate your domain to all of these name servers to enjoy the high availability of Cloud DNS and update the domain registrar accordingly. Only then are Cloud DNS name servers reachable by the client for DNS queries. You don't have any records yet, so you can postpone this step until later.

As part of DNS zone creation, Cloud DNS automatically adds two resource records: SOA and NS. Although NS is listed as part of the `describe` command, key information such as TTL values are not present. Listing 13-4 uses the record-sets command to list all the details of these two resource records.

Listing 13-4. gcloud DNS Command to List All Record Sets in a Managed Zone

```
$ gcloud dns record-sets list --zone=cloudplatformbook
NAME                    TYPE  TTL    DATA
cloudplatformbook.com.  NS    21600  ns-cloud1.googledomains.com., ns-cloud2.googledomains.com.,
                                     ns-cloud3.googledomains.com., ns-cloud4.googledomains.com.
cloudplatformbook.com.  SOA   21600  ns-cloud1.googledomains.com. dns-admin.google.com. \
0 21600 3600 1209600 300
```

Let's start by adding new DNS records to the DNS zone `cloudplatformbook.com`. The first step is to build a transaction object. Cloud DNS introduces the concept of *transactions* to satisfy the requirement that a resource record-change operation (delete or add) should be an atomic operation. This means Cloud DNS serves either the old record or the new record but never returns a void result. The transaction object state is maintained using the `transaction.yaml` file in the current directory. There can be only one pending transaction at a time. Listing 13-5 starts the transaction, and Listing 13-6 lists the contents of `transaction.yaml`.

Listing 13-5. gcloud Command to Start a Transaction Object

```
$ gcloud dns record-sets transaction start --zone=cloudplatformbook
Transaction started [transaction.yaml].
```

Listing 13-6. Listing the Contents of the Transactions Objects File

```
$ pwd
/Users/cloudplatformbook

$ ls -la transaction.yaml
-rw-r--r--  1 cloudplatformbook staff  380 Mar 15 14:52 transaction.yaml

$ cat transaction.yaml
---
additions:
- kind: dns#resourceRecordSet
  name: cloudplatformbook.com.
  rrdatas:
```

```
  - ns-cloud1.googledomains.com. dns-admin.google.com. 1 21600 3600 1209600 300
  ttl: 21600
  type: SOA
deletions:
- kind: dns#resourceRecordSet
  name: cloudplatformbook.com.
  rrdatas:
  - ns-cloud1.googledomains.com. dns-admin.google.com. 0 21600 3600 1209600 300
  ttl: 21600
  type: SOA.
```

You have created a new compute engine instance to run a Wordpress-powered blog that will hold the errata for this book. This section skips the steps to set up this virtual machine instance, install the Wordpress software; see Chapter 4 "Google Compute Engine" and Chapter 7 "Google Cloud SQL" for instructions. Next, Listing 13-7 uses the `gcloud` command to list the details of the compute engine VM instance.

Listing 13-7. gcloud Compute Command to List VM Instances

```
$ gcloud compute instances list
NAME              ZONE          MACHINE_TYPE  INTERNAL_IP    EXTERNAL_IP    STATUS
cloudplatformbook us-central1-f n1-standard-2 10.240.203.206 146.148.64.211 RUNNING
```

Now, let's add a few resource records: the public IPv4 address of the compute engine VM instance as a type A (address) record and a CNAME record for the domain's `www` prefix. You then list the transaction object and commit the transaction; see Listing 13-8.

Listing 13-8. gcloud Command to Add a DNS Record of Type A in Cloud DNS

```
$ gcloud dns record-sets --zone=cloudplatformbook transaction add
--name='cloudplatformbook.' \
 --ttl=3600 --type=A '146.148.64.211'
Record addition appended to transaction at [transaction.yaml].
```

For any web site, in addition to resolving the naked domain (that is, one without a prefix in its domain name), the DNS system should also resolve the `www` alias. In this case, `cloudplatformbook.com` is the naked domain, and `www.cloudplatformbook.com` is the fully qualified domain name (FQDN). Web servers are usually set up to serve both variations of the domain with identical content. In the DNS setup, the `www` variation is created as an alias to the naked domain. This is achieved by using the CNAME DNS record type (see Listing 13-9). Then, the "*transaction describe*" command in Listing 13-10 displays the contents of the `transaction.yaml` file.

Listing 13-9. gcloud Command to Add a DNS Record of Type CNAME in Cloud DNS

```
$ gcloud dns record-sets -zone= cloudplatformbook transaction add \
-name='www.cloudplatformbook.com.' -ttl=3600 -type=CNAME 'cloudplatformbook.com.'
Record addition appended to transaction at [transaction.yaml].
```

Listing 13-10. gcloud DNS Command to Describe the State of the Transaction Object, Pending Commit

```
$ gcloud dns record-sets --zone=cloudplatformbook transaction describe
additions:
- kind: dns#resourceRecordSet
  name: cloudplatformbook.com.
  rrdatas:
  - ns-cloud1.googledomains.com. dns-admin.google.com. 1 21600 3600 1209600 300
  ttl: 21600
  type: SOA
- kind: dns#resourceRecordSet
  name: cloudplatformbook.com.
  rrdatas:
  - 146.148.64.211
  ttl: 3600
  type: A
- kind: dns#resourceRecordSet
  name: www.cloudplatformbook.com.
  rrdatas:
  - cloudplatformbook.com.
  ttl: 3600
  type: CNAME
deletions:
- kind: dns#resourceRecordSet
  name: cloudplatformbook.com.
  rrdatas:
  - ns-cloud1.googledomains.com. dns-admin.google.com. 0 21600 3600 1209600 300
  ttl: 21600
  type: SOA
```

The output shows that the two records—A and CNAME—have been successfully added as part of the pending transaction. In addition, the transaction contains an SOA record in both the `additions` and `deletions` sections. On closer inspection, you can see that the difference between the two records is the serial number, which has been incremented by one. Listing 13-11 executes this transaction.

Listing 13-11. gcloud DNS Command to Execute a Transaction

```
$ gcloud dns record-sets --zone=cloudplatformbook transaction execute
Executed transaction [transaction.yaml] for managed-zone [cloudplatformbook].
Created [https://www.googleapis.com/dns/v1beta1/projects/cloud-platform-book/
managedZones/cloudplatformbook/changes/1].
ID  START_TIME                STATUS
1   2015-03-15T07:49:59.935Z  pending
```

Cloud DNS applies the executed transaction quickly—typically within a minute. You can see whether the transaction is successful by listing the changes to the DNS zone and by describing an individual change. Listing 13-12 and Listing 13-13 show the commands and corresponding responses.

Listing 13-12. gcloud DNS Command to List All Changes Committed to a DNS Zone

```
$ gcloud dns record-sets --zone=cloudplatformbook changes list
ID  START_TIME                STATUS
1   2015-03-15T07:49:59.935Z  done
0   2015-03-15T04:27:13.300Z  done
```

Listing 13-13. gcloud DNS Command to Describe the Changes Committed in a Transaction ID

```
$ gcloud dns record-sets --zone=cloudplatformbook changes describe 1
additions:
- kind: dns#resourceRecordSet
  name: cloudplatformbook.com.
  rrdatas:
  - ns-cloud1.googledomains.com. dns-admin.google.com. 1 21600 3600 1209600 300
  ttl: 21600
  type: SOA
- kind: dns#resourceRecordSet
  name: cloudplatformbook.com.
  rrdatas:
  - 146.148.64.211
  ttl: 3600
  type: A
- kind: dns#resourceRecordSet
  name: www.cloudplatformbook.com.
  rrdatas:
  - cloudplatformbook.com.
  ttl: 3600
  type: CNAME
deletions:
- kind: dns#resourceRecordSet
  name: cloudplatformbook.com.
  rrdatas:
  - ns-cloud1.googledomains.com. dns-admin.google.com. 0 21600 3600 1209600 300
  ttl: 21600
  type: SOA
id: '1'
kind: dns#change
startTime: '2015-03-15T07:49:59.935Z'
status: done
```

You can also list the resource records to see the current list of DNS records that is served for your DNS zone, as shown in Listing 13-14.

Listing 13-14. gcloud DNS Command to List the DNS Records for a DNS Zone

```
$ gcloud dns record-sets list --zone=cloudplatformbook
NAME                       TYPE TTL   DATA
cloudplatformbook.com.     A    3600  146.148.64.211
cloudplatformbook.com.     NS   21600 ns-cloud1.googledomains.com., ns-cloud2.googledomains.com.,
                                      ns-cloud3.googledomains.com., ns-cloud4.googledomains.com.
cloudplatformbook.com.     SOA  21600 ns-cloud1.googledomains.com. dns-admin.google.com.
1 21600 3600 1209600 300
www.cloudplatformbook.com. CNAME 3600  cloudplatformbook.com.
```

Let's add some other types of DNS records required for the Wordpress-powered blog setup. You need a MySQL database as the storage back end. This example uses the Cloud SQL product from the Google Cloud Platform for this purpose. You have created a database instance and assigned an IPv4 address to it. Cloud SQL automatically assigns an IPv6 address to each Cloud SQL instance. Again, this section skips the details of setting up a Cloud SQL instance; see Chapter 7 "Google Cloud SQL" for setup details. The commands in Listing 13-15 and Listing 13-16 list the details of the Cloud SQL instance.

Listing 13-15. gcloud SQL Command to List Cloud SQL Instances

```
$ gcloud sql instances list
NAME              REGION     TIER  ADDRESS          STATUS
cloudplatformbook us-central D2    173.194.242.117  RUNNABLE
```

Listing 13-16. gcloud SQL Command to Describe an Individual Cloud SQL Instance

```
$ gcloud sql instances describe cloudplatformbook
<snip>
ipAddresses:
- ipAddress: 173.194.242.117
ipv6Address: 2001:4860:4864:1:199b:32da:e624:20e2
<snip>
state: RUNNABLE
```

Based on these details, you can add the two IP addresses to the Cloud DNS setup. The gcloud DNS commands in Listing 13-17, Listing 13-18, and Listing 13-19 start a new transaction and add the IPv4 and IPv6 addresses.

Listing 13-17. gcloud DNS Command to Start a New Transaction

```
$ gcloud dns record-sets --zone=cloudplatformbook transaction start
Transaction started [transaction.yaml].
```

Listing 13-18. gcloud DNS Command to Add a DNS Record of Type A to a Transaction

```
$ gcloud dns record-sets --zone=cloudplatformbook transaction add \
--name='sql.cloudplatformbook.com.' --ttl=3600 --type=A '173.194.242.117'
Record addition appended to transaction at [transaction.yaml].
```

Listing 13-19. gcloud DNS Command to Add a DNS Record of Type AAAA to a Transaction

```
$ gcloud dns record-sets --zone=cloudplatformbook transaction add \
--name='sql6.cloudplatformbook.com.' --ttl=3600 --type=AAAA
'2001:4860:4864:1:199b:32da:e624:20e2'
Record addition appended to transaction at [transaction.yaml].
```

Suppose you made an error in a previous record, and you want to fix it. For example, the A record for your domain should point to 146.148.64.212 instead of 146.148.64.211. You can use the transaction process to remove the old record and add the new one as a single atomic operation. Listing 13-20 shows the update of the A record and continues using the open transaction.

Listing 13-20. gcloud DNS Commands to Replace an Existing Record by Removing the Old Record and Adding a New One

```
$ gcloud dns record-sets --zone=cloudplatformbook transaction remove \
--name='cloudplatformbook.com.' --ttl=3600 --type=A '146.148.64.211'
Record removal appended to transaction at [transaction.yaml].

$ gcloud dns record-sets --zone=cloudplatformbook transaction add \
--name='cloudplatformbook.com.' --ttl=3600 --type=A '146.148.64.212'
Record addition appended to transaction at [transaction.yaml].
```

After a while, when you list the DNS records in the managed zone, you should see the updated A record showing the correct IP address.

Let's create a few more commonly used/required DNS records for domains. E-mail is the predominant form of communication on the Internet today. E-mails are sent and received by software system called *mail servers*. The locations of the mail servers need to be defined in the DNS setup. You do so by declaring *MX records*. Just like name servers, there is usually more than one mail server handling a domain; and unlike name servers, there is a priority among mail servers. Hence, when declaring an MX record, you need to include the priority values as part of the declaration. For the domain `cloudplatformbook.com`, Google Apps is handling e-mail. Listing 13-21 and Listing 13-22 add MX records to the DNS zone and point them to the Google Apps mail servers. This example also shows that you can add multiple values for a single DNS record.

Listing 13-21. gcloud DNS Command to Add Multiple Record Sets of the MX Record Type

```
$ gcloud dns record-sets --zone=cloudplatformbook transaction add \
--name='mx.cloudplatformbook.com.' --ttl=3600 --type=MX '1 aspmx.l.google.com.' \
'5 alt1.aspmx.l.google.com.' '5 alt2.aspmx.l.google.com.' '10 alt3.aspmx.l.google.com.' \
'10 alt4.aspmx.l.google.com.'
Record addition appended to transaction at [transaction.yaml].
```

Listing 13-22. gcloud DNS Command to Commit the Transaction You Have Built So Far

```
$ gcloud dns record-sets --zone=cloudplatformbook transaction execute
Executed transaction [transaction.yaml] for managed-zone [cloudplatformbook].
Created [https://www.googleapis.com/dns/v1beta1/projects/cloud-platform-book/
managedZones/cloudplatformbook/changes/6].
ID  START_TIME                STATUS
6   2015-03-15T11:12:15.621Z  pending
```

Although e-mail has made it possible for people to communicate almost instantaneously, it has its own annoyances in the form of spam and phishing, which reduce the credibility of the system. In order to counter this, a new standard called the Sender Policy Framework (SPF) was created. SPF records are part of the DNS setup and list the authorized e-mail servers for a particular domain. By using SPF records, you can whitelist hosts that are permitted to send e-mails on behalf of the domain. It is a good practice to declare SPF records for a domain; usually, MX and SPF records are declared together. If you prefer to use a wizard-style system to construct a valid SPF record for a domain, see `www.spfwizard.net`.

Listing 13-23 and Listing 13-24 add the SPF record for the domain cloudplatformbook.com. Outgoing e-mail is permitted from servers listed in MX records and from the server hosting the domain. You need to start a new transaction, because as you have committed (and closed) the previous one.

Listing 13-23. gcloud DNS Command to Start a New Transaction

```
$ gcloud dns record-sets --zone=cloudplatformbook transaction start
Transaction started [transaction.yaml].
```

Listing 13-24. gcloud DNS Command to Add a DNS Record of Type SPF to the Open Transaction Object

```
$ $ gcloud dns record-sets --zone=cloudplatformbook transaction add
--name='cloudplatformbook.com.' --ttl=60 --type=SPF 'v=spf1 mx a'
Record addition appended to transaction at [transaction.yaml].
```

The last record type you can add to a DNS domain is a TXT record. As the name implies, it is used to publish arbitrary information about the domain. In this case, Listing 13-25 publishes a teaser about this book.

Listing 13-25. Cloud DNS Command to Add a TXT Record

```
$ gcloud dns record-sets --zone=cloudplatformbook transaction add \
--name='cloudplatformbook.com.' --ttl=60 --type=TXT \
"Building Your Next Big Thing with Google Cloud Platform by Dr. S. P. T. Krishnan and
Mr. Jose L Ugia Gonzalez (Apress). ETA May 28 2015, 978-1-4842-1005-5."
Record addition appended to transaction at [transaction.yaml].

$ gcloud dns record-sets --zone=cloudplatformbook transaction execute
Executed transaction [transaction.yaml] for managed-zone [cloudplatformbook].
Created [https://www.googleapis.com/dns/v1beta1/projects/cloud-platform-book/
managedZones/cloudplatformbook/changes/7].
ID  START_TIME                STATUS
7   2015-03-15T15:41:37.441Z  pending
```

After a bit, you should be able to list the DNS record you just added. The console output in Listing 13-26 shows the TXT records for the domain, extracted using dig tool running on a Mac OS X laptop.

Listing 13-26. Listing the TXT Records from a Desktop Using the dig Tool

```
$ dig txt cloudplatformbook.com
; <<>> DiG 9.8.3-P1 <<>> txt cloudplatformbook.com
;; global options: +cmd
;; Got answer:
;; ->>HEADER<<- opcode: QUERY, status: NOERROR, id: 37865
;; flags: qr rd ra; QUERY: 1, ANSWER: 1, AUTHORITY: 0, ADDITIONAL: 0

;; QUESTION SECTION:
;cloudplatformbook.com.        IN    TXT

;; ANSWER SECTION:
cloudplatformbook.com.    60    IN    TXT    "Building Your Next Big Thing with Google
                                              Cloud Platform
by Dr. S. P. T. Krishnan and Mr. Jose L Ugia Gonzalez (Apress). ETA May 28 2015,
978-1-4842-1005-5."
```

```
;; Query time: 31 msec
;; SERVER: 192.168.1.1#53(192.168.1.1)
;; WHEN: Sun Mar 15 21:36:16 2015
;; MSG SIZE  rcvd: 207
```

Let's look at an optional but useful DNS record type called a *pointer record* (PTR). A pointer record maps an IP address to a domain. This process is called *reverse DNS lookup / reverse DNS resolution* (rDNS), and it is the inverse of determining the IP address of a domain name (sometimes known as *forward DNS resolution*). The root of the Internet reverse DNS database is the Address and Routing Parameter Area (`arpa`) top-level domain. The second-level domains of IPv4 and IPv6 are `in-addr.arpa` and `ip6.arpa`, respectively. However, you determine the domain name associated with a given IP address using the Internet's Domain Name System (DNS).

You want to add a PTR record for the compute engine VM instance because it is designed to send e-mail in addition to the Google Apps system. Following are the high-level steps required to create a PTR record. Listing 13-27 through Listing 13-32 give the Cloud DNS commands:

1. Determine the target IP address.
2. Reverse the IP address, and split it into two octets.
3. Create a new managed zone following a special convention.
4. Add a new DNS record of type PTR.

Listing 13-27. Step 1: Determining the Target IP Address (IPv4 in This Case)

```
$ gcloud compute instances list
NAME               ZONE          MACHINE_TYPE  INTERNAL_IP    EXTERNAL_IP    STATUS
cloudplatformbook us-central1-f n1-standard-2 10.240.203.206 146.148.64.211 RUNNING
```

Listing 13-28. Step 2: Reversing the IPv4 Address and Splitting It into Two Parts

```
Reverse_External_IP = 211.64.148.146
1st, 2nd parts = 211, 64.148.146
```

Listing 13-29. Step 3: Creating a New Managed Zone

```
$ gcloud dns managed-zones create rdns-64-148-146 --description='Reverse DNS Zone for
Google Cloud Platform Book' --dns-name='64.148.146.in-addr.arpa.'
Created [https://www.googleapis.com/dns/v1beta1/projects/cloud-platform-book/
managedZones/rdns-64-148-146].
NAME             DNS_NAME                  DESCRIPTION
rdns-64-148-146  64.148.146.in-addr.arpa.  Reverse DNS Zone for Google Cloud Platform Book
```

Listing 13-30. Step 4.1: gcloud DNS Command to Start a New Transaction

```
$ gcloud dns record-sets --zone=rdns-64-148-146 transaction start
Transaction started [transaction.yaml].
```

Listing 13-31. Step 4.2: gcloud DNS Command to Add a DNS Record of Type PTR to a Transaction

```
$ gcloud dns record-sets --zone=rdns-64-148-146 transaction add \
--name='211.64.148.146.in-addr.arpa.' --ttl=60 --type=PTR 'cloudplatformbook.com.'
Record addition appended to transaction at [transaction.yaml].
```

Listing 13-32. Step 4.3: gcloud DNS Command to Commit the Transaction

```
$ gcloud dns record-sets --zone=rdns-64-148-146 transaction execute
Executed transaction [transaction.yaml] for managed-zone [rdns-64-148-146].
Created [https://www.googleapis.com/dns/v1beta1/projects/cloud-platform-book/
managedZones/rdns-64-148-146/changes/1].
ID  START_TIME                STATUS
1   2015-03-16T13:06:35.210Z  pending
```

You can verify whether the DNS records have been successfully added to the two managed zones by listing the current records using the commands in Listing 13-33 and Listing 13-34.

Listing 13-33. Listing DNS Records Using the Cloud DNS gcloud Tool

```
$ gcloud dns record-sets --zone='cloudplatformbook' list
NAME                          TYPE   TTL    DATA
cloudplatformbook.com.        A      60     146.148.64.211
cloudplatformbook.com.        NS     21600  ns-cloud-c1.googledomains.com.,
                                            ns-cloud-c2.googledomains.com.,
                                            ns-cloud-c3.googledomains.com.,
                                            ns-cloud-c4.googledomains.com.
cloudplatformbook.com.        SOA    21600  ns-cloud-c1.googledomains.com. dns-admin.google.com.
19 21600 3600 1209600 300
cloudplatformbook.com.        SPF    60     "v=spf1" "mx" "a"
cloudplatformbook.com.        TXT    60     "Building Your Next Big Thing with Google Cloud
                                             Platform by
Dr. S. P. T. Krishnan and Mr. Jose L Ugia Gonzalez (Apress). ETA May 28 2015, 978-1-4842-1005-5."
mx.cloudplatformbook.com.     MX     60     1 aspmx.l.google.com., 5 alt1.aspmx.l.google.com.,
5 alt2.aspmx.l.google.com., 10 alt3.aspmx.l.google.com., 10 alt4.aspmx.l.google.com.
sql.cloudplatformbook.com.    A      60     173.194.242.117
sql6.cloudplatformbook.com.   AAAA   60     2001:4860:4864:1:199b:32da:e624:20e2
www.cloudplatformbook.com.    CNAME  60     cloudplatformbook.com.
```

Listing 13-34. Listing DNS Records Using the Cloud DNS gcloud Tool

```
$ gcloud dns record-sets --zone='rdns-64-148-146' list
NAME                           TYPE  TTL    DATA
64.148.146.in-addr.arpa.       NS    21600  ns-cloud1.googledomains.com.,
                                            ns-cloud2.googledomains.com.,
                                            ns-cloud3.googledomains.com.,
                                            ns-cloud4.googledomains.com.
64.148.146.in-addr.arpa.       SOA   21600  ns-cloud1.googledomains.com. dns-admin.google.com.
1 21600 3600 1209600 300
211.64.148.146.in-addr.arpa.   PTR   60     cloudplatformbook.com.
```

The final step in the process of setting up a DNS server for your domain using Cloud DNS is to declare the Cloud DNS name servers for the domain in the domain registrar's panel. Depending on the domain registrar, the web interface will vary. Once the changes are made, you should be able to resolve the domain using standard tools.

Summary

In this chapter, you learned about a fundamental Internet technology: DNS. You also learned about the Cloud DNS service from Google Cloud Platform that enables you to publish various domains. The chapter began by examining the building blocks of Cloud DNS, after which you deployed a real-life domain (the domain for this book). Finally, you verified that the domain you set up is accessible over the Internet by querying its record. This chapter should have provided you with sufficient information to get started using Cloud DNS.

CHAPTER 14

Google Cloud Endpoints

The production and sale of electronic devices connected to the Internet has exploded in recent years. In 2014, enough mobile devices were sold to connect one sixth of the world's population. And this is just the beginning. Big players in the market are working on alternatives to meet the needs of communities and countries where, due to socioeconomic factors, the penetration of mobile devices is still low. Most importantly, it is not the number but the diversity of devices we are seeing that demonstrates the need to connect them all in an organized way. Intelligent houses, cars, home automation systems, sensor boards, and the rest of the spectrum covered by the term *Internet of things* are generating huge amounts of information about our world. But who is going to orchestrate all that?

This may be an ambitious and unnecessary problem for most system architects, developers, and other engineers to solve, at least this year. Nevertheless, when you design a system nowadays, it is relevant—and necessary in some cases—to account for transparently connecting different devices: mainly computers, but also mobile devices. This generally means if you develop an API to connect and sync all your clients, you need to enable each of them to communicate with your API in the cloud. This can become an arduous amount of work if you develop native applications. Suppose you add one endpoint to your API, you then need to write logic to communicate with this endpoint from each of your clients.

This is the point at which this chapter becomes useful to you. Google Cloud Endpoints is a service built on top of Google App Engine that allows you to reduce the overhead of creating, maintaining, and connecting to a RESTful API from your clients. One of its main features is the ability to decorate your API with the necessary information to extract access endpoints, request methods, the version of your API, request parameters and allowed client IDs, and so on. This information is then used to describe your RESTful API and automatically generate client libraries for Android, iOS, and JavaScript clients that you can import onto each platforms for which you develop. As mentioned, Cloud Endpoints operates on top of App Engine, and it is available for Java and Python; therefore, you can access all the APIs, services, and features that App Engine provides, some which are discussed in Chapter 5.

Cloud Endpoints and ProtoRPC

In Python, Cloud Endpoints uses the protocol RPC library. This library is one of the frameworks you can use to build your application; others are webapp2 and Flask. This framework allows you to implement HTTP-based remote procedure call (RPC) services, each made up of a collection of message types and remote methods to interact with web applications. Details about this library are not included in the chapter because most of it is abstracted away by the Cloud Endpoints library.

As you learned in Chapter 5, App Engine uses NDB in Python to control your data storage system or database. Recently, in order to integrate Cloud Endpoints without needing to deal with ProtoRPC messages to exchange information, a new library called `endpoints-proto-datastore`[1] was introduced. This library is used to simplify the logic of applications and improve readability.

In this chapter, you build an API similar to the one in Chapter 5. If you have not read that chapter yet, don't worry; you see every part of the application involved in the process.

Setting Up Your Environment: The SDK

■ **Note** You can skip this section if your system is ready to start working on a new application.

The Python SDK includes all the tools you need to build, test, and manage your application code, data, and indexes. You do that locally first, by using the development server included in the SDK. You operate the local server from the Google App Engine Launcher, a small UI-based application that helps organize App Engine projects, run them locally, access logs, explore their status through a browser-based console that resembles a small part of what you can expect from the online dashboard, and finally deploy them to the world. Alternatively, you can use the `dev_appserver.py` and `appcfg.py` commands to perform these and other tasks. We mention them throughout the book when you need their specific functionality. Also note that you can use these commands to integrate and automate specific operations in of your own development/deployment process.

You can find the Python SDK at `https://cloud.google.com/appengine/downloads`. It comes in the form of an installer file for Mac and Windows, and a zip file for Linux. Installing the SDK on Mac and Windows also gives you access to the Google App Engine Launcher UI.

As of this writing, App Engine only supports for Python 2.7. If your code is written in Python 2.5, which is now deprecated, consider migrating to 2.7. You can find a complete guide to how to do that at `http://cloud.google.com/appengine/docs/python/python25/migrate27`.

To make sure Python is installed on your computer, simply run the following command on your console or terminal:

```
python -V
```

If the output looks something like `Python 2.7.x`, you are good to go. Otherwise, you need to go to the Python web site to download and install Python 2.7 on your machine: `https://www.python.org/downloads/releases/python-279`.

The Foundations of Your Application: app.yaml

As a quick reminder, the application you are building in this chapter is a replica of the API for the LunchMates application, which you built on App Engine in Chapter 5. LunchMates is a service that helps individuals who share a common interest in a given topic to get together to learn and share knowledge about that topic. Users are expected to create informal meetings such as lunch, drinks, brunch, and so on, and define a place and time for their events; potential lunch mates can check the map of their area to look for meetings. They should be able to send requests to join meetings and be accepted or rejected as quickly as possible.

---

[1]You can find `endpoints-proto-datastore` in this repository on GitHub: `https://github.com/GoogleCloudPlatform/endpoints-proto-datastore`.

The app.yaml file is the entry point for each request. In it, you specify the version, application identifier, libraries, and request handlers, but it is also the place to configure many other application features. For details, see Chapter 5.

For this API, the app.yaml is as follows:

```
version: 1
runtime: python27
threadsafe: yes
api_version: 1

handlers:

# Endpoints handler
- url: /_ah/spi/.*
  script: main.app

# Endpoints libs
- name: pycrypto
  version: "2.6"
- name: endpoints
  version: 1.0
```

In the first group of parameters, the version helps differentiate iterations of the application. handlers are the agents that process requests. For Cloud Endpoints, the handler prepended with /_ah/spi/ is the one that manages requests. Note that the URL specified must not change, because this is a preconfigured value.

Finally, you are importing two of the libraries included in the SDK. pycrypto is used to deal with signatures and tokens, and endpoints contains the necessary logic to take advantage of this service.

Your API and api_server

According to the app.yaml file you just defined, the script that handles Cloud Endpoints requests is called main.app. This looks for the variable app in the main module (main.py):

```
import endpoints

# Controllers
from controllers import base

from controllers import meetings
from controllers import meeting_requests
from controllers import users
from controllers import auth

# Endpoints API
app = endpoints.api_server([base.lunchmates_api], restricted=False)
```

Cloud Endpoints is expecting an instance of endpoints.api_server. The classes added to the first argument of this method determine the submodules that conform to your API. These submodules are classes that inherit from remote.Service and implement endpoints.api directly or are decorated as api_classes of a parent endpoints.api. Set the restricted keyword to False so that external clients can access your API.

■ **Note** If a single class defines your API, it is recommended that you put the code for your API class and API server in the same file. Not only is your code easier to read, but both objects share common library symbols and imports. For example:

```
# imports
....
@endpoints.api(name='lunchmates', version='v1', description='LunchMates API')
class LunchMatesApi(remote.Service):
    # methods
....
app = endpoints.api_server([LunchMatesApi], restricted=False)
```

Going back to the API you are building, the `endpoints.api` object is referenced as an instance variable (`base.lunchmates_api`) instead of a class (`LunchMatesApi`). This is because this instance is simply a placeholder variable that decorates each of the API classes that conform your multiclass API. In this case, you want all the controllers—`meetings.Meetings`, `meeting_requests.MeetingRequests`, `users.Users`, and `auth.Auth`—to be part of the same API. Therefore, they are all decorated with `@lunchmates_api.api_class(....)`. This API variable is defined in a file called `base.py` in `controllers/`, along with a couple of utility methods used by the rest of the endpoint controllers:

```
#!/usr/bin/env python

import endpoints
from model.model import UserData

# Client IDs
WEBAPP_CLIENT_ID = 'your-webapp-client-id.apps.googleusercontent.com'
IOS_CLIENT_ID = 'your-ios-client-id.apps.googleusercontent.com'
ANDROID_CLIENT_ID = 'your-android-client-id.apps.googleusercontent.com'
ANDROID_AUDIENCE = WEBAPP_CLIENT_ID

lunchmates_api = endpoints.api(name='lunchmates', version='v1',
                               description='LunchMates API',
                                allowed_client_ids=[
                                       WEBAPP_CLIENT_ID,
                                        IOS_CLIENT_ID,
                                        ANDROID_CLIENT_ID,
                                       endpoints.API_EXPLORER_CLIENT_ID],
                                audiences=[ANDROID_AUDIENCE])

def authenticated_user_data():

    current_user_data = UserData.query(
        UserData.auth_user == endpoints.get_current_user()).get()

    if current_user_data is None:
        raise endpoints.UnauthorizedException()

    return current_user_data
```

`lunchmates_api` defines the main aspects of your API. `endpoints.api` accepts the arguments listed in Table 14-1.

Table 14-1. *`endpoints.api` Arguments*

Argument	Description
`name`	Used to construct the path you need to query to access your API. The name must start with a lowercase letter and match the following regular expression: `[a-z]+[A-Za-z0-9]*`. All services in your API share the same path. In the previous example, this would be `<app-id>.appspot.com/_ah/api/lunchmates/<version>/<service-method-path>`
`version`	Determines the version of your API.
`description`	A short description of your API, which is used, for example, in the API's discovery service. This service allows you to make requests and test your API.
`allowed_client_ids`	Specifies which clients are allowed to access information exposed through authentication. Only these are granted an access token when requested. You can create identifiers for your clients in the Developers Console by selecting the project or creating a new one, navigating to APIs & Auth ➤ Credentials, and clicking Create New Client ID. To read more about OAuth2 and client IDs, see Chapter 3.
`audiences`	Helps you avoid token requests to access your API coming from unwanted sources in your Android device. The audience for your Android client is the client ID for your web application.
`canonical_name`	Used to name API classes in the automatically generated client libraries.
`documentation`	A string containing the URL where users of the libraries can find documentation about them.
`owner_domain`	The domain name representing the entity that owns the API: for example, `lunchmates.com`. The full package path is generated from the combination of this field and `package_path`, in reverse order. That is `com.lunchmates` for this example.
`owner_name`	The name of the API's owner.
`package_path`	A set of string values separated by a forward slash (/) to further specify your package. Used in conjunction with the owner domain, it determines the full package name used in your client libraries. For example, if your `owner_domain` is set to `lunchmates.com` and the `package_path` is `api/tasks`, the resulting package name is `com.lunchmates.api.tasks`.
`scopes`	The list of scopes to be used when authorizing access from Cloud Endpoints. If you do not specify anything, the default value is `https://www.googleapis.com/auth/userinfo.email`. To read more about OAuth, scopes, and the authorization process, check Chapter 3.
`hostname`	Specifies the hostname of your App Engine application. The default value is `<application-id>.appspot.com`. For this example, that is `lunch--mates--endpoints.appspot.com`.
`title`	The text used to display a title for your application in services like APIs Explorer (`<app-id>.appspot.com/_ah/api/explorer`) or discovery services.

The method `authenticated_user_data` is useful when a specific part of your application needs to retrieve the associated metadata for a given user.

The model: A Bridge between NDB Datastore and Cloud Endpoints

Python has always been one of the programming languages leading the development process for App Engine. Because of that, it receives services and features before Java, Go, or PHP, and its libraries are in a more advanced development state. NDB Datastore is a good example. This is the layer that allows you to communicate with Google Cloud Datastore, a schema-less, noSQL data-storage system build on top of Google Cloud BigTable to perform and scale. NDB Datastore includes features like internal memory caching to speed up requests, a wide set of properties for models that helps you optimize how you store and retrieve data, support for transactions and asynchronous operations, and so on.

On the other hand, Cloud Endpoints makes it very easy to generate API code and take advantage of automatic client-library generation to reduce the friction and investment of targeting multiple native platforms at once. However, as mentioned earlier, Cloud Endpoints is built on top of ProtoRPC services, leaving an important gap in terms of integration and migration for applications using any of the other common frameworks used in App Engine—webapp2, Django, Flask, and so on—and/or relying on NDB to build the model.

This is where `endpoints-proto-datastore`[2] becomes really useful. This library provides you with tools to develop your application without having to think too much about ProtoRPC messages. Instead, you can use your own NDB models to operate your services directly. As of this writing, this library is not included in Cloud Endpoints. Therefore, to use it, you need to add it to your application.

■ **Pro Tip** If you do not want to contaminate your code repository, you can add `endpoints-proto-datastore` as a submodule or dependency so that the source control and life cycle of your code and external libraries remain independent. For example, in `git`, you can add a submodule running the command `git submodule add https://github.com/GoogleCloudPlatform/endpoints-proto-datastore` from the folder where you intend to store your libraries—for example, `libs/`.

Before taking advantage of the potential of `endpoints-proto-datastore`, there is only one thing you need to do. Your model objects need to inherit from `endpoints_proto_datastore.ndb.EndpointsModel`. That simply means replacing `ndb.Model` with `EndpointsModel`, because the latter inherits from `ndb.Model`.

Whether due to further optimizations or type inconsistencies between ProtoRPC messages and NDB Datastore, you also need to migrate a few properties to `endpoints-proto-datastore`, as listed in Table 14-2.

---

[2]You can find the Endpoints Proto Datastore in this repository on GitHub: `https://github.com/GoogleCloudPlatform/endpoints-proto-datastore`.

Table 14-2. *Properties to migrate from ndb.Model to endpoits-proto-datastore*

Property in NDB	Property in Proto Datastore	Reasoning
DateTimeProperty, DateProperty, and TimeProperty	EndpointsDateTimeProperty, EndpointsDateProperty, and EndpointsTimeProperty	New properties in Proto Datastore that allow a keyword argument with the string_format of the date, to handle serialization internally.
ComputedProperty	EndpointsComputedProperty	Used to explicitly set the type of the value generated in this property, because it cannot be extracted from the implementation of ndb.ComputedProperty. If no property_type argument is specified, the default is used: messages.StringField.
UserProperty	EndpointsUserProperty	The final entity remains unchanged. EndpointsUserProperty takes care of retrieving the authenticated user using the endpoints library: endpoints.get_current_user().
IntegerProperty and FloatProperty	EndpointsVariantIntegerProperty and EndpointsVariantFloatProperty	Allow custom serialization of integers and floats, respectively, by accepting variant types if they were used to create a message field.

This is what the model used in the API for the LunchMates application built in Chapter 5 looks like now:

```
#!/usr/bin/env python

import unicodedata

from protorpc import messages

from endpoints_proto_datastore.ndb import EndpointsModel
from endpoints_proto_datastore.ndb import EndpointsAliasProperty
from endpoints_proto_datastore.ndb import EndpointsDateTimeProperty
from endpoints_proto_datastore.ndb import EndpointsComputedProperty

from google.appengine.ext import ndb

DATE_FORMAT_STR = '%Y-%m-%dT%H:%MZ'
```

```
class BaseModel(EndpointsModel):
    created = ndb.DateTimeProperty(auto_now_add=True)

class UserData(BaseModel):

    def normalize(self):
        return unicodedata.normalize(
            'NFKD', unicode(self.name)).encode('ascii', 'ignore').lower()

    _message_fields_schema = ('created', 'id', 'auth_provider', 'name', 'email')

    auth_provider = ndb.StringProperty(
        choices=['google', 'facebook'], required=True)

    name = ndb.StringProperty(default='')
    search_name = EndpointsComputedProperty(normalize)
    email = ndb.StringProperty(required=True)
    auth_user = ndb.UserProperty()

class Meeting(BaseModel):
    owner = ndb.KeyProperty(kind=UserData, required=True)
    venue_forsquare_id = ndb.StringProperty(required=True)
    location = ndb.GeoPtProperty()
    earliest_possible_start = EndpointsDateTimeProperty(
        required=True, string_format=DATE_FORMAT_STR)
    latest_possible_start = EndpointsDateTimeProperty(
        string_format=DATE_FORMAT_STR)
    topic = ndb.StringProperty(required=True)
    type = ndb.StringProperty(required=True, choices=['drink',
                                                      'lunch',
                                                      'brunch'])
    tags = ndb.StringProperty(repeated=True)

    @EndpointsAliasProperty(property_type=messages.IntegerField)
    def owner_id(self):
        return self.owner.id()

class MeetingRequest(BaseModel):

    meeting = ndb.KeyProperty(kind=Meeting, required=True)
    state = ndb.StringProperty(default='pending', choices=['pending',
                                                           'accepted',
                                                           'rejected'])
```

As you can see, most of the logic remains the same. The model now inherits from `EndpointsModel` instead of `ndb.Model`. `EndpointsDateTimeProperty`-ies include a default date format that is used to serialize without your needing to care about it, and `search_name` is now an `EndpointsComputedProperty`.

■ **Pro Tip** Override the value for `_message_fields_schema` in `EndpointsModel` to set a custom message schema used to serialize your model objects into ProtoRPC messages. You can assign a dictionary, a list, a tuple, or an instance of `MessageFieldsSchema` to it. If it is set to `None`, all properties and alias properties are included in the message.

If you take a closer look at the `Meeting` class, you see a method with a decorator that you have not seen before. `EndpointsAliasProperty` can be used to decorate methods that represent properties of your model that you do not want to persist in Cloud Datastore. This property can look similar to `ComputedProperty` in the sense that it allows you to serialize and access volatile information, potentially constructed from other properties in the model. In this case, there is a bit more to it. `EndpointAliasProperty` exposes a keyword to define a `setter` that is called every time a new value is assigned to the property. You can use this as a pre-hook to do some work before a new value is assigned. Notice that the same applies at read time: every time the property is accessed, the method you decorated with `EndpointAliasProperty` is called. Here is an example, extracted from the final model in the `LunchMates` Cloud Endpoints API:

```
class MeetingRequest(BaseModel):
....

    def ParentMeetingSet(self, value):
        meeting_key = ndb.Key(Meeting, int(value))

        # Assign key to meeting. Scenario A: new entity
        self.meeting = meeting_key

        # Add the key to query info. Scenario B: fetch entities for a given meeting
        self._endpoints_query_info.meeting = meeting_key

    @EndpointsAliasProperty(required=True, setter=ParentMeetingSet,
                            property_type=messages.IntegerField)
    def meeting_id(self):
        return self.meeting.id()
```

The method `meeting_id` has been decorated with `EndpointsAliasProperty`. This means every time this property is accessed—`meeting_request.meeting_id`—the value read is the result returned by the method in question. In this case, it returns the identifier from the key of the associated meeting. Also notice that a `setter` keyword has been provided, pointing to a method defined just before. This method is called when the property is set, which can happen either internally or from your own code. When the meeting ID for a request is set, this method creates a key with `kind=Meeting` and the identifier provided and assigns it to the meeting's `ndb.KeyProperty` in the model. In addition, the same key is added to the model's query information.

This can be confusing. Why is all that happening? The answer is simple. We'll explain it from the perspective of each of the use cases. There are two situations where you may want to set the `meeting` property in your model:

- When you create a new meeting request for a given meeting: In this case you need to create a `Key` for the given `meeting_id` and assign it to the new entity's `meeting` property.
- When you are querying for meeting requests for a given meeting ID. In this case, you want to make sure you specify the meeting that you want to use to filter your query.

Note that although this approach can be confusing at first, it holds a lot of potential for the way you develop your application. In the next section, you discover why `EndpointsAliasProperty`-ies are so powerful in the context of Cloud Endpoints Proto Datastore.

■ **Note** As you have seen, `EndpointsAliasProperty`-ies can also be assigned inherited keywords such as `repeated`, `required`, `default`, and or `name`.

Services and Request Handlers

If you have read Chapter 5 of this book, you probably remember the concept of *request handlers* as classes that process and respond to requests depending on their path, method, and parameters. The same idea applies to ProtoRPC and Cloud Endpoints. In this case, the handlers are referred to as *services*. These services contain methods that are responsible for processing incoming requests and returning a result. In Cloud Endpoints, in single-class APIs, services are decorated with the `endpoints.api` method. When your API has multiple `remote.Service` classes to process requests, you decorate each of them with `<your_api>.api_class`. This method accepts parameters similar to those of the `endpoints.api` method—`resource_name`, `audiences`, `scopes` and `allowed_client_ids`—but in this case they are only applied to the scope of the defined class. In addition to those mentioned, you can also provide a `path` argument that is added to the URL path and prepended to each method of the service. If you do not specify it, it defaults to `None`, which causes it to be omitted in the path. Suppose, for example, that based on the configuration of your API, your base URL is

```
lunch--mates--endpoints.appspot.com/_ah/api/lunchmates/v1/.
```

Now you add two new services to your API. The first one contains its own path:

```
@lunchmates_api.api_class(path='meetings')
class Meetings(remote.Service):

    @endpoints.method(....)
    def list(self, query):
        ....

    @endpoints.method(....)
    def create(self, meeting):
        ....
```

These methods can be accessed with the following URLs, respectively:

```
lunch--mates--endpoints.appspot.com/_ah/api/lunchmates/v1/meetings/list
lunch--mates--endpoints.appspot.com/_ah/api/lunchmates/v1/meetings/create
```

Next, consider a service for which you do not specify a path:

```
@lunchmates_api.api_class()
class Auth(remote.Service):
```

```
    @endpoints.method(....)
    def authenticate(self, user):
        ....
```

Because a path is not specified in api_class, this method is accessed using its name:

```
lunch--mates--endpoints.appspot.com/_ah/api/lunchmates/v1/authenticate
```

■ **Note** `endpoints.method` accepts a `path` argument. As you can see in the previous example, if this argument is not specified, the name of the method is used to construct the URL path.

The previous examples show how you must decorate your methods for Cloud Endpoints to be able to generate client libraries that can access them. `endpoints.method` accepts the arguments listed in Table 14-3.

Table 14-3. *Accepted arguments in the* `endpoints.method` *decorator*

Argument	Description
`Request Message Class`	The message class corresponding to the ProtoRPC request used in the method. This argument accepts the class itself or its name.
`Response Message Class`	The message class corresponding to the ProtoRPC response used in the method. This argument accepts the class itself or its name.
`path`	A string with the path that is appended to the URL to access this method. If you do not set this argument, the method name is used.
`name`	An alternative name for this method. The name must start with a lowercase letter and match the following regular expression: `[a-z]+[A-Za-z0-9]*`.
`http_method`	HTTP method of the incoming request. Defaults to `POST` if not set.

■ **Pro Tip** Avoid collisions between the `resource_name` of your API and the `name` of your methods. For example, when generating the client library for Java, the part of the method name before the dot (`.`) is an inner class of the API resource name. Therefore, an API class with `resource_name='meetings'` and a method with `name='meetings.create'` would create a conflict and not be able to build.

In addition to the arguments in the table, you can specify the keywords `audiences` and `allowed_client_ids` at the method level, in which case they override the values specified in the API. You do so through `endpoints.api()` or `endpoints.api_class()`.

However, because you are using the Endpoints Proto Datastore API on top of Cloud Endpoints, most of the time you will not decorate with `endpoints.method` directly. Instead, the Endpoints Proto Datastore API provides two methods that simplify your requests by handling queries and serialization of Cloud Datastore model objects into ProtoRPC messages for you. Because of that, you do not need to specify the classes for the request and response `Message` objects.

■ **Note** Both `EndpointsModel.method` and `EndpointsModel.query_method` act as wrappers around `endpoints.method`, which is called at the end of both implementations.

EndpointsModel.method

`EndpointsModel.method` takes the `EndpointsModel` class specified and uses it to serialize and deserialize the entity into RPC messages. In addition to the arguments for `endpoints.method` listed previously, you can also set the arguments in Table 14-4.

Table 14-4. *Accepted arguments in the `EndpointModels.method` decorator*

Argument	Description
`request_fields*`	List of fields used to define the ProtoRPC message for the request.
`response_fields*`	List of fields used to define the ProtoRPC message for the response.
`user_required`	Accepts a `boolean` value. When set to `True`, an authenticated user is required to proceed with the request. If no user is present, the request responds with `401 Not Authorized`.

**Both `request_fields` and `response_fields` are optional arguments that accept a list, a tuple, a dictionary, or an entity of the class `MessageFieldsSchema`. If not set, messages are built using the variable_`message_fields_schema` in your `EndpointsModel` class or the properties in the model definition if the schema is not set.*

Here is an example of a `POST` method used to create new meetings in the application:

```
from protorpc import remote

from base import lunchmates_api
from base import authenticated_user_data

from model.model import Meeting

@lunchmates_api.api_class(resource_name='meeting')
class Meetings(remote.Service):

    @Meeting.method(path='meetings', name='meetings.create', user_required=True)
    def create(self, meeting):

        meeting.owner = authenticated_user_data().key
        meeting.put()
        return meeting
```

The Meeting class—which inherits from EndpointsModel—is used to decorate the method. As explained earlier, this defines the underlying ProtoRPC message used in the request and response based on the Meeting model. The rest of the arguments are common to endpoints.method. Notice that an authenticated user is required to execute the request. Also note that the path is set to 'meetings'. Hence the URL to access that method is

```
POST [localhost | <your-application-id>.appspot.com]/_ah/api/lunchmates/v1/meetings
```

The meeting object that is passed as an argument of the method you define is the result of deserializing the body of your request into the class specified on its decorator, Meeting. All that is left is persisting the object. In the previous example, the owner of the meeting is set using the currently authenticated user before the entity is persisted.

EndpointsModel.query_method

In contrast to the previous method decorator, query_method is intended to help you work with Cloud Datastore queries. As a result, only GET requests are allowed. When using this decorator, a query is created based on the parameters passed and is made available to you through the query property on your decorated method definition. In this method, you can modify the query as you wish—for example, adding a default sort order. You must return the query at the end of the method. This causes the query to be executed. In the response body of your requests there are two fields:

- items is an array of results of the type of the EndpointsModel class used to decorate the method. The number of results is limited by default, but you can configure it through the method's keyword arguments.
- nextPageToken is used as a means of pagination. You can use this value, adding it as a query parameter to your method so that if the caller sets it, it is converted into a cursor and used to return the next page of results.

This is an example of a simple GET method to fetch meeting requests:

```
import endpoints
from protorpc import remote

from base import lunchmates_api
from model.model import MeetingRequest

@lunchmates_api.api_class(resource_name='meeting_request', path='meetings')
class MeetingRequests(remote.Service):

    @MeetingRequest.query_method(path='requests', user_required=True,
                                 name='meeting_requests.list')
    def list(self, query):
        return query.order(-MeetingRequest.created)
```

Notice that the only modification to the query is adding an order clause. In this case, the results are sorted by the created property in descending order. Because created is a date, new records are returned first.

In addition to the arguments included in endpoints.method, query_method accepts the keyword arguments listed in Table 14-5, all of them optional:

Table 14-5. *Accepted arguments in the EndpointModels.query_method decorator*

Argument	Description
query_fields	Determines the fields used to construct the query. Each field specified is expected to affect the results of the query. Because of that, the fields have to refer to properties that are part of the model in question—@Model.query_method—whether they are regular properties or EndpointsAliasProperty-ies. For example, to retrieve meetings of the type lunch, adding the query field type allows requests of the kind request_url?type=lunch. This adds the filter to the query for you and returns the results you are looking for. Note that this behavior only applies to equality filters. If you need something more elaborate, you can use EndpointsAliasProperty-ies with a setter to define the details of your query. Check out the MeetingRequest model to see an example.
collection_fields	Determines the fields to return for each item in the response results. If not specified, it defaults to the model schema.
use_projection	A boolean value that, when set to True, queries for a projection of the entity instead of the entire entity. The projection is defined using the collection fields. Projection queries are faster to retrieve and transfer, but remember that they need an index on each of the fields specified. You learn more about projection queries in Chapter 9.
limit_default	Determines the number of records to be returned in the response body when no limit clause is specified on the query. Defaults to endpoints_proto_datastore.ndb.model.QUERY_LIMIT_DEFAULT, currently set to 10.
limit_max	Sets the maximum allowed number of records to be returned in the response body. If a query attempts to limit the number of results with a number greater than the value specified in this argument, an endpoints.ForbiddenException is raised. Defaults to endpoints_proto_datastore.ndb.model.QUERY_LIMIT_MAX, currently set to 100.
user_required	Accepts a boolean value. When set to True, an authenticated user is required to proceed with the request. If no user is present, the request responds with 401 Not Authorized.

EndpointsModel includes three convenient EndpointsAliasProperty-ies that you can use as query_fields in query_method like this:

```
@YourModel.query_method(query_fields=('limit', 'order', 'pageToken'), path='your_path')
def yourQueryMethod(self, query):
    return query
```

These alias properties process the three query fields so that, when added as query parameters in the request URL, they are used to modify the query that returns the results you are looking for. Therefore, if you access this method with the following URL, your query returns five results from the selected page ordered by the created property:

```
<method_url>/?limit=5&order=created&pageToken=<token-urlstring>
```

Use these predefined `EndpointsAliasProperty` methods[3] as an inspiration to construct your own based on your needs.

Here is an example of a query method with an `EndpointsAliasProperty` used in the `LunchMates` API.

In the endpoint that handles meeting requests, there is a method that fetches all requests for a specific meeting, passing the ID of the meeting as a parameter in the URL:

```
<api_host>/_ah/api/lunchmates/v1/meetings/<meeting_id>/requests
```

You can now access this property—`meeting_id`—by specifying it as a `query_field` in your method definition:

```
@MeetingRequest.query_method(query_fields=('meeting_id',),
                             path='{meeting_id}/requests',
                             user_required=True,
                             name='meeting_requests.list')
def list(self, query):
    return query.order(-MeetingRequest.created)
```

Now, in your model, you can define an `EndpointsAliasProperty` with a setter so that every time `query_method` is called, the property `meeting_id` is assigned. Because of that, the setter you define in the model is executed. Finally, in this setter, you can filter the potential query to fetch meeting requests, using the meeting ID provided, like this:

```
class MeetingRequest(BaseModel):

    ....

    def ParentMeetingSet(self, value):

        meeting_key = ndb.Key(Meeting, int(value))

        # Assign key to meeting. Scenario: new entity
        self.meeting = meeting_key

        # Add key to the query info. Scenario: fetch entities for a given meeting
        self._endpoints_query_info.meeting = meeting_key

    @EndpointsAliasProperty(required=True, setter=ParentMeetingSet,
                            property_type=messages.IntegerField)
    def meeting_id(self):
        return self.meeting.id()
```

---

[3]Line of the code in the `endpoints-proto-datastore` repository where the predefined `query_fields` aliases are defined: `https://github.com/GoogleCloudPlatform/endpoints-proto-datastore/blob/master/endpoints_proto_datastore/ndb/model.py#L826`.

EndpointsModel.method and EndpointsModel.query_method can be very powerful assets to make the methods in your services react wisely based on the type of requests your application receives and the data you are exposing. Experimenting with them as concepts of query_fields, EndpointsAliasProperty, and the internal wiring of Cloud Endpoints can make them a bit hard to learn and adopt at first. Here are some resources that can help you throughout the process:

- endpoints_proto_datastore code repository: https://github.com/GoogleCloudPlatform/endpoints-proto-datastore
- endpoints source code: http://code.metager.de/source/xref/google/appengine/python/lib/endpoints-1.0
- Introduction to the Endpoints Proto Datastore API: http://endpoints-proto-datastore.appspot.com

Finally, do not miss the documentation at Google Developers. This is a living entity that is regularly updated with the latest additions and pieces of advice.

The APIs Explorer

The APIs Explorer is a tool that allows you to browse, explore, and perform requests against most Google APIs in a visual way. It is very helpful when you are working with concrete APIs and need to experiment and see the details of each request you are interested in, such as the full URL path, the parameters allowed, the responses you can expect, and so on. You can access Google APIs Explorer at

```
https://developers.google.com/apis-explorer
```

It is even more useful in the context of developing your own API or application. To access the APIs Explorer for the application you are currently working on, simply navigate to the following URL when the development server is running:

```
http://localhost:<port>/_ah/api/explorer
```

You can also access the APIs Explorer for your deployed API by replacing the local host with its deployed counterpart:

```
http://<your-app-id>.appspot.com/_ah/api/explorer
```

For example, for the LunchMates API you have been working on throughout the chapter, it is as follows:

```
http://lunch--mates--endpoints.appspot.com/_ah/api/explorer
```

From there you can see all your services and API versions and test your methods through the endpoints generated based on the configuration of your API.

Generating Client Libraries for Your Application

One of the major benefits of Cloud Endpoints is the ability to generate client libraries that connect and make requests to your API. This is useful in the initial phase of client development and also in scenarios of continuous development and iterative approaches. When your API is still changing, Cloud Endpoints allows you to circumvent the need to manually change your client libraries according to API updates.

■ **Pro Tip** Because you are using the command line and common build tools to generate your libraries, you can easily automate this process with continuous integration tools like Jenkins and Travis. You can add hooks to your API code repository[4,5] so that every time the production branch is updated, the client libraries are automatically generated and made available to your client developers.

The command-line tool `endpointscfg.py` allows you to generate API discovery docs for your application as well as the client library you need to use in your client to connect to the API you just created. For example, to create the API discovery doc for application, do the following:

```
$ endpointscfg.py get_discovery_doc --format rpc
                controllers.auth.Auth controllers.users.Users
                controllers.meetings.Meetings controllers.meeting_requests.MeetingRequests
```

You use the same command to generate the client library for your Android application, by using `get_client_lib` instead of `get_discovery_doc`:

```
$ endpointscfg.py get_client_lib java -bs gradle
                controllers.auth.Auth controllers.users.Users
                controllers.meetings.Meetings controllers.meeting_requests.MeetingRequests
```

As you can see, the structure of the command is as follows:

```
endpointscfg.py <command> <language> <options> [services-list...]
```

Where:

- `command` can be either `get_discovery_doc` or `get_client_lib`, depending on whether you are generating the discovery docs or a client library for your application.
- `language` determines the target programming language in which you want your client library to be exported. This is only applicable to `get_client_lib`.
- `options` specifies the associated options that you can add to the two commands.
- `services-list` represents the list of services that conform your API.

---

[4]Git push hooks in Travis: `http://docs.travis-ci.com/user/getting-started/#Step-four%3A-Trigger-Your-First-Build-With-a-Git-Push`.
[5]Git push hooks in Jenkins: `https://wiki.jenkins-ci.org/display/JENKINS/Git+Plugin#GitPlugin-Pushnotificationfromrepository`.

These subcommands have a few options in common, as listed in Table 14-6.

Table 14-6. *Available options in the endpointscfg.py command-line tool*

Argument	Description
Common to Both Subcommands	
-a or --application	Specifies the path for the directory where endpointscfg.py looks to execute the desired command. By default, this is the current directory. Remember that this path must point to the root directory of your application—that is where your app.yaml file is placed.
--hostname	Determines the hostname of your application. The default is used if it is not specified. This is helpful, for example, when you need to test your application locally or you are using a different host than the default one: <application-id>.appspot.com.
-o or --output	Indicates the directory where the output files should be placed. By default, this is the current directory.
Specific to get_client_lib	
-bs or --build_system	Describes the type of bundle that is produced based on the build system you are working with. Currently, the options for Android are gradle and maven. If you omit this option, the default bundle is used. This bundle contains only the dependency libraries and a source.jar.
Specific to get_discovery_doc	
-f or --format	Selects the API protocol type used to export the discovery docs. Options are rest (the default) and rpc.

The process of using client libraries to access your API is different on each platform. For example, you can generate a Java client library directly using the endpointscfg.py command, whereas on iOS you need to generate your library from Xcode. Conversely, in JavaScript, you can dynamically load your API into the JavaScript-provided library. This chapter explains the Android case. For the JavaScript[6] and iOS[7] versions, refer to the documentation at Google Developers.

Accessing Your API from Your Android client

The first thing you need to do is export the client libraries in Java using the get_client_lib command:

```
$ endpointscfg.py get_client_lib java -bs gradle
            controllers.auth.Auth controllers.users.Users
            controllers.meetings.Meetings controllers.meeting_requests.MeetingRequests
```

[6]"Using Cloud Endpoints in a JavaScript Client," https://cloud.google.com/appengine/docs/python/endpoints/consume_js.
[7]"Using Cloud Endpoints in an iOS Client," https://cloud.google.com/appengine/docs/python/endpoints/consume_ios.

The bundle is generated, compressed, and saved in the output folder you specify or your current directory. Once generated, you can decompress this file and add it to the root folder of your Android application. In this case, a Gradle module was generated. In order for your Gradle build script in Android Studio to recognize this module, you need to include it in your `settings.gradle` file:

```
include ':app', ':lunchmates'
```

Here, app is the module of the application and `lunchmates` is the API for the `LunchMates` application you just generated. Once defined, you can go into the `build.gradle` script in your application module (app) and add it as a dependency:

```
....
dependencies {
    ....
    compile project(':lunchmates')

    compile 'com.google.api-client:google-api-client-android:1.20.0'
    compile 'com.google.android.gms:play-services:7.0.0'
    compile 'com.android.support:appcompat-v7:22.0.0'
}
```

Notice that you need to add two more dependencies to your project:

- Google Play Services libraries allow you access the Account Manager, which helps you handle the authentication process.
- The API client for Android includes a set of libraries that help you interact with Google and other APIs. When you use Cloud Endpoints, your API is built using similar conventions and technologies as APIs in Google, therefore this dependency also simplifies access to your API in tasks like networking, serialization, authorization, and so on.

In your manifest, make sure to add a permission to access the Internet. If you need to make authenticated requests, also include `get` accounts from the accounts service and generate authorization tokens using the Account Manager with `USE_CREDENTIALS`:

```
<manifest xmlns:android="http://schemas.android.com/apk/res/android" ....>

    <uses-permission android:name="android.permission.INTERNET"/>
    <uses-permission android:name="android.permission.GET_ACCOUNTS"/>
    <uses-permission android:name="android.permission.USE_CREDENTIALS"/>

    <application ....>
        ....
    </application>
</manifest>
```

To make requests on behalf of a user with an account set up in the Android device, you use the class GoogleAccountCredential, which deals with the entire process of obtaining an access token for the selected account:

```
private static final String ANDROID_AUDIENCE = "server:client_id:<your-web-client-id>";

private GoogleAccountCredential credential;
private SharedPreferences sharedPreferences;

@Override
protected void onCreate(Bundle savedInstanceState) {
    super.onCreate(savedInstanceState);
    setContentView(....);

    sharedPreferences = PreferenceManager.getDefaultSharedPreferences(this);
    credential = GoogleAccountCredential.usingAudience(this, ANDROID_AUDIENCE);

    checkSelectedAccount(sharedPreferences.getString("account_name", null));
}
```

To avoid users needing to select their preferred account every time they open your app, you store their selection in SharedPreferences,[8] Once the credentials and SharedPreferences members are instantiated, you can check whether a user already selected an account to authenticate your requests—in which case you try to fetch the current list of meetings—or prompt the user with the available accounts to start the authentication process:

```
private static final int ACCOUNT_PICKER_REQUEST_CODE = 2;

private void checkSelectedAccount(String accountName) {
    if (accountName == null) {
        startActivityForResult(credential
            .newChooseAccountIntent(), ACCOUNT_PICKER_REQUEST_CODE);
    } else {
        setupLunchmatesApi(credential, accountName);
        fetchMeetingsList();
    }
}
```

[8]SharedPreferences is a simple storage for keys and values on disk. This means of storage is very convenient for small, unstructured amounts of information that you need to persist across sessions. For more information, refer to the documentation at http://developer.android.com/reference/android/content/SharedPreferences.html.

If there is not an account already stored, a new `Activity` is started to show the user the available accounts in the Android device. When an option is selected, the `Activity` closes and calls back the original `Activity` through `onActivityResult`:

```
@Override
protected void onActivityResult(int requestCode, int resultCode, Intent data) {
    super.onActivityResult(requestCode, resultCode, data);

    switch (requestCode) {
    case ACCOUNT_PICKER_REQUEST_CODE:
        if (data != null && data.getExtras() != null) {
            String accountName = data.getExtras().getString(AccountManager.KEY_ACCOUNT_NAME);
            if (accountName != null) {
                checkSelectedAccount(accountName);
            }
        }
        break;
    }
}
```

If an account was selected, `checkSelectedAccount` is called, persisting the current account and creating the API object that you can use to make requests:

```
private void setupLunchmatesApi(GoogleAccountCredential credential, String accountName) {
    credential.setSelectedAccountName(accountName);
    storeAccountName(accountName);

    Lunchmates.Builder lunchmates = new Lunchmates.Builder(
            new NetHttpTransport(),
            new JacksonFactory(),
            credential);

    lunchmatesApi = lunchmates.build();
}
```

In this method, you set the selected account in the `credentials` object and construct your API object with it. You also persist the currently selected account in `SharedPreferences` with `storeAccountName(accountName)`.[9]

Finally, the method `fetchMeetingsList` retrieves a list of meetings from your API:

```
private void fetchMeetingsList() {
    ...
    try{
        MeetingCollection meetings = lunchmatesApi.meeting().meetings().list().execute();
```

[9]This and other methods have not been included in the book. To see the full source code of this Android application go to `https://github.com/GoogleCloudPlatformBook/lunchmates-android`

```
        final String result;
        if (meetings.get("items") != null) {
            result = meetings.getItems().size() + " meetings";
        } else {
            result = "0 meetings";
        }
        Log.i("# of meetings", result);
    } catch (IOException e) {
        e.printStackTrace();
    }
}
```

This code should not run in the main thread, because it blocks execution until the request returns a response. Among the alternatives, consider using `AsyncTask`, `Loader`, or `ThreadPoolExecutor`. If you need requests to execute and wait until a response is given even if the application is sent to the background, consider using a service. Keep in mind that services help you to execute logic independently of the lifecycle of your views or `Activity`-ies. However, a service runs in the main thread; thus you still need to handle executing the operations in separate threads.

You can find, test, and contribute to the example application from the associated GitHub repository: `https://github.com/GoogleCloudPlatformBook/lunchmates-android`.

Summary

In this chapter, you have seen the power of App Engine combined with Cloud Endpoints, which together give you the ability to develop your API and client-side logic in much less time than with the usual approaches. The combination of these two services is powerful when you target more than one platform at the same time and also helps you make your API-side logic simpler, more maintainable, and flexible in the face of potential changes in your business logic.

Now you have the tools you need to build an entire application or service from scratch. It is your duty to experiment and try the list of projects, ideas, and prototypes you have had in mind for a while but never had the resources to address.

PART VI

Google Cloud Platform - Management and Recipes

CHAPTER 15

Cloud Platform DevOps Toolbox

Google Cloud Platform provides several tools that aid in managing the lifecycle of other types of resources such as compute, storage, analytics, and orchestration. This chapter introduces you to a few of these core tools. The primary tool you learn about is the Google Cloud Deployment Manager. After that, you're introduced to tools that assist in source and binary code management and that can help you discover security vulnerabilities and identify performance bottlenecks.

Google Cloud Deployment Manager

Cloud computing platforms like Cloud Platform break down IT resources into small, individual, atomic units. This approach is followed industry-wide so that users don't have to pay for resources they don't yet need but can deploy those resources when the need arises. Users over time develop "recipes" that bring together different types of IT resources in a certain order to produce the final solution. Experienced architects may be able to repeat the same steps again and again, and the process itself is mundane—which can lead to errors. After all, "To err is human."

Cloud Deployment Manager is an infrastructure management service that makes it simple to create, deploy, and manage Cloud Platform resources. You can create static or dynamic templates that describe the configuration of your Google Cloud environment and then use Deployment Manager to create these resources as a single deployment. Just like other Cloud Platform products, Deployment Manager is supported through Developers Console, the `gcloud` command-line tool, and APIs. In this section, you use the `gcloud` command-line tool.

Building Blocks

The following components are the building blocks of Deployment Manager:

- *Resources*: A resource represents a single Cloud Platform resource. For example, a Google Compute Engine instance is one resource type; a Cloud SQL instance is another resource type, and so on. Deployment Manager supports many Cloud Platform resources. You can get a list of the currently supported Cloud Platform resource types using the command "`gcloud beta deployment-manager types list`".

- *Configuration files*: A configuration file defines the structure of your deployment. It defines a list of resources including types, properties, and specific settings of your deployment, such as the zone. Optionally, configuration files can also import and use templates to provide flexibility and reuse. Configuration files are written in YAML syntax, and you must always have one to create a deployment. Deployment Manager then deploys a configuration using the configuration file and through the Deployment Manage service.

- *Templates*: A template file contains either Python code or a Jinja template as a separate file that also defines a set of resources. The template is not usable by itself and must be imported into a configuration file. A template may include other templates; the Deployment Manager service recursively expands them to create the entire configuration. Templates allow you to further separate your configuration into files that you can plug in and take out as necessary for your deployment.
- *Deployments*: A deployment is the instantiation of resources as described in a configuration file. All resources specified in a configuration file are deployed and managed together.
- *Manifest*: Each deployment has a corresponding manifest. A manifest is a read-only, fully expanded list that describes all the resources in your deployment and is automatically created with each new deployment. A manifest is not the same as a configuration file but is created based on the configuration file. For each deployment, there is a single manifest file, and it is not modifiable.

Launching the Compute Engine VM using Deployment Manager

Let's start with a simple Cloud Platform deployment that consists of a single Compute Engine–based VM with a persistent disk attached, in the Asian region. Listing 15-1 shows the entire configuration file, after which we dissect it into sections.

Listing 15-1. YAML-Based Configuration File to Launch a Compute Engine VM

```
resources:
- name: ce-vm-by-cdm
  type: compute.v1.instance
  properties:
    zone: asia-east1-a
    machineType: https://www.googleapis.com/compute/v1/projects/cloud-platform-book/zones/
asia-east1-a/machineTypes/n1-standard-2
    disks:
    - deviceName: boot
      type: PERSISTENT
      boot: true
      autoDelete: true
      initializeParams:
        diskName: pdisk-cdm
        sourceImage: https://www.googleapis.com/compute/v1/projects/debian-cloud/global/
images/
debian-7-wheezy-v20150325
    networkInterfaces:
    - network: https://www.googleapis.com/compute/v1/projects/cloud-platform-book/
global/networks/default
```

Deployment Manager does not accept configurations through standard input. Hence, you need to save this configuration as a file: call it `ce-vm.yaml`. Listing 15-2 shows the deployment command and corresponding output.

Listing 15-2. Creating a Deployment Using the `deployment-manager` Command-Line Tool

```
$ gcloud beta deployment-manager deployments create simple-ce-vm --config ce-vm.yaml
Waiting for create operation operation-1430123706966-514b09f89dff1-dea7cd03-a54d9700 to
complete
...done.
Create operation operation-1430123706966-514b09f89dff1-dea7cd03-a54d9700 completed
successfully.
NAME          TYPE                  ID                   UPDATE_STATE  ERRORS
ce-vm-by-cdm  compute.v1.instance   4353203017605990993  COMPLETED     -
```

Let's take a look at this deployment by using the "`deployments describe`" command; see Listing 15-3.

Listing 15-3. Details of a Successful Deployment

```
$ gcloud beta deployment-manager deployments describe simple-ce-vm
creationTimestamp: '2015-04-27T01:35:07.768-07:00'
fingerprint: ''
id: '3013753110558427732'
manifest: https://www.googleapis.com/deploymentmanager/v2beta2/projects/cloud-platform-book/
global/deployments/simple-ce-vm/manifests/manifest-1430123707768-31eeeb9d-63af-4e50-a89f-
e5b051c2fd47
name: simple-ce-vm
state: DEPLOYED
resources:
NAME          TYPE                  ID                   UPDATE_STATE  ERRORS
ce-vm-by-cdm  compute.v1.instance   4353203017605990993  COMPLETED     -
```

You can inspect just the resources deployed as part of a deployment by using the `resources list` command; see Listing 15-4.

Listing 15-4. Listing the Resources Launched in a Deployment

```
$ gcloud beta deployment-manager resources --deployment simple-ce-vm list
NAME          TYPE                  ID                   UPDATE_STATE  ERRORS
ce-vm-by-cdm  compute.v1.instance   4353203017605990993  COMPLETED     -
```

Each deployment creates a manifest. You can view the manifest for more information about a deployment. The command `gcloud beta deployment-manager manifests --deployment simple-ce-vm describe MANIFEST-ID` return the complete manifest. A `MANIFEST-ID` is a unique ID for a manifest and is of the format `manifest-RANDOM-HASH`. You can determine the manifest ID by getting information about the corresponding deployment or by listing a deployment's manifests. Listing 15-5 shows the command and corresponding output to describe the manifest for your earlier deployment.

Listing 15-5. Describing the Manifest for a Deployment Using the Manifest ID

```
$ gcloud beta deployment-manager manifests --deployment simple-ce-vm describe
manifest-1430123707768-31eeeb9d-63af-4e50-a89f-e5b051c2fd47
config: "resources:\n- name: ce-vm-by-cdm\n  type: compute.v1.instance\n  properties:\n\
  \    zone: asia-east1-a\n    machineType: https://www.googleapis.com/compute/v1/projects/
cloud-platform-book/zones/asia-east1-a/machineTypes/n1-standard-2\n\
  \    disks:\n    - deviceName: boot\n      type: PERSISTENT\n      boot: true\n\
  \      autoDelete: true\n      initializeParams:\n        diskName: pdisk-cdm\n\
  \        sourceImage: https://www.googleapis.com/compute/v1/projects/debian-cloud/
global/images/debian-7-wheezy-v20150325\n\
  \    networkInterfaces:\n    - network: https://www.googleapis.com/compute/v1/projects/
cloud-platform-book/global/networks/default\n\
  \    "
creationTimestamp: '2015-04-27T01:35:07.770-07:00'
evaluatedConfig: |
  resources:
  - name: ce-vm-by-cdm
    properties:
      disks:
      - autoDelete: true
        boot: true
        deviceName: boot
        initializeParams:
          diskName: pdisk-cdm
          sourceImage: https://www.googleapis.com/compute/v1/projects/debian-cloud/
global/images/debian-7-wheezy-v20150325
        type: PERSISTENT
      machineType: https://www.googleapis.com/compute/v1/projects/cloud-platform-book/zones/
asia-east1-a/machineTypes/n1-standard-2
      networkInterfaces:
      - network: https://www.googleapis.com/compute/v1/projects/cloud-platform-book/
global/networks/default
      zone: asia-east1-a
    type: compute.v1.instance
id: '8723829954981153364'
layout: |
  resources:
  - name: ce-vm-by-cdm
    type: compute.v1.instance
name: manifest-1430123707768-31eeeb9d-63af-4e50-a89f-e5b051c2fd47
selfLink: https://www.googleapis.com/deploymentmanager/v2beta2/projects/cloud-platform-book/
global/
deployments/simple-ce-vm/manifests/manifest-1430123707768-31eeeb9d-63af-4e50-a89f-
e5b051c2fd47
```

Developing Configuration and Template Files

Let's take apart the configuration you used in the previous deployment to launch a single Compute Engine VM. We have added line numbers and duplicated the code here for easy reference:

```
1 resources:
2 - name: ce-vm-by-cdm
3   type: compute.v1.instance
4   properties:
5     zone: asia-east1-a
6     machineType: https://www.googleapis.com/compute/v1/projects/cloud-platform-book/zones/
      asia-east1-a/machineTypes/n1-standard-2
7     disks:
8     - deviceName: boot
9       type: PERSISTENT
10      boot: true
11      autoDelete: true
12      initializeParams:
13        diskName: pdisk-cdm
14        sourceImage: https://www.googleapis.com/compute/v1/projects/debian-cloud/global/
        images/debian-7-wheezy-v20150325
15    networkInterfaces:
16    - network: https://www.googleapis.com/compute/v1/projects/cloud-platform-book/global/
        networks/default
```

A basic configuration file starts with the resources property as the first item, followed by a list of resources. You must always provide a name and type to define a resource type. The type is of the format `type: <api>.<api-version>.<resource-type>`. Lines 1–3 from the configuration file declare the resources keyword, name, and resource type.

You can get a list of all supported types using the following command:

```
$ gcloud beta deployment-manager types list
autoscaler.v1beta2.autoscaler
bigquery.v2.dataset
bigquery.v2.table
compute.v1.address
compute.v1.backendService
compute.v1.disk
compute.v1.firewall
compute.v1.forwardingRule
compute.v1.globalForwardingRule
compute.v1.globalAddress
compute.v1.httpHealthCheck
compute.v1.image
compute.v1.instance
compute.v1.instanceTemplate
compute.v1.network
compute.v1.route
compute.v1.targetHttpProxy
compute.v1.targetInstance
compute.v1.targetPool
```

```
compute.v1.urlMap
container.v1beta1.cluster
replicapool.v1beta1.pool
replicapool.v1beta2.instanceGroupManager
resourceviews.v1beta2.zoneView
storage.v1.bucket
storage.v1.bucketAccessControl
storage.v1.defaultObjectAccessControl
storage.v1.objectAccessControl
storage.v1.object
sqladmin.v1beta4.instance
sqladmin.v1beta4.database
```

After providing a type, you can set the properties of the resource, as indicated by the `properties` section. You can define for your resource any writable property indicated in the API reference documentation for the resource type. Some APIs require a minimum set of properties in order to create a resource. For more information, review the product's documentation. Your configuration file can also define multiple resources from different products in a single deployment.

Lines 4–6 declare the zone and machine types of the Compute Engine instance. Similarly, line 14 declares the boot image for this instance. You can list all possible values for these options using the `gcloud` tool. The commands and output in Listings 15-6 to 15-8 show the current values.

Listing 15-6. Listing All Compute Engine Zones

```
$ gcloud compute zones list
NAME            REGION       STATUS NEXT_MAINTENANCE TURNDOWN_DATE
asia-east1-c    asia-east1   UP
asia-east1-b    asia-east1   UP
asia-east1-a    asia-east1   UP
europe-west1-c  europe-west1 UP
europe-west1-b  europe-west1 UP
europe-west1-d  europe-west1 UP
us-central1-a   us-central1  UP
us-central1-f   us-central1  UP
us-central1-c   us-central1  UP
us-central1-b   us-central1  UP
us-central2-a   us-central2  UP
```

Listing 15-7. Listing All Machine Types in the `asia-east1-a` Zone (Remove the `zone` Flag to List All Machine Types Worldwide)

```
$ gcloud compute machine-types list --zone asia-east1-a
NAME           ZONE         CPUS MEMORY_GB DEPRECATED
f1-micro       asia-east1-a 1      0.60
g1-small       asia-east1-a 1      1.70
n1-highcpu-16  asia-east1-a 16    14.40
n1-highcpu-2   asia-east1-a 2      1.80
n1-highcpu-32  asia-east1-a 32    28.80
n1-highcpu-4   asia-east1-a 4      3.60
n1-highcpu-8   asia-east1-a 8      7.20
n1-highmem-16  asia-east1-a 16   104.00
n1-highmem-2   asia-east1-a 2     13.00
```

```
n1-highmem-32  asia-east1-a 32  208.00
n1-highmem-4   asia-east1-a 4    26.00
n1-highmem-8   asia-east1-a 8    52.00
n1-standard-1  asia-east1-a 1     3.75
n1-standard-16 asia-east1-a 16   60.00
n1-standard-2  asia-east1-a 2     7.50
n1-standard-32 asia-east1-a 32  120.00
n1-standard-4  asia-east1-a 4    15.00
n1-standard-8  asia-east1-a 8    30.00
```

Listing 15-8. Listing the Boot Images Available in Cloud Platform

```
$ gcloud compute images list
NAME                                     PROJECT            ALIAS                DEPRECATED STATUS
centos-6-v20150325                       centos-cloud       centos-6                        READY
centos-7-v20150325                       centos-cloud       centos-7                        READY
coreos-alpha-660-0-0-v20150423           coreos-cloud                                       READY
coreos-beta-647-0-0-v20150415            coreos-cloud                                       READY
coreos-stable-633-1-0-v20150414          coreos-cloud       coreos                          READY
backports-debian-7-wheezy-v20150325      debian-cloud       debian-7-backports              READY
debian-7-wheezy-v20150325                debian-cloud       debian-7                        READY
container-vm-v20150129                   google-containers  container-vm                    READY
container-vm-v20150305                   google-containers  container-vm                    READY
container-vm-v20150317                   google-containers  container-vm                    READY
opensuse-13-1-v20141102                  opensuse-cloud     opensuse-13                     READY
opensuse-13-2-v20150315                  opensuse-cloud     opensuse-13                     READY
rhel-6-v20150325                         rhel-cloud         rhel-6                          READY
rhel-7-v20150325                         rhel-cloud         rhel-7                          READY
sles-11-sp3-v20150310                    suse-cloud         sles-11                         READY
sles-12-v20150310                        suse-cloud         sles-12                         READY
ubuntu-1204-precise-v20150316            ubuntu-os-cloud    ubuntu-12-04                    READY
ubuntu-1404-trusty-v20150316             ubuntu-os-cloud    ubuntu-14-04                    READY
ubuntu-1410-utopic-v20150318c            ubuntu-os-cloud    ubuntu-14-10                    READY
ubuntu-1504-vivid-v20150422              ubuntu-os-cloud                                    READY
windows-server-2008-r2-dc-v20150331      windows-cloud      windows-2008-r2                 READY
windows-server-2012-r2-dc-v20150331      windows-cloud      windows-2012-r2                 READY
```

Templates

A basic configuration file is suitable only for simple scenarios. Your configuration file will become large and unmanageable if you have complex deployments. A single configuration file also impedes your ability to share parts of your configuration in multiple configurations. In these cases, you can break your configuration file into templates.

As an example, consider the previous YAML configuration file that deployment a VM. You can break it into a template and a configuration file. In the Jinja templating language, the same structure is used for both configuration and template files. Let's create a `ce-vm-template.jinja` file that has the same properties as the VM instance.

Once you have created a template, you need to import it into your configuration file. Importing a template is straightforward and requires a single `imports` property. For example, you can import your VM template from the previous step. Note that importing a template isn't enough to invoke the template; once you import a template, you can use it as a type. You can mix and match imports of multiple templates, regardless of whether the templates are Jinja or Python. The updated configuration file is shown in Listing 15-9.

Listing 15-9. New Configuration File Using Templates to Launch a Compute Engine Instance

```
imports:
- path: ce-vm-template.jinja

resources:
- name: ce-vm-cdm-2
  type: ce-vm-template.jinja
```

Notice that there is a `name` property in the configuration file and also in the template file, which defines the name of the resource. The distinction between the two `name` properties is that in the configuration file (the YAML file), it is the custom name used to reference the template, whereas the `name` property in the template is the name of the resource that will be deployed.

Deploy the Compute Engine instance using this configuration file and template file, as shown in Listing 15-10.

Listing 15-10. Launching a Compute Engine Instance that Is Defined in the Configuration and Template Files

```
$ gcloud beta deployment-manager deployments create second-ce-vm --config ce-vm-2.yaml
Waiting for create operation operation-1430129121010-514b1e23da150-7026f579-d1299501 to
complete
...done.
Create operation operation-1430129121010-514b1e23da150-7026f579-d1299501 completed
successfully.
NAME      TYPE                 ID                   UPDATE_STATE  ERRORS
ce-vm-2   compute.v1.instance  8508817604311496457  COMPLETED     -
```

Property Parameters

One of the advantages of using templates is the ability to use parameters for properties. Instead of hard-coding a property value, you can define the property with a parameter and then set the parameter in your configuration file. This allows you to create dynamic, flexible templates that can be modified as needed for your deployment.

In Jinja, you can define a parameter name using the syntax "`{{ properties["parameter-name"] }}`. For example, to define the zone as a parameter in the template describe previously, replace all instances of the zone with `properties["zone"]`. Similarly, you can replace the variable portions of the `machineType` property as well.

Environment Variables

In addition to parameters, templates can also use environment variables. Deployment Manager replaces the environment variables with actual values from your environment and populates this information in your deployment manifest. By specifying environment variables, you can reuse templates across different Cloud Platform projects or with different deployment names.

The following are valid environment variables:

- `project`: Your Cloud Platform project
- `name`: The `name` property in the configuration file for the template
- `deployment`: The deployment name
- `type`: The type defined in the configuration file

In Jinja, you can define an environment variable using the syntax `{{ env["project"] }}`. Once the parameters and environment variables have been defined in your templates, you can set the values of these variables in your configuration file.

Property References

References help you to define a property once and refer to it from several resource declarations. Using references, you can avoid using hard-coded values. In addition, references are useful because certain values are not defined until a configuration is deployed, such as a resource's `selfLink` or system-generated ID. In these cases, you can still point to these properties using a reference.

Creating a reference to another property creates a dependency between these two properties. Deployment Manager resolves these dependencies in order, and if any references do not resolve successfully, that could cause your template to be invalid.

References are declared using the format `$(ref.RESOURCE_NAME.PROPERTY)` and defined like regular resources. In the example, you centralize the definition of the network resource and refer to it from the VM definition. You will launch two VMs to show the usefulness of the reference feature.

Now you can define the parameters—zone and machine type—environment variables, and references in your template and define the corresponding values in your configuration file. Listings 15-11 to 15-13 show the contents of the updated template and configuration files, deploy the resources, and show the corresponding output.

Listing 15-11. Updated Template for Launching Compute Engine Instances Using Parameters, Environment Variables, and References

```
{% set NETWORK = env["name"] + "-network" %}

resources:

- name: {{ NETWORK }}
  type: compute.v1.network
  properties:
    IPv4Range: 10.240.0.0/16

- name: ce-vm-3
  type: compute.v1.instance
  properties:
    zone: {{ properties["zone"] }}
    machineType: https://www.googleapis.com/compute/v1/projects/{{ env["project"] }}/zones/
```

```
{{ properties["zone"] }}/machineTypes/{{ properties["machinetype"] }}
    disks:
    - deviceName: boot
      type: PERSISTENT
      boot: true
      autoDelete: true
      initializeParams:
        diskName: pdisk-ce-vm-3
        sourceImage: https://www.googleapis.com/compute/v1/projects/debian-cloud/global/
images/
debian-7-wheezy-v20150325
    networkInterfaces:
    - network: $(ref.{{ NETWORK }}.selfLink)
      accessConfigs:
      - name: External NAT
        type: ONE_TO_ONE_NAT

- name: ce-vm-4
  type: compute.v1.instance
  properties:
    zone: {{ properties["zone"] }}
    machineType: https://www.googleapis.com/compute/v1/projects/{{ env["project"] }}/zones/
{{ properties["zone"] }}/machineTypes/{{ properties["machinetype"] }}
    disks:
    - deviceName: boot
      type: PERSISTENT
      boot: true
      autoDelete: true
      initializeParams:
        diskName: pdisk-ce-vm-4
        sourceImage: https://www.googleapis.com/compute/v1/projects/debian-cloud/global/
images/
debian-7-wheezy-v20150325
    networkInterfaces:
    - network: $(ref.{{ NETWORK }}.selfLink)
      accessConfigs:
      - name: External NAT
        type: ONE_TO_ONE_NAT
```

Listing 15-12. Updated Configuration File Defining a Zone and Machine Type

```
imports:
- path: ce-vm-3.jinja

resources:
- name: ce-vm-cdm-3
  type: ce-vm-3.jinja
  properties:
    zone: asia-east1-a
    machinetype: n1-standard-2
```

Listing 15-13. Deploying Two VMs Defined Using Parameters, Environment Variables, and References

```
$ gcloud beta deployment-manager deployments create third-ce-vm --config ce-vm-3.yaml
Waiting for create operation operation-1430185335584-514bef8e3f501-c70b6ee1-9a402195 to
complete
...done.
Create operation operation-1430185335584-514bef8e3f501-c70b6ee1-9a402195 completed
successfully.
NAME                  TYPE                  ID                   UPDATE_STATE  ERRORS
ce-vm-3               compute.v1.instance   5896613980873644946  COMPLETED     -
ce-vm-4               compute.v1.instance   2625345568575282066  COMPLETED     -
ce-vm-cdm-3-network   compute.v1.network    1540334360275934098  COMPLETED     -
```

Managing Deployments

You have already seen how to do a deployment. As the complexity of the templates and configuration file increases, it is inevitable that there will be errors in resource declarations and definitions. Depending on the location of the errors, it may take a few minutes for Deployment Manager to detect them. More important, Deployment Manager may have partially deployed some resources by this time.

In order to save valuable time and money, you can test the configuration and template files using Deployment Manager before you actually instantiate Cloud Platform resources. You do so by using the `--preview` option to the `deployments create` command. This option fully expands your configuration file and any imported template files, creating a manifest. Creating a manifest involves no resource-deployment activity on the server side—that is, no Cloud Platform resources are created.

Listing 15-14 and Listing 15-15 preview the example deployment of launching two VMs and show the output.

Listing 15-14. Previewing a Cloud Deployment Before Instantiating the Resources

```
$ gcloud beta deployment-manager deployments create --preview third-ce-vm --config ce-vm-3.
yaml
Waiting for create operation operation-1430267266410-514d20c592611-2ca35474-4f76abbd to
complete
...done.
Create operation operation-1430267266410-514d20c592611-2ca35474-4f76abbd completed
successfully.
NAME                  TYPE                  ID                   UPDATE_STATE  ERRORS
ce-vm-3               compute.v1.instance   5578641432944417640  PENDING       -
ce-vm-4               compute.v1.instance   6569519005498710888  PENDING       -
ce-vm-cdm-3-network   compute.v1.network    1516290785466489704  PENDING       -
```

Listing 15-15. Listing All Deployments (Notice the `PREVIEWING` State for Your Deployment)

```
$ gcloud beta deployment-manager deployments list
NAME         STATE       INTENT  ID                   DESCRIPTION  MANIFEST  ERRORS
third-ce-vm  PREVIEWING  -       1706880805329087175  -            -         -
```

If the preview is successful, you know the configuration and template files are good. At this stage, you can proceed to do an actual deployment. After a preview is finished, you can do a `deployment update` to instantiate the resources in your configuration. Listing 15-16 shows the output for the previously previewed configuration, and Listing 15-17 lists the deployments.

Listing 15-16. Deploying a Previewed Configuration

```
$ gcloud beta deployment-manager deployments update third-ce-vm
Waiting for update operation operation-1430267335011-514d2106feab9-95c5aab6-6c6ac55d to
complete
...done.
Update operation operation-1430267335011-514d2106feab9-95c5aab6-6c6ac55d completed
successfully.
NAME                  TYPE                  ID                   UPDATE_STATE  ERRORS
ce-vm-3               compute.v1.instance   5578641432944417640  COMPLETED     -
ce-vm-4               compute.v1.instance   6569519005498710888  COMPLETED     -
ce-vm-cdm-3-network   compute.v1.network    1516290785466489704  COMPLETED     -
```

Listing 15-17. Listing All Deployments (Notice the DEPLOYED State for Your Deployment)

```
$ gcloud beta deployment-manager deployments list
NAME  STATE  INTENT  ID  DESCRIPTION  MANIFEST  ERRORS
third-ce-vm  DEPLOYED  -  1706880805329087175  -  manifest-1430267267458-4be13f82-e12b-
491d-b476-963c102dbd26  -
```

Although previewing and creating a deployment are useful to ensure that the required IT resources have been launched, the requirement could change frequently—that is, you may want to add more resources to or remove resources from a deployment on the go. Deleting and launching a new deployment may not be an option if some of the resources are in use. To satisfy this need, Deployment Manager has an `update` option to the `deployment` command. We will now introduce you to the *update* option using an example of removing deployed resources. In the following commands, we will deploy 2 instances and 1 network and then shrink the deployment by deleting 1 instance.

Listing 15-18. Deploying 2 Compute Engine Instances using the Listing #15-11

```
$ gcloud beta deployment-manager deployments create sixth-ce-vm --config ce-vm-3.yaml
Waiting for create operation operation-1431073106819-5158dac2df7b8-40b2ae14-6317e280 to
complete...done.
Create operation operation-1431073106819-5158dac2df7b8-40b2ae14-6317e280 completed
successfully.
NAME                   TYPE                  ID                   UPDATE_STATE  ERRORS
ce-vm-3                compute.v1.instance   5516648961619906488  COMPLETED     -
ce-vm-4                compute.v1.instance   2109741715427545016  COMPLETED     -
ce-vm-cdm-3-network2   compute.v1.network    5504360587739647928  COMPLETED     -
```

You should now update *Listing #15-11* and remove the stanza that defines Compute Engine instance "ce-vm-4". Once this is done, rerun the previous command replacing the "*create*" option with "*update*" option. We now show you the output from this execution.

```
# Shrinking the previous deployment by using a modified Listing #15-11
$ gcloud beta deployment-manager deployments update sixth-ce-vm --config ce-vm-3.yaml
Waiting for update operation operation-1431073497256-5158dc3739041-1128b460-7495fc42 to
complete...done.
Update operation operation-1431073497256-5158dc3739041-1128b460-7495fc42 completed
successfully.
```

```
NAME                   TYPE                ID                  UPDATE_STATE  ERRORS
ce-vm-3                compute.v1.instance 5516648961619906488 COMPLETED     -
ce-vm-cdm-3-network2   compute.v1.network  5504360587739647928 COMPLETED     -
```

Releasing unneeded resources is a core attribute of cloud computing. By simply deleting a deployment, you can release all resources that have been launched through that deployment in a single step. Let's delete the deployment that launched two VMs:

```
$ gcloud beta deployment-manager deployments delete third-ce-vm
The following deployments will be deleted:
- third-ce-vm

Do you want to continue (Y/n)?  Y

Waiting for delete operation operation-1430188598599-514bfbb619d58-c6ee4cbe-cc5f31a6 to
complete
...done.
Delete operation operation-1430188598599-514bfbb619d58-c6ee4cbe-cc5f31a6 completed
successfully.
---
endTime: '2015-04-27T19:37:41.220-07:00'
id: '6726339243701128408'
insertTime: '2015-04-27T19:36:39.405-07:00'
kind: deploymentmanager#operation
name: operation-1430188598599-514bfbb619d58-c6ee4cbe-cc5f31a6
operationType: delete
progress: 100
selfLink: https://www.googleapis.com/deploymentmanager/v2beta2/projects/cloud-platform-book/
global/operations/operation-1430188598599-514bfbb619d58-c6ee4cbe-cc5f31a6
startTime: '2015-04-27T19:36:39.849-07:00'
status: DONE
targetId: '373709088201333655'
targetLink: https://www.googleapis.com/deploymentmanager/v2beta2/projects/cloud-platform-
book/
global/deployments/third-ce-vm
user: cloudplatformbook@gmail.com
```

You can choose to re-create a deployment using the original configuration file, but note that this is considered a new deployment with new resources.

Source and Binary Code Management

This section gives you a brief overview of some of the hosted services from Cloud Platform for managing your application's source codes and binary blobs.

Cloud Repositories

Cloud Repositories are fully featured Git repositories hosted on the Cloud Platform. Every Cloud Platform project has an associated Cloud Repository. Cloud Repositories are free and can store up to 500MB of source files.

You can configure a Git repository on your workstation to use the Cloud Repository as its remote or you can connect hosted Git repositories from GitHub or Bitbucket to your Cloud Repository. Cloud Repositories support the standard git commands, including `push`, `pull`, `clone`, and `log`. For more information on Cloud Repositories, visit `https://cloud.google.com/tools/repo/cloud-repositories`. If you are not familiar with the Git source code management system, see `http://git-scm.com`.

Push-to-Deploy

Push-to-Deploy is a hosted change-management service from Cloud Platform that is applicable to Google App Engine applications. Push-to-Deploy monitors a Cloud Repository—the master branch by default—and when a new source code commit is registered, triggers the automated process of building, testing, and deploying a new version of your App Engine application.

Pushing to the master branch of your Cloud Repository either directly from a local Git repository or via a web-hosted repository triggers any configured automated deployment. Push-to-Deploy uses the Jenkins continuous integration tool to configure and manage automatic build and deployment.

Jenkins, along with programming language–specific build and test tools and the Google Cloud SDK, should be installed on a Compute Engine VM instance to be used with the Push-to-Deploy service. You can use Push-to-Deploy with App Engine applications developed in Java, Python, and Go languages. For more information on Push-to-Deploy, please visit `https://cloud.google.com/tools/repo/push-to-deploy`.

Source Code Tools

Developers Console, along with Cloud Repositories, includes several built-in tools that help you to securely browse, edit, and troubleshoot the source code in your Cloud Repositories using a web browser. The following is some of the functionality:

- *Inspecting source code:* Using a web browser, you can view and modify a file or directory. By default, Developers Console displays the master branch of a Cloud Repository, but you can switch branches easily with the Developers Console UI. You can also do a diff of the current version with any of the historic versions.
- *Deploying an instant fix:* Developers Console allows you to edit and commit changes to files that are hosted in Cloud Repositories. Making an edit and committing the change triggers the automated deployment, if any, associated with your project.
- *Linking log events to source code:* If you use Cloud Repositories to store App Engine applications, then Cloud Platform automatically links stack traces in App Engine logs to the actual line of code. You can use the App Engine Logs Viewer to examine this. This feature is currently available for App Engine applications developed in the Java, Python, and PHP programming languages.
- *Viewing commits and commit history:* Using a web browser, you can see the latest commit, commit time, and author for each file or directory. You can also view the full contents of any particular commit in your repository.

For more information about source code tools, see `https://cloud.google.com/tools/repo/source-tools`.

Google Container Registry

Docker provides a free public registry to store Docker images. These Docker images are accessible to all users in these platforms. In many cases, you may not want to store your images where they are publicly accessible. In this case, you need to use a private registry.

Cloud Platform provides a secure, private Docker image storage called Google Container Registry. The registry can be accessed through an HTTPS endpoint, so you can pull images from any machine, whether it's a Compute Engine instance or your own hardware. Your private registry location is defined by appending your project's ID to the `gcr.io` domain: `gcr.io/your-project-id`.

Hosted Security Services

This section provides a brief overview of some of the hosted security services from Cloud Platform.

Cloud Debugger

The Cloud Debugger lets you inspect the state of a Java application at any code location without stopping or slowing it down. The debugger makes it easier to view the application state without adding logging statements. The debugger adds less than 10ms to the request latency only when the application state is captured. In most cases, this is not noticeable by users. The Cloud Debugger requires access to your application source code, which must be stored in the Cloud Repository associated with your project.

You can use the Cloud Debugger with

- Java App Engine applications running on a Managed VM
- Any Java application running on a Compute Engine instance

Cloud Security Scanner

The Google Cloud Security Scanner identifies security vulnerabilities in App Engine applications. Cloud Security Scanner crawls an App Engine application, follows all links within the scope of the starting URLs, and attempts to exercise as many user inputs and event handlers as possible. Only regular App Engine instances are supported. This means you cannot use the Cloud Security Scanner with App Engine Managed VMs, Compute Engine, or any other compute services. The Cloud Security Scanner tests for cross-site scripting vulnerabilities, mixed content over HTTP and HTTPS and other such class of vulnerabilities.

Cloud Trace

Cloud Trace allows you to view the remote procedure calls (RPCs) invoked by your App Engine application, typically called in response to incoming queries. An App Engine RPC is a round-trip network call between your application and an App Engine service. Examples of App Engine services include data store calls, Memcache calls, and URL fetch. You can view and analyze the time taken to complete each RPC.

Cloud Trace selects a representative subset of requests to your application and traces all RPCs made by your application when handling those requests. The traces can help you find performance bottlenecks in your application. Examples of bottlenecks include unnecessary service calls, service calls fetching the same data repeatedly, and serial service calls that can be batched or executed in parallel.

Cloud Trace generates a visual distribution of latencies for a set of requests. You can extract trace samples for different latency percentiles by analyzing the traces and generate reports. You can also compare the performance of two sets of requests. For example, you can compare the performance of your application before and after a release by comparing the traces for requests received.

Summary

In this chapter, you primarily learned about the Cloud Deployment Manager service. Using Deployment Manager, you can launch and manage the entire lifecycle of a set of Cloud Platform resources as a group. In addition, you can change the configuration of a deployed system to accommodate changing IT demands.

Following this, you learned about several other tools you can use to manage the lifecycle of your source code and binary builds. The primary tool is the Cloud Repository, which serves as the back end for several other tools. Finally, you learned about security and performance tools that help you discover security vulnerabilities, debug your application, and identify performance bottlenecks. You should now have a good understanding of the tools that will help you with resource deployment and code management.

CHAPTER 16

Architecture Recipes for Google Cloud Platform

In this concluding chapter, we take a broader look at Google Cloud Platform technologies and approach Cloud Platform from an architectural perspective. We propose solutions for real-life example use cases using applicable Cloud Platform products. You see how to design simple architectures and progressively enhance them so that they are more scalable and fault tolerant than the previous generation.

The example scenarios are a representative subset of actual Internet-scale web applications that developers are likely to deploy on cloud computing platforms, including Cloud Platform. The proposed architectures are suitable to a wide variety of audiences from individual developers and startups to enterprises. We refer to these architectures as "suggested" and not "recommended" because it is possible to design a wide variety of architectures that essentially produce the same end result.

Use Case 1: Using an Unmanaged Infrastructure to Host Internet-Scale Web Apps

Organizations are increasingly using online applications to support their operations. These applications may be self-developed, but many organizations are adopting open source applications as well. The lean IT model that is becoming prevalent means organizations are hosting their applications in third-party datacenters, and the adoption of the public cloud is also rapidly increasing. This use case uses the example of a content management system (CMS).

A CMS is a computer application that manages the lifecycle of a piece of content—creating, organizing, publishing, updating, and deleting—from a dashboard interface, usually web-based. Content varies in type from text and images to videos. A CMS is often used to run web sites containing blogs, news, and so on. The value proposition of a CMS is that it disconnects the content from the presentation so that developers don't need to hand-code a web site. Moreover, CMSs are increasingly used as workflow-management systems.

This scenario uses WordPress (`https://wordpress.org`), a popular open source CMS. You deploy WordPress on Cloud Platform and subsequently scale it to be able to handle a large number of simultaneous requests. WordPress has been developed using the PHP programming language (`http://php.net`) and uses a relational database to store a persistent state. Although WordPress can be installed on any operating system that can support PHP, it is typically installed on a Linux-based operating system such as Debian (`www.debian.org`). On the database side, an open source MySQL database server (`www.mysql.com`) is typically used.

Think Big, Start Small, Scale Fast

Let's take the example of three individuals: Adam, Brad, and Clif. Adam is an individual developer who works as a freelance consultant and is cost conscious. Brad works for an Internet startup and juggles multiple tasks such as projects, system administration etc; he wants his IT infrastructure to be reliable and moderately scalable while being affordable. Clif works as an architect and IT administrator at a large enterprise that has customers in multiple time zones and geographies. Response times and infrastructure reliability are critical. Although cost is not a concern for his employer, Clif insists on getting the best ROI. Let's suppose that each of them has been tasked with setting up a CMS and has decided to use WordPress.

Architecture 1: Start Small—Web Apps Using Google Compute Engine and Google Cloud DNS

Let's suppose you fit the profile of Adam. Having made the software choice, you would like to know how to go about installing it for your one-man shop with Cloud Platform. In addition, you would like to have a web presence ASAP and also minimize the cost, because you are not expecting a lot of traffic initially.

In order to run a web app such as WordPress, all you need is a single server. This server can be a physical system or a virtual machine. Using Cloud Platform, you can create a single Compute Engine instance (a VM) and install the entire software stack on it. This would meet your objective of going live ASAP at a minimal cost.

Google is a big proponent of open source software and makes it easy to consume community-developed software on Cloud Platform by providing a full software stack installer called Cloud Launcher (`https://cloud.google.com/launcher/explore`). Cloud Launcher hosts software installers from Bitnami Inc. (`https://bitnami.com`) and Google Cloud Deployment Manager (`https://cloud.google.com/deployment-manager`).

We recommend that you use the Cloud Launcher (click-to-deploy version) to set up WordPress on Compute Engine in a single step. The following is the software stack that click-to-deploy sets up:

- Debian 7 Linux
- Apache HTTP server
- PHP language runtime
- MySQL database
- WordPress CMS 4.x

For more information on installing WordPress using click-to-deploy, see `https://cloud.google.com/solutions/wordpress/click-to-deploy`. If you are keen to know what happens in the background when you click the button, read the deployment-details article at `https://cloud.google.com/solutions/wordpress/deployment-details`.

Cloud Launcher provides a pre-composed and managed software stack so that sysadmins can easily deploy an application and all its prerequisites. Some sysadmins prefer a manual approach and are not comfortable using a managed service. These are the steps to manually set up WordPress on a single server, followed by some best practices:

1. Launch a Compute Engine instance using a Debian OS disk image.
2. Set up the required system software stack: Apache, MySQL (client and server), and PHP.
3. Install and configure WordPress.
4. Assign a static network IP address.
5. Configure a domain using Cloud DNS.

When using Compute Engine, you can launch instances that vary according to the number of CPU cores and memory. We recommend using a machine size of at least n1-standard-2 for your VM. The 2 in the name refers to the number of virtual CPUs; and because Google uses hyperthreaded two-core CPUs in its Cloud Platform, instantiating a two-core CPU means you have an entire CPU to you. Instances that use single-core CPUs may be impacted by other instances if the applications on them are CPU bound. See Chapter 4 for a detailed introduction to Compute Engine and `https://cloud.google.com/compute` for complete product details.

We recommend using Cloud DNS (`https://cloud.google.com/dns`) to serve domain-name records that point to applications hosted on Compute Engine. Cloud DNS is a reliable, inexpensive, authoritative, hosted DNS solution. See Chapter 13 for a detailed introduction to quickly understand this hosted DNS service.

Let's look at the merits and shortcomings of the infrastructure that you have just set up. The setup uses two Cloud Platform products: Compute Engine and Cloud DNS. Using these two reliable and high-performance products means your site has world-class infrastructure. The cost is low because you are using a single VM to power your entire web site. Cloud Platform is also cheaper than Amazon Web Services as of today. See the blog post at `http://googlecloudplatform.blogspot.sg/2015/01/understanding-cloud-pricing.html` for an excellent guide to understand cloud pricing.

There are several shortcomings in this design:

- Regardless of the initial size of the Compute Engine instance, if the actual traffic is higher than expected, your web site infrastructure will not be able to scale to meet demand.
- Hosting the MySQL server inside a VM means you have to perform database-management tasks likes backups, restoration (if required), and software updates. This is in addition to regular system-update tasks. File system corruption means your database is also affected.
- Again, having the MySQL server inside a VM means it will be difficult to architect advanced architectures such as using a load balancer or autoscaler because in such cases WordPress software in other VMs might need to access this instance. Opening software ports for critical software like MySQL might reduce the security posture, especially if SSH access is enabled for this VM.

Hence, the suggested architecture is sufficient for you to get started hosting a web app, but it is not recommended for production environments. In the next architectural evolution, we address the primary shortcoming of this architecture: hosting MySQL in a Compute Engine instance. You will move MySQL off the Compute Engine instance.

Architecture 2: Scale Fast—Web App Using Google Compute Engine, Google Cloud SQL, and Google Cloud DNS

In this scenario, your requirements are aligned with Brad, who works at an Internet startup. In this architecture evolution, you use the hosted MySQL service from Cloud Platform, Cloud SQL. Cloud SQL is a fully managed relational database service and is 100% binary compatible with MySQL. For a detailed introduction to Cloud SQL, read Chapter 7; and refer to `https://cloud.google.com/sql` for complete product information. The following is the updated installation sequence:

1. Launch a Compute Engine instance using Debian OS disk image.
2. Create a Cloud SQL instance with the appropriate technical specifications.
3. Set up the required system software stack: Apache, MySQL client, and PHP.

4. Install and configure WordPress using Cloud SQL.
5. Assign a static network IP address.
6. Configure a domain using Cloud DNS.

This architecture is more scalable and reliable compared to the previous one, and some of the important (but mundane) tasks such as database backup and restoration and software updates are taken care by Cloud Platform. This architecture will also serve as the foundation for further architectural evolutions that will be required to support an even higher-traffic web site.

On the shortcomings side, all incoming web requests are served by a single instance, and hence the performance of the web site is directly related to the computational resources in the VM: CPU capacity, disk, and Internet bandwidth. When the traffic pattern changes, replacing the instance with a higher-capacity instance is an option, but this means the web site is not available during reboots and the process itself is manual, limiting the response time to spiky traffic.

Let's continue the architectural evolution and build a next-generation architecture that can respond to changing traffic automatically and with less latency.

Architecture 3: Think Big—Web App Hosting Using Compute Engine, Load Balancer, Autoscaler, Health Checker, Cloud SQL, and Cloud DNS

In this scenario, assume your needs are aligned with Clif, who works for a multinational corporation. A few characteristics are essential for an infrastructure that is able to automatically respond to changing traffic requests:

- Split incoming requests to a VM cluster.
- Automatically add and remove VMs from an instance group.
- Automatically check the health of VMs.

Compute Engine provides all these facilities to enable you to construct an autoscaling infrastructure that responds to varying incoming web requests. In this architecture, you use the following technologies from Cloud Platform in addition to Compute Engine and Cloud SQL from the previous architectural iteration:

- *HTTP load balancer:* The HTTP load balancer is a global resource in Cloud Platform. This means its scope is not limited to a region or zone. It provides a single IP address–based entry point for your web application. You can use this IP address to configure the DNS records for your domain. This way, you don't need to do DNS-based round-robin load balancing. The HTTP load balancer can also do latency-based routing. This means it is able to route the traffic to your VMs in the nearest Cloud Platform region.
- *Autoscaler:* Autoscaler has the ability to add or remove VMs depending on the volume of incoming requests. It launches new VMs instances using user-defined instance templates. Autoscaler detects the health of the individual instances and uses only healthy instances to distribute incoming traffic.
- *Health checks:* Cloud Platform can also do periodic health checks of VMs to detect whether they are able to continue servicing incoming requests.

Cloud Platform has a presence on three continents: North America, Europe, and Asia. Using Developers Console or the `gcloud` tool, you can set up VMs in any or all these regions. Organizations typically choose a hosting location based on the network latency between their infrastructure and their customers. In addition, they want to publish a single network entry point to their applications.

In this example scenario, you should set up at least one instance group in each Cloud Platform region/zone. Because instance groups are a zonal resource, you can set up more than one instance group in one region. Organizations typically do such a setup for their larger markets: for example, they may have an instance group in the Eastern United States and another in the West. Each managed instance group in a Cloud Platform region autoscales independently of other instance groups and depends only on the amount of incoming traffic to that instance group. The HTTP load balancer then distributes incoming requests to the nearest instance groups based on network latency.

Let's see how this setup is useful. As requests increase in one region/zone—say, in the United States during the day—more instances are added in the United States region. These instances are shut down at night when the load decreases. All this is done automatically without human intervention. Similarly, as the load increases in other geographies, such as Europe or Asia, instances are added to the nearest deployed region. This way, you can build a follow-the-sun IT architecture without procuring physical infrastructure on the various continents.

Although it is easy to setup a load-balancing, autoscaling infrastructure manually, Google has made it easy to create file-based configuration that you can simply execute to deploy the same resources. You can achieve this by using the Deployment Manager to configure and manage the Compute Engine virtual instances, load balancer, and autoscaler.

In this use case, we have proposed several ways of hosting web apps using different technologies from Cloud Platform. The theme underpinning this architectural evolution is the migration from user-managed to Google-managed technologies. You started with only Compute Engine and Cloud DNS and later added Cloud SQL, a load balancer, an autoscaler, and a health checker.

Use Case 2: Using Managed Infrastructure to Host Internet-Scale Web Apps

Today, full-system virtualization is used extensively in both private and public clouds. Virtualization is used to pack many VMs into a single physical machine. Although virtualization has produced significant gains in reducing server real estate, it has also introduced inefficiencies to the applications hosted on the guest operating systems. Each application instruction now needs to be translated by the guest OS and host OS. In this use case, we look at a technology called *containers* that seeks to eliminate an OS layer, and how you can use it to package and host applications in a managed way.

Architecture 1: Autoscaling Web Apps with Google Container Engine

Since 2013, there has been rejuvenated mainstream interest in packaging applications as binary containers. Although containers were invented a few decades ago in big iron mainframes, the concept is relatively new to mainstream computing, especially cloud computing. For public cloud computing providers, supporting application containers means they are able to package more applications per server.

Containerized applications appeal to both developers and IT operations staff. Applications that require different libraries, including different versions of the same library, can run simultaneously in a single operating system instance. Previously, running different OS instances, usually using VMs, fulfilled this requirement. For IT operations, managing containerized applications means the server real estate is more effectively used.

Linux is the only operating system among the three mainstream operating systems (Windows, Mac OS X, and Linux) to support application containers (as of this writing). In Linux, system-level features in the Linux kernel, some of which were invented and open sourced by Google, power application containers. Google has been using containers to launch and scale all of its products, such as Google Maps and Google Search, for nearly a decade.

Docker's format for application containers is widely accepted in the industry; Docker is also leading an industry effort to standardize the container's format and interface. In addition to individual application containers, you need a container-orchestration platform to manage a group of containers. In 2014, Google open sourced such a system called Kubernetes, which the company has been using internally.

Container Engine is the easiest and most transparent way to package your application using Docker container technology and scale your application using Kubernetes. Using the `gcloud` tool, you can package your applications as Docker containers and create a system design that automatically scales. Container Engine takes care of deployment and managed of your containerized application.

We recommend that you read Chapter 6 to learn more about Container Engine. In addition, the following URLs provide helpful further reading on the individual technologies:

- *Container Engine:* `https://cloud.google.com/container-engine`
- *Kubernetes container orchestration platform:* `http://kubernetes.io`
- *Docker container technology:* `https://www.docker.com`

Architecture 2: Managed Autoscaling with Google App Engine Managed VMs

App Engine is a platform-as-a-service (PaaS) product and was the first Cloud Platform product. App Engine's application execution environment was simply called the *sandboxed runtime*. App Engine mandated that applications follow a specific architecture to take advantage of the platform's scalability. Although this requirement was easily satisfied by new applications, it was difficult for legacy and proprietary applications to use App Engine as an execution platform. One of the difficulties most cited by App Engine developers is the inability to write to the local file system. This is because in the sandboxed execution environment, the local file system is read-only. Modern applications like WordPress auto-update themselves over the web and host plug-ins that extend the core functionality. Both of these features require scratch space; hence the need for a writable local file system.

Google has satisfied many of these developers' wishes in the Managed VMs runtime of App Engine. In this runtime, proprietary and legacy applications are fully supported, and each instance of the runtime has a writable local scratch disk. In addition, the Managed VMs runtime fully supports Docker containers. This means you can package your application as a Docker container, and App Engine takes care of the rest.

See the section on Managed VMs in Chapter 6 for a detailed introduction to this exciting new App Engine runtime. For information on the product, refer to the product documentation at `https://cloud.google.com/appengine/docs/managed-vms`. WordPress is also available as a Docker container at `https://registry.hub.docker.com/_/wordpress`.

In this use case, we shifted gears and used two completed managed platforms—Container Engine and App Engine Managed VMs—for hosting web apps. In the next use, we will share with you the Cloud Platform technologies that you can use to analyze Big Data whether it is generated from your Cloud Platform resources or from external sources.

Use Case 3: Doing Big Data Analytics, Google Style

Big Data is more than a buzzword today. Organizations are realizing that they can produce better value for themselves and their customers and shareholders by mining the data they have accumulated over the years. In addition, because the cost of storage keeps falling, organizations can capture and store more data for future analysis than ever before. Moreover, as more organizations adopt the lean IT model of using public infrastructure and add more applications for automation, more log entries will be generated. Sysadmins find it essential to regularly parse the logs to detect any application or system issues.

There are two big challenges when handling Big Data: data storage and retrieval/processing. It is not uncommon for organizations to have data that spans multiple years. Storing (that is, making a copy for analysis) such massive and growing data is a Herculean task, and retrieving and processing it in real time to produce valuable information is equally challenging. These challenges inhibit developers from assembling a solution using foundational technologies like Compute Engine and persistent disks.

Google provides a dedicated product called Google BigQuery that you can use to capture, store, and analyze multi-terabytes of data in minutes if not seconds. Let's consider a scenario in which you would like to analyze the access logs generated by the Apache web servers that you set up in use case 1. Let's also suppose that the application software you are using is WordPress and the operating system is Debian Linux.

There are two predominant forms of data analytics: historic and real-time data analytics. Historic or time-lagged analytics is about analyzing old data, perhaps using new queries or machine-learning models, with the objective of discovering comprehensive trends. Real-time data analytics, on the other hand, is about doing quick analysis to classify events into different categories, usually good and bad.

The first step in doing data analytics with BigQuery (or any other tool) is to prepare the data using the extract, transform, load (ETL) philosophy. For historic data analysis, the extraction phase simply involves copying the access logs over and performing the transformation to load the data into BigQuery. Several tools are available that do the transformation; following are two that you can use to import data into BigQuery. You can install either of these open source applications in the VMs, process the access and error logs, and load the transformed data into BigQuery:

- *Fluentd:* Open source data collector, unified logging layer (`www.fluentd.org`)
- *Logstash:* Open source log management (`http://logstash.net`)

At the same time, more organizations are performing real-time log analysis. This is useful from a security perspective as well and is typically used to detect a cyber attack or an intrusion. BigQuery supports live streaming of data as well. See the article at `https://cloud.google.com/solutions/real-time/fluentd-bigquery` to learn how to use Fluentd and BigQuery to do real-time data analytics.

In Chapter 10, we cover BigQuery in a detailed way and show you how to perform data analytics using the command-line tool.

Use Case 4: The MVP Approach

It is interesting and exciting to see the rise and fall of innovative ideas, projects, and prototypes—especially those that try to capture and tackle problems in ways that have not been attempted before. Whether the unknown relates to the market, technology, audience, usefulness, or feasibility, there is a need to test theories and assumptions in an effort to burn as few resources as possible. The minimum viable product (MVP) as a concept has helped enormously to realize concepts at a very low cost, by making us understand that it is possible to create something that is miles from a final product but that is sufficient to address some of the unknowns that cannot be proven in theory. This concept is supported by initiatives and efforts from companies, individuals, authors, and other parties that enable creators, entrepreneurs, inventors, and professionals with the tools they need to put this in practice. Google is one of these parties—and not the only one—and provides a handful of products, services, training, and other resources that are crucial to the success of approaches based on MVP, fast development, quick iterative processes, or the lean movement in general.

It feels almost like fiction that you can have thousands of machines at hand in a matter of seconds to run whatever you wish. It makes us think of the scene in *The Lion King* when Mufasa tells his son, "Look, Simba: everything the light touches is our kingdom" while the sun rises on the horizon. And you have access not only to machines, but also to clever intelligence that can orchestrate these machines for you. In summary, this means if you can give up control in order to benefit time and resources, you can build your MVP in a matter of days, if not a single weekend. This is precisely the case here, where control is not necessary but time is precious. After all, MVPs are equally valuable whether they are used for further development or end up in the trash bin. This is because the win situation is not keeping everything you build but learning what works and what does not work for your product, idea, or test.

In this use case, the goal is to assess building a mobile application with an API, from an architectural standpoint, in the least amount of time and using the fewest resources possible. The application is called Mobbo, and what it does is much nicer than its name. Mobbo is a mobile application that allows users to share their location privately and anonymously so that it can be processed and aggregated massively to extract interesting results, but mainly to show where "the people" are right now. Note that you are not sharing locations with names—only anonymous data. The options are wide, but this can be useful in various scenarios. For instance, imagine you are planning a trip by car and you want to make sure you avoid the common traffic jams in your city; you can check the map and avoid busy routes. Or you plan to go for a drink with friends tonight, and you want to know what venue is hot in the city.

The target cost of the project is 0, and the time to develop is a weekend. You can see the potential of such an approach, because you are getting to test something that has a tangible application in a very economic way.

■ **Note** The numbers estimated are not optimistic. They represent the real costs and time necessary to build this prototype. This application is open source and available in this book's GitHub profile. You can find the API at `https://github.com/GoogleCloudPlatformBook/vulgus-api` and the Android application at `https://github.com/GoogleCloudPlatformBook/vulgus-android`.

Let's define the requirements of this specific project so that we can extrapolate them to more generic cases. The requirements for the API are as follows:

- Serving information.
- Reading information about the current status of the city—that is, where is everybody?
- Writing the anonymous position of the user.

To fulfill these needs, first you need to choose the technology for the API. Remember that you want to build something as quickly and in the most straightforward manner possible. For this purpose, App Engine is a great option. With 4 to 6 files and not more than 100 effective lines of code, you can create a fully managed, auto-scalable, worldwide API with a couple of endpoints, secure access, a data store to persist data, and a handful of other features. To read more about App Engine, see Chapter 5.

Using App Engine also helps you benefit from a very convenient service included in the platform. Search API,[1] in addition to featuring full-text search, also works with locations in such a way that you can perform distance queries; that is, given a geolocated point, you can query for elements within a radius of your choice. This is very useful for an application like this.

[1]Documentation for Search API: `https://cloud.google.com/appengine/docs/python/search`.

Another relevant aspect of choosing App Engine for this kind of project is its free usage tier. This means you can use App Engine to develop your application for free, because most of the time you will not exceed the free quota when developing an MVP.

Summarizing, your API uses the following:

- App Engine for hosting, securing, and serving.
- Search API to work with locations

■ **Note** Due to the nature of this application, if the number of stored locations grows to a certain level, it could be counter-effective to handle and send all of them to connected clients. Because of that, it can be very useful to add Google Cloud Dataflow to the package, to process incoming locations from users and generate aggregated and reduced information, which is then stored using Search API so that clients can access this information later. Nevertheless, it is not healthy to optimize MVPs and prototypes for massive use, because doing so collides with the definition of prototyping.

On the mobile side, the idea is to build an application in Android due to the flexibility of the system, the cost to share and distribute internal builds, and the integration with Google APIs. In the rare instance of needing to prototype on more than one mobile platform at a time, it is sensible to consider cross-platform approaches like Cordova,[2] Xamarin,[3] and so on, such as directly exposing a web site optimized for mobile.

These are the requirements for your Android app:

- Show a map with points and/or polygons.
- Communicate with an API.

Even though these are very basic requirements, there are ways you can accelerate and enhance the development experience. You have to show a map; the Android SDK and your phone are well equipped for that. Integrating a Google Map[4] in your Android application is straightforward.

When developing an MVP (and most of the rest of the time) it is crucial to write as little code as possible, benefiting from well-developed and -tested code. A vast number of libraries are out there that do an impressive job of what they intend to solve. Two examples are OkHttp,[5] a networking library for Android that you can use to quickly begin making calls to your API, and Gson,[6] a library that makes it quick and easy to serialize objects into JSON format.

If you plan to develop for more than one mobile client, consider using Google Cloud Endpoints, which helps you annotate your API in App Engine to dynamically generate client libraries to connect to your API from JS, iOS, and Android clients. This removes a lot of friction and repetitive work when your application is living in a highly changing environment. To read more about Cloud Endpoints, see Chapter 14.

That's it: two primary technologies, two days of work, an API, and a mobile platform, and your MVP is running and can be used by a fair number of users—enough to give you the insights you need to choose your next steps, look for supporters, test your assumptions, and/or simply have fun developing something new.

---

[2]Cordova is a platform for building native mobile applications using HTML, CSS, and JavaScript, `https://cordova.apache.org`.

[3]Xamarin, `http://xamarin.com`.

[4]Integrating Google Maps in your Android application, `https://developers.google.com/maps/documentation/android`.

[5]Networking on Android using OkHttp, `http://square.github.io/okhttp`.

[6]Gson, a JSON serialization library, `https://code.google.com/p/google-gson`.

Use Case 5: LunchMates—Getting the World to Learn During Lunch

Social applications are, by default, applications with the potential to be used by many users at the same time. I know, the first word that comes to your mind is *scalability*, but that is just one of the challenges you must tackle, and possibly not the hardest. Your application needs to work for almost every user who decides to give it a try, from the perspectives of usability and user experience—and remember that these two concepts leave room for connectivity latency, relevance of the information, and so on—and you need to make sure your back-end infrastructure is responsive when communicating with the different agents involved, independently of the average Internet speed in the countries where some users use your product. In summary, this kind of application is demanding from almost any perspective; and, most important, many aspects are directly or indirectly related to how you build your infrastructure.

■ **Pro Tip** At this point, you should have heard the name of this application a few times. If you have not, we encourage you to read the rest of this book.

LunchMates is a social application that helps individuals with similar interests to connect and exchange ideas, discuss them, or simply have a relaxed chat about a certain topic while they do something they must do every day: have lunch. Users of this application can create lunch, drinks, or other kinds of meetings based on topics they are interested in. These meetings appear on the map so that other users can join.

■ **Note** This application is used throughout this book to illustrate examples in the various technologies covered. Even though this use case does not add content from a technical standpoint, it serves as a wrap-up of what the final picture of the cloud stack looks like and how to assemble the pieces.

LunchMates meets the first and possibly most important requirement of any product: it is simple and easy for potential users to understand. Whether that simplicity is also present in the guts of the service is a different story. This application is developed for Android and iOS, and the API is hosted in App Engine. Let's start with the API. This is the list of planned features:

- API to host data and communicate with clients
- Memory cache to speed up user requests
- Location search
- Deferred tasks and internal messaging to perform operations in the background
- File storage to enable users to upload files about their meetings
- Analytics about usage

Several architectures apply to this scenario. From those, we are going to choose the fully managed option while also taking advantage of the platform App Engine. This time, the rational decision tends toward having the ability to use integrated services like Google Cloud Datastore and Search API, as well as taking advantage of the simplicity of the platform and its ability to scale.

To persist data, you can use Cloud Datastore, a storage system for metadata that performs fantastically in the context of scalability and availability if compromises are made properly during the design phase. One important aspect to keep in mind is how to structure your data from a consistency standpoint. Strong, consistent information always returns up-to-date versions of your data, but that comes at the price of reduced throughput: around one write per second. Entity groups always operate with strong consistency; in addition, when you fetch an entity using its key (`Key.get()`) the results are also strongly consistent. In all other cases, your data operates in an eventually consistent fashion: that is, the results returned to you may not be the most up-to-date snapshot of your data, but this structuring enables your data store to operate with larger-scale datasets. To read more about Cloud Datastore, see Chapter 9.

Even if your system scales properly, reducing the number of times your application accesses the disk has a clear impact on performance. Memcache is a distributed object memory-caching system integrated in App Engine. Use Memcache to speed up queries that are commonly requested and that do not change much, or when showing relatively outdated information is acceptable. For example, in this application, the request to retrieve meetings that are currently active in a specific city is a perfect candidate for in-memory caching. Even if you specify a short time-to-live for the record, the benefits can be substantial. Check out Chapter 5 on App Engine to learn more.

Probably the most important aspect of this application is its ability to present meetings that are currently open to join in your area. As suggested previously, you can do this by querying meetings, specifying a location, and returning the options available nearby. Just as in the previous example, the Search API is a great choice for that purpose. Assuming that your data is persisted in Cloud Datastore, you can use the Search API to store the coordinates for the location where the meeting takes place and the key of the record holding the rest of the information in Cloud Datastore. That way, you can retrieve meeting metadata using the keys in the results returned by the location query in the Search API. To fetch many entities at a time using a list of keys, you can use the method `ndb.get_multi([list_of_keys])` in Cloud Datastore.

Having the ability to perform tasks in the background, especially when the outcome is not immediately relevant for users, is a great way to improve the overall responsiveness of your application. Sending e-mails, processing files, and reminding users about specific events are great candidates for this kind of task. In App Engine, you can use task queues and scheduled tasks to execute logic in the background. In addition, if you need your application to communicate across services in a way that is independent from the caller and receiver, you can use Google Cloud Pub/Sub to exchange messages in a publisher-consumer fashion. This is especially useful when working with independent events that may come from different systems or platforms, which requires your application to perform some work. To learn more about Cloud Pub/Sub, see Chapter 12.

Another important feature of LunchMates is giving users the ability to upload documents that complement the content of their meetings. For example, suppose you create a meeting about snakes. You may want to attach a document that explains the evolutionary path of this animal. To do that, you can use Google Cloud Storage. This service allows you to store files in buckets hosted in durable and highly available object storage. Among its features is the ability to upload files from almost anywhere; Cloud Storage exposes a complete API to do that. Even though this API can be accessed from practically anywhere, it is still simpler to operate from your App Engine application. Chapter 8 dives deep into the details of Cloud Storage.

Finally, you can get insights about how your users experience your application by analyzing the access logs they generate. This is only a small example that shows you how to treat and process information in order to obtain useful insights that help you make future decisions about where to take your product. As discussed in Chapter 11, you can use Cloud Dataflow to analyze big chunks of information and generate results based on them. You can measure practically anything you can think of. In this example, you periodically take the contents of your `access.log` file and use Cloud Dataflow to generate a report based on the requests your users are making against your API and the results they are obtaining. As of this writing, Cloud Dataflow can use other services in Cloud Platform as data sources and sinks, such as Cloud BigQuery, Cloud Storage, and Cloud Pub/Sub.

On the mobile side, this app supports iOS and Android and provides the following features:

- Show a map with meetings nearby.
- Provide the ability to upload files.
- Connect with your API.

Similar to the previous use case, you can use Google Maps to provide location capabilities to your mobile applications. Note that Google Maps is also available for iOS, although it is a fair choice to go with the native option if you think platform consistency is more important than a wider feature set.

You can use networking libraries to upload files and connect to your API. As mentioned earlier, OkHttp is a great option for Android, combined with Gson for JSON serialization. On iOS, AFNetworking is a widely known and used networking library.

Note that in this instance, you can also take advantage of Cloud Endpoints to simplify the construction of your API and dynamically generate client libraries that you can use in your JS, iOS, and Android clients in order to connect to it.

Finally, you can take advantage of many of the APIs that Google exposes to improve the overall experience of your application. For example, when a new user finds a meeting on the map and decides to join, you can request directions to the place where the meeting takes place using the Directions API. Similarly, you can use the Calendar API to add a calendar entry with the date and place of the meeting so that users do not miss events. Chapter 3 shows you how to access APIs in Google; check it out for more information.

As you can see, we have constructed a demanding application using services and APIs in Google that incorporate much of the knowledge you have acquired in this book. Note that this does not necessarily mean this is a unique approach to tackle your challenges. Other companies and communities are operating in this same market and providing powerful solutions to problems you may encounter when building your next big thing. Carefully assess and choose the alternatives that fit your needs as more and more providers give you the ability to use their services independently of your platform or architecture. However, note that some services perform better if they operate using their internal network, as is the case for some services in Google.

Remember, all that matters in the end is that you find the right tools to achieve your objectives, regardless of whether you connecting your house with sensors that communicate with each other, building a fantastic internal application that makes the employees of your company twice as productive, prototyping your ideas just for fun, or building your next big thing that addresses the needs of millions.

What's Next in Google Cloud Platform

In this section, we share our vision of the capabilities and features we expect Google to build in the next generation of Cloud Platform. The intention of this section is to provide content for reflection and discussion that you can continue online. We would love to hear your thoughts on this matter. Note that this is *not* an official road map, but the personal—and questionable—opinions of the authors.

Google Compute Engine

- *More regions and zones:* It is no secret that Google owns a private fiber network that spans continents and oceans. In addition, Google has a substantial number of datacenters distributed worldwide to support its core products like Search and Maps. We would like to see more Cloud Platform regions and zones made available in Google's datacenters.
- *Support for ARM architecture:* Compute Engine currently allows developers to launch VMs that feature x86 architecture-based virtual CPUs. ARM architecture, which is used ubiquitously in mobile devices, primarily due to its low power consumption, is making inroads in server rooms. We would like to see Google support ARM-based VMs in Compute Engine.
- *Instances with GPGPU Accelerators:* General-purpose graphical programming units (GPGPUs) are used to perform large-scale scientific analysis. We would like Google to provide this capability so that the academic and scientific communities can run their workloads efficiently.

Google App Engine

- *Version 2.0:* Today, App Engine hosts more than 4 million active applications. Most of them run on the classic sandboxed runtime. The shortcomings of this runtime are well known. Google is currently experimenting with a container-based runtime called Managed VMs. We explained Managed VMs in Chapter 6 and also used it in reference architecture in the previous section. Managed VMs is promising in that it addresses several shortcomings. At the same time, as you can tell from the name, containerized applications run inside a managed VM. In addition, the startup time is an order of magnitude higher, compared to the sandboxed runtime. We don't see the need for this VM and believe it is a transitional step before App Engine manages containers natively. We look forward to App Engine 2.0, which is based on containers and lets you use any standard language runtime, permits local disk writing, and allows live debugging over SSH while launching instances in a second as in the sandboxed runtime.
- *Asian region:* Today, when launching App Engine applications, developers can specify their hosting region as either the European Union or United States. Once this choice is made, App Engine makes sure applications only scale and store data in the respective datacenters on these continents. This is because of the strong privacy laws in effect in both the European Union and United States. We would like to see an Asian region added to the scope as well.

Google Container Engine

- *Bare-metal execution:* Our wish here is similar to that for App Engine. Today, container pods run in a Compute Engine instance, and each instance can host one or more container pods. This means the allocation of resources is based on instance sizes and not pod sizes. Moreover, each physical machine is likely to host more than one Compute Engine instance. We don't see a need for the intermediate Compute Engine VMs as they add to the inefficiency in executing applications. We look forward to a future generation of Container Engine that eliminates the use of Compute Engine instances and executes the application container on the host OS directly.

Google Cloud SQL

- *Support for non-MySQL databases:* Currently, Cloud SQL supports only MySQL. Developers use other database like PostgreSQL, SQL Server, and Oracle as the back end for applications. We want Cloud SQL to support additional database software in a future release.
- *Replication and throughput:* Currently, Cloud SQL is capable of acting as a master only in a replication architecture where external MySQL instances are involved. We would like Cloud SQL to support the slave role as well so that sophisticated architectures like master-master replication can be set up. In addition, Cloud SQL should support large databases. We look forward to these features in the near future.

Google Cloud Storage

- *Support for external mounting:* Persistent disks can be mounted in read-write mode on one Compute Engine instance or in read-only mode in several Compute Engine instances. Developers innovate around this restriction by mounting the persistent disk in read-write mode in one instance and then exporting it other instance through NFS. This solution works but is far from ideal. First, persistent disks are limited in scope to a Cloud Platform region and cannot be shared globally. Second, contents stored in persistent disks cannot be cached at edge nodes. Cloud Storage addresses these shortcomings by providing integrated object caching at edge nodes and access control lists (ACLs) for sharing with a global audience. However, it is not currently possible to mount cloud storage in Compute Engine instances. We would like this feature to be added to either Compute Engine or Cloud Storage.

Google Cloud DNS

- *Asian nodes:* The Cloud DNS architecture uses multiple nodes in both the United States and European Union regions. We would like to see Asian nodes added to this architecture. This could further reduce network latency for DNS queries.

Summary

In this closing chapter, we assessed typical scenarios of hosting web applications in the cloud. We designed several architectures, each of them enhancing the previous generated and eliminating shortcomings. We combined technologies that we covered in this book and provided links to external articles and tools that may be useful to you.

We also included a brief section in which we reflected on and discussed what we consider to be natural steps for cloud computing technologies, specifically for Cloud Platform in this case.

We hope you have learned from this book and enjoyed reading it as much as we enjoyed writing it. During this process, some existing Google products have changed and improved while others have been added. We have done our best to keep up with this pace by updating content, code snippets, and strategies until the last possible moment. Additionally, we have open sourced each piece of code[7] used in this book, not just for reference but also so that we can update it as the technology evolves and as we receive your contributions.

It is now time for you to show the world what you can do with this vast array of computing power and services. In the end, what you build is what gives meaning to all this and ultimately what powers the world and pushes it forward.

[7]Find all the code used throughout the book in the repositories under the GitHub user CloudPlatformBook – *https://github.com/GoogleCloudPlatformBook*.

Index

A

Access control lists (ACLs)
- default/predefined, 204–207
- permissions/scopes, 202–203

Android key, 29
Apache access log files
- AccessLog declaration, 240
- commas as delimiters, 242
- CSV, 241
- CustomLog directives, 239
- environment variable declaration, 240
- Github code-hosting platform, 242
- JSON-encoded text file, 241
- loading transformed data, 243–245
- location, 241
- log entry, 240–241
- querying data, 245–250
- replacing tabs with string TAB, 242
- tab characters as delimiters, 242

apply method, 271
Auth
- API keys, 28–30
- OAuth 2.0 (*see* OAuth 2.0)

Autoscaler
- autoscaled managed instance groups, 81
- autoscaling integrations, 77
- gcloud CLI tool, 80–81
- instance template creation, 78
- managed instance group, 76, 79
- target utilization level, 77
- utilization metric, 76

AvroIO class, 265

B

Big Data analytics, 235–236, 355
BigQuery
- ad-hoc system, 236
- Apache access log files
    - AccessLog declaration, 240
    - commas as delimiters, 242
    - CSV, 241
    - CustomLog directives, 239
    - environment variable declaration, 240
    - Github code-hosting platform, 242
    - JSON-encoded text file, 241
    - loading transformed data, 243–245
    - location, 241
    - log entry, 240–241
    - querying data, 245–250
    - replacing tabs with string TAB, 242
    - tab characters as delimiters, 242
- columnar layout and distributed storage, 236
- containers, 237
- creating views, 252
- data types, 238
- date/time string, 238
- Dremel research technology, 236
- exporting data, 250–253
- importing data, 238–239
- interactive system, 236
- petabytes size, 236
- scalability, 236
- shared multi-tenant architecture, 237
- tree architecture, 236
- Unix timestamp, 238

BigQueryIO class, 265
Bigtable, 211
Browser key, 29

C

Capital expenditures (CapEx), 6
Cloud Dataflow
- construction
    - access.log file, 267
    - AllowedOptions, 267–268
    - input and output command, 268
    - PipelineOptions, 267
- data sources and sinks
    - AvroIO class, 265
    - BigQueryIO class, 265
    - Cloud Pub/Sub messages, 265

Cloud Dataflow (*cont.*)
PCollection objects, 264
TextIO class, 264
execution
Cloud Storage, 268
Count transform, 270
ExtractLogExperience, 269
filtering operation, 269
FormatResultsFn, 272
options and application, 275
runner parameter, 273–274
TopCodes, 271
Extract Logs UX, 268
PCollection, 259
pipelines, 255, 258
setup, 256
streaming data channels, 255
transformation (*see* Transformation)
Cloud Datastore indexes
autoGenerate property, 222
Bigtable, 220
configuration file, 221
cost optimization, 229
datasets
cursors, 227–228
data repositories, 227
LIMIT, 227
OFFSET, 227
exploding, 222–224
filtering, 229
index.yaml, 222
properties, 220
queries, 224–226
querying ancestor, 220
and SDK, 221
sorting, 230
Cloud deployment manager
configuration, 333
beta deployment-manager types, 337
boot images, 339
compute zones, 338
machine types, 338
resources property, 337
deployments management, 334, 343–345
environment variables, 341
manifest, 334
parameters, 340
references, 341–343
resources, 333
single compute engine VM, 334–336
templates, 334, 339
Cloud domain name system (DNS)
benefits, 295
change requests, 296
entities, 296
gcloud tool, 306
publishing internet identity
adding IPv4 and IPv6 addresses, 302
adding multiple record sets, 303
creating managed zone, 296–297
listing Cloud SQL instances, 302
listing DNS records, 295–296, 302, 306
open transaction, 303
PTR record, 305
rDNS, 305
SPF records, 303
transaction object, 298–300
TXT record, 304
TTL, 296
Cloud endpoints
API, 311–314
api_server, 311–314
APIs explorer, 324
app.yaml, 311
client libraries generation
authentication process, 328
endpointscfg.py, 326
fetchMeetingsList, 329
GoogleAccountCredential, 328
gradle module, 327
onActivityResult, 329
EndpointsAliasProperty, 317
NDB Datastore, 314
protoRPC, 309
SDK, 310
services/request handlers
EndpointModels.query_method, 321–324
endpoints.method, 319
EndpointsModel.method, 320–321
Cloud management system (CMS)
autoscaler, 352
cloud launcher
advantages, 351
click-to-deploy, 350
cloud DNS, 351
disadvantages, 351
WordPress, 350
cloud SQL, 351
definition, 349
health checks, 352
HTTP load balancer, 352
Cloud platform resources
cloud client libraries, APIs, 21–23
Developers Console
permissions and auth, 17–20
web-based interface, 16–17
gcloud Tool, SDK, 20
projects, 13–14
regions, zones, resources, and quotas, 14–16

Cloud publisher-subscriber approach, 265
  lifecycle, 278
  messages, 286–288
  processing messages
    pull subscriptions, 288–290
    push subscriptions, 290–291
  project and topic identifiers, 279
  subscriptions
    acknowledgement deadline, 285–286
    pull, 284–285
    push, 283–284
    Python client library, 283
  system, set up, 278
Cloud storage
  access control, 190–192
  ACLs (*see* Access control lists (ACLs))
  advantages, 188
  API access, 186
  applications, 189
  automation, 209
  billing, 186
  gcloud tool, 186
  gsutil
    bucket creation, 187
    cleaning, 188
    execution, 187
    installation, 185
    uploading files, 187
  handling errors, 200
  lifecycle management, 208–209
  resumable upload, 192–196
  signed URL
    gsutil command-line tool, 197
    signature, 198–200
    structure, 197–198
  strong consistency, 189
Comma-separated values (CSV), 241
Compute Engine
  autoscaler
    autoscaled managed instance groups, 81
    autoscaling integrations, 77
    gcloud CLI tool, 80
    instance template creation, 78–79
    managed instance group, 76, 79–80
    target utilization level, 77
    utilization metric, 76
  global multi-datacenter web tier
    Asian nodes, 75
    backend services, 70
    content-based load balancing, 75
    gcloud commands, 72–73
    global forwarding rules, 70
    health check, 73
    HTTP load-balancing service, 72
    instance groups, 71
    Linux commands, 71
    load-distribution algorithm, 71
    target HTTP proxy, 70
    URL maps, 70, 76
  load balancer
    definition, 65
    forwarding rules, 65
    HTTP load balancing, 65
    load-distribution algorithm, 66
    network load balancing, 65
    target pools, 65–66
  PD, 55
  VM (*see* Virtual machine (VM))
Container engine, 353–354
Container_exec tool, 152
Core transformations
  combine, 263
  Flatten, 264
  GroupByKey, 263
  ParDo, 262

■ D

DevOps initiatives
  Container Engine
    cluster, 134
    firewall rule, 137
    gcloud command, 137
    Kubernetes pod, 136
    node, 134
    Single Node Cluster, 134–135
    Wordpress installation, 137–138
  containers
    computational resources, 125
    hypervisor models, 124–125
    LXC, 126
    namespaces, 126
    operating system-level
      virtualization, 126
  Docker
    client, 127
    containers, 128
    daemon, 127
    hub, 127
    images, 127
  Kubernetes
    DNS, 134
    Docker model, 132
    Kubernetes cluster manager, 129
    Kubernetes model, 132
    labels and annotations, 131
    namespace, 133
    orchestration system, 129
    pods, 129
    replication controller, 130
    service, 133
    VolumeMounts property, 130

DevOps toolbox
cloud deployment manager (*see* Cloud deployment manager)
hosted security services
cloud debugger, 347
cloud security scanner, 347
cloud trace, 347
source and binary code management
cloud repositories, 345
Google Container Registry, 347
Push-to-Deploy, 346
source code tools, 346
Docker container technology, 354
Domain name system (DNS), 295

■ E, F

EndpointsAliasProperty, 317, 323

■ G

gcloud bq command, 238
gcloud command-line interface (CLI), 160
GetResponseCodeFn class, 269
get_result() method, 97
Google APIs
access control, 27
Auth (*see* Auth)
OAuth 2.0, 27
OpenID Connect, 27
Translate API (*see* Translate API)
Google App Engine (GAE), 361
api_version, 85
application outputs errors/uncaught exceptions, 86
deployment, 120
e-mail, 107–109
handlers host, 85
integrated frameworks and libraries, 86–89
key properties and ancestor paths
batching and asynchronous operations, 96
Cloud Datastore, 95
meeting request, 95
ndb.KeyProperty, 95
queries, 99–102
request routing, 98–99
transactions, 102
logs, 120
Memcache, 105–107
Python 2.7, 85
scheduled tasks
cron configuration, 119
parameters, 118
periodic format, 119
specific timing format, 119
SDK, 83
storing information
additional arguments, 93
BlobKeyProperty, 91
BlobProperty, 90
BooleanProperty, 90
ComputedProperty, 92
data models, 90
DateProperty, 91
DateTimeProperty, 91
DynamicThing class, 93
Expando models, 93
file structure, 89
FloatProperty, 90
GenericProperty, 92
GeoPtProperty, 91
Google Cloud Datastore, 89
Google Cloud SQL, 89
Google Cloud Storage, 89
IntegerProperty, 90
JsonProperty, 92
KeyProperty, 91
LocalStructuredProperty, 91
PickleProperty, 92
StringProperty, 90
StructuredProperty, 91
TextProperty, 90
TimeProperty, 91
task queues
administration console, 115
deferred tasks, 116–117
deleting tasks, 116
handling tasks, 113–115
push queues, 110–112
threadsafe, 85
user management, 103
version number, 85
web applications, 84
YAML configuration files, 84
Google BigQuery. *See* BigQuery
Google Cloud Datastore
ancestor paths, 214–216
availability, 212
cross-group transactions, 219
eventual consistency, 217
identifier, 216
indexes (*see* Cloud Datastore indexes)
keys
App Engine Python NDB, 215
entity retrieval, 217–218
locality, 218
Node.js (JSON) API, 215
path, 216
protocol buffers, 215
transactionality, 218

limitations, 211
for LunchMate app, 213
model.py, 213
operation speed, 212
pricing, 231
properties, 213
scalability, 211
strong consistency, 217
test case, 219
Google Cloud DNS, 362. *See also* Cloud domain name system (DNS)
Google Cloud Platform
Amazon Web Services, 11-12
economic innovations, 10
hardware innovations, 8
software innovations, 8-10
Google Cloud SQL, 362
features, 159
master Cloud SQL instance
configuration steps, 174
my.cnf, 178
MySQL server software, 175
MySQL slave status, 179
MySQL Users, 178
mysqldump, 177, 179
server-id, 179
MySQL database (*see* MySQL database)
performance-measuring, 181
Google Cloud Storage, 362
Google Compute Engine, 361
Google Container Engine, 362
Google Translate, 41
Gradle, 257, 273-274
grep, 166

H

Health-check requests, 154

I, J

iOS key, 29
IP-per-pod model, 132

K

Keys-only query, 229
Kube-proxy, 133
Kubernetes container technology, 354

L

Linux containers (LXC), 126
LunchMates application
advantages, 360
architectures, 358
cloud datastore, 359
features, 358
Memcache, 359
networking libraries, 360
requirements, 358
scalability, 358

M

main method, 272
Minimum viable product (MVP) approach, 355
Mobbo application, 356
MySQL database
Cloud SQL instance
binary logs, 170
database backup, 169, 171
gcloud CLI tool, 160
installation, 164
IPv4 Address, 162
read replica, 169, 171
SSL connection, 165
Wordpress CMS, 172
mysqldump, 177
MySQLslap, 181-182

N

named() method, 259
Namespaces, 126
Network address translation (NAT) router, 247

O

OAuth 2.0.
access request procedure, 30
application authentication, 31
user authentication
client_secrets_json_path, 35
discovery classes, 36
manual access token, 36
parameters, 35
redirect, 36
refresh_token, 37

OAuth 2.0. (*cont.*)
3-legged OAuth 2.0 user authentication flow, 33–38
2-legged, 38–40
urn\:ietf\:wg\:oauth\:2.0\:oob, 36
urn\:ietf\:wg\:oauth\:2.0\:oob\:auto, 36
OpenID Connect, 27
Operational expenditures (OpEx), 6

P, Q

PARSE_IP function, 247
Persistent disk (PD), 55
Pointer record (PTR), 305–306
Private IP addresses, 247
processElement method, 270
Projection queries, 230
Public cloud
business benefits
growth patterns, 7
pay-per-use business model, 7
self-service, 7
time to market, 6
economic benefits
CapEx, 6
economies of scale, 5
OpEx, 6
ROI, 6
TCO, 5
technical benefits
expertise, 5
resource utilization, 5
uptime, 4
put() method, 97

R

RESTful services, 25
Return on investment (ROI), 6
Reverse DNS lookup/reverse DNS resolution (rDNS), 305
Round-robin method, 66

S

Sandboxed runtime, 354
Scalability, 7
Sender Policy Framework (SPF), 303
Server key, 29
ssl-certs describe command, 165

T, U

Tablets, 212
TextIO class, 264
Three-legged authentication (3LO), 19
Time to live (TTL) parameter, 296
Total cost of ownership (TCO), 5
Transformation
core transformations
combine, 263
Flatten, 264
GroupByKey, 263
ParDo, 262
Count transform, 270
Developers Console, 260
ExtractLogExperience, 262
single transformation, 261
Top transform, 271
Translate API
access
batch query and response, 43
HTTP GET method, 41, 43
HTTP POST method, 43
HTTP query, 42
HTTP response, 42
phrases, 41
query words, 42
translate method, 41
translation request without source language, 42
using client programs, 47
discovering languages
English sentence, 46
language query response, 44
retrieving language codes, 44
source language detection, 45
Spanish input, 46
specified target language, 45
URI template, 44
web-based Developers Console, 41
2-legged OAuth 2.0 user authentication, 38–40

V, W, X, Y, Z

Virtual machine (VM), 139
automatic scaling, 153
configuration elements, 154
CPU cores, 53
definition, 54
Docker containerization processes, 140

features, 139
firewall configuration, 153
gcloud command-line tool
    Apache web server, 64
    command sequence lists, 59
    default specifications, 60
    external IP address, 64
    firewall rules, 62
    Google authentication screen, 58
    Google login screen, 57
    ingress network access, 60
    instance creation, 59
    instance deletion, 65
    long URL and code, 59
    project selection, 59
    zone flag, 61
health-check requests, 154
instance types, 54
load balancer
    forwarding rule, 69
    health checks, 66, 68
    index.html file, 67
    new instance creation, 66
    target pool, 68–69
    web browser, 67
networks and firewalls, 55
resource settings control, 153
sandboxed App Engine, 143
sandbox environment, 139
SSH debugging, 149
standard and custom runtime, 140
<standard-runtime> options, 152

Printed in the United States
By Bookmasters